Other books by Robert Morrissey

A Cop's Gotta Laugh

Humorous Beat

2nd Humorous Beat
Actual funny Police Stories

Vagabonds

Four Young Soldiers And Sergeant Doyle

©2011 by Robert Morrissey

Cover Design by Mary Morrissey

WRB Publishing
Palm City, FL 34990
wrb1174@att.net

ISBN-13: 978-0-9844198-8-3

Four Young Soldiers

And

Sergeant Doyle

By

Robert Morrissey

DEDICATION

To every American who took their turn wearing, with honor,
the uniforms of the United States Armed Services

A SOLDIER

It is the soldier,
Not the reporter,
Who has given us the freedom of the press.
It is the Soldier,
Not the poet,
Who has given us freedom of speech.
Not the campus Organizer,
Who has given us the freedom to demonstrate.

It is the Soldier,
Who salutes the flag.
Who serves beneath the flag.
And whose coffin is draped by the flag,
Who allows the protester to burn the flag.

It is the Soldier

By: Father Denis Edward O'Brien M.M. U. S. Marine Corps.

ACKNOWLEDGMENTS

I want to thank my wife Mary for her encouragement and art work.

In Biblical times, a man and his name were so intimately related that "to cut off the name" of an individual amounted to the same thing as killing him.

Author unknown

PREFACE

It was the early 1950's. The pace of life was slow and carefree...a comfortable time to be a teenager. The football games on Friday night, sock hops, and hanging around the soda shops.

Few seemed to have a care. Sure, the Korean conflict was going on, but that was thousands of miles away. For most people, it didn't affect them. The newspapers and radios referred to the war as a "police action." For thousands of young American soldiers, most of them teenagers, it was a bitter, full-fledged war where many lost their lives in a country they had never heard of.

This is the story of four young men drafted into the army during the Korean War. Hillbilly was an easy going southern boy from the mountains of Tennessee; Zug, a jazz musician, found a way to carry his saxophone wherever he went, even into combat: Mike, a good athlete came from a religious family. Then there was Rick. A street smart kid who had only one thing in life, his name. God help the person who called him something other than his name.

Journey with these four young men through Basic Training. The humorous incidents that happened on overnight passes and R&R in Japan. Go into combat with them and get a first hand view of how soldiers react and perform in war time. Be with them through the happy, tragic and sad times. After you read this book you'll have a better understanding of the American soldier from the forgotten war. Veterans will relate to this story, because they lived through war too. Americans should have a place in their hearts for the men who defended them and their American way of life.

Chapter 1
Leaving for the Army

Mrs. Ryan pushed the door closed with her elbow as she shuffled through the morning mail. One letter stopped her. She stared at the bold print. UNITED STATES SELECTIVE SERVICE. Her eyes dropped to the addressee, Michael Ryan. She immediately sat down in the overstuffed chair and tears welled in her eyes as she thought back to the day her son was born, his first day of school and when he became an altar boy. The many times his name was in the paper for playing high school football. Could it really be possible? Was he old enough to take his turn as a soldier? He had been such a help since his father passed away, now everything will change. Mike will go to war. She paused and slowly shook her head, *"Take care of him Lord! Please!"*

"Hi Mom, how you doing?" She quickly turned her head trying to act normal. He saw part of the brown envelope she was concealing under her apron. He knew what it was, but asked anyway. "What you got there mom? I saw you hide it." She hesitated a moment then handed it to him. "Well I'll be darned, I must be an important person getting a letter from the United States Government. Can you imagine that?"

"Michael, I know what it is. If only you would have gone to college on one of those football scholarships."

"Mom, I didn't want to go to college. There's things a man wants to do, and there's things a man doesn't want to do. I'm sorry."

She forced a smile as she looked at his young face. "Just like your father, bless his soul."

Mike went into the kitchen and quietly opened the letter.

"It doesn't do any good to hide it Michael. How long do you have?" Mike didn't answer. "How long, Michael?"

"Two weeks, Mom." He slowly walked back to the front room. "I feel bad about leaving, but I think it is the right thing to do. I must go, it's my turn. It will be a good experience. Don't you remember how Dad and Uncle Tim were proud when they went? Every time they got together and had a couple of drinks that's all they'd talk about."

"Yes I know Mike."

"Well Mom, let's not talk about it anymore. I'll be Okay and I'll be back soon."

She looked up nodded and in a soft low voice. "Okay, Michael."

Two weeks passed like lightning and the day came to leave. He walked into the kitchen where breakfast was waiting. He sat down and sensed his mother's sadness. She kept busy, always with her back to him, trying to hide the redness in her eyes. "Mike, your Uncle Tim is coming over to drive us to the bus station."

"Oh, that's great." Mike tried to eat but couldn't. He was relieved when he heard the knock on the door.

Uncle Tim came in. "Where's that soldier boy?"

Mike smiled. It was good to see him. Uncle Tim had a way that made everyone cheer up. When he walked into a room it was like someone turned on bright lights.

"You know son, it wasn't too many years ago that your Dad and I were leaving. Yes sir, I'm proud of you Mike." He looked at his sister, "Yeah Maggie, it was a lot of fun, Mike will enjoy himself, just like we did."

She looked at him, then managed to smile. "I hope you're right Tim." She stood for a moment, then turned. "I'll powder my nose, then we'll go."

When she left the room Uncle Tim sat in a chair next to Mike. "How's she taking it, Mike?"

"Okay, I guess. I never felt so bad in all my life."

"Now you leave this up to me, she'll be all right, I'll see to it. You take care of yourself, because they got one hell of a war over there in Korea. Remember what I told you, keep your head down so you don't get shot. When you get them in your sights, squeeze that trigger slow and smooth. You play this war thing just like football, to win."

"Okay Uncle Tim, I understand."

"You got any money, Michael?"

"Yeah, I'm all set."

Tim reached into his back pocket, took out his wallet and threw a fifty dollar bill on the table. "This will hold you until your first pay day."

Mike pushed the money back toward his uncle. "Naw, I don't need it, Uncle Tim."

Tim picked up the bill and stuffed it into Mike's shirt pocket. "You take this and I don't want to hear any more about it."

Mike could tell his uncle was driving slow so they wouldn't have to stand around in the bus station. The car was quiet, hardly any conversation. They no sooner entered the station when it was announced that the bus leaving for Cleveland, Ohio, was boarding.

Mike turned to his mother and uncle, "Well, I guess it's that time."

Uncle Tim grabbed Mike's hand and shook it. "You take care of yourself, Michael, and remember what I told you, and don't let them drill sergeants get the best of you. They can be mean."

"I won't." Mike turned to his mother. He tried to say something but words wouldn't come.

She stared at him. "Michael, you be careful, write home, and be sure to attend mass on Sunday. I'll be praying for you, Son."

"Okay, Mom, I will. I promise." He tried to say more but choked.

She hugged and kissed him on the cheek "Goodbye Son."

Mike got an empty feeling in his stomach and fought the tears welling in his eyes. "Goodbye Mom. Don't worry, everything will be all right." He kissed her forehead and patted her on the back. He reached down, grabbed his bag and climbed the steps into the bus. He took a seat near a window where he could see his mother and uncle. He waved at them and they waved back.

The bus made a hissing noise and pulled away from the station. All the way to Cleveland he stared out the window, seeing nothing. His only thoughts were how his mother was taking it. He felt he had made a mistake and acted selfishly by not going to college for her sake. His spirits were low, knowing she was home alone worrying about him.

Chapter 2
Guy in a Zoot Suit

The large bus swayed from side to side as it entered the driveway to the Cleveland station. As soon as it stopped, some of the people popped up from their seats and grabbed their luggage from the overhead racks. The driver looked back and yelled, "We'll be in Cleveland for fifteen minutes and then on to Louisville, Kentucky. Anyone wishing to stretch and freshen up may leave the bus." Mike stayed in his seat and continued to stare out the window. It was the most empty, lonesome feeling he had ever experienced. His trance was broken by loud singing coming from the front of the bus.

"You're in the army now. You're not behind the plow. You dig in the ditch, you son-of-a bitch you're in the army now." Mike could not believe what he was seeing. A young man, in the front of the bus was marching and singing. He was dressed in a Zoot Suit and a black pork pie hat with a large pink band wrapped around it. His shirt was pink with a white tie. His long black jacket hung down to his knees. His pants were black and white checked. They were so tightly pegged it's a wonder he got his feet through them. His shoes were white bucks. A large gold chain hung from his belt down to his knee then up to his pant pocket. He carried an overnight bag that was painted silver with a large gold star stenciled on it. He continued to sing as he marched down the aisle.

People stared at him as he marched past their seats. He stopped next to Mike. He looked down. "Hey man, you going in the Army too?"

Mike stared at the Zoot Suit. He hesitated, then stuttered, "Yeah, yeah, I'm going into the Army ."

The guy slid into the seat next to Mike and held out his hand. "Well, I'm glad to meet you. My name's Rick Miller."

Mike grasped his hand. "I'm glad to meet you Rick. I'm Mike Ryan."

Rick threw his bag in the overhead rack and sat down.

"So your friends and neighbors stuck it to you too."

Mike squinted. "What do you mean?"

"Man, didn't you read the letter Uncle Sam sent you? It said your friends and neighbors on it didn't it?"

Mike laughed. "Oh yeah! I remember. Your friends and neighbors selected you to serve in the United States Armed Forces."

"Well, when I got that damn letter everyone laughed like hell and told me the Army was going to change me."

Mike stared at his clothes and asked. "Do you dress like that all the time?"

"Nah, not all the time! I thought this would be a good occasion." He smiled. "Don't you think so?"

"Well, I don't know too much about it Rick, but from what I've heard, the first few weeks are pretty rough. They told me it's not a good idea to give them any reason to get on your case."

Rick shook his head. "No, I've got two years to serve and I'm going to serve them my way. No bastard is going to break me like a wild horse and ride me."

Mike shrugged his shoulders and didn't say anymore.

The bus started to move and Mike again stared out the window. The large buildings of downtown Cleveland gave way to smaller ones and soon the bus was passing farms fields. Inside the bus was quiet. Mike leaned his head back and almost fell asleep. A loud yell caused him to lunge upright. He looked and Rick was standing in the aisle, pointing out the window, shouting. "Look Mike, out there in that field."

Mike got out of his seat and hunched over so he could see what Rick was pointing at. A large bore hog was on top of a sow. Mike quickly slid back in his seat.

"Did you see that Mike? He's mak'in bacon."

Mike sank lower into the seat, blood rushed to his face. It felt like every pair of eyes on the bus were staring at him.

Rick continued to stand in the aisle snapping his fingers and laughing. "Yes sir! You got to give that old hog credit, he adapted to the situation." He sat down and shouted again "You got to give that old boy credit, he adapted to the situation.

That's what life is about."

Embarrassed, Mike turned toward the window, he heard people whispering and giggling.

Rick shouted. "Ha, ha, this is going to be good times. I can tell. Can't you?" Mike remained silent and Rick leaned forward and looked at Mike. "Hey Mike! How come your face is so red? Are you blushing? Come on man, don't worry about these people. They're you're friends and neighbors."

Mike looked him in the eyes. "Do you always act this way?"

"As long as I can remember. You see, you got to adapt to the situation. This Army bit could be a bad scene if you let it. But all you got to do is don't let it bother you. Always remember my motto. You adapt to the situation and you'll be all right. You get it Mike?"

"Yeah, but don't you care about these people riding on this bus?"

"Hell no! I don't care. You think they don't like me for what I say and the way I dress? You watch."

Mike threw up his hand. "Don't do anything crazy. Settle down, I just want to ride this bus to Louisville without any trouble."

Rick jumped up. "Aw man, there ain't going to be any trouble." He stepped into the aisle and stared at the people sitting in their seats. Everyone became silent. They seemed concerned and thought he was going to do something nuts. He smiled and laughed out loud. His arms began going up and down and he started reciting. *"Little fly on the wall don't you have no clothes at all. Don't you have no Bee Vee Dees, aren't you afraid your ass will freeze?"* He took a bow and sat down. A few people clapped and he immediately jumped up and bowed again.

Mike looked to the front of the bus and saw the driver's concerned face in the mirror.

Rick slapped Mike's knee, "Well how did you like that?"

Mike shook his head. "Oh, you were great."

"You know Mike, when I was standing in the aisle I saw a couple of sharp broads sitting in the back. What do you say we go back there and put the moves on them?"

"No! No! That's all right. You go back there. I'm sure they'll be glad to talk to you."

"Hey Mike you're blushing again. Where the hell you from?

"Toledo."

"Toledo huh?"

"No. Toledo, Ohio."

He smiled, "You're a commodian. You get it a commodian?"

"Yeah, I get it."

"Come on, those two broads are waiting for us."

Mike shook his head. "No way, I don't want any part of that. I'm sitting right here. I don't need any problems. Believe me I have enough."

"Well Mike, if you're not going, will you watch my bag?"

"Sure. But I think you'd be better off, if you took it with you. If you need it, it would be close to your new seat."

Rick smiled. "You know it sounds like your trying to get rid of me."

"You could say that."

"I know your just kidding Mike. I'm like MacArthur I shall return." He got up and started strutting to the back of the bus. It became quiet. People in the aisle seats leaned away from him when he passed. The bus driver stared at him in his rear view mirror.

Mike felt relieved the guy was gone. He leaned his head back and exhaled, everything was normal except for the loud laughter coming from the back of the bus. His thoughts drifted to home and his depression returned. The dull vibrations from the bus lulled him to sleep.

"Hey Mike! Hey Mike! Wake up."

Mike blinked a couple of times and looked up. Rick had his arm around a girl's shoulder. "Ain't she a beauty, Mike? She wants to meet you." Rick patted the seat next to Mike. "Sit right here you doll. Mike, this is Ella May. Ella May, this is Mike."

The girl sat down. "I'm pleased to meet you, Mike."

Mike looked at her and stuttered. "I'm, I'm glad to meet you. " A warm feeling came to his face and he tried not to blush.

Rick tapped her on the shoulder a couple of times. "You just sit here with Mike, Ella May, and enjoy yourself. He's a good buddy of mine and he'll treat you right. You have to watch him though, he blushes easy so watch what you say and do. I got to get back to Mary Bell. We're hitting it off real good."

The pretty girl looked at Mike, "Your friend is really persistent."

Mike stuttered "Oh, no! He's not my friend, I just met the guy. He got on in Cleveland and sat next to me. I swear I never saw him before." He looked at her. She was beautiful. Her eyes were big and blue. Long blond hair hung to her shoulders. Her southern accent complemented her beauty.

She smiled, "That old boy Rick is something else. I sure never met anyone like him before."

Mike nodded. "Your definitely right there. Where are you headed Ella

May?"

"I'm going to Louisville. I live there. I suppose you're going to Fort Knox?"

"Why do you say that?"

"Well, any boy around your age on a bus to Louisville, Kentucky usually means he's going into the Army."

Mike smiled. "That's good logic and you're right." The conversation continued and Mike started admiring her. She had such a plain, wholesome way and he enjoyed every minute with her. She radiated a friendly warmth.

"Mike, where are you from?"

"Toledo, Ohio."

"You know, I have to believe your friend, Rick. You are shy."

"Oh no. Wrong on both counts. First of all that guy is not my friend and second, I'm not shy."

"Well Mike, I've been doing most of the talking and you just answer."

"I'd rather look into those beautiful eyes and hear that pretty southern accent you have. You're the best thing that has happened to me in a long time."

Ella Mae tapped his shoulder, "You're really flattering me Mike." Her face turned red.

Mike laughed, "Who's shy and blushing now?" Every time the bus passed a mile marker he regretted it because it meant less time with her. The warm conversation continued until the bus pulled into the station. He looked out the window and saw all the men in Army uniforms.

"See what I told you Mike? This is an Army town."

"Yeah, I see what you mean."

The bus came to a stop and she smiled at him. "Well Mike, it sure was nice meeting you. I have to go to the back and get my luggage. I really enjoyed talking to you. I hope you make it home safely." She begun to walk back and he grabbed her wrist.

"Wait just a second. There's time, sit down please." She sat back down puzzled. Mike hesitated "Ella May, I know we've only known each other for a couple of hours, but I would like to see you again if it could be possible. I'll probably be at this camp for a short time and maybe we could go out."

She smiled, "Sure. I would be glad to see you again."

"Will you write your address and phone number down?"

She reached into her pockets and brought her hands out palms up.

8

"Sorry, I don't have a paper or a pencil."

Mike shook his head, "Gee, I don't either. Maybe the bus driver will loan us his."

He started to stand up and a little lady sitting in front of them turned around. "That won't be necessary, Sonny." She handed him a pad with a pen. They all laughed and Mike took the pad, and gave it to Ella Mae. She wrote her name and phone number, and handed him the slip of paper. Mike returned the pad and pen to the lady. The lady winked and smiled. "Good luck to the two of you."

Ella Mae jumped up, "We better hurry Mike, this bus is almost empty."

Walking to the rear of the bus Mike saw Rick still sitting and a young woman quickly making her way down the aisle to the front of the bus. "I'd introduce you to her Mike but she won't talk to me."

The woman bumped into Mike with her luggage and yelled. "Hurry up, Ella Mae, I got to get away from that crazy sex maniac."

Mike looked at Rick who was smiling. "What happened?"

"Oh, nothing. I was adapting to the situation."

Ella Mae had a worried look. She quickly grabbed her bag and rushed down the aisle after her friend.

Mike watched her pass. "Good bye Ella Mae." She turned and said good bye. Mike looked down at Rick. "Man, you really made her mad. What did you do to make her act that way?"

"Well, Mike, did you ever hear of a quickie?"

" A quickie - what do you mean a quickie?"

" Do you remember a little ways back when that hog was making bacon."

Mike looked at him and shook his head. "You mean you were going to try that right here on this bus with all these people around you?"

"Oh yeah, we were in the last seat. Where there's a will there's a way. You know Mike, where we're going there ain't going to be any broads for a long, long time."

"Man, I can't figure you out. Rick, those girls aren't that type. You never should have tried that."

Rick laughed out loud and mimicked Mike. "Those girls aren't that type. They're not that way. Boy you sure are from Toledo."

Mike ignored him, grabbed his overnight bag and rushed off the bus.

He saw Ella Mae and her friend walking fast and talking. He shouted, "Ella Mae." She turned, looked at him and then hurriedly went into the bus station with her friend. He started to run after her, then stopped. *What's the use?* He looked at the paper with her name and phone number, crushed it and threw it down.

ALL NEW US ARMY INDUCTEES GO TO LOADING AREA DD.

A large red arrow pointed straight ahead. Mike stared at the sign and started walking and saw an olive drab colored bus with a bunch of young men his age milling around it. He continued to walk when he heard a familiar voice.

"Hey Mike, wait up. No hard feelings." Mike continued to walk. "Wait Mike, they were just a couple of broads, man, why worry about it." Mike heard the voice getting closer. "Come on Mike, I said I was sorry, let's just forget about it. We'll be friends again."

Mike stopped abruptly turned and pointed at Rick who was out of breath. "Now, you listen, I don't understand you at all. I do know you draw trouble and I don't like trouble, I don't need it because I've got enough of my own. So you go your way and I'll go mine."

"No Mike you got it wrong. Hell, we'll be going to the same place. You saw that sign back there. We're both going on that silly looking bus."

Mike looked at him. "That's right, we're both getting on that bus. You sit in the front and I'll sit in the back. I'm keeping a long ways away from you."

The young men waiting by the bus saw Rick in his Zoot Suit. They stopped talking and just stared at him. One of them said. "Is he going with us? Man, that's asking for problems."

Rick ignored them and kept chasing after Mike. "Aw come on Mike, don't be that way." Rick continued to talk but Mike walked to the bus and got on. Most of the seats were empty but a few had men sitting by the windows. Mike quickly got into an aisle seat next to a man by the window. Rick followed him on the bus and stood over him looking down. "Listen Mike, I said I was sorry and I meant it. There won't be any more bullshit I promise."

Mike shook his head and looked up. "No sir, I'm sitting here and you can do what you want, just leave me out of your plans. I don't know you."

Rick mumbled and sat directly behind him by the window. The conversation stopped as the rest of the men got on the bus. Mike felt the hardness of the seat and stared at the drab khaki color of the bus. *This is the first touch of reality of being in the Army.* A couple of guys up front kept asking the driver questions like what to expect when they get to the camp? The driver didn't offer much information and gave the impression he had driven this bus a thousand times and had been asked the same questions as many times.

The bus pulled away from the station. It was unusually quiet, everyone was in deep thought. They traveled for about ten miles when someone yelled. "Hey, that guys pissing out the window."

Mike didn't turn around. He knew who it was. Everyone in the seats ahead of him were looking back. He slowly turned. There stood Rick with his hat pushed back standing on the seat leaning into the open window. He looked down at Mike and kept urinating. "Man, what you going to do? If you got to go, you got to go. I had to adapt to the situation."

Mike quickly turned around and yelled at him. "I don't even know you. Do what you got to do."

Chapter 3
Surprise

The bus slowed as it turned to go through the large metal gates leading into the Camp. Two Military Police waved it through with their white gloves. It again picked up speed. On both sides of the street were tan wooden barracks that all looked alike. Soldiers crowded the sidewalks. They too looked alike dressed in their khaki uniforms. Mike thought if khaki is our color what is the oppositions color. He, like the rest of the guys on the bus, stared out the windows and watched their new environment unravel.

The brakes squealed a little and the bus pulled to the curb and stopped. The driver opened the front door and a sergeant with a clipboard, fresh crew cut, starched shirt, and shiny combat boots climbed the steps and stood at the front. His build indicated he was in good condition. His muscles strained the material of his tailor made uniform. The bus became quiet. No one said a word. He continued to stand and stared from one young man to another. He paused a little more and when he was sure he had everyone's attention. He said in a soft calm voice. "I'm Sergeant Mardoon, and I'm very pleased to meet you. I'm going to be with you while you're here at Fort Knox. You'll probably be here for about five days and then onto another camp for basic training." He seemed like a nice courteous man. The young men smiled and relaxed.

The sergeant paused again. He stared a moment, stomped his combat boot and screamed, "GRAB YOUR OVERNIGHT BAGS AND GET THE FUCK OFF THIS BUS!" Everyone jumped out of their seats. "I SAID MOVE, HURRY, HURRY, GET YOUR SORRY ASSES OFF THIS BUS." The aisle was full of young men trying to run to the door. There was panic and fear in their eyes. He screamed again. "DO YOU HEAR ME SHITHEADS?"

No one answered they continued to stampede to the front of the bus. The Sergeant yelled again. "STOP YOU STUPID WET DREAMS" The men in front heard him and they stopped immediately. The ones in the back continued to push forward crushing the mass in the front. The Sergeant squirmed above the squeezing bodies. He threw his clip board at the men in the rear. "YOU

BASTARDS BACK THERE, KNOCK IT OFF. QUIT THAT FUCK'IN PUSHING." This time every one heard and they stopped. He shoved the squeezing bodies away from him.. All motion stopped, no noise, everyone was confused and scared. The Sergeant shouted. "Listen you Shitheads, when I ask a question you better sound off like you got a pair of balls. If you don't have any, we'll put you in the WAC's. Do you hear me Shitheads?" The men were confused, they didn't understand what this man was talking about. Again. "DO YOU HEAR ME SHITHEADS?" Still no answer everyone was tense and scared.

All at once a voice directly behind Mike pierced the silence. "THE BIG MOUTH SERGEANT IS A FAIRY."

The silence remained for a short time till the Sergeant convinced himself he heard it. A sort of animal groan then, "WHERE YOU AT SON-OF-A-BITCH? I"M GOING TO RIP YOUR FUCKT'IN TONGUE OUT OF YOUR HEAD." He dove into the mass of bodies like a charging bull, knocking men into seats and onto the floor. He stopped at where his instincts told him the voice came from. He stared into Mike's eyes. His face was beet red, the veins in his neck were swelled and pulsating. In between breathing heavily he yelled out. "YOU THE NUMB NUT WITH THE BIG MOUTH?"

Mike shook his head. "No sir."

"You know who did then, don't you? Point the son-of-a-bitch out."

Mike stuttered. "No sir, I don't know." Mike felt like it was eternity till the sergeant quit staring at him. He pushed Mike aside. The sergeant was standing directly in front of Rick. He squinted, with his head going up and down staring at the Zoot Suit.

He shouted. "What THE HELL ARE YOU? WHO DRESSED YOU THAT WAY? YOU'RE THE SILLIEST LOOKING JERK I EVER SEEN. ASSHOLE, WHAT'S YOUR NAME?"

Rick put his hands on his hips twisted his head and blinked. In a very feminine voice, "Well cute sergeant of the United States Army, I'm going to tell you who I am. I'm Rickey the civilian, and I don't appreciate my hard earned tax dollars being spent on a big mouth klutz such as you."

The sergeant's eyes strained, his face wrinkled and his mouth twitched. He shouted in Rick's face. "LISTEN YOU FUNNY LOOKING BASTARD. I'll BREAK YOUR BACK AND THROW YOUR ASS RIGHT THROUGH ONE OF THOSE WINDOWS." He raised his arm as though he was going to carry

13

out his threat.

Rick boldly stood there and smiled. "Sergeant, you so much as swing once and you'll see those stripes come off your arms so fast it'll be like a gallon of bleach thrown on a zebra. I will go to the Inspector General of this camp and then call my Congressman and tell them how you are treating United States citizens." Rick pointed at the other guys on the bus. "If you can comprehend, Sergeant, not one of these men has an Army uniform on. None of them has been sworn in as a U.S. soldier, in other words you're talking to U.S. civilians. Now knock off your bullshit and name calling."

The Sergeant was lost for words. Rick could not leave well enough alone. "Furthermore, from now on you better refer to us as men and not Shitheads. The Sergeant stood dumbfounded. He breathed hard, mumbled, turned and walked off the bus. Slowly the men followed.

The Sergeant took a position in front of a ribbon of concrete. He shouted "Give me four straight lines." The men formed the lines. He stared at Rick with a mean look. "We're going to that white building over there. I want you to march if you can. If you can't, try." The men marched out of step but they made it to the building. He ordered them to break ranks and enter. Inside, they were directed to a gym-type room. A large American flag hung on the wall. The men were positioned in front of it.

A smartly dressed officer walked in front of the group and welcomed them. He advised them they were going to take the oath to become members of the Army. "Men, before I administer this oath are there any questions?"

A young freckled faced kid asked, "Sir, what if I was drafted and I don't want to become a soldier?" The officer looked at him and smiled.

"Son, have you ever heard of a federal penitentiary called Leavenworth?"

The young man looked at the Officer and said, "I get what you mean."

Mike was waiting for Rick to say something but he kept quiet. After they were sworn in they went for a break in the hallway. A few of the guys who were on the bus came up to Rick and warned him to watch out now that he was sworn in. Rick smiled. "Well you guys, don't worry about it, you just adapt to the situation."

The men once again assembled in the large room. The officer spoke. He motioned for the Sergeant to come to the front of the room. "As you all know this is Sgt. Mardoon who you met earlier." Everyone looked at Rick, smiled, and then back at the officer. "Sergeant Mardoon is going to take you to the Medical Center where you will have your physical examinations. So long and good luck."

The Sergeant saluted the Officer and with a calm voice said "Ok men, follow me." The group left the room. Mike and Rick were the last ones out the door. As soon as they got outside Sgt. Mardoon was waiting. "Hey you, Shithead, with the funny looking clothes." Rick ignored him and continued to walk. He yelled again. "Hey, Shithead, who now is a soldier."

Rick looked back. "You mean me?"

"Who the hell do you think I mean? You're the only sorry son-of-a-bitch with funny clothes on."

"Well, Sergeant Margoon, that all depends on how you interpret funny clothes. I don't think my clothes are funny. I don't try to understand your stupid ways."

The sergeant shouted, "Shithead the name is Mardoon. I'll tell you what is funny looking, and what isn't funny. Do you understand?"

"Oh, I understand that. But I have to tell you my right name. It's not Shithead. It's Rick Miller. My mother named me that. Somewhere along the line you got me mixed up with some other guy. I would appreciate if you would call me Rick."

Sergeant Mardoon's nose was now touching Rick's. His teeth were gnashing. "Shithead, one more word and you'll be in that mess hall the rest of the time you're here. Now get your ass in that line with the rest of those men."

Rick was ready to say something. Mike thought, I better get away from this guy and get in line. Instead he grabbed Rick's arm. "Come on Rick, do as he says." Rick stared at the Sergeant. His eyes were full of anger. Mike pulled harder and Rick slowly got in the line behind Mike. "Hey Rick, you better let up man, that guy is really mad. He can get you in a lot of trouble."

Rick's squinted, a concerned look came on his face. He thought, Mike cares about me. He didn't say anything, then in a low voice. "Okay, Mike."

The group entered the large building and went upstairs where the odor of alcohol and disinfectant greeted them. After being herded into a room with benches along the wall Sergeant Mardoon shouted. "Take a section of the bench and remove your clothes except your shorts."

The young men were now standing in front of the bench with only their shorts on. They waited for further orders. The Sergeant didn't say anything. He was staring at one of the men in the line. They turned and there stood Rick. Instead of having white jockey shorts on like everyone else, he had knee length fire-engine red ones with large white ants printed on them. Sergeant Mardoon ran to him cussing. "Well I'll be goddamn, the asshole has silly clothes under his silly clothes. Where in the hell did you get them shorts, Shithead?"

Rick smiled. "Well, Sergeant, these shorts are army issue. You see I used to be a Soldier Ant and I lived in a colony. We used to go on furlough at picnics." Everyone laughed.

Sergeant Mardoon stared at the recruits and they became silent. Mardoon's face was beat red. He was inches away from Rick's. "Goddamn it, when I ask you a question you better answer me right. Do you hear me?" Rick just stared at him. "Shithead do you hear me?" The room was silent and no one moved. Everyone was waiting for Rick's answer.

The sergeant pressed his face into Rick's. "Are you talking to me Sergeant?"

Sergeant Mardoon screamed, "Yes I'm talking to you, Shithead and you better answer."

"I'm sorry Sergeant. I keep hearing you call out for that fella shithead. I think you got me mixed up with him. Like I keep trying to tell you my name is Rick Miller, You know RICK MIILLER, that's me. I'm sure if you call me that name you won't have any problem."

Sergeant Mardoon made a fist and was about to swing when the door at the far end of the room flew open. A major dressed in white hospital scrubs yelled. "Who the hell is making all that noise? It sounds like a football stadium." He walked to Sergeant Mardoon who was still staring at Rick.

Rick saw the Major coming. "Sir, this sergeant has lost someone and he can't seem to find him. He's been calling him all day. I've been trying to help, but there's something the matter with him."

The major glared at Sergeant Mardoon. "What's the matter with you Sergeant?"

"Nothing, Sir, nothing."

Rick shrugged his shoulders. " But Sergeant, you keep yelling for that person. Maybe the doctor can help you. Heck, I remember this guy back home he kept seeing these little people and the doctor cured him."

The doctor stared at Sergeant Mardoon. "Are you sure you're all right?"

"Yes Sir, everything is all right. Sir."

"Okay, bring the men into the next room for examinations. Sergeant Mardoon whispered through clenched teeth to Rick. "I ain't done with you bastard." The men entered the examination room. Sergeant Mardoon ordered them to form a straight line and face the doctor. Mike noticed Sergeant Mardoon glaring at Rick waiting for him to do something wrong. He thought of all the times he heard how tough drill sergeants were. This man was no exception, but Rick was slowly driving him crazy.

Two doctors moved behind the inductees. Sergeant Mardoon continued to stand in front of the group.

The doctor nodded at Sergeant Mardoon. "Ok, Sergeant."

Sgt. Mardoon shouted. "Ok men, drop your shorts, bend over and spread your cheeks." Everyone did except Rick. He dropped his shorts, and spread his facial cheeks. Sergeant. Mardoon saw him. He ran to Rick and shouted. "Well I'll be goddamned, you are the dumbest son-of-a-bitch I've ever saw. I ought to kick you in the ass so hard your nose will bleed."

The doctor saw what was happening and interceded. "Wait, Sergeant, that's no big thing, the man didn't understand what you told him. You got to make yourself clear." The doctor looked at Rick. "What's your name, son?"

"Rick Miller. Sir."

The doctor explained what he was going to examine and that is why he wanted him in that position. Rick quickly bent over and grabbed his butt. "Sorry Sir, I didn't understand. I do now Sir. Thank you, Sir."

The doctor turned away from Rick and looked at Sergeant Mardoon. "See Sergeant, you just have to make yourself clear. You can't use army language on these new men and expect them to know what you're saying."

Rick smiled and winked at Sergeant Mardoon. The Sergeant glared at him. The doctor again asked. "Did you hear me Sergeant?"

Sergeant Mardoon kept staring at Rick who was mocking him. Reluctantly he slowly looked at the major, "Yes Sir." And turned around and went to the front of the room.

After the examinations, they returned to the other room for their clothes. The young men dressed and were escorted to another building with swinging doors at both ends. Sergeant Mardoon pointed to a aisle. "You'll get some of your army clothing in this building. When you go past those racks yell out your sizes."

The men went down the aisle. At the first bin a man yelled. "Give me your pants size." Mike replied and a pair of olive drab colored pants were thrown to him. The next station a shirt. When he got to the end of the room his arms were full of army clothes and two pair of combat boots. After getting their issue of clothes they were herded upstairs to a room and ordered to put on a pair of fatigue pants, white tee shirt, and combat boots.

Sergeant Mardoon shouted, "You will sit on the floor and wait for an Army instructor to come in and advise you further. After he is done you will walk through those swinging doors and another instructor will talk with you. For now, get dressed and sit on the floor and wait till the instructor or myself comes back. Do you understand, Shitheads?" Every one replied except Rick. Sergeant Mardoon left the room. Mike could see the metamorphosis taking place before his eyes as the young men put on their army uniforms.

Someone blurted out. "These pants don't fit."

Someone else yelled. "Wear them any way. Who the hell cares." The whole group was now dressed in olive drab fatigue pants, white tee shirts and the large heavy combat boots. Some men were sitting leaning forward with arms over their knees and their chins resting on their arms. Others sat erect and stared at the ceiling thinking.

The room was quiet. Mike looked at Rick who was shaking his head. "What's the matter Rick? You got that sergeant on your mind.?"

Rick's expression was serious. "Yeah, I got him on my mind. "What goes with these people here? Why do they have to be hard asses? They never saw us before and right away they have to start that name calling. What goes with this shithead, numb nuts and all those goofy names? Why can't they call us by our names?"

"Don't let it bother you, Rick. Don't take it personal. Ignore it. It will be a lot easier."

"No, Mike, that's not how it is. This really bothers me. I won't take it."

"Rick, it's silly letting it get to you. What's the big deal? "It's only a name. Nothing else seems to bother you. Why get up tight over a name?"

Rick shook his head and squinted. "You don't understand. It's easy for you guys." He stuttered and looked to the floor. "Never mind you wouldn't understand. I'm not going to take it. I'll get even with every one of those bastards who don't call me by my right name." Rick stood up and went to a window and stared out. Mike felt Rick wanted to talk some more but he couldn't. This name calling really upset him.

18

Mike didn't ask any more questions. His thoughts went back to home and his mother. The more he thought the more depressed he got. He shook his head. *I've got to get these thoughts out of my mind. I know uncle Tim will help her, I'll call her as soon as I can.* He put his head back and tried to get a quick nap. His eyes shut and he was dozing off when he heard a loud thump and laughing. His head shot forward and his eyes opened wide.

Rick was laying on his back in the middle of the floor. Everyone was laughing. Rick got up and walked to the wall. He bent over and threw his feet in the air. He was now standing on his hands with his feet pointed to the ceiling. He shouted, "I'll bet anyone five bucks I can make it across the room without falling."

A hillbilly accented voice yelled. "You're on boy." Rick's hands were alternating in front of him. Sometimes fast, and sometimes slow trying to maintain his balance. He gained speed as he came to the far end of the room. His body struck the wall and he fell backwards. The large combat boots he wore slammed to the floor, making a loud pounding noise. He immediately jumped up and shouted. "Okay sucker, where you at? Who bet the five bucks?"

Again the hillbilly voice. "Right har."

Rick walked to him with his palm up. "Place the money right here."

The guy stood up and he was big. "Okay, man, you win but aren't y'all going to be a sport about it and let a man get a chance to get his money back?"

Rick studied him for a second. "Okay, big boy, if you can go farther than I did we're even."

The big guy stared at him. "That sure is right nice of you." He went to the spot Rick started from and got up on his hands. He went about five feet and his body started to wobble. His arms gave out and he came down with a crashing boom. He laid on the floor, moaned a little then laughed and crawled back to the wall.

Rick stood in the center of the room with his hands on his hips shaking his head. "Man, it ain't going to do any good. Stay on the floor. I'm the champ and nobody can beat me."

Almost in unison voices shouted, "Bull Shit" Twenty young men were now up on their hands trying to walk across the room. They fell and the large combat boots hitting the floor sounded like the beats of bass drums. A lot of cursing and loud laughing filled the room as they kept trying to get the hang of it. Mike was laughing so hard his stomach begun to cramp.

19

He was about to try it when the swinging doors flew open. Two officers stared at what was going on. The young men falling and laughing weren't aware they were being watched. They continued trying. One of the officers yelled. "ATTENTION." The startled young men crawled and walked back to the wall. Again the officer yelled. "When you hear attention you get to your feet and stand at attention." Everyone in the room stood up and stiffened their bodies. "What in the hell is going on in here? "We're having a conference downstairs and it sounded like the ceiling was coming down. We thought it was an earth quake. I'm warning you people that if I hear one more sound, I'll make sure you don't have enough energy to make another one. AM I CLEAR?"

A loud answer. "Yes Sir." The officers glared at every man, then left the room. One by one the young soldiers slowly eased themselves down and sat. A corporal entered the room. The young men jumped to attention.

"No, no. You only come to attention when an officer comes into the room. I'm a corporal. You men and the group in the next room will have to wait for about a half hour. At that time you will be escorted by your sergeant to the Mess Hall for lunch." He left through the swinging doors and talked to the group in the next room.

"Mike, those two officers were really pissed."

"Yeah, they sure were, I bet that did make a lot of racket down there."

Rick looked around the room and his expression got serious. He stared at the big guy with the hillbilly accent. He jumped up and walked on his tiptoes to him. "Hey man, you owe me five bucks."

The big guy shook his head. "No way man, I didn't get a fair chance. Them old boys came in here all hot and bothered. I didn't get a chance to practice."

Rick stared at him. "Well, go practice now."

"Boy, you're plum out of your cotton-picking mind. They'd hang me by my ass if I made a noise. Them boys are mad."

Rick looked at the swinging doors at the far end of the room. He walked to the doors and slightly parted them. He saw the other group of inductees sitting against the walls. He went back to the big guy. "Hey, Hillbilly, want to get even?"

"Sure do. But I sure as hell ain't getting up on my hands again."

"No man, you don't have to get up on your hands. You see them swinging doors leading into that other room?"

"Yeah, I. see them."

"Okay, all you have to do is open them wide when I tell you and we'll be even."

The big guy got up. "That's fair enough." He walked very quietly to the doors and looked over his shoulder. Rick was hunched over in the middle of the room. He motioned with his finger.

"Okay Hillbilly, open them doors." The big guy pushed them open. Rick leaned forward and now was standing on his hands. "Okay Hillbilly, keep them open wide, I'm coming through."

The big guy saw him coming on his hands. "Ah, shit, man you're nuts. I don't want no part of this crap." Rick made it through the doors and walked on his hands across the other room. Hillbilly shook his head and walked on his tip toes to his spot by the wall. "No, sir, I all don't want any part of that mess. What's the matter with that boy?"

Rick was the center of attention as he completed his journey to the far end of the next room. All the men were staring at him. He took great care getting to his feet not to make any noise. A few men started to clap. Rick threw up his hands. "No clapping, or cheering it's not necessary. I just want to tell you who I am. I'm Rick Miller." He pointed to the room he came from. "I just won the championship of walking on my hands in that room. I'm looking for some fresh competition, but after seeing you guys I don't see anyone in here who can beat me." The room came alive.

A shout from someone. "Your ass, who do you think you are? I can beat you." Other guys started hollering.

Rick shook his head. "No yelling. You guys practice, then have a run off. Whoever is the best in this room will go up against me, the champ. I don't care how good you think you are. No one from this room can beat me."

Again they started to shout. "Well if you're so damn good, let's put some money on it."

Rick again quieted them down. "If you guys want to lose your money it's all right with me."

They laughed. "We'll be ready in a short time. We'll show you who the champ is."

Rick smiled and slowly walked through the swinging doors and sat next to Mike.

"What did you start up in there?"

21

"Just sit back and watch the fireworks."

Mike started to ask him another question but was interrupted by familiar sounds. Thuds, loud shouting and laughing came from the other room. Mike stared at Rick. The noise increased and the floor vibrated. Mike shook his head, "Oh no. You better get in there and put a stop to that."

Rick got up and quietly walked to the doors and peeked in. He smiled and motioned for Mike to come. Mike threw up his hands and shook his head. "No way, I don't want any part of that." The noise that was coming from the other room was deafening.

Rick quickly backed away from the door and sat next to Mike. "It won't be long now."

He no sooner said it than the swinging doors blasted open. The two officers were back yelling. "ATTENTION." The men jumped to their feet. The officers had puzzled looks when they saw no one was making any noise. That look was short lived when they heard the racket coming from the next room. They ran through the swinging doors. The noise was so intense the officers had to yell, attention, three times before it got quiet. One of the officers shouted, "So you damn fools think this is a joke, do you? I'll show you the Army means business. Just because you're new is no excuse you're going to get away with this."

Sergeant Mardoon walked into the room where Mike and his group were. He heard the commotion coming from the next room. He walked to the swinging doors and looked in. An officer saw him. "Sergeant Mardoon."

"Yes sir."

"I want you to take these men down to the parking lot and give them short order drill for a few hours. I want them to learn how to obey orders."

"Sergeant Mardoon stuttered a little and pointed to the other room where Mike and Rick were. "Sir, my men are in..."

The officer didn't let him finish. "Sergeant you heard what I said. That's an order. Take these men to the parking lot and give them short order drill, immediately. Do you hear?"

"Yes Sir."

The two officers came back through the room where Mike and Rick were. The older officer said while he was walking out, "Now it will be quiet."

A lot of yelling, and cursing came from Sergeant Mardoon in the next room. The group of men filed out with the Sergeant behind shouting, "You

Shitheads get in trouble and I get punished. You bunch of slope headed bastards."

Mike looked at Rick. "If he ever finds out what you did he'll kill you."

"No sweat Mike, you just adapt to the situation. He deserves it. Maybe he'll stop that name calling."

Ten minutes passed and another sergeant came into the room. He was younger than Mardoon. "Men, I'm Sergeant Carlie, and you are my group. I will be with you for the next couple of days till your assignments to another camp for basic training come through. Any questions?"

Rick raised his hand. "Sergeant, we had Sergeant Mardoon. What happened to him?"

"I don't know. They told me to come to this group and I'm here. The army works in strange ways sometimes. I don't question orders."

Rick elbowed Mike. "Well, we got rid of that name calling jerk."

"What do you mean we?"

More questions were asked. One small blond haired kid asked. "Where do you think we'll end up sergeant?"

"This is not official, but I would guess that ninety percent of you will be going to Korea. The rest will stay Stateside, or Europe."

Mike elbowed Rick. "Where do you want to go?"

"Home."

The Sergeant answered a few more questions, then said it was dinner time. He walked out of the room and everyone followed. They exited the building and were stopped by Sergeant Carlie who wanted his group to let a ragged bunch of men trying to march go by. Sergeant Mardoon was by the side of the formation shouting. "Your left, your left, your left ."The men were all out of step. Sergeant Mardoon ran to the front of the group and threw up his hands. "COMPANY HALT. LISTEN YOU BUNCH OF SHITHEADS, YOUR LEFT FOOT IS ON THE SAME SIDE OF YOUR BODY AS YOUR LEFT ARM. DO YOU HEAR ME SHITHEADS?"

"YES SIR."

The march was on again, "Your left, your left." Sergeant Mardoon looked tired and disgusted.

When they passed, Sergeant Carlie shouted to his group. "Okay men, let's go." They were approaching the mess hall when Sergeant Mardoon's voice got louder. His group had turned around and were coming back to where Mike and the rest of the men stood in front of the mess hall. Mike looked at Rick and saw his expression. He knew he was going to do something crazy. He quickly moved away from him and mingled with a few guys by the door to the mess hall. When Sergeant Mardoon's ragged group passed, Rick shouted.

"Hey Mardoon, you're nothing but a stupid Shithead." He quickly blended into a group waiting to go into the mess hall.

The sergeant's head snapped around. He stared but couldn't determine who had yelled He squinted and grumbled some cuss words. Hillbilly saw this and he whispered to Rick. "Boy you don't know when you're well off. You all better keep that bullshit to yourself. That old sergeant is looking like he's fit to kill."

The mess hall was a Quonset hut. The smell of food greeted them as they entered. Sergeant Carlie ordered them to grab a metal tray and get in line. As they passed the steam table men were standing gripping large spoons. The group held their trays out and the servers slammed food on it. They went to a table and sat down. Mike looked at the white watery food oozing out of one section of the tray into another. He turned to Hillbilly. "Don't look too good does it?"

Hillbilly looked up from his tray. "Hell man, we give better swill to the hogs." The rest of the men made faces as they stared at their trays.

Rick grabbed the large soup spoon and started shoveling the food into his mouth. He looked up. "Man this is better than home cooking." The men stared at him with disgusted expressions. They couldn't believe it. Rick shouted at Hillbilly. "Shit, Hillbilly, this is better than southern cooking. You ought to try it."

"I'm telling you boy, you are plum crazy. How did you all get into this army? They're only supposed to take sane people?"

Mike got up with most of the men from the table and walked to the dump can. He slammed the tray on the inside and placed it on a pile of dirty ones. He went outside and mingled with the other men who couldn't eat. Rick was the last one out. He yelled. "That was the best meal I ever had." He walked to Mike.

Mike shook his head. "You really didn't like that, did you?"

He smiled. "Hell no, I hated it. Did you see the looks on those guys? A couple of them almost puked."

"You sure are something Rick. Don't you ever quit?"

"Like I told you before Mike. You can make this army thing a bad scene or make it a fun thing. All you got to do is adapt to the situation and everything will come out all right."

Mike shook his head. "Boy, I wonder about you. I never met anyone like you."

Chapter 4
Who Won The World Series

Mike, Rick and Hillbilly were sent to Camp Carson. When they exited the plane Rick yelled, "Man look at those hills."

Hillbilly hit him on the back. "Man, don't you know nothing, those aren't hills they're the Rocky Mountains."

Rick, laughed. "If anyone should know you would. I bet you walked on so many hills your one leg is shorter than the other."

Hillbilly, with his jolly way, smiled. He looked to the mountains. "You know what this hilly country tells you? Mike and Rick nodded. "We're all on our way to Korea the land of the Frozen Chosen. They say the country around here is exactly like it is over there."

Rick smiled. "I bet it's a lot quieter around here." The conversation ended and they continued to stare at the mountains.

"FALL IN! HURRY UP!" A sergeant quickly walked to the group of men who had just gotten off the plane.

Hillbilly, looked at Mike. "I guess that means us." They joined the other men and formed four lines.

The sergeant stood in front of them. "Welcome to Camp Carson, Colorado. I'm Sergeant Welever and I'm going to be your drill instructor for the next sixteen weeks. I'm going to make soldiers out of you Shitheads. I want you to know that your soul belongs to God but your ass belongs to me, and I intend to work it off." Mike and Hillbilly cringed. They knew what's coming.

A familiar voice from the assembled men. "I'll be goddamned. Another idiot." The Sergeant hadn't heard the voice and continued to give his well rehearsed speech.

Mike wondered how many times he had given this speech to new men. He went on and on using large words trying to impress the inductees. After a hour he finally concluded. "And that men is what you can expect while you're here at Camp Carson. Are there any questions?"

Rick raised his hand. The Sergeant glared at him like he was the first recruit to ever ask a question. He pointed his finger at Rick. "Yeah. You there Shithead, what do you want?"

"Yes, Sergeant I have a question."

"Go ahead!"

"Who won the world series last year?"

"What the hell does that got to do with basic training? You idiot."

Rick smiled. "It doesn't. You asked if anyone had a question and I was wondering about baseball and I forgot who won the series. Oh, and Sergeant could you explain to me what a Shithead is?"

Sergeant Welever glared at Rick. Mike bit his tongue not to laugh. The quietness and the staring of Sergeant Welever at Rick was too much. Someone behind Mike busted out laughing and it was like a chain reaction. The whole group laughed. Sergeant Welever shouted. "ATTENTION." The laughter stopped and he walked through the ranks and positioned himself in front of Rick. "So you're one of those smart bastards, huh?" He stared right into Rick's eyes and talked through gritted teeth. He pushed his face to about an inch away from Rick's. "Now, Asshole, you got anything to say?" Rick watched the beads of sweat forming on the sergeant's forehead. "Well Shithead, say something."

"Yes, Sergeant, I have something to say. I don't think you brushed your teeth this morning. Your breath is pretty bad. If you don't mind I would appreciate if you'd moved back a few inches, or feet." Sergeant Welever rolled his hand into a fist and was drawing back to hit Rick in the face. Rick didn't flinch. He kept his hands to his side. "If I were you Sergeant, I wouldn't get violent. I've heard of many instances where men have lost their rank for striking a recruit."

The sergeant froze in his position and slowly unraveled his fist and pointed his finger at Rick. "Listen Shithead I got you for sixteen weeks and you're going to regret every second of it. Do you hear me, Shithead?"

"Oh, I hear you Sergeant and so did every man here. I believe you are threatening me. In the event you have any intentions of carrying out those threats, I will go immediately to the Inspector General's office and give him all the details. I will also request these men be called into the investigation so they can testify that you threatened me the first day at this camp."

Sergeant Welever stared a while longer, then looked both ways and whispered in Rick's ear. "I'll get you, Bastard." He walked back to the front of the group.

The men were marched to a large Quonset hut. "OK men, this is the Personnel Building. Enter in a single file. They're going to ask you questions. You answer as best you can. Once inside, follow the arrows and go to the desks where the sergeants are sitting. Does anyone have a question?"

Mike looked at Rick. He was going to say something but Mike shook his head. "Don't do it Rick. He's going to make it rough on all of us."

Rick mumbled. "Okay, I won't."

The Sergeant looked at Rick. "Are there any questions?" Rick stared at him and whispered a foul name. The Sergeant didn't hear it. "Okay, go in."

Mike, Rick and Hill Billy went to the back of the line. The men relaxed and laughed at what Rick had done. Hillbilly slapped his leg, "Boy I almost pissed my pants when you asked that sergeant those questions. That old boy was sweating and talking an hour about the army, and you ask him who won the World Series. I never saw anything like that before. I'll remember it for the rest of my life."

Rick stared at Hillbilly with a concerned look. "You tell me that after two years and I'll be a happy man Hillbilly."

Hillbilly blurted out. "Hey, what you mean by that?"

Mike joined in. "Yeah, what did you mean by that?"

Rick turned away, shrugged his shoulders and didn't say anything. Hillbilly shouted. "Boy I can't figure you out, one minute you're raising all kinds of hell. The next minute you're as serious as a heart attack. What goes with you man?" .

Rick turned around. "Lets just drop it, we've got to answer a bunch of questions in that building so I don't want to answer questions out here. Didn't you hear what that half baked Sergeant said."

The line moved slowly. About an hour later they finally went through the front door. The heat inside was unbearable. Rick was first. He walked to a desk where a heavy set sergeant was wiping perspiration from his neck and face with a towel. He asked in a hoarse mean voice, "What's your name?"

"Rick Miller."

The Sergeant kept staring at the paper and holding his pencil in one of the question blocks. He shouted. "You a girl?"

"The last time I looked I wasn't." The sweating sergeant glared. "If you're not a girl Shithead, sound off like you got a pair." His pencil went back to the block on the paper. "What's your name Numb Nuts?"

Rick looked offended. Mike and Hillbilly both shook their heads. It was too late. Rick cupped his hands around his mouth, leaned over next to the Sergeant's ear and shouted as loud as he could. "RICK MILLER." Everyone in the room jumped.

The Sergeant stared at him and tapped his pencil on the desk. "Now Asshole, I got your name, where do you live?"

Rick again cupped his hands to his mouth and shouted his address. A captain came out of an office and ran to Rick. "What are you yelling about?"

Rick pointed down at the heavy Sergeant. "Sir, that Sergeant told me to do it."

The captain's stare went from Rick to the Sergeant. "What the hell is the matter with you telling him to yell like that?"

The Sergeant came to attention and stood speechless. His uniform was wet with perspiration. The captain spoke again, "I don't want any more noise, is that understood Sergeant?"

"Yes Sir."

The captain walked back to his office. The sergeant slowly sat down all the time glaring at Rick. "Now listen Slope Head I don't want any more bullshit. When I ask you a question you answer it. Is that understood?"

"Oh yes, Sergeant, I'll answer any question for you. Please look at my name at the top of that paper where you wrote it down and use it. If you do, there won't be any more problems."

The sergeant picked up his pencil and put it in one of the blocks again. "Shithead, how far did you go to school? "

"Three blocks."

"Asshole, what was the last grade you attended?"

"Sergeant, my name is Rick Miller not Asshole. Don't you people understand? Rick's the name. Just call me by my name and there will be no trouble."

The Sergeant started to get up. He looked at the captain's office and sat back down. He put his pencil back in one of the boxes and wrote third grade. He wiped the sweat from his forehead with his shirt sleeve. "Where were you employed, Shithead?"

"I was a salesman."

"What did you sell, Shithead?"

"I sold do-it-yourself volcano kits. Not everybody can have lava running down their front yard and onto their sidewalk."

Mike and Hillbilly tried not to laugh but they couldn't hold it back. The sergeant climbed up on the desk broke his pencil and dove at Rick's throat yelling, "I've had enough. You silly son-of-a-bitch, I'll kill you." He had Rick by the throat and was squeezing. Three other sergeants rushed to him and pulled his hands from Rick's neck."

The Captain ran out of his office. "WHAT'S GOING ON HERE?" The Sergeant who was being restrained shouted. "LET ME LOOSE I'LL KILL THAT SMART BASTARD."

Rick stood with a defiant expression. "There he goes again. I've got a name and why can't he use it?"

The Captain ordered the men to release the Sergeant. "Sergeant sit down at your desk. What is the problem here?"

"He's a wise guy, Sir. I asked him what he did for a living and he got cute."

Rick looked at the Captain. "Sir, can I tell you my side of the story?"

The Captain pointed his finger at Rick. "Listen, you Wise Ass. You don't have a side. Now tell him what you did for a living?"

Rick glanced at Mike and shrugged his shoulders. He turned and looked directly into the Captain's eyes. "I used to smuggle bananas into the Virgin Islands."

The Captain glared at him. The big Sergeant jumped up. His chair fell back. "JUST LET ME HAVE THAT JERK FOR A COUPLE OF MINUTES!"

Mike tried not laugh but he did. He turned away and Hillbilly saw him. He too broke out laughing.

The Captain yelled at another sergeant. " Take these men to the mess hall."

Hillbilly pointed at himself. "Me, I didn't do nothing."

The Captain shouted. "You two thought he was funny. You can be entertained by him while you're doing K.P."

The three of them were marched to the mess hall. The Mess Sergeant was told the Captain sent them. He smiled. "I'm glad, I was running out of screw-ups." He motioned for the three of them to follow him into the kitchen. He pointed to a stack of metal food trays covered with garbage. "Get your asses to that sink and get busy."

Rick smiled "Sergeant, do you have rubber gloves? I don't want to get dish pan hands."

"Listen Shithead, the only rubber you'll get is a rubber club which I'll break over your stupid head."

"Hey there's that name again. I heard it before." Rick was about to get into a heated argument.

Mike grabbed his arm. "Come on Rick, we're in enough trouble as it is." They grabbed the dirty trays and put them into the soapy water. Two hours passed and the last tray was washed. They were drying their hands on their pants when Hillbilly saw a large dishwasher on the other side of the kitchen.

"Hey Sergeant, why didn't you tell us you had a dishwasher?"

The Sergeant laughed. "You didn't ask, Shithead." Rick started to say something. Mike and Hillbilly got in front of him. They warned him he better not.

Hillbilly yelled. "Hey Sergeant, we're done can we leave?"

"You boys, grab those mops and wash down the eating areas."

Hillbilly squinted. "The eating area, holy cow, look at the size of it!"

"Never mind the bullshit. Grab those mops and buckets and get to work."

Hillbilly shook his head in disgust. "Hell man, it will take hours to wash that floor."

The sergeant laughed. That's the idea, Shithead. Now get your asses behind those mops and move it." They started mopping and cussing under their breath.

About three hours passed and Rick asked if he could get a drink. The sergeant yelled, "I said mop the damn floor. Not drink water. When you get the floor done I might consider letting you."

Rick glared, then shook his head. He mumbled. "I'll get even, you meat-head."

They continued to mop and were almost done. Mike looked at Rick and Hillbilly. "We only got a little ways to go now."

Hillbilly smiled. "We got it made in the shade. Let's give it hell and get out of here." Their feeling of accomplishment was short lived. The doors flew open and hundreds of soldiers with dusty combat boots ran to the pile of metal trays. Dirty shoe prints marked the clean floor. The three of them leaned on their mops and stared in disbelief.

The sergeant saw them and laughed. "Guess what you Shitheads will be doing after they get done chowing down? Get your asses behind that counter. I need servers." He pointed at Mike. "Grab that large spoon and put potatoes on their trays when they come by." He shouted at Hillbilly. "You, put a square of ice cream on their tray." He looked at Rick and smiled. "And you Shithead, take that dipper and put gravy on their potatoes."

Rick knew he was being baited. He glared at the sergeant and did everything he could not to punch him. Mike and Hillbilly again calmed him down.

Mike handed him the dipper. "Come on Rick do what he says."

Rick continued to stare at the Sergeant. Three other men were put behind the counter to help serve. The mass of men formed a single file and were moving past the servers. Mike dug into the large bucket of mashed potatoes and scooped up a heaping spoonful and dropped it in the front section of the tray. The soldier yelled "Hit the spoon on the tray." He wanted every morsel that stuck to the spoon. Mike hit the spoon on the tray for him. Hillbilly put the ice cream on their trays. They kept asking for two squares. He continued to give them one and tried to explain he was ordered to only give one. They kept arguing for two.

Rick poured the gravy on the potatoes and they wanted two dips, so they could soak their bread. He gave it to the ones who asked. He didn't care. More men came and the line got longer. It was nerve racking. The soldiers were becoming more demanding. They bitched louder and threatened the men behind the counter.

Rick shouted. "Mike, I had enough of this shit." He walked to a chair and sat down. The line stopped and the men started banging their trays on the counter.

The Mess Sergeant heard the commotion and came running. "What the hell's going on back there?"

Mike saw him. "Hey Rick, get up, the Sergeant's coming."

Rick just sat. The sergeant saw him sitting in the chair with his head leaning on the wall, with his eyes closed. "Hey, Shithead, wake up, what the hell do you think you're doing?"

Rick's eyes slowly opened. "I'm tired and I need a break."

"Break my ass. Get up and serve these guys, The only break you'll get is when I break your damn neck."

Rick was mad and Mike could tell. "Come on Rick, let's get this over with. Don't say anything. We want to get out of this place." Rick slowly got up and walked back to his position at the steam table.

Rick started putting gravy on the potatoes again and the line started to move. It wasn't fast enough for the sergeant. He yelled. "Hey Numb-Nuts back there, hurry it up. You guys who got your food put it in your mouths and chew it later. Get the hell out of here." Mike wiped the sweat from his forehead with the back of his hand. The Sergeant kept yelling and the soldiers continued to argue for more food.

A soldier pushed his tray in front of Rick. Rick looked at him and slowly moved the dipper over the ice cream and poured.

The guy shouted "Why you son-of-a-bitch, you put that gravy on my ice cream on purpose."

Rick smiled. "Sir, that's what your order said."

He tried to yell at Rick but the guys behind shouted for him to move. He cussed, and walked away.

The next man put out his tray waiting for gravy. Rick again poured hot gravy over the ice cream. The soldier threw a spoon at Rick and missed. Rick laughed. "I hope you can shoot better than you throw."

Someone in the line yelled. "Come on jerk move it. We're not going to have time to eat." The next man placed his hand over the ice cream and stared at Rick. Rick sunk the ladle deep in the hot gravy and pulled it out. He moved the dipper over the man's hand. They both stared at each other. Rick poured the hot gravy.

"Yeeow— you scalded me." He danced and shook the hot gravy from his hand than wiped his hand on his pants. He threw the tray at Rick. Rick ducked. The tray flew over his head and hit the wall.

Rick smiled at him. "You got to aim before you throw." The guy climbed on the counter and tried to kick Rick in the face. Rick grabbed the guy's leg and twisted. The guy lost his balance and the seat of his pants landed in the mashed potatoes. Another server grabbed his ankles and pushed him till he fell off the front of the counter. He hit the floor hard. The men in line laughed at him. He jumped up and swung at whoever he could hit. The battle was on. Rick scooped up a spoonful of hot mashed potatoes and slung it hitting one of the battlers in the face. He screamed, wiped his face with a quick downward motion and jumped on the counter and tried to dive on Rick. Hillbilly smacked him in the head with the large metal tongs and he dropped on

33

the counter then rolled off on the floor. Rick kept slinging mashed potatoes and laughing. Everybody in the place was fighting. When one of the battlers tried to scale the counter he would be knocked back to the other side by the servers.

The sergeant came running and shouting. "Stop, stop, attention. No one paid attention. They kept punching. The sergeant became frustrated. He grabbed men and pulled them away from the brawl. He grasped a big soldier by the shoulders and tried to yank him away from the guy he was fighting. The big guy thought someone was going to hit him. He quickly spun around and swung a powerful right hook that hit the sergeant flush on the chin. The sergeant hit the floor and slid under a table.

Rick shouted. "That was the prettiest sight I ever saw."

The brawl had spread throughout the mess hall. Men were throwing food and banging trays over each other's heads. Military police entered the hall with helmets on and billy clubs in their hands. Rick yelled to Hillbilly and Mike, "Hurry, let's get the hell out of here." Mike and Hill Billy hesitated, Rick grabbed their arms and pulled them out the back door. "Believe me you guys, it's best to get out of here now."

Mike yelled. "Boy if they catch us skipping out, we'll be in all kinds of trouble."

Rick shook his head. "Don't worry, it's best you'll see. Trust me."

They ran for a couple of blocks and hid behind a warehouse. Mike kept pacing back and forth. "We better go back."

Rick shook his head. "Hell no, we get as far away from here as possible."

Mike stared at him. "What are you getting at? What do you mean get as far away from here as we can?"

Rick pointed to a large fence that surrounded the camp. "Well, you see that fence. We climb it and become civilians again."

Mike grabbed him by the shirt. "That is the dumbest thing I ever heard of. We'll be AWOL and they'll court martial us. Don't even think about it."

Rick shrugged his shoulders. "Well I guess this is where we part. Say good bye to Civilian Miller. You guys stick around and take all that name calling and them chicken shit sergeants. He broke loose and ran toward the fence. Mike tackled him. They hit the ground and Mike wrestled on top. He drew back his fist to punch him.

Hillbilly grabbed Mike's arm. "Don't do it Mike. It won't do any good."

"Turn me loose Hillbilly, I'm going to knock some sense in this crazy fool. I never been in so much trouble in all my life." Mike kept staring at Rick, then slowly got up. He shook his head then reached down and picked Rick up. "I'm sorry I lost it. We're in so much trouble I can't even think." He patted Rick on his shoulder. "I don't want to see you go over that fence and ruin your life."

Hillbilly nodded his head. "He's right Rick you'll end up in the federal pen. Man, you don't need that. Let's try to get this mess straightened out."

Rick stared at them. "You guys care about me. You don't want me to get in more trouble. You don't want me to go AWOL because you like me. You really care about me. His head turned to the side. He kept taking deep breaths to fight off his emotions. He tried to talk but words won't come out. Mike and Hill Billy stood speechless. Rick got control again. "I'm sorry I got you guys in this mess. I'll get you out of it no matter how hard."

Mike stared at him. "I think the best thing to do is go back and face the consequences."

"Hell no, we got a perfect excuse. We were scared. Those guys were going to kill us in that fight. We were outnumbered and they were coming over that counter like pirates and swinging those metal trays trying to knock our heads off. We adapted to the situation and got out of there. If we tell them that they'll let us go."

"There you go again with that damn adapt to the situation. It's not that simple. Mike raised his hands. "We got to think this out. Man, if they find out we ran out of there, we'll end up in the brig."

"Now listen you guys have faith in me and everything will be all right. I have experience in these type of things."

Mike shook his head. "Oh no, you don't give a damn. I just wanted to come in this army and do my time and get it over with and no problems. I've only been in a few days and I'm in all kinds of trouble. Ever since I met you Rick I don't know what's going to happen next."

Hillbilly agreed. "You're sure right there Mike, that old boy will get you in all kinds of trouble and you don't even know you're getting into it."

Mike paced back and forth staring at the ground talking to himself. "I don't know. I've got to think this out"

"Aw come on you guys. I know I can work this out. Just have faith in me and everything will be all right."

Mike pointed at him. "OK: what's your plan?"

35

"We go back to that Quonset hut where all this trouble started and we act like we did our punishment and get processed and that's all there is too it."

Hillbilly asked. "What about that big fight we were in at the mess hall. They'll be looking for us."

"That big fights is the answer. It will take those MP's about a hour and a half to straighten that mess out. By that time we'll be processed and out of the Quonset hut." "What do you think Mike?"

"Man, I don't know. I can't think of anything. It might work till one of those sergeants calls him a Shithead. By the way what makes you so mad when they call you a name?"

Rick turned away. "Never mind, it just bothers me. Don't worry I won't cause no more trouble if we go back. I promise." No one said anything, they just stared at one another.

"Mike, We don't have a choice. Let's go with this crazy fool. If he starts trouble in there I'll knock his head off."

"Okay Rick, We'll go. But what Hillbilly said goes twice for me. I don't care what they call you. You ignore it. I don't know what your problem is with this name calling, but I don't want any more trouble." They approached the Quonset hut and the line was still long.

Mike and Hillbilly were concerned. Rick was calm. It was like this was an everyday thing for him. Mike sensed Rick really didn't care. "Rick I want you to understand something."

"Yeah what, is it Mike?"

"If you cause any trouble in there I'm going to punch you so hard you'll never forget it."

"Aw, I promised you Mike. I wouldn't do anything that will get you or Hillbilly in any trouble. You're my friends."

Hillbilly pointed at Rick. "You don't do anything to get yourself in trouble either. You hear?"

Rick lead them to the front of the line. He talked with a couple of the men and conned them. He told them they were here before and they had to do some work for the general. The general told them to go back in line where they were before. The men looked at them suspiciously, then motioned for them to get in front. Rick walked up to Station #1 and came to attention and saluted the fat sergeant who he had the problem with.

The sergeant stared at him. "Listen Shithead you only salute officers. It

36

looks like you learned your lesson. I want you to know I am goddamn tired. I don't want any of your bullshit. If you do I'll pull your fuck'en head right off your shoulders. Do you understand Shithead?"

Mike and Hillbilly held their breath. Rick faked like he was scared. "Yes sir. No more trouble. Sir, I'm Rick Miller, I come to you to answer all your questions. Yes sir, I've learned my lesson. I promise I will never talk bad to a sergeant again. I'm sorry, Sir."

The sergeant pulled a clean sheet of paper and asked him questions. He answered everyone without a smart remark. When the sergeant completed the form he stacked it on a large pile of other completed forms. He looked up and smiled. "Well Shithead, that K.P. is only a mild taste of what you're going to get if you fuck up again, do you understand?"

Rick heard Shithead. He stared at the sergeant and then at Mike. Mike shook his head and made a mean face. The sergeant again asked. "Do you hear me Shithead?"

Rick paused. Mike and Hillbilly were tense. Finally he said. "Yes Sergeant."

The sergeant pointed at another desk. "Get your sorry ass over there and talk with that man." Rick slowly walked away. Mike and Hillbilly were processed without any problem. After going through all the stations they were ordered outside where other young soldiers were waiting.

The three of them got together. Hillbilly puckered up his lips and let air out. "Boy, I never dreamed we'd get out of there." Man, I thought any minute they were going to throw us in a room and call the M.P's"

Mike looked serious. "We're not out of it yet. Let's hope that door doesn't fly open and that fat sergeant comes running at us. What do you think Rick?"

"You know that pile of forms that were made out about us and the rest of these guys? I saw a soldier pick up that pile and go out the door. If we can make it out of here I think we'll be in the clear."

CHAPTER 5
My name is Rickey

The waiting group became quiet when a new sergeant walked up. He shouted. "Fall in." The young men quickly formed five lines. "Men, I'm Sergeant Carter and I'm going to be with you while you're taking basic training here at Camp Carson. What we're going to do now is take you to your quarters. I want you to try to look organized. When I say forward march, you step off on your left foot. Every time I say hup, try to have your left foot hit the ground. I know it will seem awkward at first but you'll catch on. Look around you. These men standing next to you will be your unit known as "A" company. We'll be competing against other companies. I'd like to have the best unit. Men, let's have pride in our group. As long as you have to be here, why not be the best? Okay, I said what I wanted. The rest is up to you. Good luck."

Mike thought this sergeant knew how to talk and motive people, like a good coach. He looked at Rick. Rick nodded his head and winked. Sergeant Carter shouted. "Okay men here we go. Forward march." Most of the men stepped off on their left foot. Others got mixed up and stumbled and tried to skip to get in step. The formation looked like a large sheet with dogs and cats fighting under it. The sergeant called the group to a halt. "Okay men that wasn't bad for the first time. Now again, when I say forward march step off with your left foot. You can do it. Just relax and think left foot. Again Sergeant Carter shouted. "Forward march. Everyone stepped off on his left foot. Sergeant Carter walked along the side of the formation and kept repeating hup, hup. The men were smiling because they were in unison. Sergeant Carter kept yelling encouragement between the hups.

"You got it men. You're doing great. Hup, hup, hup." Mike could feel the pride of this unit being born. He looked at Rick who was caught up in it too. He was actually trying.

Everything was going well till Hillbilly talked out of the side of his mouth. "Mike, look back at that Quonset hut."

Mike slowly turned and squinted and saw two Military Police cars parked in front. He knew they were inquiring about the fight in the mess hall.

He shouted. "Hey Rick." Rick turned. Mike lifted his thumb over his shoulder and pointed at the police cars. Rick looked back. He smiled and nodded his head.

Hillbilly said. "What you all going to do now? We're in a real mess."

Rick laughed and made a smirk and formed a circle with his thumb and index finger. He stretched his body so he could see above the men in front of him. He saw another company about fifty yards in front of his group. He called out to Sergeant Carter. The Sergeant kept in step and moved next to Rick.

"What is it soldier?"

"What is double time sir?"

"Double time is getting the formation to a place faster. Why do you ask that soldier?"

"Well sir, our group is doing so good. I was wondering if we could do double time and pass that bunch in front of us."

Sergeant Carter looked at the group in front of him. "Men, stay in step. Let's show that outfit in front of us how good we are. We're going to pass them. Can we do it?"

A loud shout. "Yes Sir."

"Okay men, "Double time hoe." The hups were coming faster and the men kept in step. In no time they were overtaking the other company. The men could detect that Sergeant Carter was yelling cadence louder and there was pride in his voice as they passed the other company. When they were about a hundred yards ahead of the pasted company Sergeant Carter returned to normal cadence. He shouted. "That was great men. We'll show everybody we're the best." He directed them down a street on the left. It was lined with two story tan colored barracks with ladders nailed to the back for fire escapes. Sergeant Carter halted them if front of the third one. He told them to be at ease. The whole company was bending over grasping to catch their breath in the thin Colorado air.

One of the young soldiers in between pants blurted out at Rick. "What the hell is the matter with you? Telling him to go double time. That kind of shit will kill you, if you're not used to this thin air."

Rick smiled. "I'm gung ho. I want to be a good soldier."

Mike heard this and shook his head. While his head was turned he saw the Military Police at the company that they had passed. They were walking through the ranks. He figured the fat sergeant back at the Quonset Hut told the

M.P.'s that the last group that left the processing center was the company that had the guys who started the fight in the mess hall. He knew now, why Rick asked for double time, and why he wanted to pass that other company. He hit Rick on the shoulder and pointed at the M.P.'s. Rick nodded his head and smiled. "Like I told you Mike, you adapt to the situation."

Sergeant Carter called the men to attention. "I want to tell you men I'm proud of what you did today. There's no doubt you are going to be the best company on this post. I never experienced a group who responded to marching the way you did." He continued to heap praise on them. A large tough looking Master Sergeant walked out of a barracks and up to Sergeant Carter. "What's going on with these Shitheads." Hillbilly and Mike saw Rick squint and mumble something.

"Mike, Rick heard that name. He's going to do something nuts."

"I know. There's nothing we can do about it."

Sergeant Carter explained to the Master Sergeant how fast the men learned to march. He pointed at Rick. "That soldier asked if we could do double time. We passed another company without losing a step."

The two sergeants approached Rick who was standing at attention. Sergeant Carter ordered. "At ease soldier." Rick continued to stand at attention and very ridged. The Master Sergeant yelled.

"You heard the sergeant. At ease, Shithead." Rick continued to stand at attention. The Master Sergeant shouted again. "At ease relax you stupid idiot. What's your name?"

A big smile came on Rick's face. He put his hands on his hips, blinked a couple of times and in a very feminine voice. "Rickey."

The Master Sergeant jumped backwards and glared at Rick. He had a dumbfounded look. He gained his composure and immediately pointed his finger in Rick's face. "You son-of-a- bitch. If you ever talk like that to me again, I'll rip your tongue out of your head." Rick was still standing at attention. The Master Sergeant looked at Sergeant Carter. "Let that silly bastard stand that way till the blood runs out of his empty head." He walked away cussing.

" I told you Mike. I knew he was going to do something nuts. That boy can't leave well enough alone. He's not happy unless he's got everything stirred up. Let someone call him a name and all hell is going to break loose."

Sergeant Carter led them into the barracks. "Okay men line up on both sides of the aisle. When I call out your name go to the bed I assign you." The young soldiers looked at their new living quarters. Everything was made of raw wood. Huge pillars came out of the floor and held up large wooden beams that crossed the ceilings. Mike's name was called. He was assigned a top bunk. Rick got the bunk below him. Mike heard this and he shook his head and thought, Oh, no. Mike climbed up and sat on his bunk and let his legs dangle. He stared at Rick as he walked to the lower bunk.

Rick looked up at him. "Damn, I was hoping to get one with a view, or by the pool."

"Hey Rick don't you ever slow down? One of those guys is going to tear your head off. That sergeant was really mad. He was ready to give you praise for that double time trick. Why did you make him mad?"

Rick didn't answer right away. He shook his head. "You ask me why I made him mad. You tell me why they can't use my real name. What goes with this Shithead stuff. I don't like it and I'm not going to take it. I'll get even with everyone of those idiots who calls me a name."

"What's the big deal. Just ignore it. Don't take it personal. They're calling all of us names. It's no big deal."

Rick stared. His eyes watered a little and he turned. "Maybe it's not a big deal with you. But I—I—I can't. Oh never mind." He walked away.

"Rick, come back. Tell me." Rick went out the door and sat on the step to the porch. Mike saw he didn't want to talk anymore and wanted to be left alone. Mike laid back and fell asleep.

Mike woke up. His bed was bouncing up and down. He looked over the side and saw Rick down below with his feet on the underside of his mattress pushing up. "What's the matter with you? What do you want?"

Rick kept pushing up on the mattress. "I was wondering, how do you like the army?"

Mike was getting mad but he thought what's the use. "I got seven hundred and fifteen days till I get discharged. And if you keep messing up, I'll have to do more. Does that answer your question?"

Rick laughed and laid back. His eyes just closed when the door flew open. Sergeant Carter was standing in the door way. "Attention men, I want everyone out of the barracks and into formation in the back."

A few moans and bitching but the men raced out the door. Sergeant Carter stood in front of the men. "We're going to march to that platform in the middle of the parade field. You are going to meet the Company Commander.

He's going to brief you on what to expect for the next sixteen weeks." The group stood in front of the wooden platform. Mike thought it felt funny not walking on grass. The surface of the parade field was small stones and sand. The group was standing at ease and Mike looked at the beautiful mountains in the distance with the sun setting on them. He thought how nice it would be to explore and climb them. To sit in the peaceful valleys and listen to the fast running water of the streams. This was the first time he had seen mountains. He couldn't wait to get closer to them.

His day dreaming continued till he heard someone shout. "Attention." The gravel under the mens' shoes made a scuffing sound as their shoes came together.

A short man dressed in a Class A uniform climbed the steps and walked to the front of the platform. His uniform was pressed. The silver bars on his shoulders flickered in the dying sun light. His eyes were close together. Mike thought he looked like a sparrow hawk. The man didn't talk. He kept staring at the men standing at attention below him. It seemed like he enjoyed standing above the men who were below him. It was unbelievable how long he continued to stare without saying a word. This staring and silence made the men uneasy. Someone said in a low voice. "The ass hole must be a mute."

Finally a screeched voice pierced the silence. "I am Captain Thimp. I'm the Company Commander of Able Company. That means I'm the most important man in this unit. Whatever I say you will do. I'm going to make you the greatest fighting machine ever. I will work you from dawn to dusk and then some. I will not tolerate any back talk. If you go against any of my rules or the United States Army rules, you will be punished. I will tell you when to eat, sleep, and when to wake up. There will be no overnight passes for sixteen weeks. I don't believe in passes. They're only trouble. Every minute will be directed to you becoming the best soldiers on this camp." He continued to demand and threaten. The men were getting tired at standing at attention. It seemed like the Captain enjoyed it. He continued and the young soldiers appeared hypnotized by his close set eyes staring at them as he preached. From his lecture they determined he was mean and no one wanted to cross him. No matter how painful it was they stood rigid. Fear was being instilled in them. Maybe not all of them.

The hypnotic trance of the men was broken when the noise of pressurized water hitting small pebbles was heard. Someone whispered "Hey, he's pissing." Mike squinted and thought oh, no. Some of the men started to turn around but caught themselves since they were at attention. Sergeant Carter who was standing at the front of the formation right below the platform heard the squirting water hitting the ground. His neck turned red but he didn't turn around. The sound of the running water stopped and just above a whisper a familiar voice.

"Aw, I feel better. You got to adapt to the situation." Mike made up his mind he was not going to laugh even though it was hard.

The speech was finally coming to an end. Captain Thimp wanted to reinforce what would happen if anyone went against his orders. "I want it understood that I feel sorry for anyone who messes up. Do you understand!"

"Yes, Sir."

The small man with the mean look and the hawk eyes continued to stare. He looked down. "Sergeant Carter take charge of these men."

Sergeant Carter waited for the captain to descended from the platform, then he shouted, "At ease." The group sighed and rubbed their sore muscles from standing at attention for so long. "Men, I want you to go back to your barracks. I will be there in fifteen minutes." The group broke ranks and started to walk back to the barracks.

Hillbilly ran up to Mike. "Man, I don't believe what he was doing back there. That old nasty captain was telling all the mean things he was going to do to us if we messed up, and that fool Rick took a piss while he was talking." Mike shook his head and they both laughed.

The men were relaxing on their bunks. Sergeant Carter shouted. "Attention." The men jumped from their beds and scurried to the aisle and stood at attention. Sergeant Carter walked up and down the aisle staring at the men. "All right, who was the wise guy that pissed out there when the Captain was talking? If you would of got caught I can guarantee, you would of been court martial" He stopped talking and his eyes stared at a wooden beam. Everyone looked up and saw a small microphone. Mike felt the sergeant wanted to let everyone know the barracks was being monitored. "Men, you will get cleaned up and ready for supper. Mess formation will be in a half hour. Is that understood?"

"Yes, Sir."

Mike grabbed his towel and started for the shower. Rick was laying on his bunk. Mike bent over and whispered. "You know that Sergeant knew who did that out there. "

"Yeah, I could tell. He stared right at me when he was talking."

"Well he seems like a fair guy. Don't give him any guff."

"Yeah, I agree with you Mike. As long as he don't start that name calling like the rest of those idiots. I'll get along with him."

"What goes with you and this name calling? It's only a name. They are not hurting you. They've been doing it so long it's a habit."

Rick squinted, and got a mean expression. "You don't understand, Mike. Someday I'll tell you about it. I just want to be called by my name. This name calling by these bird brains galls me. Is it too much for them to call me by my name?"

Mike could tell that even talking about this name calling was making him mad. "Well you can adapt to the situation." Rick smiled.

Hillbilly walked up and hit Rick on the shoulder. "You know Rick I think you met your match today. That little old chicken shit Captain looks like he's mean and is going to be pretty rough." He wanted to say more but Mike put his finger over his lip. He pointed to the microphone hooked to the large beam. Hillbilly's eyes widened.

Rick saw this and he cupped his hands around his mouth. He shouted as loud as he could. "Screw that short chicken shit captain."

Hillbilly shut his eyes and shrugged his shoulders. He tiptoed back to his bunk. Mike ran to the shower room.

After supper the men were assembled back in the barracks. Sergeant Carter explained how the army demands that their beds be made a certain way. How their equipment will be displayed in the foot lockers. After he was done he asked. "Are there any questions men?" Mike and Hill Billy looked at Rick. He didn't say anything. Sergeant Carter left the barracks.

Hillbilly tapped Mike on the shoulder. "Man I thought that sapsucker Rick was going to ask a dumb question to piss that Sergeant off."

"If you noticed. Sergeant Carter didn't call us any names."

"Damn, you're right. That old Rick don't take to that name calling. I wonder why?"

Mike climbed up on his bunk. He stared out the window at the beautiful mountains. Darkness was crawling up them but the peaks were still in sunlight.

Chapter 6
The hidden mike

A clicking noise and everyone looked up at the speaker. "This is Captain Thimp. In a half hour all lights will be turned off. There will be no noise, that includes talking. I can hear a pin drop in your barracks. I'll have your ass if you go against me. Do you understand?" The young soldiers stared at the speaker afraid to say anything. The Captain's voice again. "Are you stupid or deaf? Do you hear me?"

Everyone in the barracks shouted. "Yes sir."

Rick was in the latrine. He looked up at the speaker and right next to it was a microphone. He stepped onto a toilet and in a low voice. "Ain't this a bitch we can't talk. Dip shit, haven't you heard of freedom of speech. Listen Mickey Mouse, You can kiss my ass."

Captain Thimp shouted. "What barracks are you in? I'll find you, and when I do, you'll never talk like that again."

"Shut up, you phony little Shithead. You're so short you should be in the boy scouts."

Captain Thimp was screaming like a wild man. Mike knew someone was talking back to the Captain. He looked around and didn't see Rick. He ran to the shower room and saw Rick laughing, standing on a toilet with his hands cupped to his mouth and talking into a small mike. Mike grabbed him and pulled him down. He put his hand over Rick's mouth. He whispered, "He's trying to keep you talking so he can find out what barracks you're in. Don't say any more."

Captain Thimp shouted again. "Where you at bastard?"

Rick was going to shout something. Mike put one hand over Rick's mouth and made a fist in his face. "No more."

Rick whispered. "Just one more time." Mike shook his head and drew back his fist. From Mike's expression Rick knew he better not.

The Captain shouted again. "I got sixteen weeks to get you bastard and I pity you when I do." Mike stared at Rick who was dying to shout back. Mike kept his fist in Rick's face and kept shaking his head.

The young soldiers were asking each other what was going on. They couldn't understand why the Captain was so mad. A couple of them asked Mike when he came from the head. Mike shrugged his shoulders and climbed up into his bunk. The lights went out and he immediately fell asleep.

The shrill sound of a whistle shocked him out of his sleep. The bright lights were on and in between blowing the whistle the sergeant shouted. "Get your assess out of those beds" Mike looked at his watch. It was four o'clock in the morning.

Someone yelled. "Four o'clock, man, I used to be coming home at that time."

The bitch box came alive. Captain Thimp shouted. "You have three minutes to get dressed and be outside in formation." The men were frightened. They jumped out of their bunks looking for their clothes. Not use to lacing the high combat boots, they skipped holes. The barracks was total confusion, men were shouting and swearing. Captain Thimp hollered again. "You have a minute and a half. Anyone not in formation will be punished." The confusion accelerated.

Rick stared at the nervous men shaking and trying to get dressed. He knew what kind of man this Captain was. He had seen his type before. "You now have twenty seconds." Loud thumping noise filled the barracks as the young men ran to the door in their heavy combat boots.

Rick shook his head. He looked up at the microphone. "Hey, Captain Pimp. Put that stop watch up your ass."

Captain Thimp screamed. I WILL GET YOU BASTARD. If ANYONE KNOWS WHO IS TALKING BACK, COME FORWARD. I WILL MAKE YOUR NEXT SIXTEEN WEEKS VERY ENJOYABLE." A hesitation then he shouted again. "GET YOUR ASSES OUTSIDE."

The men stood at attention. Mike felt the cool damp morning air chill his body. Sergeant Carter called roll call. The men shouted yes sir, when their names were called. When he was convinced everyone was present, he smartly turned around and faced the large trumpet shaped speakers attached to wooden poles. The speakers crackled and Captain Thimp yelled. "Able Company report."

Sergeant Carter, shouted. "All men present and accounted for, Sir."

Other captains called their companies and the sergeants in charge responded. "All present and accounted for, Sir."

It was dark but Mike could tell there were a lot of soldiers on the parade field. Sergeants' voices were heard from the far end of the field. Captain Thimp shouted again. "You men were slow getting out of your bunks this morning. I guarantee, you will be faster tomorrow. I again heard the smart mouth this morning. When I catch you mister, you'll be one sorry person. I repeat my offer. Whoever turns in this wise guy will have a very easy sixteen weeks. I will continue to monitor the barracks and I will find you. After you men complete your physical fitness this morning, you will get an army haircut. A rifle will be issued to you and the rest of the day will be marching. I want every man to pay attention to what the instructors say. I will not put up with any slackers. Our unit will be the best on this camp. When you go to the mess hall and eat, you get your food and eat as fast as you can. There will be no time wasted there. Is that understood."

A loud shout from the many men assembled on the parade field. "YES SIR."

Sergeant Carter ordered, "At Ease. I want every man to take off his fatigue shirt and drop to the ground and give me twenty five pushups." The white tee shirts seemed to glow in the darkness. Some of the men hadn't exercised for a long time. They grunted and gasped when they pushed their bodies off the ground. Mike had no problem. More exercises were ordered. The men tried but most struggled. Captain Thimp shouted over the speakers. "I'm watching, you're a sorry bunch. Listen to all that hard breathing. Sergeants you get them in shape no matter what. We want to win the P.T. competition. We will be the best and we'll set the record for this camp. Is that understood?" The men were gasping in the thin Colorado air and didn't respond. "Listen you soft sissies. Did you hear me?"

This time a loud shout. "YES, SIR." Then an undertone of grumbling and cursing.

Sergeant Carter put them through the rest of the exercises. He called them to attention. The odor of cooking food filled the air. Everyone was hungry and couldn't wait to get in the mess hall for breakfast. Sergeant Carter ordered the group to put their fatigue shirts back on. When everyone was properly dressed, He shouted. "Mess is being served. Company dismissed." No matter how tired the men were, they still had enough strength to race to the mess hall.

There was a jam up at the mess hall door. A sergeant appeared and

47

restored order. "You men will form a single line. There will be no pushing." The young soldiers quickly formed the line. When the sergeant was convinced there would be no more rush he let them in. The men grabbed metal trays and walked to the serving line. Captain Thimp with his hawkish eyes was standing at the beginning of the counter. Everyone stopped. No one said a word. He shouted. "You get your food and eat as fast as you can, then exit this building and form a formation outside. Do you hear me? You soft sissies."

"Yes, Sir."

Mike and Hillbilly noticed Rick didn't yell yes sir. Instead he had a disgusted look "Man I don't know about you Mike. I'm going to the end of this line. That Sapsucker is going to do something crazy."

"I think you're right. I'll go with you."

Captain Thimp stood behind the steam table and stared at the men with his beady little eyes. The men were nervous and looked down at their trays when they passed him. Captain Thimp had a smirk on his face like he enjoyed this.

Rick put his tray on the metal rails. He looked right in the Captain's eyes and his heels clicked when he slammed his combat boots together. He came to attention and saluted. He shouted as loud as he could. "Sir, Private Rick Miller, reporting for mess, Sir."

Captain Thimp was startled. He jumped back and shouted. "What the fuck is the matter with you?"

Rick stayed at attention. Sir, request permission to eat my breakfast."

The captain was dumbfounded. He stared at Rick standing at attention. He felt he had really instilled fear in this man. "Soldier, you don't have to salute when you're in line for mess. Come to at ease, and get your food."

Rick shouted. "Yes, SIR. I will come to at ease and get my food. Sir, I ask permission to talk with you, Sir."

The captain looked bored. "Go ahead. What do you want?"

Sir, It is a privilege to be trained by you. You remind me of Napoleon, one of the greatest soldiers in history. It would be a privilege to go into combat under your leadership."

Captain Thimp stared at Rick. The servers stood idle holding their large spoons and tongs. The line came to a standstill. Hillbilly stood on his tip toes so he could see what the holdup was. He saw Rick talking to the Captain. "Oh, damn, that boy is at it again. He's doing something up there. I'm glad we're back here."

Rick kept buttering up the Captain. The Captain was taking it all in. It seemed like no one ever gave him praise. It went on for about ten minutes. Captain Thimp finally realized the line was not moving. He shouted. "That's enough, that's enough. What the hell is the matter with you? You keep this up and I'll see to it that you get a Section Eight."

Rick again came to attention and saluted. The Captain started to salute. He quickly put his arm down. He pointed at Rick. "You get your food and get the hell out of here." Rick put his head down and pretended he was scared. Every once in a while he looked back at the Captain. The Captain pointed his finger at him and shouted. "Keep your ass moving!"

Mike and Hillbilly put their trays down on the table next to Rick. Hillbilly asked. "Hey boy, what was you and that hard ass captain talking about?"

Rick pointed his fork at him. "I told him that you were the one that was talking back to him. I want the rest of my time in Basic Training to be easy."

"You what? Man, what in the hell is the matter with you. That man will hang my ass."

Mike laughed. "Take it easy Hillbilly. He's joking you."

"Kidding my ass. Mike that boy is completely crazy. You don't know what he's going to do next."

Mike was concerned. "Tell him Rick, you were only kidding."

Rick started laughing. He pointed his fork again at Hillbilly and winked. "I got you."

The first eight weeks passed and still no over-night pass. Rick continued to aggravate the Captain over the microphone. The Captain was now offering money to whoever would tell. Everyone was expecting a pass to go into town. They had been working hard and they were one of the best companies on post. They believed they deserved a pass. The bitch box came alive. The young soldiers eyes looked up at the speaker. They smiled and someone said. "We're finally going into town."

The Captain's voice sounded like he was smiling. "Men I have good news. I have volunteered our company for two more weeks of bivouac. We're going to be involved in operation Seek And Destroy. We're going to be the company who will hide in the mountains. Two other companies will try to locate us. If we are successful and stay concealed we will surely win the best company award. They were going to transport us by truck into an area so we could set up camp. I told the general that I wanted my company to hike in. That way no one could give out our location. Men if we pull this off we'll be number one."

The men looked at each other and shook their heads. Everyone was talking at once. Someone said,"This is a crock of shit. He volunteered our overnight passes away. He didn't do it for the company. He did it to make his record look good. The bastard is bucking for a promotion. We have to march in and that little son of a bitch will ride on a jeep. We don't get a pass cause of that bastard."

The bitch box came alive again. "I heard every word you men said. You have three hours to get your equipment ready. Any man who is late will be punished. Remember you will be in full pack and in formation at 0005 hrs."

Mike looked at Rick. "Rick, that's 12:05 in the morning. We're going to be marching in the dark." Rick was staring out the window and didn't say anything. Mike knew something was really wrong. Rick didn't cuss over the microphone. "Rick, what you up to?"

He didn't reply. Instead he walked to his foot locker and started putting his personal stuff into a pillow case. "Rick, don't even think about it. You're crazy sometimes but the guys think you have a lot of guts. Hey, you're the most liked guy in the company. When they feel down they look to you for a laugh. This Captain is making it rough on everybody. He will really make it tough on us if you go AWOL. It would put a blemish on his record and that would ruin his chances for best company and also a promotion for him. Don't do it Rick." The rest of the guys in the barracks huddled around Rick's bed. They all nodded to what Mike said.

Rick slowly sat down on his bed. He looked up at the guys and didn't say anything. Everyone went back to his area and started packing. Rick got up slowly and started putting his clothes in his pack.

The young soldiers milled around in the darkness waiting for the Captain to come to the platform and get the march started. A voice from the darkness. "Hey guys, look out there at them lights in Colorado Springs. We should be down there having a beer with some sharp looking broads."

Rick's voice from the darkness. "What you talking about? If you went into town you'd probably wake up with a mean hangover. The broad might of gave you a good dose of the clap. You'd be wishing you would of took this nice walk with the captain."

"We don't even need to see you, Miller. Keep your bullshit to yourself."

Two portable lights illuminated the platform. Captain Thimp climbed the steps and went to the edge and stared down at the men assembled below. As usual he gaped for a long time with his beady little eyes. Finally, "Men as you can see it is very dark. I picked this time so no one will see us leaving the camp. You will be on both sides of the road. You will keep a distance of six feet between you. There will be complete silence. That means no talking. We will be under combat conditions. You must follow my orders." The Captain kept rattling on. The sound of pressurize water hitting the small stones on the ground. Everyone below the platform knew who was pissing in ranks. The Captain ended his speech. "There will be no noise is that understood?"

A weak, "Yes, Sir."

The men started down the road in the darkness. The only noise was the thumping of the combat boots coming down on the loose stones on the unpaved road. It was so dark Mike could hardly make out Hillbilly's pack going side to side as he walked in front of him. Some of the guys were bitching in low voices. The tiring hike continued for hours. Mike felt like he was going to fall asleep on his feet. The sky was turning a slate gray as dawn broke through the darkness. He came alert when someone shouted. "Company - Halt." A scraping sound as the men's' combat boots stop on the gravel. "Men take a five minute break. Get off the road"

Mike walked down into a dry drainage ditch. He leaned against the side and put his head back and pulled his helmet over his eyes. Hillbilly and Rick dropped next to him. Hillbilly whispered "Man my feet are sore."

Mike mumbled. "Don't talk, get some rest when you can." The three of them were sound asleep in a matter of seconds. A loud clanking and hissing sound caused Mike to raise his helmet. A metal canister was gushing white smoke. His eyes burned. He grabbed his gas mask and shouted. "Gas." Rick and Hillbilly jumped to their feet as the white smoke clouded the ditch. Rick got his mask on but Hillbilly started climbing out.

Rick grabbed him. "Don't get out. Hold your breath and put your mask on." Hillbilly was choking. Mike quickly crawled to him and pulled him down the ditch away from the smoking grenade. Hillbilly managed to get his mask on. Rick was in front leading the way. When they got about twenty five yards away from the gas he looked up from the ditch. Two sergeants were pointing their rifles into the gas coming from the ditch. Rick stared at them laughing. He thought those sons-of- bitches threw that grenade. If we had panicked and crawled out they'd of said they shot us like the enemy would of." He reached into his pocket and pulled out a clip of Ml red tipped blank shells. He loaded his rifle and ran behind the two sergeants who didn't see him coming. He fired two shots and shouted. "I got you. You didn't cover your back or your flanks."

The sergeants turned around and Rick was laying prone and pointing his rifle at them. One of the sergeants shouted. "Who gave you permission to fire that gun?"

Rick shouted back. "We're simulating combat conditions. I don't need permission."

Someone from the ditch shouted. "Oh, shit here comes trouble." Both the sergeants and Rick saw the jeep speeding toward them leaving a cloud of dust behind it. Captain Thimp was standing up with his hands on the windshield. The driver stopped and Captain Thimp jumped out. "Who in the hell is shooting?" The two sergeants pointed at Rick who was laying prone still aiming his rifle at the sergeants.

Captain Thimp pointed his swagger stick at Rick. "Soldier, get on your feet and explain yourself. Why did you fire your weapon?"

Rick jumped up and came to attention. "Sir, we were ambushed by these two sergeants. They threw a gas canister into our position. You instructed us that when we are surprised to use it to our advantage when we can. Those two sergeants thought they had us in a situation where we could not defend. I let them think that way for a moment then I surprised them by firing on them. Yes sir, that was good training you gave us, it really worked. Just like you said, Sir."

Captain Thimp had a blank expression. He turned to the sergeants and then back to Rick. Rick nodded his head. "Sir, I think these sergeants learned a lesson. If they're going to surprise attack, they should follow through and not stand around and laugh. They should of watched their rear and flanks. Maybe they weren't listening when you instructed them."

Captain Thimp stared for awhile then said. "That was good thinking soldier. Yes it was good thinking. I'm glad you learned what 1 taught you."

"Thank you, Sir. I listen to every word you say. You're just like Napoleon. If ever I go into combat I want you to be my leader. Yes Sir, I really learned from you." Rick kept heaping praise on him.

Captain Thimp threw up his arms. "That's enough soldier." He walked back to his jeep and was driven to the front of the formation.

The two sergeants stared at Rick. "We're not done with you, Shithead."

Rick smiled.

The march continued and they finally got to their destination. A green valley between two large mountains. Captain Thimp shouted for the men to gather around him. He pointed to the high hills on both sides of the valley. "You men, see those hills? You will put your tents on the sides of them. There will be no tents or walking in the level part of the valley. The reason for this is the enemy can see you in the open flat land. On the hills you will be covered by the trees. Remember we have to be quiet. We do not want to be detected by those other companies looking for us. Remember sound travels a long distance in this type of terrain."

The company was divided into four groups. Two groups took one hill and started assembling their tents on the side of it. The other two groups set up on the opposite hill. Mike and Rick climbed their way up the hill. "This looks like a nice spot Rick. What you say right here?" Rick nodded his head. They both dropped their packs and took out their half of the tent. They put their halves together and tied the ropes to the tent stakes.

Rick stared at the tent. "Home sweet home for the next two weeks. Man, we could of been in that town raising hell with some broads. That little asshole Captain. He's a sadist. The no good bastard."

Mike laughed. "Hey Rick that isn't what you were calling him a few hours ago. 'Captain you're just like Napoleon.' You remember that?"

"Yeah, I remember. Napoleon was a sawed off runt that was half baked. That's what I meant. This guy is nuts. Why are mean people born? All my life I had to deal with them. Why are they put on this earth?"

"What you talking about, Rick?"

Rick shook his head and crawled in the tent.

Mike took out his field glasses and climbed higher on the hill. He gasped at the beautiful scenery. "Hey Rick, come up here, you gotta see these mountains. It's unbelievable I never saw anything like it. Rick did you hear me? What you doing in there brooding?"

"I'm not brooding. If you see one mountain you've seen them all."

Mike scanned the hill across from his. The men were still putting up their tents. Half way up he saw the two sergeants who threw the tear gas grenade. "Hey Rick come out of the tent. I want to show you something you might be interested in."

"Mike like I said before. Mountains, valleys and all that other nature shit don't interest me."

"No Rick, remember those two sergeants who threw that grenade. I'm looking at them pitching their tent on the other hill."

The flap to the tent flew open. Rick came crawling out. "Where's those assholes?" He quickly climbed to where Mike was and grabbed the field glasses. "Well I'll be damned. There they are. I got to mark the spot so I can visit them after dark."

Mike pulled the field glasses away from him. "Hey, I didn't show you those two guys so you can start trouble."

"Like I told you before. All you got to do is adapt to the situation. Everything is going to be perfect."

"Oh, no, I heard that before and every time it's trouble."

"Mike, you worry too much. Let me handle this."

Mike saw Hillbilly below waving his mess kit. "Hey Rick, it must be time to eat. Hillbilly is motioning with his mess kit."

Rick cupped his hands around his mouth and shouted. "It's okay Hillbilly. You yell up here whenever you want us. Don't worry about that captain." Hillbilly quickly turned around and put his mess kit under his shirt and ran down the hill. Mike tapped Rick on the shoulder.

"Hey, we were ordered not to make any noise. What's the matter with you?" Rick didn't answer he walked down and got Mike's and his mess kits out of the tent.

"Come on Mike let's go eat." They made their way down the hill to a two and a half ton truck camouflaged with pine branches. A line had formed with soldiers holding their mess kits. Mike and Rick got at the end and waited their turns to pass in front of the servers who were behind the truck. As usual Captain Thimp was standing next to the servers. When the men got served the Captain stared at them. He had his finger up to his mouth and spoke in a whisper. "Remember no noise, or lights tonight." The men nodded, too scared to say anything. Rick stood in front of the captain. He can't be content by nodding his head.

"Sir, we all got your message on how important it is to be quiet tonight. I'm going to do everything possible to help you make it quiet." Rick pointed his finger to where his tent was pitched. "You see up there Sir? That's my tent. I did everything you told me. I pitched it under those pine trees. You remember me don't you Captain. I was the guy who turned that gas ambush around. You know those two sergeants who didn't follow through. They left their guard down because they wanted to laugh. Sir, they should of listened to you." The Captain had a bored expression but he kept nodding his head when Rick talked.

Rick kept rambling on. The Captain's patience ran out. He shouted. "Damn it. That's enough soldier." The sound of the Captain's voice echoed through the valley. Soldiers eating put their mess kits down and stared at the Captain. He realized what he did and a frighten look came on his face. Rick was still standing in front of him.

"Sir you know your voice carries a long way in this terrain. Remember you told us that earlier."

The Captain glared at Rick and pointed his finger at him. Through gritting teeth. "You listen to me soldier. You take your food and get the hell away from me. Do you understand?"

"Yes sir. I understand. "I'll be extra quiet tonight. I promise there will be no noise and no lights." He walked away repeating. "No noise and no lights. Yes sir."

Rick sat on the ground with his mess kit balanced on his knee between Hillbilly and Mike. Hillbilly was still laughing. "Man if that Captain ever finds out your playing with his mind there will be hell to pay. I thought that old boy was going to have a heart attack when he yelled and then realized what he did. You silly fool, Rick, you're going to drive that man crazy. Why you do shit like that? Can't you leave well enough alone?"

Rick didn't say anything for awhile then he looked at Hillbilly. "You want to have some fun tonight?"

"What you mean some fun?"

Rick pointed to the large hill. "You remember those two sergeants who threw that gas grenade. Their tent is half way up. I'm going to pay them a visit tonight. Do you want to come along?"

"Boy, I don't know what kind of bullshit you're up to. I don't want any part of it. I don't even want to know what you're going to do up on that hill. No sir, count me out."

Later in the evening the men gathered on the side of a hill. A short training lesson by a lieutenant and Captain Thimp. Captain Thimp walked in front of the group. "I have one thing to say. Those two companies are out there searching to find us. No lights and no noise. Do not respond. As like I said before, sound travels a great distance in these valleys. You are now dismissed. Go to your area and stay there."

The sun was still shining on the peaks of the mountains. The valleys were becoming dark. Mike stared and enjoyed the beauty. Rick tapped him on the shoulder. "Come on nature boy let's go back to the tent. I don't want to hear about mountains, waterfalls and pine trees. If it wasn't for that little shrimp Napoleon we'd be sitting in some nice bar with a couple of broads having a great time. That no good son of a bitch'en, mealy mouthed bastard volunteered us for this bullshit to make himself look good. The dirty little chicken shit-son-of-a bitch, I'll show him."

Mike saw Rick getting madder. "Hey, cool it. When we get back to camp we'll get a pass. Don't get all worked up and do something stupid that will jeopardize it." Rick kicked the ground and sat on a rock glaring across the valley at the other hill. Mike thought it was best to let him alone to cool off. He crawled into the tent and laid on his sleeping bag.

Chapter 7
The rock fight

"Rick, you better get in here and get some sleep. They'll be waking us early." There was no answer. He quickly threw the flap to the tent back and crawled out. He looked around and Rick was gone. *OH, no, he's up to something.* He walked around and called his name low. Mike realized he couldn't find him in the dark so he quietly crawled back into the tent and hoped Rick would come back without causing any trouble.

Rick squinted trying to get accustomed to the darkness. He visualized the hill from what he remembered when it was light. He slowly descended from his tent area. A couple of times he nearly fell as loose stones slid under his feet. Luckily he grabbed some pine branches and got his balance. At the bottom of the hill he felt for the mess truck. He made it through the flat area and started up the other hill. His eyes were getting acclimated to the darkness. He climbed half way up the hill. He started to breath hard so he sat down without making any noise and took a few deep breaths. The men were talking low in their tents. He smiled, *They'll be yelling in a few minutes.* He made his way to a large boulder at the top of the hill, dropped to his knees and felt for rocks the size of baseballs. A couple of times his hand passed over cactus plants and he almost screamed. He gathered the rocks and piled them at the base of the large boulder. A couple more trips and he felt he had enough. He looked down and made out the tents. He managed to pinpoint the sergeants' tent and smiled. *Don't want to hit those jerks yet.* He picked a tent at the base of the hill and threw a rock. It made a slashing noise as it went through the pine trees then a loud thud as it hit the side of the tent.

A voice in the darkness shouted. "What the hell was that?" Rick laughed and started peppering more tents down at the base of the hill.

Men crawled out and yelled. Rick climbed down halfway and shouted, "This is your sergeant. We're under attack from the men above. Put on your metal pots and return fire."

The group at the lower level put on their metal helmets and were feeling for rocks. Someone shouted, "Give it to those wise guys up there."

The men in the tents above yelled, "What the hell is the matter with you guys? Are you crazy?" The soldiers at the base heard the voices and threw at the sound. The whole hill was now in an enormous rock fight. The tents got hit making loud thumping sounds. The metal helmets made a pinging noise when struck. This was mixed with shouting and cussing.

Rick thought it was time to get out of there. He slid down the hill almost out of control. A few thrown rocks narrowly missed him. On the flat land he heard Captain Thimp. "What in the hell is going on. Son-of-a-bitch they found us." Rick quickly climbed to his hill. Outside his tent he dropped to his knees and caught his breath.

"Rick, is that you?"

"Yeah Mike, everything under control."

Mike stuck his head out. "What's going on over there? It sounds like a riot"

"Ain't that the prettiest noise you ever heard? Just listen to that cussing and shouting. I bet that little jerk wished he would of let us have our passes. Let's be quiet and enjoy this."

Light beams from flash lights danced around on the far hill looking for a good target. Captain Thimp shouted, "You men quit. Do you hear me it's an order. Sergeants bring this under control. God damn it, quit."

Rick started sliding down the hill. "Where you going Rick?"

"I'm going back over there. Now's the time to hit that little bastard with a rock."

Mike grabbed him. "You did enough. Don't even think of going back over there."

"Mike let go. Now is the perfect time. No one will know who hit him. We owe that little goof that."

"No way, just sit down. We're going to catch hell for this mess you started."

A half hour passed and it's brought under control. Rick and Mike could hear the Captain's voice all the way to their area. "Who in the hell started this mess. I want an answer and I want it now."

Another voice. "Sir, we were ordered by the sergeant."

More voices chimed in. "Yes sir, the sergeant ordered us to throw rocks."

Captain Thimp screamed. "Sergeant come here now. Did you instruct these men to throw stones?"

"No sir. I don't know how this started."

Rick laughed. "He's chewing out one of those name calling idiot sergeants. This is great."

Everything calmed down. The Captain wasn't convinced the other companies didn't start the uproar. He ordered a full alert. Sergeant Carter told his men to dig in on top of the hill and to report any movement that might be the other companies. Rick asked, "How we supposed to see them in the dark sergeant?"

"Smell them."

Mike and Rick climbed to the top of the hill. The wind blew much stronger. "Mike it's cold up here, I'm freezing my ass off."

"I know, Let's dig a small trench so we can shield some of this wind."

"I got a better idea. Let's build a roaring fire. That chicken shit captain would have a heart attack if he saw the flames."

"Don't get any funny ideas. It's bad enough now. If you give him a reason he'll have us up here all the time." The rest of the night was quiet. Morning came and the beauty of the mountains was spectacular. Mike started to say something but Rick interrupted.

"I know they're beautiful. I don't care how pretty they are, I would rather be in a nice warm hotel room with a broad I picked up if I would of got a pass."

Sergeant Carter climbed up. "You men go down and get some chow." They half ran and slid down the hill. They joined the line waiting to be served. Rick pointed to a couple of helmets the men in front of them were wearing that had white scratches on the sides of them.

"Them are the guys who caused all that trouble last night. We got blamed for them acting like a bunch of fools throwing stones." One of them turned around.

"You got something to say to me jerk?"

"Yes I got a lot to say to you. You acted like street gangs last night. Why can't you be good soldiers like Captain Thimp is trying to make us. We're going to be the greatest fighting machines in the world. You heard Captain Thimp say that."

One soldier shouted. "Screw you and Captain Thimp." He swung his mess kit at Rick. Rick ducked and drove his fist into the guy's stomach. The other soldier started to punch Rick and Mike grabbed his arm.

"Hey, you guys that's enough. We didn't get any sleep last night. If you keep this up we won't get any tonight."

The guy pulled his arm from Mike's hold. "You're right." He reached down and picked up his friend.

Mike pointed his finger at Rick. "No more trouble."

They got their food and sat on a rock. No sooner than they started to eat and someone said, "Here comes the asshole." Captain Thimp walked through the men eating. He had a clean set of fatigues on. He struck his swagger stick on the side of his pants as he walked. He didn't say anything to anyone. Someone behind Mike and Rick said. "Look at the mean look on that son-of-a-bitch."

When the Captain was sure everyone saw him he motioned to Sergeant Carter. Sergeant Carter shouted. "Attention" Every man in hearing distance got up and came to attention.

Captain Thimp did his usual stare from one man to another. "You men were a disgrace last night. Grown men throwing stones at one another. You can be sure I will get to the bottom of this before you're done with basic training. We're still under full alert. Put your food away and get back to your positions."

The men looked at the food in their mess kits and then looked at one another. Captain Thimp shouted "Empty those mess kits and get back to your positions." Some of the men walked to the garbage can and dumped their meal.

Rick looked at his food and shouted, "Captain Sir. Isn't there something in the general orders that states a man has the right to eat his food." The look that came on the Captain's face was unbelievable. He couldn't believe what he heard.

He ran to Rick and pointed his swagger stick at him. "When I give an order you will obey it. You will never question an order I give. Sergeant Carter, take this man to the mess truck and see to it he works all day. He will think the next time before he opens his mouth."

"Sir, this is the next time. Be advised that when I get back to camp I'm going directly to the Inspector General's Office. I'm then going to send a letter to my congressman about this."

Captain Thimp's mouth twitched and he motioned the sergeant with his swagger stick. "Get this man out of here. You other men get back to your positions." Mike trudged up the hill and looked down at Rick being led to the mess truck.

Darkness set in and the Captain nervously walked from one position to another. He questioned the men if they heard or seen anything. Hillbilly threw a rock up next to Mike. Mike looked and Hillbilly was pointing down the hill. He talked in a soft voice. "Here comes Rick. He's walking like he's tired. He looks plenty mad."

Rick slung his rifle into the tent. "I'll get even with that rotten little son-of-a-bitch if it's the last thing I do."

Hillbilly and another soldier came up to Mike and Rick's tent. The guy with Hillbilly said. "I heard you talking about that old cold-blooded Captain. You best quit getting into that man's stuff. He'll hang your ass." Rick didn't say anything he just stared at the guy.

Hillbilly laughed. "Oh, I want you guys to meet Zug. He's a good old boy who plays a mean sax. This here is Mike and that guy is Rick. You listen to Mike and you'll be all right. That boy there Rick is something else. If you like trouble see him."

Mike stood up and shook Zug's hand. "I'm glad to meet you Zug." Rick remained on the ground and raises his hand.

Zug reached down and shook.

"I'm sorry Zug, I'm too tired to get up."

"Man, that's cool. I saw you and that Captain making some bad scenes this morning. I bet he worked your butt off."

"Yeah, he did that but I'm not done with that little runt."

Hillbilly slapped his knee. "Boy, don't you know when to quit. Can't you be good for a couple of days?"

Rick didn't answer. He stared at the ground and every once in awhile he grabbed a hand full of dirt and threw it.

Hillbilly told how good Zug was on the sax and how he managed to bring the horn with him. He looked at Zug. "Ain't that right?"

"Sure stuff, man, wherever I go, my piece goes with me. It's like part of my body."

Mike asked. "What good is it if you can't play it? We're on full alert and that Captain will hang you if he hears any noise."

"Well, you see man, I'll drop off in the bushes and I'll find me a place where I can make some sounds. You see, man, that's what keeps me with it. I've got these tunes in me and they have to come out. I'll have my own little jam session. Where there's a will, there's a way."

Rick's face lit up. He liked what Zug said. "You know Zug I got the perfect place for you to play that sax. You and I are going to be talking later." Rick then crawled into the tent and passed out from fatigue.

Hillbilly and Zug went back to their tent. Mike sat in the darkness thinking of home. Sergeant Carter came up the hill and told the men there would be a formation at the bottom of the hill. The Captain wanted to talk with them. Mike reached in the tent and grabbed Rick's leg. "Rick, We got to go down the hill, there's a formation. Come on we got to go." Rick finally woke up and followed Mike down the hill.

Men were sitting on the ground. Captain Thimp walked back and forth in front of them. He didn't say anything he just squinted and stared. Someone in a low voice said. "That silly son-of-a-bitch looks like a queer bantam rooster strutting around like a damn fool."

The Captain finally stopped. "You men know we're on full alert. Those companies are close and we know it. We were lucky last night when the damn fools acted like they were crazy. Tonight be exceptionally quiet. I want to warn you. We will catch anyone who makes a noise. Are there any questions?" Mike looked at Rick and feared he was going to say something. Rick was sleeping. Everyone else looked angry. They were all thinking how this man beat them out of their overnight passes. No one said anything. "Okay, go back to your positions. Keep your ears and eyes open and keep your mouths shut."

Mike and Rick were sitting on top of the hill. Rick had his rifle on his lap and he was leaning against a tree root, sound asleep. The night was quiet Mike looked in the distance. *Is his mother making it? If he had gone to college how would he of been doing playing football? What is that pretty girl he met on the bus doing? Was going into the army the right decision?* He stood up and took a couple of deep breaths. He looked down at Rick. *This guy don't care about anything except when someone calls him a name. He never talks about his mother or family. Never mentions anything about his friends or school. I really don't understand the guy.*

A twig snapped. Mike dropped down and grabbed his rifle. He shook Rick. "Wake up, there's someone out there. Rick wake up" Mike shook him and at the same time put his hand over Rick's mouth. "Don't say anything. There's someone out there."

62

"Okay Mike, I'm awake." Both of them got into the prone position with their rifles aimed in the direction of the sound. The quietness lingered and then a low voice.

"It's okay men, it's me Sergeant Carter." A body formed from the darkness. He sat next to them. "Good to see you're both awake and alert. Has there been any activity up here?"

Mike answered. "No sir, it's been real quiet." "What about you Rick?"

"Hell, everyone is too tired to hear anything the way that chicken shit little son-of-a-bitch is running us day and night. I can guarantee you one thing Sergeant. If I was in town tonight I would be able to report a lot of activity. Man, that Captain is a mean bastard."

Mike could tell from the Sergeant's expression he agreed with Rick but due to his rank he couldn't say anything against the Captain.

Sergeant Carter stood up and tapped them on their helmets. "You're doing a great job soldiers. Keep up the good work." He disappeared in the darkness.

"What time is it Mike?"

"It's o two hundred hours.

"Man, don't give me that army shit. What time is it in sane language."

"Mike laughed. It's two o'clock in the morning."

"Damn, ain't this a bitch. Two o'clock in the morning sitting in a fox hole freezing your ass off, waiting for some silly ass to sneak up on you. Man I can think of better things to do." He leaned back against the tree root and pulled his helmet over his eyes. He tried to sleep but couldn't He jumped up and crawled out of the hole.

"Where you going Rick? I don't want any trouble. Why don't you just stay here and sleep? I'll wake you if I hear anything."

"I'll be all right. I want to slide down to Hillbilly and talk with him. I'll be back in a little while."

Hillbilly and Zug heard someone coming down the hill. Zug asked, "Hey man what's your bag? I hear you out there."

"It's me, Rick. I want to talk with you guys."

Zug's voice again. "Come on in the crib. We haven't swept it for a while."

Rick slid into the hole. Hillbilly pointed at him. "What you up to boy? We don't need no bullshit down here. Everything is nice and quiet. If you're going to do something crazy you get back up there in your position."

Zug laughed. "Man, If I had a taste I'd offer you some. What's your bag man?"

"Well, it's awful quiet around here. I'd like to hear some music. How good are you on that sax?"

Hillbilly jumped up and put his hands in the air. "There ain't gonna be any horn blowing around here. No way am I gonna be any part of that bullshit. No way." Zug went to his tent and came out with a sax. He ran his fingers up and down the valves. Hillbilly put his hand over the mouthpiece. "You ain't letting that crazy man talk you into playing that horn here."

Rick patted Hillbilly on the shoulder. "Don't worry he isn't going to play it here. We're going to the other hill."

"Man, you are plum out of your mind Rick. And you are worse Zug, if you go over there and start up trouble with him. That hill caught hell last night. That Old Captain will hang both your asses."

Rick grabbed Zug by the arm. "Come on Zug, I want to hear some nice loud sounds."

"Zug, you listen to me. That fool Rick will get you in all kinds of trouble. I only knew that boy for a couple of weeks and I never got in so much trouble in all my life. You best put that horn away and stay in this hole."

"Don't listen to him Zug. Everything is going to be all right, you follow me. I got it all figured out."

Hillbilly started to say something but Zug said. "Okay man, I know how to follow." They both started down the hill.

Hillbilly yelled, "Remember what I told you Zug. "You're going for trouble."

Rick looked back at Zug. "Now we got to be quiet. Make sure you don't slip and start rocks sliding down the hill."

"I got you man. I can handle it. You just watch where you're going and I'll be behind you." They made their way to the bottom of the hill. When they went past a large tent they saw Captain Thimp and some other officers standing over a table. The Captain was cupping a flash light with his hand and they were studying a map. Rick was tempted to make a noise like a mountain lion. The flash light went out and the officers came out of the tent.

"Rick grabbed Zug by the arm and whispered. "Don't move they won't be able to see us."

The Captain talked to the other officers. "It's a good night, nice and dark and the men are quiet. They'll never find us in this darkness." A few yes sirs and the men made their way to their tents. Rick and Zug waited till everyone was settled down. They then climbed the hill to a clump of bushes and pine trees.

"This is the perfect place. Now I want to hear some real sounds. You aim that sax right down into that valley at the Captain's tent."

"Okay man, your got any requests?"

"Yeah, can you play *Far A way In Africa?*'

"You mean *Skokiaan?*"

"Yeah, I remember it as *Far Away In Africa.* What's the difference just play it loud." Zug lifted the sax to his mouth. He tapped his foot a few times then bellowed the horn. The song *Skokiaan* pierced the still night. It echoed off the rock walls of the hills. Rick patted him on the back. "Hey Zug you're great. Where did you learn to play like that? Keep it going. I love it." This encouraged Zug and his body rocked back and forth and his foot tapped with the beat.

The large flap of the Captain's tent flew open. He shouted into the darkness. "What the hell is that?" A sergeant ran to his side. "Sir, that sounds like a horn."

"I know it sounds like a horn. Who the hell is playing that god damn horn at three in the morning?"

Other officers and sergeants ran to the Captain's tent and asked him what was going on. Captain Thimp screamed, "I don't know what the hell it is, put a stop to it."

Back on top the hill. "That's great Zug. Man, that's the best I ever heard that song played."

"Thanks cat. This is where it's happening. I love this horn and it feels good to play it."

"You're right Zug. Get with it, only louder. Man I love that music."

Hillbilly climbed up to Mike. "Mike you hear them damn fools over there?" Mike was laughing so hard he couldn't answer.

He finally stopped laughing. "That Zug can really play a horn and he's loud. Did you put them up to doing that Hillbilly?"

"Aw Mike, don't even say anything like that. I tried to stop them, but you know how crazy Rick is. You can't tell him anything."

When a song stopped and there was a pause Captain Thimp yelled,

"Stop that god damn racket. Find that son-of-a bitch." The horn started up again and it sounded louder. Flashlights were aimed to where the music was coming from. The horn stopped and the lights went out. A short time later the music started up at a different place. Captain Thimp kept cursing and threatening. The flash lights lit up again trying to locate the horn blower.

"You know Hillbilly, I can't understand how they can move so fast in this darkness."

"I don't know either, but I can tell you one thing. They better keep moving fast. If that old boy gets hold of them damn fools they won't be moving for a long time."

"Rick you like any other song?"

"Not really, I do like that *Far Away In Africa.* But go and play anything you want."

Zug put the sax back to his mouth and played jazz. "Hey that sounds good too. Keep it up." The beams of the flashlights bounced off the trees above them. "Stop Zug they're getting close. It's time to move."

Down in the valley the Captain was pacing back and forth in his under shorts and combat boots. "Who in the hell could that son-of-bitch be?"

One of the sergeants ran up to him. "Sir, do you think it might be one of those companies that is trying to find us?"

"Why in the hell would it be one of them?"

"Well, Sir, in Korea when the gooks were going to attack they'd liked to blow horns."

"You're right, Sergeant. They're trying to imitate the enemy. He cupped his hands around his mouth and shouted, "Douse those god damn lights. Come back down here. Don't give our position away. Do it now." The officers and sergeants came down and regrouped around the Captain. "Men, it's the enemy. You should have never shined those lights. Sure as hell they blew that damn horn so we would be tricked into showing our position. They wanted us to chase them so we would divide our company. Keep the lights out and go back to your positions and stand by."

Zug was playing his fourth song. He pulled the horn from his lips. "Hey man what's happening? They turned off the lights and old cold blood down there isn't rapping his jaws."

"I don't know. Lets move. They got behind a large boulder. "Okay Zug give it hell. Play *Far Away In Africa* again."

"Man, I told you the name of that song is *Skokiaan*. Don't you hear, man?"

"Who cares what the name is. Play it."

The Captain heard the familiar song. "Why is it the same song? It must be some type of signal. The bastards must have us surrounded. I tried so hard and they found us." He stood waiting for the search companies to come in.

Zug finished the song. Everything was quiet. What now Rick?"

"I don't know, it ain't any fun without them trying to find us and that little shrimp yelling. They're up to something. Let's get back to our positions."

When they got back Zug slid the sax into his tent. Hillbilly and Mike stood and stared at them. Rick smiled. "How did you like the jam session Hillbilly?"

"Something is really the matter with you, boy. Now you got Zug crazy. You had that Captain talking to himself. He thought you guys were the other companies. That boy is crapping his pants. He believes he lost his major's promotion."

The rest of the night was quiet. When the sun came up the Captain was in his undershorts and combat boots running from one tree to another putting his field glasses to his eyes scanning the hills for the two companies.

Rick saw him and shouted, "There's the enemy company!" Everyone froze. An hour passed and when it was clear the other companies didn't find them, word came up the hill it was time for mess. Rick, Mike, Hillbilly and Zug got their food and sat on the side of the hill. They heard other soldiers talking about the horn blowing. Someone said,. "I don't know who it was but he shook hell out of that ass hole Captain. Did you notice he's not around this morning messing up our meal. The bastard got so tired last night he passed out in his tent. I hope he sleeps for a week."

For the remaining time on bivouac the Captain walked around in a daze. He constantly looked at the top of the hills waiting for the other companies to appear. Rick went along with the program since no one called him names. On the last day of bivouac the Captain assembled the men. He went through his normal routine walking back and forth staring with his beady little eyes not saying anything. He stopped abruptly and raised his arms skyward. "MEN WE ACCOMPLISHED OUR MISSION. We were not found. I want you to be good soldiers like I taught you. We're going to march back to camp and when we go though those gates I will be leading you. Raise your heads high when we do. We won the contest and we'll probably be the best company on base. Go up to your areas and pack. Square those packs like you were instructed. We're going to look sharp when we march down the streets to camp. As soon as we get back you'll get your overnight passes."

The young soldiers ran up the hill so fast they defied gravity. The tents went down and the equipment packed in record time. Voices were shouting. "Hurry you guys. We're going into town. Man can you believe it. We're getting away."

The young soldiers were assembled for the long march back to camp. Captain Thimp had fresh starched fatigues on. The jeep he was riding in had been washed. He grabbed the windshield and stood up. "Okay, men, remember we straddle both sides of the road. Keep a distance of six feet between each other. When we get close to camp we will regroup and march in formation. We will go in with our heads high. Okay, let's get going your passes are waiting for you."

Moral was high. The men were singing. They were tired but the thought of that pass into town gave them strength. They walked for hours and finally saw the camp in the distance. Captain Thimp's jeep stopped. The men were assembled.. He got out and carefully put a back pack and metal helmet on. Someone said. "Look at that phony bastard. He rode all the way back and now he puts on a pack and helmet. He's going to lead us into camp like he hiked back with us."

Hillbilly said, "Who cares as long as we get our pass."

Captain Thimp led the march through the gates. He counted cadence extra loud so everyone on the sidewalks would hear him and look. Able company marched onto the parade field. Captain Thimp kept the men at attention. He was waiting for a high ranking officer to come and congratulate him. No one showed up. He climbed the platform with a disgusted look. "You men will get your pass as soon as all weapons are cleaned and inspected. That includes the heavy mortars." He had a half smile on his face. The men moaned.

Rick clenched his fists and gritted his teeth. He mumbled, "You chicken shit, spiteful sadist. I ought to come up there and kick hell out of you."

Mike grabbed him. "Rick control yourself. Let's hurry and get those weapons cleaned. It won't take long if we all work together." They were discouraged but the thought of going into town gave them new energy. They ran into the barracks and grabbed the weapons. Rick picked up an air cooled machine gun.

"Mike I'll clean this machine gun and the Browning Automatic Rifle and you take care of those rifles. Is it a deal?"

"You're on."

Rick took off his clothes and was a sight standing naked with a machine gun and a Browning Automatic Rifle. Mike stared at him. "Rick what are you doing.?"

"I'm going to give these guns a shower. He wants them clean. I'll make them clean."

"You can't put them under water."

"Why not, it gets me clean?" Mike knew it wouldn't do any good to argue with him once he made up his mind. He just shook his head.

Rick walked naked with the two guns in his arms down the crowded aisle with men sitting on the floor cleaning weapons. They stared at him but didn't say anything. He went past Hillbilly and Zug. Hillbilly shook his head. "What is that fool going to do now?" Some of the men followed him into the shower room. They wanted to see what this naked guy was going to do with a machine gun and a Browning Automatic Rifle in the head.

Rick broke down the machine gun and picked up the barrel. He turned on the water in the shower and walked under it. He ran water through the barrel. The men made a painful face when they saw water running out the barrel. One of them shouted. "I'm out of here. If they see us in here with that fool we'll all get court martial." Rick laughed and aimed the water running out of the barrel at their feet. He took a bar of soap and lathered up the barrel. Seeing this, the remaining men left the latrine. Rick took the other parts of the guns and put them in the shower and soaped them up and rinsed them He dried every part with a towel and talked to them.

"You babies are my pass into civilization. Baby if I had some powder I'd rub you with it so you'd smell good for crazy Napoleon."

He walked back to his bunk. The men on the floor didn't look up at him when he passed. They didn't want anything to do with a naked nut who might jeopardize their overnight pass.

"Hey Mike I'm all done. All I got to do is put some oil on these babies and I'm ready for inspection. Do you want me to take care of those rifles for you?"

"No thanks, I'll do it the army way,"

Three hours passed. Captain Thimp's voice came over the bitch box. "You men can bring your pieces to the weapons room for inspection now."

Rick grabbed the mortar and the machine gun. "Come on Mike let's get these weapons inspected and head into town." He went out the door and Mike was right behind with the rifles. They got in line and waited their turn.

A group of men came out the door carrying their weapons with discouraged looks. Someone asked. "What happened?" They didn't reply and walked back to the barracks with their weapons mumbling.

"Rick those guys worked a long time cleaning those guns. They should of passed with no problem."

Rick didn't say anything. He tried to see what was going on in the weapons room. The line was moving fast and everybody came out rejected. Mike and Rick finally got to go inside. Two men in front of them placed a couple of mortars on the table. The Captain had a flash light in one hand and a screw driver in the other. A sergeant placed a sheet of toilet paper on the head of the screw driver. Captain Thimp pushed the paper into every crack and indentation of the mortars and rubbed. He took the toilet paper from the head of the screw driver and spread it out and put it over the head of the flash light. He pointed to a piece of dirt the size of a pencil tip.

"Take it back and clean it. Don't bring it back till it's clean."

"The young soldier's eyes filled with tears. "Captain I did my best."

"Get your ass out of here. Dirt, dirt, bring it back when it's clean." The two young men walked out rejected shaking their heads.

Rick reached down and picked up the machine gun and set it on the table. Captain Thimp ordered the sergeant to turn the gun on its side. He took the screw driver with the toilet paper on it and rubbed it on the underside of the leg of the tripod. He held the paper up and shouted, "Dirt, this gun is filthy. I don't even have to stretch out the paper to see it."

"Sir, I also had a mortar to be inspected. That gun is heavy and I had to wait in line. I put the gun down because it was too heavy to hold. Check the other parts that were not on the ground."

"I said dirt Shithead, now go clean it."

Rick, glared at him. Mike knew Rick was going to do something that would get him in a lot of trouble. He quickly slid in front of Rick and dropped the rifles on the table then picked up the machine gun and handed it to Rick. "Take it back to the barracks and I'll help you clean it."

Rick took the gun and continued staring at the Captain. Mike gave Rick a slight push. "Take it back Rick, we'll work it out. Rick slowly turned and walked out the door. The captain took one of Mike's rifles. He pushed the paper into every crack. He couldn't find any dirt. He took another piece of paper and rubbed it on the stock till a little oil came off.

"This gun is dirty."

"Sir, that's oil. I was told to put a light coat of oil on the stock."

The captain pointed his finger. "Don't you argue with me. Take these guns and go back and clean them. Do you hear me soldier?"

Mike glared at him. He was doing everything he could to control himself. He slowly shook his head and said. "Yes sir." He picked up the rifles and went back to the barracks. The captain smiled.

Mike noticed the machine gun sitting in the middle of the floor. He walked to it and Rick shouted, "Let it alone. You might as well put them rifles in the rack. That little bastard isn't going to give any passes out tonight. He's getting his beanies by turning everyone down. The sick son-of-a-bitch don't have anywhere to go so he's going to screw us. The only way I'm going back with that machine gun is if it's loaded. I swear I'd blow that sadistic bastard's brains out." Mike walked to the gun rack and stood the rifles up in the slots. He went to his bunk and laid down and watched the other guys come back and drop to the floor and take their weapons apart and clean them again. They reassembled them and rushed out the door only to come back depressed.

Rick yelled at them. "Leave them damn guns alone. Don't go over there. Let that son-of-a-bitch keep his passes. Don't give him the satisfaction of turning you down." Some guys listened but others continued to go back only to be rejected.

Hillbilly took his Browning Automatic Rifle in five times. He came back and slammed the gun to the floor. "That little old cold blood over there is really enjoying himself. I wouldn't go back there if he offered a two week furlough. What makes a man mean like that? I'm not playing his game anymore."

Rick laughed out loud. "You're finally getting smart Hillbilly."

"Yeah, I think you're crazy but this time you're right. The next time that sap sucker sees that B.A.R it will have two inches of dust on it."

"You sound like you're mad Hillbilly?"

"I sure am. You know that man is just doing that so we won't be able to go into town. He's evil."

"Well, how would you like to get even with that mean ass hole?"

"Oh no, I don't want any part of that. He might not give us a pass but he hasn't taken our sleep away yet. I'm still tired from not sleeping out there on bivouac cause of that confusion. Right now I'm going to plop in that bed and get me some sleep."

Mike nodded. "Hillbilly's right. I'm tired too, so don't start anything with that captain or he'll have us up the rest of the night with a detail." Mike, Rick, Hillbilly and Zug laid in their bunks. A few men continued to clean their guns and go back. They repeatedly came back rejected.

At two o'clock in the morning one of the soldiers came running in the barracks shouting. "He accepted it. I got a pass." He ran to his locker and grabbed his towel and headed for the showers.

Rick raised from his bed. "Big deal what the hell you going to do at two in the morning. There's no buses running and the bars close at two thirty."

The young soldier sat on a foot locker with his head bowed. He tapped the pass then threw it over his shoulder. "Boy, what makes a man like that. We did everything for him."

The speaker came alive. "This is Captain Thimp. Due to the fact that you men worked so hard on your weapons bring them to the weapons room and turn them in. You will receive your passes as soon as you do." The Captain continued talking. Rick got up and walked to the other men in the barracks. He whispered into their ears. After he talked to everyone he gathered them below the speaker. The Captain ended his speech and in a loud tone. "Do you hear me?"

Rick was moving his hands up and down. He shouted "One, Two, Three."

Everyone in the barracks yelled. "Put your pass up your ass."

Rick clinched his fist and raised it to the ceiling. He shouted "Again!" "Put your pass up your ass."

A bewildered voice spoke over the speaker. "Wha -wha, barracks did that come from. I demand to know which barracks yelled that." The men in the barracks stared at each other. Rick raised his middle finger and aimed it at the speaker.

The young soldiers turned to the open window when they heard the other barracks shouting. "Stick your pass up your ass." The men in the other barracks continued to yell. Sergeants were ordered into the barracks to quiet the men. Captain Thimp ordered a formation to form at the platform. It's was three fifteen in the morning.

The men stood at attention. Captain Thimp shouted, "If there is any more conduct like we just experienced, there will be short order drill the rest of the night." He yelled on and on threatening.

While he was ranting, the familiar sound of squirting water hitting the small stones was heard, then Rick's voice. "Oh, I feel so much better."

Disappointment and exhaustion set in. The men dragged their tired bodies back to the barracks and dropped into their beds. They were too tired to make any noise. At six o'clock a sergeant came running through the barracks blowing his whistle shouting, "Get out of those sacks."

Mike looked at his watch. "Only two hours of sleep. This is unbelievable. We haven't slept a full night's sleep in over two weeks." He slowly got out of bed. Again he had to pull Rick out. The company was taken to the parade field and forced to do calisthenics The men were so tired the sergeants had to keep yelling at them to keep them going. During breakfast the men fell asleep at the tables. They were ordered outside and marched to the infirmary for shots. They formed a line outside waiting for the doors to open. Another company was brought in behind them.

Some guys from the other company shouted wise remarks. "That's Able Company in front of us. It's the most chicken shit outfit on post. They got nothing but misfits in that company. They volunteered to give up their passes so they could be gung ho." The smart remarks kept coming but the guys from Able Company were so tired they ignored them.

The door was opened and a wooden fence met them. An officer shouted "Stay within the fenced area. There will be medics at stations along the way. You stop and they will give you a shot. Move on to another station to get another one. When you are done leave the building and go to the front of the building and reassemble with your company."

Rick spoke out loud. "I hope theses needles are sharp. The last time they had to use a hammer to punch them into my arm. One medic was throwing the needle like a dart."

Sergeant Carter yelled. "Knock it off Miller."

Able company's men got their shots. Everyone went to the front of the building except Rick. He walked to the other company that was behind them.

Rick sort of staggered and acted like he was in pain. He had his hand over his eye. One of the men in line asked. "Man what's the matter with you? How many shots did they give you?" All the men waiting by the door were staring at Rick, waiting for his answer.

Rick shook his head. "I had shots before but nothing like this time."

"Man what the hell you talking about. How many shots did you get?"

"I got three shots with the biggest needles I ever saw. They gave me one in the arm. One in the ass. Ah, I don't even want to talk about the other one."

"Man where in the hell did you get the third one? Come on we want to know. We got to go in there."

Rick shook his head and kept his hand over his eye. "I couldn't believe it. The medic told me to stare at the point of the needle and not to blink because if I did it would fuse to my eyeball. He then stuck that big needle in my eye. I never felt so much pain in all my life? "

"The mother fucker, stuck a needle in your damn eye?"

"Yeah. Remember don't blink. It hurts like hell when he squirts that needle in there but don't blink." Three men fainted and the rest of the line mumbled and looked at one another. Rick staggered back to his company still with his hand over his eye.

Mike looked at Hillbilly. "Don't even ask what he did over there."

Chapter 8
Sorry Sir, I'm Exhausted

The rumor around camp was Able Company was going to be the winner. Captain Thimp pranced around like a peacock. He bragged to other officers. "All my company has to do is pass the physical fitness test and we'll win." He was confident because he had a lot of athletes in his company. He had tested them before and they almost broke the Army record for physical fitness.

Rick heard this and talked to the men the day before headquarters sent their evaluation team to test Able Company. Captain Thimp gave the men a pep talk. "You men are the best conditioned company on camp. Show these examiners what good shape Able Company is in."

One by one the men were called to do push-ups. The first one dropped into the push up position. Captain Thimp looked at the chart of the last time the man was tested by his sergeants. He smiled when he saw he did seventy-five. The examiner gave the order to start. The young soldier did three and then struggled to do four. His chest dropped to the ground and he didn't come up again.

Captain Thimp knelt and shouted in the man's ear. "Soldier you got seventy-one more to go. Get up, you can do it."

The man got to his feet. "Sorry sir, I'm exhausted." The examiner wrote four.

Every man after that did only five push-ups at the most. The captain screamed. He was ordered to go back to his quarters till the testing was done.

The number of pull ups, sit ups and all other exercises was extremely low. It must have been the lowest score a unit in the army ever made. Needless to say Able Company didn't win first place.

The remaining days of Basic Training passed without incident. Captain Thimp sulked about losing the top company award. He let his cadre run the show for the remaining days. Rick had no reason to get even and was a model soldier. On graduation day the men put on their Class A uniforms. They marched onto the parade field and it was a cold. Mike looked at Rick who was marching next to him and had his hands in his pockets. The band played some songs and the company assembled in front of a stage. The camp commander gave a long boring speech and everyone was tired and cold but he kept up. The familiar sound of pressurized water hitting the small stones. A smile came on the young soldiers faces. The General thought they were smiling at him. He smiled back and thought he gave a good speech.

The men were loaded onto buses and taken to the train depot in Denver. When they entered the train Rick was waiting. He pointed at Captain Thimp who was standing at ease in front of his cadre. In a low voice Rick gave them instructions. He told Zug to get his sax out of his duffle bag. Mike saw him. "Don't do anything crazy Rick. We're out of the hell hole."

"You worry too much Mike. I got it under control."

The train started to move. Captain Thimp called his cadre to attention. The men inside the train rushed to the windows. Captain Thimp started to salute. Rick yelled. "Now". Every man on the inside of that train raised his middle finger and pressed it against the windows. Captain Thimp's arm went limp and dropped to his side. The cadre who were behind him were laughing. Zug stood on the connector platform between cars. He stuck the sax out just far enough so no one on the platform could see him. He tapped his foot a couple of times and bellowed out *Skokiaan.* Captain Thimp shouted, "Son-of-a-bitch" and chased the train trying to see who was playing that horn. He couldn't catch up and the young soldiers cheered.

The train rambled through the Rockies. Mike enjoyed the peaceful ride and the beautiful scenery. *I'd like to take my mother on a trip though these mountains. She wouldn't believe her eyes.* He noticed the farther north they traveled the trees got larger and greener. The streams next to the tram were clear and running fast. Mike was content looking out the window. Rick and Hillbilly were busy playing cards. Zug had his own jam sessions in the bar car. The train slowed as it entered a city. The young soldiers gathered their luggage. A faint screech and the train came to a stop. They exited the train and soldiers wearing rain gear escorted them to waiting busses. One of the escorting soldiers shouted. "Get your ponchos ready. You're going to Fort Lewis, Washington. It rains so much there you grow webbing between your toes."

The bus traveled up winding roads lined on both sides with tall pine trees. Mike was almost lulled to sleep by the monotonous clapping of the windshield wipers. Once on camp, they were driven to a processing area. They got off the bus and the rain was coming down hard. Someone shouted. "Next stop Korea."

A sergeant stood in front of a large white wooden building. He pointed to a spot. "Form a line here." The men did. There was no protection from the heavy rain. The group looked at an overhang on a building that was parallel to their line. They wondered why there was a lot of luggage under it and why they couldn't get beneath it. One of them asked the sergeant. "Sir, why can't we get out of this rain and go under that roof?"

"I'm sorry you men have to stand in the rain. I know you're going overseas and I wish I could do something. That luggage belongs to officers. And you know rank has its privileges. You'll find out you'll get wet every day in this state. Just hang in there. This processing goes pretty fast."

As the line moved Rick stared at the officers' luggage. Mike watched him. "Hey, what you going to do? Don't mess us up. We're close to getting a pass."

"Mike don't they know when it rains it comes down on us too? What's more important us or them officer's duffle bags?"

"Well, there is more of us than officers. They try their best so I guess we got to put up with it."

They didn't say anymore. Rick kept staring at the officer's luggage. He noticed an amber colored neck of a bottle sticking out of an overnight bag. He jumped out of line and unzipped the bag a little more and pulled out a fifth of whiskey and quickly got back in line. Mike saw what had happened. "Hey, hey Rick, put it back. That belongs to an officer."

"What the hell's the difference, it'll get us warm. That officer put it in that bag so we would see it. He knew it was raining and he felt sorry for us. He's a nice guy." He laughed and unscrewed the cap and put the bottle to his mouth and let the whiskey run down spreading warmth though his body. He took a deep breath and let it out, hitting Mike in the back of the neck. Mike smelled the breath and immediately turned around and lifted up his duffle bag.

"Man, I'm getting away from you. You're crazy enough when you're sober; I don't want any part of you when that stuff gets a hold of you."

Rick grabbed Mike's arm, "Okay, I promise I won't drink any more. I was so cold and wet it made me feel warm. Here Mike take a swig. You'll see what I mean. It'll warm you up."

"No way Rick. They said we get a pass after this processing and I don't want to end up in some mess hall doing K.P. or going to the brig. I want to see the outside of an army camp before we go overseas. It's been sixteen weeks since I was off base. Now knock it off."

"Okay Mike, I won't touch it anymore; If I do, I'll go to the back of the line away from you. You just watch me."

Mike stared at him with a concerned look. "Okay, but you heard what I said. I don't want any trouble. I don't want to hear you say after you get us in trouble, you adapt to the situation."

"I promise you, Mike. You're my best friend and I mean what I say."

Rick kept his word. Their turn came and they entered the large building and an older heavy set Master Sergeant with a red face motioned Rick and Mike into his office. Mike looked at Rick. "Remember, no crazy answers no matter what he calls you. I want everything to go smooth."

"I promise, Mike." They looked at the many stripes running up the Master Sergeant's forearm. "Mike, this guy is really an old timer, look at all those hash marks. He must of been in the Civil War." Mike glared at him and pointed his finger. "You promised there would be no wise answers."

The old sergeant smiled. "I'm Doyle, and what might your names be, lads?" Mike squinted at Rick. They both looked confused. The old Sergeant spoke again. "What's the matter son?"

Rick shook his head. "You don't know his name and you don't know mine?" He pointed to other soldiers being processed. "And you don't know their names?"

The old sergeant kept his smile. "And what might you mean by these questions?"

"Well sergeant, every other place they called us Shitheads, Wet Dreams, Numb Nuts and every other filthy name they could think of."

The old sergeant shook his head and got a serious expression. "Not here me boy. It isn't fitting to call one names when in a short time he'll be fighting for his country. We both wear the same uniform. We're like one big family."

Rick was lost for words. He stuttered and in a soft voice, "Mike, I can't believe this." His voice quivered and he wanted to say more but he choked up.

"Now listen men. As soon as you're done here you'll be receiving your pass. But if you just as soon talk I got all day. They got some nice places downtown just waiting for you."

Mike smiled. "No Sir, we're looking forward to getting that pass. We haven't had one for sixteen weeks. My name is Michael Ryan."

"Oh, so it be. That's a fine Irish name." He reached into the pile of folders. "Here it is, he opened it up. He read a few of the typewritten papers. I see here you're a football player Mike."

"Nothing big, Sir. I played high school."

"Your record shows you made All State. I'd say you must be pretty good." He studied a few more papers and shoved them back in the folder. "Everything is in order Michael. Why don't you take a chair and wait for your friend." Mike stared at the old Sergeant. *He's the kindest man I met since coming in the army.*

Sergeant Doyle looked at Rick. "And what might your name be son?" Rick stood up and could only stare at the old sergeant. "My, my name is Rick Miller, Sir." Mike couldn't believe the respect Rick was showing this man.

Rick's folder was opened and the contents were spread out on the desk. Mike noticed Rick's papers were different than his. Rick looked concerned. Sergeant Doyle seemed like he was reading from every sheet. He looked up at Rick. "And how did basic training go?"

"Okay, Sir."

Sergeant Doyle stood up and grabbed Rick's hand and shook it. "I'm glad for you, son. Keep up the good work. Your papers are in order."

Rick stood there. His eyes watered. He smiled and his mouth quivered. He managed to say "Thank you, Sir." Mike never saw him act this way. He felt good for him till He pulled the whiskey bottle from his coat. "Hey Sergeant Doyle, let's have a drink to that."

Mike leaned to the front of his chair. "No Rick, put that damn thing away."

Sergeant Doyle pulled a drawer open and came out with a large coffee cup. He slid it in front of Rick. "So be it." Rick unscrewed the cap and filled the cup half way. He started to pull the bottle away from the cup and the old Sergeant said, "I thought you said a drink son. Where I come from a drink is when the glass is full."

"Sorry about that, Sarge." He poured the cup full.

"Now that's better."

Mike was nervous and watched both ways. He could not believe what was happening and kept staring at the doors. Sergeant Doyle raised the cup and

Rick tapped the bottle to it. "Here's to a safe journey across the sea. May you come home to your families."

Mike watched Rick put the bottle to his mouth. "Rick, remember what you promised?"

"I know. But this man is something special. You know all those other mean bastards. This man is good. I'll give the bottle to Sergeant Doyle when we're done with this toast."

The door opened and a major walked in. Mike motioned for Rick to hide the bottle. Rick quickly stuffed it into his coat. Sergeant Doyle continued to drink from his cup. He showed no emotion. Mike held his breath and could feel the blood rushing to the back of his neck when the Major walked up to Rick. "What's your name, Soldier?" Rick just stared. This time the major shouted. "I said what's your name Soldier?"

Sergeant Doyle smiled. "The lad be Rick Miller, a good friend of mine, Major. He was just doing me a favor. You see I haven't seen him since he was a young boy. His father was a hell of a soldier. We served in Europe together. What a great man he was." The Major just glared at him. The old Sergeant smiled and winked at him. The Major walked to his office in the back of the room. Before opening the door he hesitated and looked back at Rick and the sergeant. Sergeant Doyle raised his cup and toasted him. The Major went into his office and slammed the door.

"Now are you ready to have that drink, Rick?"

Rick slowly pulled the bottle from his coat all the time looking at the door where the major went in. He ran around the desk opened one of the drawers and put the bottle inside. "Here Sergeant you take it. I don't want any more."

Sergeant Doyle laughed. "Okay son, I'll take good care of it for you."

Mike got up. "Thanks Sergeant. That is the best thing to do. We sure would get in trouble with that stuff."

Sergeant Doyle winked at Mike, "Yeah I know. You keep up the good work Mike." Mike didn't understand what he meant by that, but he assumed it meant something about Rick. "Now that you two men are processed go to the barracks over there and get yourself a bunk and a locker. When you get in town you can go to a bar by the name of the Busy Bee. The people there will treat you right and it's not expensive. Tell them that Doyle sent you."

Rick nodded. "We'll tell them Sergeant Doyle. Thanks, Sir." The three of them shook hands. Rick kept looking back at the Sergeant's office when they went to the barracks.

"Mike, I can't believe what happened back there. That old sergeant looked that Major right in the eye and he stood up for me. That was the greatest thing that ever happened to me. Mike did you hear what I said?"

"Yeah, I heard what you said. But if you hadn't pulled that bottle out in the first place there wouldn't of been any need for him to stick up for you." They walked into the barracks with their duffle bags on their shoulders. Hillbilly and Zug were waiting in their Class A uniforms. They showed their passes.

Hillbilly shouted, "Go to that sergeant over there and tell him who you are. He'll assign you a bed and locker. Put on your Class A's and we're on our way. Hot damn." Mike and Rick ran to the sergeant.

The sergeant handed them a sheet of paper with numbers for beds and lockers. He smiled, "Do you want a pass? You know you don't have to take it." They both held their hands out. From their expressions the sergeant knew what they wanted.

Rick raised the pass to his lips and kissed it. He reached down and shook the sergeant's hand. "I could kiss you Sergeant."

"You can keep that bullshit to yourself. Now get on your way and have a good time."

Mike and Rick dashed to the locker and bed they were assigned to. They changed into their Class A uniforms in record time. Rick shouted, "Here we come town. Put all your pretty girls outside and pass them in review."

Chapter 9
Three Day Pass

Downtown Seattle was beautiful. The bright neon lights of the bars caught their eye. Rick pointed to one. "Hey, lets have a beer there. They went in and sat at the bar. Rick looked at Mike. "Man, it sure would be great to have some civilian clothes to wear. I'm so tired of this shitty khaki color."

Mike pointed at him and laughed. "You mean to say you'd like to have those clothes you had on when your came into the army? That bebop hat, pegged checker pants and red ants crawling on your undershorts." Everyone laughed except Rick.

The beer continued to flow. Rick kept talking about getting some civilian clothes. "Man, how in the hell are we going to get broads in these costumes. Every son-of-a bitch and his brother looks alike in this town with these uniforms on." Someone suggested they find another bar. Again Rick piped up. "Yeah there ain't no broads in this place."

The four of them walked down the street. Whenever they came to a bar they cupped their hands around their eyes and looked into the window. One of them always said, "Ain't no broads in there." They'd move on. When they passed a large window one of the guys from their company knocked and motioned for them to come inside. Mike looked at the large sign. TATTOO EVERY TYPE IMAGINABLE. WE DO THEM WHILE YOU WAIT.

Rick shook his head. "How in the hell else can you get a tattoo?"

The young soldier shouted when they came through the door. "Come on you guys get a tattoo." Another soldier from their outfit was sitting on a stool with his shirt off and sticking out his chest. The tattoo artist was bent over drawing a large eagle. The soldier saw Mike, Rick, Hillbilly and Zug and he pretended it didn't hurt, but every once in awhile he squinted his eyes.

Rick walked right in front of him and stared. "Come on Miller, don't start any bullshit in here. I want this man to do a good job." The artist stopped and motioned Rick to go to another part of the room. Rick walked over to where Hillbilly was looking at a board with samples. He turned to Rick and pointed to a large tiger.

"Yeah man, I'd like to get that big cat running up my arm. What do you think?"

"No damn panthers, snakes, spiders or skulls. Man you got to get something with class. Ain't that right Mike?"

Mike shook his head. "I don't know too much about tattoos. I know I don't want one."

Hillbilly shouted. "Man, just what do you call class? Tell me what you're going to get?"

"Well, I'm going to have that guy draw me a pair of red lips on my ass."

"You're going to have what?"

Rick smiled. "Did you ever see a lady put lipstick on? Well, after she puts it on, she blots it with paper. If you look at that paper there's a perfect impression of those red lips. I'm going to have him tattoo those red lips on the cheek of my ass. It'll look like some broad kissed my ass." They all laughed. "Now I'm serious. If you get one on your behind no one will see it except the guys in the shower room. And the people you show it to." They all laughed. "Now you see Mike, you won't have any problem with a tattoo like that."

"No, I've had enough needles with those shots we got back at camp."

Rick looked at Hillbilly and Zug. Hillbilly shook his head. "I don't want anybody down there with a needle. I'm going to get that panther running up my arm."

"What about you Zug?"

"No man. I'll skip that scene. I don't want anyone drawing on me."

Rick and Hillbilly walked to the man who had just finished the eagle on the soldier's chest. The artist stared at Hillbilly. "Have you decided?"

"Yeah, I want that panther on my right arm."

The artist looked at Rick. "What about you?"

"Well, you don't have what I want in your samples."

"Well, what do you want?"

"I want a pair of red lips on my ass."

The man made a face and sort of shook his head. "You drunk, or crazy?"

"I'm neither. Now here's how I want you to do it." At first the guy didn't want any part of it but Rick talked him into it. The guy agreed to do it for an extra five dollars.

83

Hillbilly went first. He sat on the stool next to the window. In no time the panther took form and was completed. All through the ordeal he tried not to show pain. He left his sleeve rolled up so he could admire the new art.

Rick got next to the stool and started to pull down his pants. The artist yelled. "Hey you don't take your pants down in front of that window. Get in back of that room divider over there."

Hillbilly laughed. "Wait till that old boy starts working with that needle on his ass. You'll hear some yelling."

"I heard that Hillbilly. There ain't going to be no noise coming from this side."

The voice from the artist. "Pull your drawers down, let's get this over with."

The three on the other side of the divider were quiet and waiting for Rick to yell. Rick sensed this. "I know you guys are waiting for me to say ouch but I'm not going to."

There was no more talk till the artist said. "All done."

Rick walked out from behind the divider holding his pants up. He dropped them and turned so Mike, Hillbilly and Zug could see the lips. "How does it look?" They laughed. "What's so funny? How does it look.?" They told him it looked all right. "Is it all right, Mike? Tell me the truth."

"Yeah, the lips are all right. But why did you have him put buck teeth over the bottom lip?"

"What the hell you talking about buck teeth. That bastard better not of put buck teeth over them lips." He straightened up and twisted his head around trying to see the tattoo but no matter how he gyrated he couldn't see it. He ran to the big bay window and dropped his pants and bent over. His head twisted around and he looked at the reflection. "Hey, Mike, why in the hell did you lie to me? That's a good looking tattoo."

The artist finished putting away his instruments and walked out from behind the divider and saw Rick with his pants down in front of the bay window. "Hey, you, what the hell's the matter with you? That's a busy street out there. Get away from that window and get your pants up. The cops will be coming in here and arrest both of us for indecent exposure."

Rick and Hillbilly paid the man and they left the parlor laughing. Rick shouted. "Hey you guys, let's go to that bar that Sergeant Doyle said to go to.

He said it was called the Busy Bee. I forgot the directions but I'm sure we can find out."

Mike saw a cab and he flagged it down. They got inside and told the driver to take them to the Busy Bee bar. After a few blocks the driver stopped in front of a bar with a picture of a large Honey Bee painted on the front window. They paid the driver and got out. Mike looked at the tavern. "This isn't the greatest looking place in the world."

Rick shouted, "Who cares as long as it's not painted khaki. Sergeant Doyle said it was a good place and that's good enough for me." They entered and sat at a large table and looked around. Rick shouted, "Hell this looks like Armed Forces Day. Shit, they got the Army, Navy, and Marines in here."

A waitress came to the table and wiped it off with a damp rag. Rick smiled at her and pointed to Hillbilly. "Ma'am will you please wash his armpits with that rag?" She didn't hesitate. She grabbed Hillbilly's arm and forced it up. She rubbed the damp cloth under it. She released that arm and grabbed the other one and did the same thing. Hillbilly's face turned beet red. He squinted his eyes and said. "Aw, man."

The waitress hugged and kissed him on the cheek. "Well what's it going to be boys?"

Mike put up four fingers. "Four beers please."

Rick raised his hand. "Wait, hold that order. We want something better than beer. We're soldiers. We're mean, fighting men just like Captain Pimp said we were." The waitress raised her eyebrows. "Oops, sorry about that ma'am."

She smiled, "Well are you going to be men or boys?"

Hillbilly shouted, "We'll be men, bring on the fire water." The others nodded. In a short time she returned with a small round tray with four glasses on it and put them on the table.

Rick was the first to lift his glass. "Let's have a toast for us fighting machines. We'll clink these glasses and put them to our lips and not return them to the table till they're empty. Mike, tell us what we're toasting."

Mike raised his glass. "To our friendship. Let it always be this way."

Zug said, "That's cool."

They touched glasses and immediately drank the whiskey. Rick slammed his empty glass down first and watched Mike. Mike did the same but started to cough. He was breathing as fast as he could. He jumped up and motioned for the waitress. She came running. He drew in a breath and shouted.

"Water". She ran to the bar and returned to the table with a glass of water. He snatched the glass and drank. The other three at the table laughed. Rick tapped him on the back.

"What's the matter, Mike didn't you ever drink whiskey before?"

Mike took a couple of deep breaths. "Whew, that stuff is hot." He started to laugh. "No I never drank that stuff before." He took another sip of water. *I can't be chicken about this.* He motioned to the waitress. "Ma'am will you give us four more of the same?"

She looked at him funny. "Would you care for water with that?"

"Yes please." The drinks were placed on the table. Mike knew what to expect this time. He raised it to his mouth and emptied it and brought the glass down hard on the table. He looked at the other three and smiled.

Mike looked toward the bar and saw the old sergeant. "Hey you guys, there's that Sergeant Rick and I were talking about." They turned and looked.

Rick said, "Sure enough that's him. He stood up and started walking to the bar. He bumped into a soldier. He noticed the soldier had the same shoulder patch as Sergeant Doyle. Rick asked. "You're stationed at Fort Lewis aren't you?"

"Yes, since I got back from Korea."

Rick pointed to Sergeant Doyle at the bar. "Do you know that old Sergeant sitting at the bar?"

The soldier looked to where Rick was pointing and got concerned. "Yeah, I know the man. You got a problem with him?"

"No, I don't have any problem with him." Rick knew the man was suspicious so he explained what happened earlier with the whiskey and the Major. "That man saved my ass. That Major was ready to stick it to me. The old man seems to throw a lot of weight. That Major didn't want any part of him."

The soldier smiled. "Well I'll tell you about Doyle. He's got brass nuts."

Rick stared at him. "What do you mean brass nuts? I've never heard of that."

"Well let me ask you this. Did you ever hear of the Medal of Honor?"

"Yeah, I've heard of the Medal of Honor. That's the highest medal you can get."

"Well Doyle has it. If he's wearing it, the god damn general has to salute him. Now tell me, if you were that major would you mess with him?"

Rick stood dumfounded. "You mean to say that nice old guy has the Medal of Honor. How did he earn it?"

"Doyle don't talk about it. But the story going around this camp has it that his company was surrounded. Guys were getting hit all around him. Doyle crawled out and pulled the wounded in so the medic could work on them. He then grabbed a Browning Automatic Rifle and grenades and held off the enemy for about four hours. When the Gooks got so thick, he gathered the wounded men in a small area and covered them with his body. He then called the artillery to fire on his position. When it was over Doyle got wounded, but there were dead Gooks all over the place. Does that answer your question?" The soldier walked away.

Rick cupped his hands around his mouth. "Hey Sergeant Doyle." The old sergeant turned around on his stool and stared into the crowd. Rick yelled louder and waved his arms. "Hey Sergeant Doyle, over here." Doyle waved and got off his stool. He picked up his beer and made his way through the crowd to Rick.

"Well, if it isn't Rick Miller. The lad that carries the good whiskey."

Rick stared at him. His eyes sparkled with admiration for the old guy. "Will you sit at our table Sergeant?"

"Sure, I would like that."

Rick led him to the table. He pointed to Mike. "You remember Mike, we were in the room together when you processed us."

"Sure I remember Mike. You're the football player." He put his hand out and Mike shook it. "And who might be these lads be?"

Rick pointed at Hillbilly. "This is Hillbilly, and that is Zug." Doyle shook hands with both of them.

"It's good to meet you men. Now that we got the formality done with, let's have some fun. I'm sure you've been waiting for this night."

The waitress came to the table. Rick yelled, "Drinks for the table." She took the order and in a short time she made her way back with a tray of drinks. Doyle saw her coming and he pulled out a roll of bills from his pocket. Rick put his hand over Doyle's hand. "No, you're not paying for anything. You see Sarge, we never got a pass all the time we were in basic training. We had no place to spend our money. This night is on us."

Sergeant Doyle shook his head. "If I'm sitting at this table we're going to do this drinking the proper way." He threw a twenty dollar bill on the table.

"Now if you boys are serious about drinking. Match that twenty." The four of them pulled out their wallets and each threw a twenty into the pot. The old sergeant rubbed his hands together. "Now let's get down to some serious drinking." He motioned for the waitress to take money out of the pot for the drinks.

She smiled. "Okay Doyle, it looks like another goodnight."

He smiled at her. "So be it."

The drinks came faster. It seemed the more they drank the smoother the drinks went down. Doyle took off his cap, loosened his tie and unbuttoned his shirt. The four young soldiers did the same thing. In a little while he rolled up his sleeves. The four young men did the same. Hillbilly stared at his tattoo of the panther. "Hey Sergeant Doyle how do you like my tattoo?"

"That's a good looking one."

Rick shouted. "Forget about that damn tattoo. Sergeant, tell us how you got the Medal of Honor."

Doyle looked startled, then became serious. "Rick it's a long story and it's in the past. Let's concentrate on the present and the friendships and memories we're making now."

"Why don't you wear it? It's the greatest honor a soldier can get."

Sergeant Doyle looked at Rick for a long time then said. "I only wear that medal on special occasions. There's many sad memories concerning it. I'd give it back along with ten others if my friends were alive today." No one at the table said anything. It became quiet and an uncomfortable feeling hovered over them. Sergeant Doyle's eyes watered and he just stared. Mike could tell he was thinking of some sad memories.

Mike looked to Rick and shook his head, meaning no more questions. He jumped up and shouted to the waitress. "Bring us a round. Make them doubles." The waitress waved, letting him know she got the order. The drinks were placed on the table. Mike grabbed his glass and stood up. He ordered the others to stand. Mike slurred. "I want to toast to our great new friend, Sergeant Doyle." They touched their glasses and nodded. The laughter started again.

The drinks kept coming and the conversation got louder, mixed with profanity. Most of it concerned Captain Thimp and what a no good he was. Doyle laughed. "I met a few like him."

Hillbilly started bragging again about his tattoo. Rick shouted. "I told you before that anyone who gets a tattoo of a spider, skull, snake, or a god damn panther ain't got no class."

Doyle put up his hands. "Now wait, Rick. We all got different tastes. Hillbilly likes panthers and that's what he got. You could of got what you wanted and I'm sure no one would of said anything."

Rick jumped up and stood on his chair and then stepped onto the table. He unfastened his belt, unzipped his pants and let them drop to his ankles and shouted. "Now I'll show you class." He shoved his shorts down and exposed his bare butt and twisted the upper part of his body around and pointed at the red lips. "Now damn it, that's class. What do you think of that tattoo, Sergeant Doyle?"

Doyle laughed. "Yeah, Rick, I would say that was different." Mike, Zug and Hillbilly laughed. Doyle stared at them. *Enjoy yourselves you don't know what you'll be facing in a few weeks. I hope all four of you will come back home and be able to do this again.*

Zug shouted to Rick, "Man, spin around a few times up there. Let everybody in the joint see that great tattoo." Rick looked at the crowd. He bent over, and slowly rotated on top of the table.

A chief from the Navy was sitting at the bar looking in the mirror and saw Rick. He turned around and Rick was aiming his bare ass at him. He elbowed a couple of sailor friends sitting next to him. They turned around and one of them said, "That ground pounder is shooting you a moon chief."

The chief didn't hesitate. He jumped off his stool and took three strong puffs on his cigar. It now was glowing a bright red. He made his way through the crowd and smashed the hot end into Rick's bare butt.

"E-E-E, yow- you, you, rotten son-of-a bitch." He tried to kick the chief in the face but his legs got caught in his downed trousers. He fell onto the table knocking glasses in all directions then dropped to the floor. He tried to maneuver his legs with his pants around his ankles to kick the chief.

Zug yelled. "Pull up your damn pants, then kick his ass." Rick reached down to get his pants up and the chief wound up and was about to punch him in the face. Doyle sprung to his feet and slammed a right cross into the chin of the chief.

The chief rolled across the table next to them and dropped to the floor. His sailor friends saw this and rushed to assist him. One of them was running directly for Doyle. Mike swung and made full contact in the sailor's face. Zug grabbed one and the sailor picked him up and threw him over a table and he slid across the dance floor. He was dazed but he managed to get up and rush back to the melee with clenched fists. A sailor, who had been decked, and was using a table to get up saw Zug coming. He drew back and hit Zug on the side of his head. Zug slid back across the dance floor on his back and this time didn't get up.

Rick saw they were outnumbered and he jumped on top of the table. He cupped his hands around his mouth and shouted. "THE UNITED STATES ARMY, AGAINST THE SHIT HEADS FROM THE NAVY."

Hearing this, everyone in uniform sprang to his feet and looked for someone with a different uniform. The whole bar was fighting. Doyle grabbed Mike's arm. "Get your friends. We're getting the hell out of here."

Mike yelled to Rick who was punching a sailor. "Rick, follow Doyle."

"Okay Mike, you get Zug and I'll get Hillbilly."

Mike ran to Zug who was lying on the dance floor. He grabbed him. "Zug, can you get up? We got to get out of here."

"Oh man, this is a bad scene." Mike got him to his feet but Zug was groggy. Mike threw him over his shoulder in a fireman's carry and ran with him to Doyle.

Doyle motioned with his arms. "Hurry Mike. We'll use the back door." Mike followed him behind the bar with Zug on his shoulders. Rick and Hillbilly were right behind. A stocky bouncer stood on the bar with a baseball bat. When he saw Rick come behind the bar near the cash register he raised the bat and was ready to swing it down on him.

Doyle shouted. "No Elmer, he's with me." The man lowered the bat and stared back at the fighting crowd. Doyle pushed the door open. He helped Mike get Zug out into the alley. "Lean him up against that wall, Mike." Mike bent over and Zug's feet hit the ground. Rick steadied him and braced him against the wall.

The fresh air brought Zug around. "Man, I was doing so good. I was really working those sailors over until I got sucker punched." He staggered up to Doyle. I did good, didn't I Sergeant Doyle?"

Doyle put his arm around him. "You were wonderful Zug. It's a good thing we got out of there. There wouldn't be a sailor standing the way you were going at them."

Hillbilly stared at him. He smiled. "Zug you took the best punch in the house." They walked out of the alley laughing. Zug continued to rub his chin. In front of the bar were five police cars. Two of them were Military. Doyle lead them across the street from the bar.

The fight was still going strong with cussing, glass breaking and chairs hitting the walls. Rick started to walk across the street to look inside. A Military Policeman raised his club. "You stay on that side of the street and keep moving."

"But sir, I never saw a real fight. Can I just take a look."

The M.P. pointed his club again. "You get your ass out of here and keep moving."

"Yes sir. I sure don't want any trouble. I'll do what you say."

Doyle yelled to Rick. "Come on, knock off that nonsense. We're getting out of here."

"Where we going Sarge"?

"To a nice quiet bar. It will do wonders for your nerves." The men followed him for about three blocks. It was a small bar but it looked clean. They walked in and sat at a large round table.

The waitress looked at Doyle. "And how be the old man tonight? Are these soldiers on their way overseas like the other ones."

"I'm feeling great, Marge. Yes these soldiers are on their way. Let me have my usual and give them what they want." She returned and placed the drinks in front of them. Doyle reached into his pocket and pulled out his wallet.

Rick who was standing pointed to a bulge in his pocket. He reached in and pulled out crumpled bills and threw them on the table.

Doyle smiled. "Now I like that. A man under duress and still has the knowledge to think of his resources."

Rick shouted, "You're damn right. I stuffed that money from the pot in my pocket when I was on that table. I kicked so that sailor couldn't get his hands on it." Everyone laughed and the whiskey flowed smoothly again. The conversation was getting louder and slurred.

Mike stared at Rick. "Why don't you sit down? You haven't sat since you got that tattoo."

"Man, my ass is hurting. I don't know if it's where I got tattooed, or where that son-of-bitch burnt me with that damn cigar." He rubbed his butt, then thought he had to examine it. He started to unbuckle his pants. Doyle grabbed the belt.

"Oh no, not in here. If you want to look at your wound, you go to the head. We had a real problem the last place you dropped them pants."

"Damn, Doyle, I don't know what hurts. The tattoo, or that burn from the cigar."

Doyle raised his glass. "Now you just have a couple more of these and the pain will disappear. If that doesn't work I have a doctor friend who will amputate." Everyone at the table broke out laughing.

Rick continued to stand. "You know I can feel two hurts down there. I can understand why the burn would hurt, but why would the tattoo?" He got a mean expression. "I bet that bastard used a dirty needle on me." Hillbilly heard this and immediately examined his arm.

Zug yelled to Rick. "Hell there's no problem figuring out what went wrong. That guy didn't wash the needle after he got done with Hillbilly."

Hillbilly pointed his finger at Zug. "You little twerp. You best keep your cotton picking mouth shut. Ya hear?"

Doyle winked at Mike. "You know Rick, if that tattoo gets infected you can be court marshaled"

"For what?"

"Well, you destroyed government property." "Destroying government property? What the hell are you talking about?"

Doyle smiled. I'm telling you the truth. You think about this Rick. You heard them call you a G.I. didn't you?"

"Yeah, I heard them call me that and a lot of other rotten names."

"Well G.I. means Government Issue. That body you got no longer belongs to you. It belongs to the government. If you injure any part of it, you're destroying government property. And that gives them the right to Court Martial you."

Rick continued to stand and shook his head. "Hey let's forget this army bull shit. Where the hell is all the broads in this town."

"You just take it easy. There are some nice looking ladies that frequent this bar. Just be patient." The words no sooner came out of his mouth and a heavy woman walked to the table.

"Well if it isn't Doyle. You're a sight for sore eyes." She bent over and gave him a kiss on the cheek.

Doyle stood up and grabbed her hand. He looked into her eyes. "Martha, you've never looked prettier." Rick looked. He squinted and stared at the woman.

He bent down to Mike. "Man, if she never looked prettier I'd of hated to of seen her before."

"Knock it off. She's a friend of Doyle's." Rick straightened up and continued to stare at the large woman.

Doyle pointed. "These are my friends. This is Mike. That's Zug and Hillbilly. And that gentleman standing is Rick." Hearing this Mike, Zug and Hillbilly shook their heads.

One of them said, "Gentleman?" They all nodded at Martha, and told her they were glad to meet her.

"And I'm glad to meet you fine looking soldiers."

Chapter 10
The Big Broads

Zug blurted out. "Hey Martha where's all your girl friends?"

"Oh, they'll be around." She talked with them a little more then went to the juke box and played some songs. She waved at them as she took a stool at the bar. When the waitress came to the table they sent Martha a drink. She held it up and smiled at them. They raised their glasses to her.

The waitress came to the table again for an order. She started to place the empty glasses on a tray. Rick said. "Hold it, leave those glasses where they're at. Bring us fresh glasses every time we order."

She looked at Doyle. "What goes with him?"

He shrugged his shoulders. "I'm sorry, honey. He's a strange lad. You'll have to ask him."

She looked at Rick. "Why?"

"Well, we're going to drink until we fill the whole top of this table with glasses."

Mike corrected him. "You mean cover the whole top of the table, don't you?"

"What's the difference fill or cover? Just leave the glasses on the table till we're done."

She looked at him and shook her head. "Whatever makes you happy. By the way. Why don't you sit down like the rest of the guys?"

"Baby, I can't explain it to you. I'll have to show you." He started to unbuckle his belt.

"Don't do that, Rick." Doyle shouted.

Hearing this, the waitress shook her head. "Never mind, I never should have asked."

An hour passed and the top of the table was being covered with empty glasses. The effects of the drinks were starting to show on the four young soldiers. Doyle continued to drink and laugh. Rick remained standing. "Hey Sergeant Doyle. How many more of these whiskies will it take before my ass gets numb?"

"I'll tell you when. Keep drinking." A group of women came into the bar. Doyle waved to them. He pointed at the four young men. "Now you guys be quiet. You see those ladies going to where Martha is sitting? They'll be coming to this table in a short time. I want you to watch your manners and be polite."

Rick looked at Mike. "What do you think? I'm half drunk and I can't see them."

Mike squinted. "Oh, they're beautiful, Rick "

"Are you sure?"

"Would I lie to you?"

"Yes."

Doyle saw them carrying on. "You fellas knock it off or you'll run them away. Do you understand?" They both nodded.

The women came to the table and said hello to Doyle. They were much older than the young soldiers. Doyle stood up. "My, you ladies look beautiful tonight. You just stand there looking lovely and I'll get some chairs for you." He motioned for Zug to help him. The whiskey got the best of Zug and he didn't respond.

"Hillbilly kicked him in the ankle bone. "Zug, Sergeant Doyle wants you to help him get chairs."

Zug rubbed his ankle. "Man, that hurt. Why do you got to inflict pain?" He managed to get up and stagger to an empty table and grab two chairs. On the way back he wobbled and looked like he was going to fall, but he managed to regain his balance. He now was just standing in the middle of the dance floor holding two chairs and smiling at the women.

Rick walked to him. He grabbed the chairs. "Give me those damn chairs, you grinning idiot, you're going to break your fool neck." Zug hung onto the chairs and Rick pulled. They both fell. Rick was on top of Zug staring in his face. "What the hell's the matter with you, Zug? Are you drunk?"

"Man, you ask me if I'm drunk. You're the dummy who fell on me." They both laid on the floor laughing. Mike started to get up to help them. Doyle put his hand on Mike's shoulder and pushed him back down.

"Never mind, Mike. You just sit there. I'll take care of them." He grabbed Rick first and stood him up and pointed to the table. Rick stumbled a couple of times but he managed to get back to the table. He didn't sit down. He leaned forward with his elbows on top of the table. His head wobbled as he winked and smiled at the women. Doyle grabbed Zug by the back of his shirt and carried him like a puppy to the table and dropped him in a chair. Zug looked up at him and smiled.

The women were all seated now. Hillbilly whispered in Mike's ear. "Mike, these are some big heifers. I bet each of them weighs three hundred pounds."

"Who cares."

Doyle rearranged the seating so a woman was sitting next to a man. He had his hand on one of the large ladies' shoulder. "This here is Mary. And Mary, he is Mike."

Mike eased up out of his chair. "I'm very glad to meet you, Mary." She nodded and smiled. Zug was introduced to Angie, and Hillbilly to Betty. The biggest one of the bunch stood next to Rick. She had on a dress, but there was no belt going through the loops. She filled the dress so completely it looked like it was going to explode at the seams. Rick squinted at her. He couldn't believe his eyes.

"Bertha, I want you to meet Rick."

"I'm glad to meet you, Rick." Rick continued to stare at her. She looked to Doyle. "What the hell's the matter with this guy? Can't he talk? Why don't he sit down?"

Rick laughed out loud. "Get close to me, you great big beautiful woman. I want to hug hell out of you." He got his arms half way around her and lost his balance and fell into a chair. She fell in his lap. He was completely covered by the huge woman. He screamed in pain. "Oh, Mike, I'm being crushed. My ass, oh, my ass, it hurts so bad. Get this big son-of-bitch'en whale off me. Come on, you guys, lift her off me. She's squashing me." Hillbilly and Mike grabbed her wrists and pulled her to her feet.

Bertha stood over Rick. Her hands were folded into fists. "Why you smart talking, insulting bastard I'll knock every tooth out of your head."

Doyle ran to her. "Wait a minute, Bertha. This can be explained"

She didn't listen, she continued to glare at Rick. "I'm going to knock your smart ass right out of that chair."

Rick was street wise and knew this woman meant business. He had seen her type whip men before. He had to get up and get her before she got him. He managed to get half way up then fell back into the chair. He sort of laughed and shouted. "Oh, Mike, I think that big broad crippled me. Grab her before she pops me. I can't get up."

Mike knew this was getting out of hand. He was drunk but he had to do something. He took a couple of deep breaths and tried to clear his head. He got up walked in front of Bertha and grabbed Rick by the shirt and pulled him up. "Rick, these women are Doyle's friends. He's been good to us. it's not right what you're doing. I'm going to get a cab and take you back to camp."

Rick nodded his head. "You're right Mike. I'm always doing wrong. I didn't mean what I said. But that hurt like hell when she squashed me." Rick looked at the big woman. "I'm sorry, pretty lady. I didn't mean what I said. I promise, there won't be any more talk like that. Believe me it was all an accident." She glared at him. He kept sweet talking her. Her fists slowly came apart. Rick saw this and he knew she was starting to calm down. He made tears come to his eyes and continued to apologize. Mike saw this and became suspicious.

Rick slowly took her hand and looked into her eyes. "Please, pretty lady. Let me explain." She continued to stare. "Pretty lady, earlier in the day I got a tattoo on my ass. About two hours ago some crazy sailor crushed a lit cigar on my ass right by the tattoo. I was standing because it was hurting there and I couldn't sit. The pain was unbearable. Believe me, pretty lady, that is why I did all that yelling when you dropped on me. Here let me show you, so you won't think I'm lying to you." He started to pull his pants down.

Doyle shouted. "That won't be necessary, Rick. Bertha, what he's saying is true. You know I wouldn't lie to you." Rick saw her anger melting. He wiped the tears from his eyes with his shirt sleeve. He looked down at Mike and winked.

Mike made a fist at him and whispered. "Knock it off, Rick."

Rick gently put his arm on Bertha's shoulder. "Come on, pretty lady, let's play some songs. You look like you got good taste in music." They walked to the juke box and smiled at each other. Rick reached into his pocket and held a handful of change in front of her. "Play some romantic music. I love being with a pretty lady and listening to that kind of music." Bertha took the coins from his palm and dropped them into the machine. She had one finger on the buttons and another finger on her lips. Every time she picked a song Rick kissed her cheek. Everyone at the table watched them, waiting for something to erupt. After Bertha was done picking the songs Rick put his arm halfway around her. "Come on pretty lady, let's don't waste a minute. I want to dance and hold you tight all night." He was wobbly but Bertha managed to hold him up. She was light on her feet. Rick tried to lead but she was too big, so he let her. Doyle laughed when he looked at them on the dance floor. Bertha was taller and wider then Rick. Doyle pointed to the other couples sitting at the table.

"Look out there you guys. Rick knows what to do. Get out there and dance with these beautiful women." The women all looked to the young soldiers and nodded. Mike managed to stand up. He pulled the chair away from the table so Mary could stand.

She smiled. "Why thank you, Mike. You're so kind." Mike could feel the effects of the whiskey as they walked to the dance floor. He never felt so dizzy. His reflexes were slow but he tried to keep in step.

Doyle stared at them dancing. Martha put her hand on his. "You really care about these young kids don't you?"

"It's good to see them having a good time. Where they're going is hell. I just hope they all make it back. The odds are against that though." Martha kissed him on his cheek and grabbed his arm and pulled him to the dance floor. He was reluctant, but he went. They all danced for five songs and returned to the table.

Rick yelled. "Hey waitress, more drinks, all that dancing made us thirsty." Doyle unbuttoned his collar and pulled down his tie. He rolled up his sleeves. The young soldiers did the same. When Hillbilly rolled his sleeve up he showed the women his tattoo. They all pretended to admire it and said nice things about it.

Rick yelled. "You girls haven't seen anything yet."

Doyle pointed at him. "Never mind Rick".

Hillbilly got up and excused himself and went to the head. Like a chain reaction the other three followed him. Mike bent over the sink and threw cold water on his face. Rick tapped him on the back. "How bad is that woman I got? Man I'm messed up. I can hardly see her."

"I really can't say. After all those drinks, I don't know much of anything."

Zug popped up. "Who the hell cares what they look like. I'm having a good time. Besides there's no one in this town that knows us. You just behave, Rick, and go out there and get your head messed up and have a good time. Tomorrow no one will know what we did."

Rick put his arm around Zug. "We're like brothers. Let's have the best time of our lives. Bring on those big broads and let's cover the top of that table with empty glasses. Right, Zug?"

"That's damn straight, man. Let's do it."

Back at the table Rick got the waitress's attention. He pointed to an empty spot on the table. She got the message. Bertha watched Rick's head wobble. "Say boy, you better slow down on that whiskey or they'll be carrying you out of here."

"Boy! boy! Who the hell you calling boy. I'm an adult fighting machine. Captain Thimp told me that. Bertha would you call King Kong a monkey?"

"Well, well no, I guess."

"Then don't call me boy." Everyone at the table laughed.

The rest of the night was fun. The empty glasses finally covered the top of the table. Doyle pointed at them. "Well men, we accomplished our mission. Do we move to another table and try to cover that one too."

Mike stared at him through bloodshot eyes. His limp hand tried to wave to tell him that he's had enough. Zug had both his arms hanging over the side of his chair. His head was slumped on his shoulder. He said something but no one understood. Hillbilly tried to talk but nothing came out. Doyle looked at Rick. "Well, what do you say?"

The message finally got through Rick's foggy brain. "You're damn right, Sergeant Doyle. Let's invade another table." He got up and took two steps forward and then reeled around and fell on the glasses atop the table. Doyle and the women tried to study the table but it tipped. Rick dropped on the floor and all the empty glasses cascaded on him

The owner of the bar came running and shouting. "No more drinks for that guy." Rick said something to him but no one could understand what he said.

Doyle grabbed a ten dollar bill and handed it to the owner. "This will take care of the broken glasses."

Bertha reached down and picked Rick up with one arm. "Come on, Sonny, we'll get you outside where you can get some fresh air."

Doyle nodded. "That's a good idea."

The young soldiers' legs looked like they were made of rubber as they walked. Once outside Bertha shouted. "Breath deep you damn fools. You drank like you were nuts. You ought to have your heads examined to get shit-faced like that." Mike nodded. *In all my life I never felt this way.* Bertha had Rick against a wall, stabilizing him. She shouted crudely. "I'm not babysitting this guy the rest of the night. This drunken fool is not my problem."

Rick's head straightened up. His eyes opened wide. "I heard that. No one takes care of me. I don't need a damn broad giving orders. He staggered to where the other guys were. "Mike, Zug and Hillbilly hear me. Get them women off your arms. We are strong United States Army fighting machines. We don't need broads to hold us up. What the hell, can't you hold your liquor? Act like the men you are." They heard this and pulled away from the women.

Mike slurred, "That's right, Rick. We can make it on our own."

Doyle shouted encouragement when he saw them walking. "Keep it up men you're looking good. Take those deep breaths through your nose."

Bertha was still irritated. She glared at them staggering. "What a sorry bunch of drunken losers. Just look at them fools wobbling all over the sidewalk. Hey, I'm hungry. Let's get something to eat. Forget about these jerks. Leave them here."

Doyle yelled. "We're not leaving them. Food and some coffee will help straighten them up. Men, at the next corner, turn right. We're going to a restaurant."

Mike was first to make the turn, he was unaware there was a steep hill. Gravity pulled him and now he was off balance running down a hill out of control. He knew he was in real trouble. He grabbed a parking meter and the momentum swung him completely around and slammed him to the sidewalk. He grasped the pipe holding the meter and hung on for all he was worth. He tried to warn the other guys but it was too late. Zug ricocheted off store fronts, than managed to dive into a doorway. Rick's legs tried to catch up with the upper part of his body. "Yow, what the hell is going on." He hit a telephone pole and dropped to the ground. He rolled down the hill but managed to grab a pole. Hillbilly saw Mike holding on to the meter. He dove on top of him.

"Mike, we're messed up. Man, I don't know if I can get up." They both laughed.

Doyle and the five women were on top of the hill looking down. Bertha shouted. "Let the damn fools lie there. I'm hungry."

Doyle was concerned, "Don't talk that way, Bertha, they might be hurt." He made his way down the hill to check on them. He saw them move and he felt relieved.

Bertha shouted., "Get your sorry asses up you drunken fools." Doyle and the women helped the soldiers get to their knees. Red flashing rotating lights and a bright spotlight swept from one person to another. Hillbilly looked at the paddy wagon.

"Oh, Mike, we're in a rash of shit."

Two officers got out and walked to the sidewalk and saw the large women standing over the soldiers on the ground. One of the officers shouted. "All right, what's going on here?"

Rick saw the police. His instincts from past experiences with police took over. He quickly shimmed up the pole and got to his feet. He tried not to slur. "We weren't doing nothing."

Luckily, Doyle knew one of the officers. "How you doing Ed?"

"They some of your boys, Doyle?"

"Yeah, they were out celebrating and they drank too much."

The other officer asked. "They shipping over?"

Doyle nodded his head and in a low voice. "They're on their way to Korea. They got three days and they'll be on a troop ship."

One officer scratched the back of his head. The other one stared at the young soldiers trying to get up. "I've seen some bad ones, but this bunch is the worst. What were they drinking, airplane fuel?"

Doyle sort of laughed. "No they just had a few. Look at them officers, they're just boys. They haven't acquired a tolerance for it yet. They were enjoying themselves with these nice ladies."

The officers squinted when they saw the women. The one named Ed, whispered in Doyle's ear. "Were these guys drunk when they met the women?"

Doyle, shrugged his shoulders. "They're good people."

The other officer walked to Mike and hauled him to his feet. Mike thanked him. The officer laughed. "Man, what did you do, try to drink the bar dry? How in the hell did you guys get tangled up with these women?" Mike shrugged his shoulders.

One by one they were helped into the back of the paddy wagon and ordered to sit on the benches and not move. Officer Ed pointed at them. "You guys don't move. I want you inside so you don't stagger into traffic."

Doyle was concerned. "Hey, Ed you're not running them in are you? They're good boys. Give them a break."

"We're not arresting them, just relax, Doyle." He pointed to the women. "Come on ladies. Get in with your boyfriends."

Bertha, shouted. "Hey, what the hell did I do? I'm not drunk."

"Oh, I know that. You're a fine citizen Bertha. You were concerned about these young soldiers. I know how nice you are. Don't give me a reason to check if there's warrants out for you or your girl friends."

Bertha's, composure changed and she smiled. "Yes, officer we were trying to be nice to these young soldiers. We'll get in and cooperate with you fully."

The officers helped her climb the steps to get into the paddy wagon. Once inside she hunched over and made her way to where Rick was sitting. He saw her coming and he put up his hands. "Don't sit on my lap." She sat next to him and he put his arm around her shoulders. Bertha smiled at him and he kissed her on the cheek.

Officer Ed saw this. "Now that's true love. I hope he feels the same way in the morning." He pointed to the other women. "Come on, girls get inside the love wagon."

Doyle and Martha, stared in the paddy wagon at the couples. Ed looked at Doyle. "You need a ride, Sarge?"

"No fellas, Martha, and I are going to have something to eat in a nice quiet restaurant."

"Okay, Doyle, we'll drop them off at the hotel by the water. They'll sleep it off and be as good as new in the morning."

The paddy wagon rolled off into the darkness. In between radio transmissions Ed asked his partner. "Jim, remember when you were a soldier their age and the second world war was going on? I bet you did the same thing, didn't you?"

"Yeah, but I sure as hell don't remember getting one that size. How about you, Ed?"

"I did some crazy things when I drank that fire water. I woke up in some strange places with some strange women. I'd give a hundred bucks to see that one guy get up in the morning next to that super big one. I'll bet he won't drink for a long time after he gets a clear sober look at her." They both burst out laughing. Jim kept driving and Ed looked through the window into the back of the wagon. "Damn, I wish I had a picture of them back there. Hey, Jim, is this wagon going awfully slow tonight?"

"It's doing its best. You got to understand it's transporting a lot of weight."

The paddy wagon pulled into a driveway and stopped under an awning. The officers got out and opened the back doors. "Okay lovers, we have arrived at your nest. Ladies will exit first." The officers reach inside the wagon and grabbed the women by their arms and helped them out. Every time one got out, the paddy wagon rose. "Okay soldiers, you're next." The officers assisted them too and told the women to come and get their partner. The couples stood on the driveway.

Bertha, grabbed Rick around the neck and kissed him. "That's my man."

Rick's head wobbled and he slurred. "You better believe it."

Seeing this, the officers made sour faces. One of them said. "No kissy stuff out here. Go inside and get it on."

Mike reached into his pocket and pulled out his wallet. "How much is the taxi?"

The officers laughed. Ed, patted Mike on the back. "No charge, son. This one is on the house. Let's say it's from two G.I's from another generation. You guys have fun and when you get to Korea give them hell and come back in one piece."

"Thank you, Sir." The four couples walked into the hotel. The officers waited to make sure there was no trouble.

As the paddy wagon pulled away Ed laughed. "Brings back old memories."

Eight o'clock and a church bell was ringing. Sunlight filtered through a nicotine stained window shade. Rick's eyes opened slowly and looked at the strange surroundings and knew right away he's wasn't in an army barracks because the walls were painted blue. He stared at the dresser and the padded chair. He didn't move and tried to figure out how he got in this room. He couldn't think too well because his head was throbbing and his butt ached. He heard loud snoring and felt heat radiating under the covers next to him. Slowly his hand went behind him and made contact with soft warm flesh. He rolled over on his back and turned his head. A woman was sleeping with her face turned away from him. He lifted the blanket and saw a big woman's naked body. A very heavy one. She was lying on her side and where her back met the mattress a large roll of fat extended away from her body. She had an enormous tattoo of a spider web which covered her entire buttocks. A big red spider was crawling out from between her huge cheeks. He thought, I got to get my ass out of here before she wakes up. He turned slowly to the other side of the bed and started to put his feet on the floor as quiet as he could. The blankets flew up and the big women sat up. "Oh Rick, come here and hug me." He couldn't believe what he saw. Her hair was greasy and messed up. Her teeth looked like a piano board. Every other tooth was rotten or missing. He was stunned. He just stared. He was in shock. He never saw anything like her. She held out her arms. "Come here, Rickey, baby, let's have some more fun."

He grabbed his clothes and shouted "goddamn, get me the hell out of here." He ran into the hall naked, banging on doors and putting on his clothes at the same time yelling for Mike, Hillbilly and Zug.

People in the rooms yelled. "Keep quiet, you damn drunk." He continued to yell until he heard Mike's voice."

"Rick, is that you out there? What's going on?"

Rick ran to the door where he heard Mike's voice. "Mike, I just got the shit scared out me. Man, you should of seen this big ugly thing I slept with last night. Mike, take a look at what's in there with you. Let's get the hell out of here. Man, we're going to catch some shit off these broads."

"From inside Mike's room a woman's voice screamed. "You smart punk. I'll come out there and mop the floor up with you. You best keep your damn mouth shut, you smart talking son-of-a-bitch."

Movement could be heard from inside the room. Mike yelled, "Take it easy, he don't mean it. He's probably still drunk. Rick, do you hear me? Don't say anymore."

Rick heard the door open where he stayed last night. Bertha came out into the hall without any clothes on. Her large breasts hung down to her belly button and her stomach covered her knees. She had a water pitcher in her right hand. Rick stared and said. "Damn" She threw the water pitcher at him. He ducked and it shattered when it hit the door Rick was standing in front of. The big woman was yelling and cussing and started to charge him. Doors opened and people stuck their heads out.

Bertha saw them and ran back into the room shouting. "I'll be right back, you bastard, I'm going to kick your ass."

"Hey Mike, hurry, lets get out of here that big broad is going to tear up this place." I'll get Zug and Hillbilly." He started pounding on doors and yelling their names.

Zug shouted through a closed door. "Go away, everything is cool in here. I'll meet you back at camp." Hillbilly too said he was satisfied and told Rick he was going to stay.

Rick ran back to Mike's door. "Mike, are you coming. I ain't got too long, that big broad is putting on her clothes and she's going to raise hell when she gets out here."

Mike immediately dressed. "I'm sorry Mary, but I have to go. He's going to get us all in a mess." He left the room and saw Rick running out the front door with Bertha chasing him with a vase. Mike ran to her. "Bertha, please, let's stop this. Here take this money and get yourself and Mary breakfast and a ride home. I'm sorry this had to happen."

"Mike, I don't care whose friend that guy is. If I get my hands on him, I'll break him in half."

Mike calmed her down and she walked back to the hotel. He caught up to Rick who was sitting on a park bench. "Rick, get up. We got to get out of here. They'll surely call the police."

Rick jumped up and held his butt when he ran. They got a good distance away and sat at a picnic table. "What brought this on Rick? Why are you acting this way?"

"Oh, Mike, I must of kissed that ugly broad. Man, I don't know what else I did with her." He made a face and started spitting. "She turned around and I thought it was King Kong without any hair. I never saw so many rotten teeth. Man, she scared hell out of me. I'll never drink again. Her face was as big as a beach ball. Man, I never saw anything like that before." He made a sickening sound. "That ain't all. You should of saw the tattoo she had. I lifted the covers and she had a tattoo of a spider web covering her big ass. A huge red spider was crawling out of you know-where. Shit, man, I wasn't drunk, I was blind and crazy. That woman looked like a beached whale laying in that bed. She got up and her belly hung down to her knees. Aw, man, I did some crazy shit, but nothing like that. I want to go to a service station and gargle some gasoline. You know all this bull shit with that broad and I got a terrible hang-over and my ass feels like it's on fire. Shit, I should of stayed in that camp. I don't know what I might of caught off that woman. I'll tell you what. If that guy used a dirty needle and got me infected I'm going back there and destroy his joint."

Mike let him rattle on. A church bell rang and he sobered. He remembered the promise he made to his mother. "Hey, Rick I got to go to church."

Rick squinted. "You got to go where? What's the matter with you? Do you feel guilty for what you did last night?"

"Nah, it's nothing like that. I made a promise and I got to keep it."

"You're serious, aren't you?"

"Yes, I'm serious. I know what we did last night wasn't right, but that's not the reason. Like I said. I made a promise. You can wait for me. I'll meet you here after the services."

"You made that promise to your mother, didn't you?"

"Yes."

"Mike, if I made that promise to your mother I would go too. Can I come with you? I've never been in a church."

Mike took his hat off when he entered the church. Rick noticed this and took his off. They walked down the aisle and stopped. Mike genuflected and Rick started to do the same. He got half way down and whispered. "Mike, I'm sorry it hurts too bad." They went into a pew and Mike knelt. Rick did the same. The services started and Mike sat, stood, and knelt like the rest of the people. Rick stayed kneeling with his face in his hands. Mike tried to encourage him to sit back. He just shook his head and whispered. "I can only kneel. It hurts too bad."

After the services, they left with the other people. A couple of old ladies came up to them and one said, "It's so nice to see you soldiers in church." Rick nodded to her. She put her hand on his arm. "Young man I never saw a person pray so hard in all my life. You're a good boy." Other people from the congregation crowded around.

Another old lady stood in front of Rick and looked him in the eyes. "You two men are refreshing. So many times we see soldiers drink, fight and pick up with women-of-the-night. You two are decent men." Rick looked at Mike and raised his eyebrows. Other people were praising them. Every time one said something nice, the rest agreed. Rick thought, I hope Bertha doesn't show up.

The little old lady who came up first grabbed both their arms. "We have a breakfast in the basement. We want you to eat with us."

Hearing this Rick's eyes opened wide. He whispered to Mike. "Let's get out of here. I got a hangover and I don't want to eat."

Mike looked down at the lady, "Ma'am, we sure appreciate the offer, but we have to get going. Thank you anyway."

She was persistent. She squeezed their arms tighter and pulled them to the basement. "We will not take no for an answer. We're going to give you a good meal and then you can go." Rick cringed.

She forced them down into chairs at a table. Mike laughed when Rick sat on the edge of the chair. The old lady saw this and grabbed Rick's shoulders and pulled him back.

"Now sit back and get comfortable. We'll get your breakfasts" Rick winced and when she left he slid back to the edge of the chair.

"Come on Mike let's jump up and run out of here."

"We can't do that. They're such nice people. It would hurt their feelings."

"Hurt their feelings? What about the feeling I'm getting from that hangover and the feelings of that tattoo and cigar burn. Mike, I never felt so bad in all my life. Let's get out of here."

"We'll just stay for a little while, then we'll leave. You made a real impression on these people the way you prayed."

"Prayed? I had my face in my hands because I was scared I was going to cry out with pain."

Three ladies came out of the kitchen. One was carrying two trays loaded with food. The other ones followed with juice, and coffee. They placed the food and drinks in front of the two. Rick stared at the scrambled eggs and sausage links. The sausages were shining from the fat oozing out of them.. He kept staring at them and felt sick. "Ma'am where is the restroom?" She pointed to the far wall and he ran to it.

The woman stared at the restroom door till Rick came out. His legs were wobbly and his eyes were bloodshot and watery. He came to the table and didn't sit down. The woman asked him what was the matter?

He stood silent with a pathetic look. He stuttered a little and in a soft voice. "I can't eat, I'm sorry. When I saw you ladies being so nice and putting that food in front of me, it reminded me how my mother did the same thing when I was home. I was overwhelmed and I didn't want to make a scene in front of you nice people. I'm all choked up inside. Please forgive me." He sobbed a little and turned his head. The ladies all dabbed their eyes with tissue.

The old lady patted him on the back. "We understand, son. You do what you have to do. We want you to remember, you're always welcomed here." She pulled his head down and kissed him on the cheek. "Such a nice boy." Rick sobbed some more and walked out the door.

Mike got up. "Please excuse me. Thanks for being so kind to us. Rick and I will never forget you. I hope you understand. I have to go to my friend."

The old lady stood on her tip toes and Mike bent forward. She kissed him on the cheek. "You're such good boys. We understand."

"Thank you ma'am"

Mike left the church and caught up with Rick. "Man, you can really lie. You sounded so sincere. You even had fake tears. What a pro. Those women were crying. Don't you feel guilty lying to them?"

"Nope."

Mike sort of laughed. "Tell me Rick, did your mother really serve you breakfast like that?"

Rick became serious. "Hell no she —, the reform school." He stopped abruptly turned his head and walked away. Mike sensed Rick blurted out something he didn't want to say. He didn't ask him any more questions.

Chapter 11
The Decision

The night before they shipped out, a sergeant stood in the aisle of the barracks and gave orders for the next morning. The men had gathered around him and were listening intently. Rick snuck off to his bunk and laid down with his hands behind his head looking up. Mike came to his bunk. "Hey, Rick, you better get packed, we're going on that cruise tomorrow."

"Yeah, Mike, I know. I just want to rest a minute." Hillbilly shouted for Mike to come to his bunk. Mike left and Rick jumped up and pulled the pillow case off his pillow. He threw a few personal things in and snuck out the door. He ran to distance himself from the barracks. He stopped and looked back to see if anyone had followed. The lights in the barracks were all lit. He listened to the laughing and loud talking coming from it. He turned around and a cold damp mist engulfed him. He pulled his collar up and sunk his hands into his pockets and walked with his head down. He turned around again and stared at the barracks. *Mike, Hillbilly, and Zug are in there. They are like brothers. They worried about me and tried to help. Sergeant Doyle called me son. I never had people like that around me.* He shook his head. *I've got to get those guys out of my mind. I want to be free. I don't want them idiot sergeants calling me names anymore.*

He looked down at the city. The lights were smeared by the cold misty rain. Everything felt chilly. He took his hands out of his pockets and started running and shouting.. "Got to get away from here. Don't think about it anymore." He tried to put everything out of his mind but it didn't work. His friends' faces reappeared, laughing. He stopped running and walked slowly. He stopped and leaned against a tree. *For the first time in my life someone cares about me. I have brothers back there and I'm running away from them.* He looked at the city. *It's like the weather, cold. Who do I know there? No one will care about me. I'll just end up in some jail.* He smiled, turned and ran back. He watched through the windows. Guys were laughing and teasing each other. When no one was looking he snuck back in and went to his bunk. He emptied the pillow case. His eyes opened wide when he saw his duffle bag packed leaning against the wall. Mike walked up. Rick pointed at the duffle bag. "Who did that?"

Mike shrugged his shoulders. "Hillbilly, Zug, and me." Rick turned, took a deep breath and tears streamed down his cheeks. He ran into the latrine.

At 0500 hrs. the men sat by their duffle bags and waited for the order to board the military buses. Mike and Rick were lying on their bunks using their duffle bags as pillows. Fifteen minutes later a sergeant came in. "Okay men, form a single file outside. Take your duffle bags and other belongings. You're now on your way to the Frozen Chosan. Be careful and good luck."

The men exited the barracks and walked to the bus. Someone said. "Good-bye, good old U.S.A." The sergeant standing at the doorway of the bus checked the soldiers' names when they entered. When the busses were loaded head lights came on and the sounds of motors got louder. One after another the buses rambled out of the camp, through the city and to the dock where a large ship was waiting. Mike's group got off their bus and they looked at the many soldiers waiting to board the ship. More buses with soldiers came.

Hillbilly's eyes looked in all directions, he couldn't believe so many men. "Man is that old boat going to hold all of us?"

Rick pointed to the far side of the dock. "Go back there and when they start boarding you stay at the end of the line. Maybe they won't have enough room for you."

"Y'all keep that bullshit to yourself, Miller."

They were ordered to get in a long line of soldiers who were boarding the ship. Mike looked at Rick. "Well I guess this is it."

"Yeah, I know Mike. I wonder what they'd do if I started running and yelling, I lost my ticket." "You're not serious are you Rick?"

"Hell no, I wouldn't miss this for all the money in the world."

Mike slipped out of line and looked toward the front. "It won't be long now and we'll be on that ship. Zug and Hillbilly are almost there."

Rick snuck a look. Hillbilly happened to be turned around and saw Rick. "Y'all ain't going to believe what's happening up here. They're going to delouse you before you get on this boat."

"They what?"

"These old boys up here got big old spray cans and they make you drop your drawers and they give you a big puff of white powder."

Rick laughed. "You and Zug need two puffs of that shit after being with them big fat ugly broads the other night. I bet you guys got creatures on you they don't even have names for." Every soldier in line laughed.

Mike and Rick finally made it to the loading platform and sure enough there were three sergeants holding large spray cans.

"Hillbilly wasn't kidding"

One of the sergeants yelled. "Okay, Shitheads, drop your pants and shorts."

An older soldier behind Mike spoke up, "This is the fourth time I went through this and every time I got sprayed with that bug powder."

Rick asked. "What's it for?"

"Just like you told your buddies. These jokers go out and shack up with any broad they can find. They don't know what they caught and they don't care. Hell, if a bunch of crabs, or bedbugs got on this ship, they'd have a field day with all these guys."

Rick stood in front of the sergeants who had the sprayers. "You heard what he said. Drop your pants and shorts."

"Yeah, I heard you, but these bugs are my pets."

"Skip the bullshit and drop your drawers." Rick did, and they started spraying him. When one of them got behind him he shouted to the other sergeants. "Hey you guys, come here and see what this joker's got tattooed on his ass."

They looked. One of them shouted. "Well I'll be damn, a pair of lips with a cold sore on them. They laughed and gave him another spray of the white powder and told him to go aboard.

Rick went aboard and pointed to his head. "Hey, you wise asses." They looked at him. "I had them take refuge up here."

One of them shouted. Keep'em, and give'em to the Gooks."

Another sergeant checked names and told them to go to the lower deck and follow the red arrows. Their bunks were there.

Rick asked, "Is it close to the pool?"

The sergeant smiled. "No, but you got a nice view."

They went into the lower decks of the ship, and Mike commented. "This ship is big. I hope we don't get lost." They followed the arrows and finally made it to their section. It was a large room with rows of beds stacked

111

five high. A sergeant yelled. "Pick a bunk." They took one and watched a steady flow of soldiers come into the room.

"Mike, it's like a stinking cattle car. When we slide into those beds our nose will be touching the one above us."

Mike laughed. "I guess we'll have to adapt to the situation."

Rick ignored him. "Come on, I can hardly breath. Let's get out of here." They threw their duffle bags on their bunks and went outside. They elbowed their way through soldiers standing on the deck to get to the railing.

"Look down, that line is as long as it was when we first got here. I wonder how many soldiers this ship can hold?"

"Too many."

Mike and Rick were joined by Zug and Hillbilly. Mike pointed at the dock "Hey, you guys, look, there's Doyle." Rick yelled, "Hey Sergeant Doyle, up here."

Doyle saw them and waved. "How's it going gang?" They nodded their heads..

Rick shouted. "You're a great guy, Sergeant, but your women don't show me much."

"You better watch your mouth, or I'll yell out what Bertha told me you and her did in that motel room."

The soldiers leaning on the railings yelled. *"Tell us. Sarge."*

Rick's face redden. "Okay, Doyle, you win."

Doyle waited till it got quiet. "Remember this is all business now. You boys get over there and do what you were trained for. Don't give that enemy a break. You're going there to win. I want everyone of you to come back."

The four of them waved. "We'll see you when we get back."

"That's what I want to hear. The Lord be with everyone of you."

The lines were unfastened from the ship and water churned behind it. A white plume of steam came from the stack and the horn blasted.. The ship slowly separated from the dock. The soldiers continued to stare at Sergeant Doyle, the lone person on the dock who was still waving.

The Sergeant watched till the ship became so small he could barely see it as it made its way to the open sea. *It's cold the way these young men are sent off to war. When I was young and sent to Europe in the Second World War, there were thousands of people lining the docks cheering and waving their soldiers off. Bands played music that made your blood tingle. Pleasure boats*

112

sailed next to the ship with people waving and yelling encouragement to their soldiers. It sure is different for these boys. It's as though no one cares there's a war in Korea. Don't they realize a lot of these kids won't be coming back? What will it take to make them aware? What happened to the spirit of our country?

Doyle walked through the empty loading area, stopped, turned and looked at the tiny speck on the horizon. He felt a chill and his eyes watered. He slowly shook his head, came to attention and saluted the tiny speck on the horizon.

Five days out into the Pacific a storm hit. The waves pounded so hard it felt like they were playing catch with the ship. Rick and Mike lay in their bunks. They felt the floor rise then free fall and hit the water with a bang. "Hey Mike, we're in front of this damn ship. It's the worst place to be. Those waves are going to pound hell out of us."

"I was thinking the same thing. It's like being on an elevator that goes to the top floor and the cable breaks and we crash to the bottom"

Another soldier said, "They say we're going through a hurricane. All the hatches are shut and no one is allowed outside."

"Mike, did you hear that? A hurricane, man, that's a hell of a storm. It's so stuffy in here I can't breathe. I feel like one of those sardines packed in a can."

"I believe it's true, the way this ship is bouncing around. Just lay still and ride it out."

Hours passed and perspiration streamed down Rick's face. He protruded his lower lip and exhaled his breath to try to cool himself. He tried to get some sleep, but couldn't. In disgust he jumped from his bunk and shouted. "I'm getting some air." He climbed the steps and grabbed the large metal handle and forced the door open. He was immediately struck in the face with a blast of wind and salt mist. He hunched over with his hands on his knees. The ship was going down in the front. He looked up and saw a monstrous wave that looked like it was about to come over the ship and crush it. He slammed the door and secured the latch. He froze on the steps waiting and wondering if he was going to survive. The ship came back up and he sighed. He walked to his bunk.

Mike asked. "Did you get some air?"

Rick was quiet, then said. "You're not going to believe this. I opened the door and a wave was so big I thought it was going to swallow us. You know where the Captain steers on top of this ship? Water was flying up there. The windshield wipers were going." He pointed to the ceiling. "When those big waves hit, water runs over the deck above us. You cannot believe what I saw out there."

"From the way we're bouncing around, I'd believe anything."

That night it became difficult to breathe because so many men were stuffed in those small quarters. Mike heard a soldier on a top bunk across from him gagging with dry heaves. He started to get up to help him. Another soldier on the lower bunk directly below stuck his head out and looked up to where the gagging was coming from. He shouted. "Hey, you up there, are you all right?" The sick soldier put his face over the side of his bunk and the dry heaves became wet. The man on the bottom shook his head as it splashed in his face. He shouted "You rotten son-of-a-bitch." He jumped out of his bunk, wiping his face with one hand. The other clenched in a fist. It looked like he was going to strike the man, but at the last second he realized the man was sick. He punched the side of the bed and ran to the head.

"Hey, Mike, did you see that? He got it right in the face."

"Yeah, I saw it. That guy is really sick." He got up and went to the sick soldier and Rick followed. Mike asked if he was all right.

"I'll be better as soon as I get rid of this sea sickness. I feel bad about letting it go on that guy's head."

Rick laughed. "That's all right. He's in the shower cleaning up. If there's any trouble when he comes back we'll handle him. Just lay there and get better."

They went back to their bunks. Mike tried to talk to Rick but he didn't answer. He jumped down. "What's the matter?" Rick was pale and looked like he was turning green. He rolled out of his bunk with his hand over his mouth and ran to a garbage can and stuck his head inside. Mike followed and asked if he could help. Rick kept his head inside the can and motioned with his hand for Mike to leave him alone. Mike walked back to his bunk and sat on the side of it.

Rick came back shaking and cussing. "Ain't this a bitch? I got a pass after sixteen weeks. I get a damn tattoo and I don't know if I got blood poison. Some fool burns my ass with a cigar. I had a hangover that felt like my head was going to cave in every time I blinked. My stomach did flip flops and some old lady wanted to stuff greasy sausages down my throat. Now I get seasick. What the hell is going on?"

114

"Tell me Rick, are you as sick as you were when you woke up and found yourself in bed with Bertha?"

"Oh, man, nothing could be worse than waking up next to that. Do me a favor and don't talk about homely broads, booze, or food until I'm over this shit."

A couple of soldiers a few bunks over heard the conversation. One of them shouted. "Hey, how would you like a thick lard sandwich with a onion on top?"

Rick heard this and made a face and shook his head. He tried not to let it bother him. Another one shouted. "Hey Miller, I got a big jar of jam and a spoon. You can eat it with a limp cooked dill pickle. How does that sound?"

Rick grabbed a combat boot and threw it at them. He ran to the gorp bucket with his hand over his mouth. When he was done he walked to the wise guys bunks.

"When I get better I'm going to pay back both you bastards. He dropped on his bunk and moaned. "Oh man, I'd just as soon be dead."

The sea kept pounding the ship. Down below it was like an epidemic. Men were getting up and running to the gorp cans. Some didn't make it and it accumulated on the floor. The smell was terrible.

Rick groaned. "This place is a shithole." Mike tried not to think about what was going on around him. He knew sooner or later it would get him. He put his head under his pillow and tried to muffle the sounds of men moaning, vomiting and complaining. Somehow he managed to fall asleep. When he woke the ship was still rocking and pounding. The sick men were still doing the same as they had the night before.

Mike got up and shook Rick. "Come on, it's time for breakfast. Eat something and you'll feel better."

"Hell no, just let me stay here. I want to die."

"Okay, I'll bring you something."

"No, don't do that. I couldn't even look at food, let alone eat it."

"Well, is there anything I can do for you?"

"Yeah, stop this son-of-a-bitching boat from jumping out of the water."

Mike hung onto the bunks as he walked to Zug. "I'm going to breakfast. Do you want to come?"

"Oh no, man, this is a bad scene. My stomach is rolling around like that damn water outside. No sir-ree I can't handle it." He sank his face into a pillow.

"Where's Hillbilly?"

Zug pointed his finger up. "He's eating. That cat must have a stomach made out of cast iron. Please knock off the talk about food. Goodbye."

Mike started up the metal steps to the mess hall. He grasped tight to the railings, as the rocking ship slammed him against the steel walls. He made it to the mess hall and it was almost empty. He grabbed a tray and put it on the track in front of the servers. Eggs, bacon and toast were placed on it. He put the tray down and stared at the food. An older soldier looked at him.

"You're not feeling too good, are you kid?"

"I was all right until I sat down. Boy it got me."

"The best thing you can do right now is go to that sailor with the white pants and tee shirt on. Ask him if he'll give you some soda crackers. Crackers will help. It always did for me."

Mike left the table and went to the sailor. "Sir, can 1 ask you something?"

"I'm not a sir, what do you want?"

"I got sea sickness and a couple of my buddies down below are really bad. I heard soda crackers will help. I'm willing to buy them."

"You're getting a little green behind the gills? He went behind a wall and came out with three packages of crackers. "Here's a couple for your friends."

"What do I owe you?"

"They're on the house."

Mike went back to the bunks. "Here Zug, eat them, they'll help you."

Zug kept his head buried in the pillow and raised his hand. Mike put a box in Zug's hand and left."

"Hey, Rick, wake up. An old timer told me how to get rid of sea sickness."

Rick looked through his blood shot eyes. "What did he give you, a gun?"

"I got some soda crackers. The crackers will help settle your stomach." He broke open a box and took one out.

The storm continued into the night. Mike munched on the crackers and they seemed to help. Morning came and it was extremely quiet. The ship wasn't rocking. The storm subsided. Men slowly got out of their bunks and smiled.

116

Most of them hadn't eaten for three days. Someone said. "It's going to be great to eat again."

After breakfast they went out on the deck. The wind howled and it was cold. Rick pulled his collar up and dug his hands into his pockets. "Damn, it's too cold out here Mike. Let's go back inside." They started walking for the door. Zug, Hillbilly and a group of men came out.

Hillbilly shouted. "Y'all aren't going in there. They got a work detail and they're cleaning up in there. They ran everybody outside until they're done."

Rick yelled. "What the hell we suppose to do freeze our asses off till they're done? Man, this is a bitch. Three days of seasickness and now the idiots are trying to make me catch pneumonia." He kept bitching and everyone laughed. He got mad, and ran to the door and kicked.

A voice inside yelled. "What do you want?"

"I want some heat. I gotta get inside I'm freezing out here."

"You keep your sorry ass outside until we're done."

"Why can't we stay inside where it's already been cleaned? It's cold out here."

This time another voice with authority. Rick recognizes the voice of the master sergeant who was in charge of his area. "Because I said so, Shithead."

"You sadistic, dumb, son-of-a-bitch. When I get inside I'm going to mop up that puke with your rotten ass." He continued cussing till he heard the latch on the other side of the door being lifted. He ran down the deck and mixed with the group. The Sergeant came out and looked around cussing. He walked to the group.

"Who the hell was the wise ass pounding the door?" No one answered. He glared at each one of them. "Pound on that door again and I guarantee I'll be pounding on your god damn head." He walked away mumbling to himself.

It got colder. Rick jammed his hands deeper into his pockets and started running up and down the deck trying to get warm. He stopped and his hands came out of his pockets. "Hey, you guys, get over here. There's heat coming from somewhere." The group walked to him. They felt the warm air.

Hillbilly stepped back. "Damn, man, that's an exhaust fan blowing from the kitchen."That stink will get into your clothes and you'll smell like a fried fish. The rest of the group walked away.

Rick continued to stand in front of the exhaust fan. "Suit yourself, I don't care what I smell like, as long as I'm warm."

The rest of the men continued to lean against the wall until they heard a door bang open on the deck above them. They eased forward and looked up. A woman from the officers' section was leaning over the railing right above Rick. Her hand covered her mouth, and her cheeks wcrc ballooned. She took her hand away from her mouth and threw up. Mike tried to warn Rick but Rick couldn't hear because of the hum of the fan. The vomit hit him on top of his head and splashed down on his shoulders. He momentarily stood and rubbed his hand on his head, bought it down and stared at it. He jumped away and looked up shouting, "Puke, puke. Some son-of-a-bitch puked on me." The woman leaned over the rail again and was gagging.

Rick saw her and ran. "You dumb bitch, you puked on me. What the hell is the matter with you?" The soldiers laughed.

The lady continued to stand at the railing gagging. She was joined by a major. He put his hand on her shoulder and started leading her back to the cabin. The lady must have explained what happened, because the major came back to the railing and yelled down at Rick who was rubbing his head and shoulders cussing.

"Soldier, come up here. I want to talk with you."

Rick looked up and saw the major. "Yes sir." He mumbled as he walked to the stairs. The soldiers sobered up when they saw the officer. They wondered what was going to happen. Rick saluted and the major led him into his cabin.

Time passed and Rick didn't come out. A soldier shouted from the work detail. "It's clean in here. You guys can come in." Everyone rushed to get inside. Hillbilly shook his head.

"Man, that old boy can get in trouble by just standing not doing nothing. I wonder what that major is going to do to him? Rick used some strong language on that woman. I'll bet she's the major's wife."

Mike shrugged his shoulders. Zug yelled. "Man, I don't care who you are. That's a bad scene when somebody heaves on your damn head. He's entitled to be pissed and say what he wants." Mike started to go to the officer's cabin to see if he could help Rick by explaining what had happened.

A voice yelled. "You just got to adapt to the situation." They looked at Rick who was smiling.

Zug shook his head. "Man, look at this cat. He's all cleaned up. You're standing tall man."

Rick looked like he had just stepped out of a shower. His hair was combed and he had on a new set of fatigues. "Man, you're so clean you could stand inspection. Tell us about the scene in the Major's room."

"That Major is a great guy. He's a doctor and he's headed for a hospital in Japan. That was his wife who puked on me. They treated me real good. They said when I go on R and R to look them up. It's nice to meet kind people."

Hillbilly asked. "What about all that bad talk you did?"

"Well, I told her I was sorry. She and her husband said they understood. Everything worked out okay. Man that shower sure felt good and I got a new set of clothes out of the deal."

Even though they were back in cramped quarters, it felt good to be in a warm place. Blankets stretched out on the floor and poker games were going on. Zug got his sax and was entertaining. A group of soldiers gathered around him swaying and snapping their fingers. The master sergeant came up. He pointed at Mike and Rick. "You two take that gorp bucket to the fantail and dump it. Rick made a face and started to say something but Mike grabbed his arm.

"Come on, Rick, if you give this guy any hassle he'll get us for every dirty detail he can find." They walked to the large garbage can and each grabbed a handle.

"Damn Mike, this thing is almost full. Oh man, it stinks, and it gets me sick thinking what's swirling around in there. I bet that work detail emptied all the other buckets into this one and they forgot to empty it, or they were scared to touch it."

"Quit talking about it. Let's get it over with as fast as we can." Mike opened the latch to the outside door. "Boy, it's dark out here, Rick. I can't even see you."

"I know what you mean. There's no moon or stars out. I never saw it so dark."

"They say if you close your eyes for awhile and then open them, you'll be able to see." They both did.

"Mike, that's bullshit, I can't see any better. I'll tell you one thing I'm not lugging this puke to the fantail, wherever that is. Let's sling it over right here. What's the difference? It's going in the ocean no matter where we throw it." Mike agreed and they lifted the top edge of the can onto the railing. Okay, Mike, hold the top and I'll get under it and push up."

"Be careful I don't want to get any of this crap on me."

"Don't worry, Mike, we just go slow and we won't have any problem." Rick lifted the bottom of the large can and the rancid liquid surged out. Mike looked down at the deck below and saw red glowing.

"Rick, there's guys below us smoking." Rick pushed up as hard as he could. The remaining waste in the can made a gushing sound and dropped in one big liquid mass.

Someone yelled. "Man, what is that shit."

Another guy hollered. "Hey, I'm all wet. Where did it come from? Smell that. What is it?"

"Some bastard dumped a gorp can on us. Let's find the son-of-a-bitch and kill him."

"Let's get the hell out of here Mike. Open that door and don't make any noise. We'll put the bucket back and go to the far end of the room." They hurriedly went inside and pulled the latch down. The guys on the floor playing cards didn't notice them as they walked by and quietly put the large garbage can down. "Hurry Mike, get back with the guys around Zug."

Someone on the outside was yelling and pounding on the door. No one paid any attention. Finally, one of the bystanders to the card game walked to the door and pulled up the latch. Ten wet soldiers rushed in yelling. "Where's the bastard who dumped that gorp can?"

Rick elbowed Mike. "Man, all hell is going to break out now." The swearing and yelling was so loud Zug quit playing and looked in the direction of the noise. The soiled men were now standing behind the guys sitting on the floor playing for high stakes. The card players were so caught up in their game they didn't pay any attention to the yelling. One of the men who got soaked went to the gorp bucket. "It's still wet inside. The bastard that threw that shit is still in this room."

One of the card players who was losing looked up and yelled. "Shut the fuck up and get out of here." A soldier wet with filth heard this and kicked the card player. The card player grabbed the soldier's leg and twisted till he fell in the pot. The card players grabbed the pot money. The wet ones fought the card players and the card players fought both the wet ones and other card players

120

who stole the pot. The Military Police rushed in and after a few swings of their clubs order was restored.

The fighters stood at attention. The Master Sergeant walked in front of them. He shouted to the Military Police. "Get everyone of their names. We got a lot of work details to be done before we get to Korea."

Rick looked at Mike. "This ship will be like a luxury liner now. That chicken shit Sergeant won't be bothering us. He's got a nice size work force."

Every day seemed longer and more boring as they continue to live in their confined quarters. One day they were leaning on the railing looking off in the distance. Zug broke the silence. "Hey Rick are you scared?"

"Scared, scared of what?"

"You know man, about that scene going on in Korea. A lot of guys are on a one way trip."

"Hey, Zug, you don't worry about that shit till we get there. When we get there you still don't worry about it because you adapt to the situation."

Mike heard the conversation. *How bad is combat? I know we trained hard but no one was shooting at us. I really don't care if something should happen to me, but how would Mom take it? I hope and pray for her sake nothing happens to me when I'm there.*

Everyone was quiet. Rick was mad. "Man, what the hell is the matter with you, Zug, talking that goofy shit? Hell man, this boat with these zillion guys on it got me crazy enough and now you're talking that crap. I'm getting the hell out of here." He left cussing under his breath. The three continued to lean on the railing staring at the open sea.

Rick walked into the head and threw water on his face. When he looked up he saw the master sergeant who was in charge of quarters shaving with a straight razor. He never saw anyone shave with this type of razor. He was fascinated and stood motionless staring at him. The Sergeant rinsed the razor and was bringing it back to his face when he noticed Rick watching him. "What you looking at, Shithead, you one of those queers?"

"I'm hoping this ship gets hit by a big wave and you'll slice your big ear off and it'll drop in that sink."

"No way, Shithead. It takes a man to use a straight razor. Half you punks never shaved so you don't know what you're talking about   Now shove off and get out of here, Shithead."

"Tell me Sergeant. Is it possible for you to call a man by his name? If you look, I have it written on my jacket. All you have to do is read it. Maybe you can't read. In that case, you can call me Rick."

The Master Sergeant spun around and pointed the razor at Rick. "Listen you wise, Shithead. If you don't get your ass out of here I'll cut your ears off and you can watch them drop in the sink. Now shove off, Numb Nuts."

Rick noticed the sergeant had a girly magazine rolled up in his back pocket. He stared at him then slowly walked away cussing under his breath. Mike, Hillbilly and Zug saw Rick running and cussing going for the door leading to his bunk area. Hillbilly yelled. "Come on you guys. We better find out what's going on. Sure as hell, that boy got into something." When they caught up to Rick he was standing next to his bunk. He was digging in his overnight bag and came out with a can of lighter fluid. He asked the guy in the next bunk if he had any. The guy pitched him a can. Rick took a couple of old T-shirts and some paper and rolled them up tight. He saturated it with the lighter fluid.

Mike asked. "Rick, what's the matter? What are you going to do?"

"This don't concern you guys. I'll take care of it myself."

"Listen Rick, we're your friends. Tell us, and maybe we can help. I mean it."

Rick stared at Mike. He explained what had happened and how the Master Sergeant called him names and threatened him. "So what are you going to do with those rags and papers soaked with lighter fluid?"

"You know those toilets in the head. There's about fifteen in a row sitting on top of a large flow pipe. The water comes in from the ocean and goes through that big pipe. I figure that big dumb Sergeant will be sitting on one of those toilets. If you guys are serious and want to help, I'll need a diversionary tactic."

Zug shouted "Hell man, I'll help you. I don't like that big mouth. What about you two?"

Hillbilly was reluctant, but he said all right. Mike was still thinking about his mother and felt he needed something to get her off his mind. "I'm in. What do you want us to do."

"That big stump will be sitting on the toilet. We look and see which way the water is running through the pipe. You guys go to the far end of the pipe where the water is running out and start yelling like you're going to get into a fight. Make the big dummy look at you guys so he won't see what I'm up to."

Hillbilly asked, "But how will you know he's going to get on one of those toilets?"

"He had one of those girly magazines. If he wasn't going to use the toilet, he wouldn't of brought it to the head with him. Now remember, I'll be upstream. And you guys do your thing downstream."

They entered the head and sure enough the Master Sergeant walked to one of the toilets. He pulled the magazine from his back pocket and was ready to sit down. Zug walked to one of the toilets and looked at the water flowing in the big pipe. He motioned with his finger the way the water was running. Rick secretly walked to a toilet about four stalls from the Sergeant. The other three went to where the water was going out of the pipe into the ocean. The Sergeant didn't notice Rick because he was so engrossed in his magazine.

Hillbilly grabbed Zug by the collar and raised him off the floor. "I ought to break your cotton-picking neck, you smart punk."

Mike shouted. "Hey, leave that little guy alone. Pick on somebody your own size."

Hillbilly put Zug down. "Who are you, big mouth? If you want some, I'll kick your ass. I'm not particular who I whip." All three of them were yelling, and threatening each other.

The Master Sergeant slammed his magazine to the floor. "Hey, Shitheads knock off the bullshit?" They glared at him. He lifted his arm so they could see his stripes. "Now get your asses out of here. They slowly walked to the door but didn't go out. They hid in a little cove.

Rick saw his chance. He struck a match and touched it to the lighter fluid soaked rags and paper and it burst into flames. He quickly dropped the fireball into the toilet and it landed on the moving water below. The current carried it toward the sergeant's toilet. Rick glanced at the sergeant who was en-grossed in the girly magazine and walked away from the toilets to a partition by the sinks. He watched as the flames belched out of the empty stools as the fiery bundle made its way to the sergeant's. The sergeant was so absorbed reading his magazine he didn't notice the flames shooting up from the empty stools next to him. The fire went under his toilet and the flames struck his bare buttock He sprang up and the girly magazine flew into the air. "Goddamn." He danced and slapped his crotch and butt. Another soldier sitting a few toilets away stared at him with a strange expression. The soldier saw the fire leaping out of the toilet next to him. He leaped off the toilet and pulled his pants up and all the time staring at the Sergeant jumping around rubbing his rear. The sergeant shouted at him. "It was probably one of those deck ape sailors trying to play a joke. I've got a few more days left on this ship and I'll find the bastard and break his neck."

Chapter 12
Welcome to Korea

Land was sighted and the men got their belongings together. The large ship slowed down as it made its way into the harbor. A lot of small fishing boats with Orientals aboard waved at them. The young soldiers were asking the older ones who had been in Korea all kinds of questions. The conversations were serious. It got quiet. Everyone listened to see if they could hear the sounds of war in the distance. The ship docked and the men noticed all the Army equipment from tanks to large raw wood crates with stenciled lettering on the sides of them stored on the docks.

"Well we made it this far, Rick, let's hope everything will go okay."

"Yeah, let's hope. But if I had my way I'd stay on this sorry ship and go back to the States."

A boarding platform was attached to the ship and the soldiers started filing down with their duffle bags on their shoulders. Rick pointed out beyond the dock area. "It sure looks desolate out there. I wonder how the night life is?"

Zug tapped him on the shoulder. "They say things are really popping out there."

They exited the ship and Rick looked back. "So long you sorry son-of-a-bitch. I have never spent so much time being sick and bored as I have with you."

Zug shook his head. "Yeah, man, that's straight stuff. Let them sailors ride that boat."

They were ordered to climb onto open beds trucks. When loaded, they rambled down a dusty road. Mike felt the cool air. "You know Rick it won't be long and winter will be setting in."

"I know Mike, and where we're going there won't be any warm places."

The trucks stopped in front of a giant Quonset hut. A sergeant shouted, "Men, as soon as you get off these trucks you go to that building. You will be getting your final orders before going to the front. Pay close attention because over here you don't get a second chance." Entering the building they were met by a large sign. "Welcome to Korea." The new soldiers took a chair and were very serious. In a short time a full bird Colonel walked up on the platform.

He pointed to the sign. "As the sign says, welcome to Korea, men. It isn't the greatest place on earth to be, but we got a job to do over here. Everything you learned back in the States will now be put into action. We're fighting an enemy who is very cunning and fierce. We are better than they, and you're here to prove it. Just remember what you were taught and do as you're told and in a short time you will be back in this building getting debriefed and on your way home. Your name will be called and you will be broken down into smaller groups and then sent north to join a unit. Good luck men, may the Lord be with you. Happy hunting."

Mike's name was called first and he was told to wait in a numbered section of the room. He went to this area and heard other names being called, none familiar to him. He wondered if he was going to be separated from the other three. Mike's section was almost filled with men. He was convinced his friends would be assigned to another outfit. Just then Rick, Zug, and Hillbilly's names were called. They ran to Mike and hugged each other.

Ml Rifles and ammunition were issued to each man, then they returned to the trucks. When loaded they headed north again. They traveled many miles on rough dirt roads. No one said anything. They stared wide eyed at the barren terrain. The trucks finally came to a stop and three soldiers came out of some underbrush. They carried their rifles at port arms. The Sergeant from the group yelled. "Men, get down from the trucks and follow us. Make sure your rifles are loaded. You will keep your eyes open and be extra alert. There are enemy in the area. We may engage in a fight so stay alert. Remember, you walk single file and keep six feet away from the man in front of you."

Trudging along the beaten paths Mike wondered how many soldiers had come this way before. And how many never returned. Rick asked, "Where's all the trees around here?"

Someone answered. "They were blown up. There are no trees to stop the wind. The wind is so strong those mountains over there are in different places every morning."

The procession of new soldiers made its way up a hill and a few tired looking American soldiers watched them approach. One of them shouted. "Welcome to the Frozen Chosan. You are a sight for sore eyes. You're our replacements. We're on our way to the States, thanks to you guys. Just a few

126

things to remember while you're here. You don't kill rats in the bunkers because they give off heat. Don't walk on top of any hills because some gook sniper will shoot out your lights. Don't leave anything laying around because the greatest thieves in the world are here. The other day a seventy five year old Popasan took the motor out of a jeep and carried it away with an A Frame. There are some good things here though. You got running water every time it rains. The incoming shells exploding keeps the mosquitoes away. The broads over here got hair under their arms three feet long and it lights up in the dark. If you get bored, you can throw rocks at low flying airplanes."

Rick shouted at the wise soldier. "You're about as funny as a boil on my ass."

The guy kept jabbering. The new men stopped in their tracks as loud rumbling sounded from their right. The sergeant shouted. "Don't worry about that, it's ten miles away. Somebody is getting shelled. You'll hear it every day." They continued walking a few more miles. The sergeant pointed to a hill with large holes burrowed in the side of it. "There is your home, men. It's not the best but you'll learn to love it." They went inside. Mike looked around and saw the wood beams holding up the rocky ceiling. The sergeant told them how hard they had to fight to get this place. "Winter is coming on and the gooks are out there thinking of a way to get it back. But we have no intentions of giving it up. This bunker doesn't look like much but it's a place to sleep and it keeps some of the cold off you. The gooks were pushed back to the Thirty Eighth parallel and they're up there regrouping. When they get ready they'll come back with thousands of reinforcements to join the ones here and mount another attack on us. We will be prepared when they come. We're not going to give up our hill."

Mike looked to Rick. "It doesn't sound too good does it?"

Rick shrugged his shoulders. "We just adapt to the situation."

"Yeah, you're right. That's all we can do. What do you think about it, Zug?"

"Like man, this isn't going to be good times. Did you see the size of those holes outside? Some cats were banging some big stuff."

Hillbilly pointed at some soldiers at the far end of the room. They were holding the barrels of their riffles over a flame coming from a small can. The four of them walked to the men. Rick asked, "What are you guys doing?"

They look at him puzzled. "Didn't they show you this in basic training?"

Rick shrugged his shoulders. "No they didn't teach us anything like that."

"Well you see this flame. It gives off soot. Anything that shines we coat with soot. The gooks shoot at anything that moves or shines. This soot will stop shiny things from reflecting. The four young soldiers quickly looked at their uniforms for any metal that might shine. The soldiers sitting laughed.

The four asked all kinds of questions. Hillbilly tapped one of the older soldiers on his shoulder. "When was the last time you were fired on?"

He didn't look up. He casually said. "This morning."

"You all mean just this morning you battled with them. Right outside that door?"

"Yeah, it wasn't a big deal. They dropped a few mortars on us and we fired back our 75's and 105's at them. Wait till the waves come, that's when it gets hairy."

"Waves, what do you mean by waves?"

"Well, right now thousands of North Koreans and Chinese are getting together to come back down here and try to overrun us. They will come at us with so many men it looks like waves. They run directly up this hill firing their guns. They don't take cover. There are so many of them they try to overwhelm us with their bodies."

"How do we stop them?"

"We use everything we got. Our heavy machine guns, mortars, 105's, 75's and if we get lucky, air support"

Mike asked what it felt like the first time they saw a wave come at them.

Someone looked up. It's hard to explain but I'll tell you one thing, the only thing that moved on me for a couple minutes was my bowels." Everyone laughed.

The older soldiers got up from the floor and extended their hands and introduced themselves to Mike, Zug, Rick and Hillbilly. They said they were glad for them to be in their company. One named Bob Marr said, "It's not all bad. In six months you get to go on R and R. Some guys call it rest and recuperation but others call it I and I."

Rick asked, "I and I, what does that mean?"

The older soldiers laughed. "Intoxication and Intercourse."

Rick nodded. "Now that's not bad either."

Someone shouted, "Attention." Everyone in the room stood rigid. A captain walked to the center of the room.

"Men, I'm Captain Marko, and I'm your company commander. I wish I had better quarters to offer you but this is the best I can do. I know it's not a lot but we have to protect it with every muscle we have. The enemy we're fighting is cunning and they don't care if they die which you will see when we engage them. We have to be strong, and we're only as strong as our weakest man. Don't be the weakest man. Another important thing I want to impress on you. Never salute an officer when we're in a combat zone. As of right now there will be no more saluting. The enemy has snipers who concentrate on watching soldiers saluting officers. Have I made myself clear."

"Yes sir."

Rick whispered to Mike. "Wouldn't it be nice if Captain Thimp was here. I would salute the bastard every time I saw him."

Captain Marko asked. "Are there any questions? Feel free to ask."

Rick raised his hand, Mike's eyes widened. Hillbilly elbowed him. "Mike, get ready for some off-the-wall-talk."

The Captain nodded at Rick. "Yes, Soldier, what is it?"

"Sir, can I go on R and R tomorrow?"

Captain Marko, laughed. "Only if you can get me a ticket on the same plane." There were no more questions. "Men, I'm glad you're with us. We'll protect one another and come out of here alive. I wish you good luck. Sergeant Mitchell here, will be your squad leader. He's a good man and he'll fill you in on whatever you want to know."

Sergeant Mitchell shouted. "Attention." The men came to order and Captain Marko left the room.

Sergeant Mitchell was all of six three and weighed about two hundred and fifty pounds. He looked in top shape. "Men, I'm not much for lectures. I will make it short. When we leave this bunker, we'll go to the top of the hill. Keep your body down so you don't give a sniper a target. I will assign you a position that will be on the down side of this hill, on the other side, there is a heavy machine gun in every position. There also are grenades and plenty of ammunition. These positions are manned twenty-four hours a day. Now remember those snipers out there are deadly. Don't expose your body and you won't get shot. It's that simple."

The new soldiers nodded.

"All right, I want to welcome you men to my squad. I will help you anyway I can, but first you have to help yourself. After mess tonight we will meet outside this bunker and you'll take your turn in the positions. Are there any questions?"

The room stayed silent. "Very well, I'll see you after mess."

Mike grabbed his Ml and went to the carbide lamp, lit the wick and started sooting his rifle. In no time Rick, Zug and Hillbilly were doing the same.

After supper the sun slowly dropped behind the high hills and darkness crawled into the valleys. Sergeant Mitchell stood in front of the bunker and the young soldiers started milling around him asking questions. "Okay men, gather up.

Again, I want to warn you to stay low. Don't give that sniper a target. Now follow me. He made his way up a worn path and when he got almost to the top he dropped to his knees and laid on his stomach. He motioned the men behind to do the same. He put his field glasses to his eyes and scanned the hills in front of him. "Okay men, I'll point to a position and two of you will hunch over and rush to it. The people there will leave the position and it will be your responsibility for the rest of the night. I'll check with you throughout the night." Mike and Rick were called and Sergeant Mitchell pointed to a Foxhole about twenty-five yards down the hill. "Okay you two make it." Mike held his breath. He imagined the enemy looking through a scope on the far hill, waiting for him to run to the position. His heart pumped pure adrenalin. He bent over and dashed down the hill past the sandbags that shielded him from the hills. When he got about ten yards from the foxhole he dove and slid in on his belly.

The two soldiers waiting in the position laughed. One of them looked down at Mike. "This your first time here?"

"How did you guess?"

Rick came in the same way. The two soldiers shook their heads, then explained where everything was. They warned them not to fall asleep because if they did, they wouldn't be waking up in the morning. They left and Mike and Rick explored the position. Rick sat behind the machine gun and swung it back and forth. He checked to see if it was loaded. Mike examined the ammunition and the grenades. "We got a lot of ammo and grenades, Rick. I'm going to put more of it up front in case we need it in a hurry."

After they familiarized themselves with the weapons they leaned on the sandbags and stared at the hills in front of them.

Hillbilly and Zug were in another foxhole about fifteen yards away and they waved. Mike scowled. "Rick, how do you feel about killing someone?"

Rick didn't say anything for awhile. "Well, I don't know those guys out there, but I do know they and us are in a situation. They're here to kill us. And we're here to kill them. I don't care to die at this time, so I guess I'll have to adapt to the situation. In other words I don't have a choice if I want to stay on this earth a little longer. I'll shoot their asses off, because if I don't they'll shoot mine off."

Mike smiled. "I knew you were going to say adapt to the situation. I guess you're right."

Darkness engulfed them and their voices got lower. They strained their eyes on the valley below and the adjoining hills for any movement. Sergeant Mitchell startled them when he crawled in. "Just hang loose you two, it's only me. I'm glad you're alert, it's a good sign. Keep it up. How's it going men?"

They both respond. "Okay, Sergeant."

"Good, stay awake and be quiet. If you hear or see anything out there it's the enemy. Do you understand?" He slid out and disappeared in the darkness.

It was extremely quiet. There were no stars or moon. It was pitch black. The tension was unbelievable. Mike kept asking Rick if he saw anything? Rick would reply, "No." In a short time Rick asked Mike the same question.

The hours passed. Mike nudged Rick and whispered. "Down there, right below us I saw a flash."

"What was it Mike?"

"It looked like someone struck a match. Hey, there it is again,"

"Yeah, I see it. Can you make out what it is? Hey, it's a fire burning down there." Rick immediately swung the machine gun and aimed it down at the fire.

"Rick I can see silhouettes of men standing around that fire." Rick started to squeeze the trigger of the machine gun.

Sergeant Mitchell yelled. "Hold your fire. Hold your fire. Those men down there are Turks and they're on our side." Rick slowly took his finger off the trigger. Sergeant Mitchell crawled from one position to another explaining what was happening. The flames from the fire leaped higher and the yellowish, red glowing light flickered on the hill sides. Music played and it sounded like some sort of whiney string instruments. More fuel was thrown on the fire and the flames were crackling and sending embers high into the air. Laughter could be heard coming from the men around the fire. Bottles were being passed around. "Man, Mike that is some strange racket. I never heard music like that. Those guys must be crazy, drinking, and raising hell around that fire. It's a wonder the gooks don't shoot at them." They kept watching and couldn't believe their eyes. The Turks formed a circle and locked arms. They danced around the fire going to the right, then to the left. "Ain't this a bitch. They told us to crawl and be quiet and them crazy fools light a big fire, drink, dance and sing."

The familiar voice of Sergeant Mitchell. "Those men are far from crazy. They're some of the fiercest fighters in the world. I'm always glad to have the Turks at our base. The gooks try to steer clear of them especially at night. You can be sitting in a foxhole and be perfectly quiet and it will be dark like it is tonight, and all at once you'll feel a hand reach into your shirt, grab your dog tags, then pat you on the helmet and disappear without making a sound."

Rick asked. "What happens if you don't have your dog tags on?"

"You'll probably have another mouth put on your throat. Those boys would rather slice you with their knives than shoot you. They're so quiet they can crawl up on an enemy position and slice one man's throat and leave without a sound. The other guys in the position wake up, see their partner dead and can't understand what happened. It sure as hell has a demoralizing effect on the ones he let live. They don't sleep for a long time."

Sergeant Mitchell, Rick and Mike leaned on the sand bags and stared down at the Turks in disbelief. The fire and music relaxed them and they talked in a casual manner and were enjoying this unexpected incident. The relaxed atmosphere was short-lived. Two bright flashes, and loud explosions near the fire shook the ground and lit up the area. Mike and Rick jumped.

"Man what the hell was that?" Four more explosions hit the same area. The music stopped and the fire was doused. Everything went quiet.

Sergeant Mitchell laughed. "Those gooks are going to catch hell now. They thought they'd be cute and lob some mortars in on the Turks. The Turks' dander is up now and the gooks are going to pay." Rick and Mike got next to the machine gun. Sergeant Mitchell left and yelled. "Remember! Be alert!" Mike and Rick could hear him talking to other soldiers in other positions.

The night went back to normal, dark and silent. Rick leaned over the machine gun with his finger on the trigger. "You know Mike, when those mortars hit, it shook the hell out of me. What about you?"

"Yeah, they sure were loud. If those were mortars the guys who fired them aren't far away, because mortars don't travel a long distance. Those North Koreans are at the most a mile away."

No more was said. Both of them stared into the darkness waiting for something to happen. "You know Rick it's quieter now than it was before the Turks started that fire."

"I was thinking the same thing. It sure is eerie."

"Did you hear that Rick?"

"Yeah, it sounded like someone screamed. Hey there it goes again." They squinted into the darkness straining their eyes and ears hoping to figure out what it was.

The rest of the night was quiet except for a scream out in the darkness every once in awhile. Dawn broke and the sky turned a slate gray. The sun came up and the tips of the hills turned a misty yellow. In a short time the light rolled down into the valleys. Mike pushed his helmet back and looked at Rick. "Well we made it through our first night in the combat zone.

Rick rubbed his eyes. "You're right I just hope the rest of them are as easy."

Sergeant Mitchell was bent over at the top of the hill. His hands were cupped to his mouth. "You men down there. Your relief is on the way. The mess truck is at the bottom of the hill. Get something to eat and hit the sack. You did very well last night, keep up the good work. Remember keep down when you leave your positions. Some gook is scanning our hill with his scope waiting to kill you." Mike and Rick crawled out and kept themselves concealed by the sand bags. They made it to the top of the hill where Sergeant Mitchell waited. He tapped every man on his helmet. "Nice going gang, get down there and get some chow."

Mike and Rick got their mess kits and were eating hot food next to a large rock. Zug and Hillbilly joined them. Hillbilly tapped Rick on the shoulder. "How did it go last night?"

Mike answered. "All right till they dropped those mortars on the Turks."

"Yeah, I know what you mean. Old Zug went up like a Jack-in-the-box when they went off."

Rick laughed. "Is that right Zug?"

"Yeah man. Those cats were getting down with their sounds. I was really getting with those tunes till them boys up north started carrying on. Man, that booming shit ain't my key." They started eating again. Mike stopped, he noticed a group of men in foreign uniforms. They were talking in a different language and standing around a man sitting on the ground.

He pointed at them. "I bet they're the Turks who got fired on last night." He put his mess kit down and walked to them. Zug, Rick, and Hillbilly followed. The foreign soldiers were pitching something to the man sitting on the ground. Mike took a close look to see what they were throwing. He quickly turned his head and walked away. Rick took Mike's place.

"Shit, man, those are ears." The foreign soldiers were throwing ears to the man sitting on ground. The guy on the ground studied them and handed money to the man who threw them. Rick walked to where Mike was. Hillbilly and Zug did the same thing. Mike went to the garbage can and emptied his mess kit. No one ate except Zug.

Rick watched him eat. "Hey Zug, how in the hell can you eat after what you saw?"

"No problem man. Those weren't my ears and I'm hungry."

Rick sat next to him. He pointed to the small pieces of meat in Zug's mess kit. "You see those pieces of meat in there?" "Yeah man, I see them."

"Well the rumor is, they have a hard time getting meat over here. And you know where that meat your eating came from?"

Zug continued to eat only slower. Rick kept it up. Zug jumped up and ran to the garbage can and slammed his mess kit inside. "You're a sick son-of-a-bitch Rick, I'll never sit next to you again."

Chapter 13
The first wave

A week passed and there wasn't much action, except a few mortars and some sniper fire from both sides just to show they're still around. The younger men continued to question the older soldiers about what to expect. Everyone was concerned about the regrouping of the North Koreans up at the Thirty-Eighth Parallel.

Next night in the position Rick noticed Mike hadn't said a word. "Mike what's bothering you?"

I don't know but something is different. It seems extra quiet. I got butterflies just like I used to get when I ran into a stadium before a game. Something is going to happen tonight, I can feel it."

Sergeant Mitchell was making his nightly rounds and he overheard the conversation. "I know what you mean, Mike. I got the same feeling. If they come, we're ready. Be alert, and if you see or hear anything yell out."

"Okay, Sergeant."

Two hours passed and Mike kept looking into the darkness not saying a word. "Hey, Mike, take it easy. You're spooking yourself. It's just another night. If something happens we'll adapt to the situation."

Mike was ready to answer when a tinny bugle sounded. Tada, tada tada in the darkness in front of them. Another bugle to the right of them. Now more bugles were blowing. An American soldier from the position shouted. "What the hell is that?"

Rick yelled. "Hey Zug, go capture those horn blowers and you'll have a brass band."

The horns stopped, voices in broken English shouted from the adjacent hills and valley. "Tonight we come Joe. You die tonight, Joe." The bugles started up again.

Rick yelled. "Hey Zug, now that's real music. Don't you wish you could play like that?"

"Shit, man, that ain't music, that's racket. Those boys sound like a broken record."

"Zug, get your horn and show them some class."

Hillbilly's voice. "Sure enough, Zug. Go get your sax and I'll hold the fort."

The bugles continued their repetitious shrill blaring. Sergeant Mitchell was crawling from one position to another calming the men. "Keep your composure, they're trying to psyche you. Just stay calm. If they decide to come we'll knock them back." Mike could tell the different tone in the Sergeant's voice. He sounded concerned.

Sergeant Mitchell crawled in with Mike and Rick. "You were right, Mike. I hate the sounds of those horns. Just once I would like to get my hands on one of those Gook horn blowers. I'd shove that horn so far down his throat music would come out his ass".

Rick asked, "What does that horn blowing mean, Sergeant?"

"It means they'll probably come tonight. But sometimes they blow them to fake an attack. Don't take any chances. Always assume they're going to come." Sergeant Mitchell went silent and leaned on the sandbags squinting into the darkness. A horn blared behind him. He quickly turned and pulled his forty five from the holster. The horn wasn't playing monotonous screechy sounds but an American song. He pointed his automatic in the direction of the music.

Rick screamed, "Hold it, Sergeant. It's Zug, one of our soldiers."

He turned to Rick. "I almost fired, I thought one of those bastards got behind us."

"Nah, it's only Zug. He takes his sax wherever he goes."

Zug continued to blow the horn and the echo bounced off the hills into the dark stillness. When he finished his first song, he paused. The Americans in their positions were clapping and cheering. The enemy bugles and yelling were silent. Mike yelled, "He's got them baffled. They can't figure out what's going on."

Soldiers in the positions were yelling for Zug to keep going. Rick yelled. "Zug, play *Far Away in Africa.*"

"Man, Rick, don't you ever learn. The name of the song is *Skokiaan.*"

"Who cares, you know what I mean. Play it."

After he got done playing *Skokiaan,* a soldier shouted, "Hey, play the *Notre Dame Fight Song.*"

"Notre Dame Fight Song? - Man, I'm into jazz."

Another soldier shouted. "Go ahead and play it." Zug hesitated then blared out the fight song. When he got done the whole hillside cheered.

The soldier who requested the song shouted, "Thanks, that never sounded better."

Sergeant Mitchell said. "I suppose, I should of stopped him but it was great for moral and the gooks don't know what to make of it."

Rick yelled, "Now that's class, give'em hell, Zug."

Zug put the sax back to his lips. He stomped his foot and the rhythm built up. He played pure jazz. The men in the positions heard the wailing of the horn. They clapped and shouted, "Go man, go."

Mike yelled, "I can hear guys cheering him a mile away."

Some American soldiers shouted to the enemy, "Hey, Dip Shits, put your horns up your asses. You've been put down. Maybe if you give up we'll teach you how to play a tune on your silly horns."

The night became silent. The soldiers were on edge. They knew a lot of the enemy were massed in the hills and wondered when they'd attack. Mike could feel the tension in the air. He paced back and forth in the position. Rick tried to settle him down. "Take it easy. We'll handle them when they come."

Mike didn't say anything. He squinted down into the valley where the bugles sounded. A loud popping sound and a small flickering projectile shot straight up from the valley floor. Someone from a position shouted. *"Trip flare in the valley"* The flickering projectile went high above the positions. It exploded and a bright white flame dangled from a small parachute. It slowly rocked back an forth as it descended to the valley floor. More flares exploded and were floating down under small parachutes The hills and valley were lit up like day exposing thousands of enemy soldiers in drab colored quilted jackets and hats, hunched over with rifles and fixed bayonets. They yelled and charged the American positions.

"Someone screamed, "Here they come."

Captain Marko shouted. "Fire. Fire at will. Fire." A deafening noise vibrated the air and ground as hundreds of weapons opened fire into the mass of humanity running through the valley charging the positions. Screams of pain as the bullets found their mark. More parachutes with burning phosphorus illuminated the battle. Rick saw a mass of enemy troops coming straight for his position. He squeezed the trigger and slowly swept the barrel back and forth directly into them. Fire spit out of the barrel of the machine gun. The bullets slammed into the charging enemy, it looked like someone with a giant sickle cut them down like clumps of grass.

Rick screamed. "Hurry Mike, another can of ammo." Mike fed a new belt of bullets into the machine gun, then tapped Rick on the helmet letting him know the gun was ready to fire again. Mike peeked over the sand bags and saw thousands of men rushing toward him. Flashes from their weapons told him they were firing at him. He quickly ducked down. In coming mortar shells were exploding all over the hill. One hit about ten feet from Mike and Rick and sprayed them with dirt. Rick kept firing the machine gun. He shouted, "I never saw so many sons-of-bitches in all my life."

The positions were firing full go. Tracers from machine guns drew straight white lines into the night telling the gunners where they were striking. Bullets hit the sandbags above Rick's head. Sand streamed down on him. "Keep your head down, Rick. Those bullets are coming close."

"I know what you mean. I can hear them zinging by."

The air was full of smoke and the stench of burnt gun powder gagged the men. Mike turned and reached for another can of bullets. Rick yelled. "Watch out, Mike, one of them is crawling in."

Mike grabbed his M1 rifle and spun around with his finger on the trigger. A North Korean was rushing straight at him with a bayonet on the end of his rifle. Mike squeezed the trigger and fire shot out of the rifle. The enemy soldier was struck flush in the face causing his head to explode. Rick's face was splattered with blood and pieces of the man's head and brains. He slapped and rubbed his face trying to get it off. "God damn, throw that son-of-a-bitch out of here." Mike lifted the limp body and pushed it over the top of the sand bags and it rolled down the hill.

Sergeant Mitchell ran and dove into the positions shouting. "They're at the base of the hill directly below us. Lob your grenades, we can't get good shots at them with our machine guns." Mike pulled the cover off the large raw wood box. They grabbed grenades, pulled the pins and reached over the sand bags and rolled them down the hill to meet the enemy who was crawling up. Loud concussions shook the hill when the grenades exploded. Piercing screams of pain followed the blasts.

"Mike, there must be a shit house full of them down there. Did you hear all that screaming?"

"Yeah, I heard it. Keep throwing those grenades or we'll be screaming."

They emptied one box and quickly slid another one forward and continued activating the grenades and rolling them down on the enemy. Sergeant Mitchell shouted. "Keep throwing those grenades, or we'll be overrun"

The grenades killed and wounded many of the enemy. Slowly, they retreated. They withdrew about a hundred yards and their mortar men went to work. The high arching trajectory of the shells enabled them to drop straight down into the positions. The whole hill seemed like it was on fire. Round after round rained in and exploded. Mike and Rick crouched close to the sand bags in the front of their position their arms crossed over the back of their necks. Wounded American soldiers screamed for the Medics.

"Rick, we got to get back to the gun." They managed to crawl to the machine gun. The men firing flares finally got them back in the air. The brightness showed some of the enemy sitting on the ground with the small mortar tubes between their legs launching shells at the positions. Rick squinted and took aim at one and squeezed the trigger and held it till the man was slammed on his back. He continued to send round after round into him making sure he didn't get that mortar working again.

Mike shouted, "That's enough, Rick. Get the one at nine o'clock." Rick quickly swung the gun to the left. He didn't wait to aim but fired as it zeroed in on the man. The guy spun around by the impact of the projectiles and lay motionless.

"Quit firing at him. The rounds hitting him are making him look alive. Get that bunch coming over the hill to the left of us." Rick kept firing as he swung the gun to the left. The bullets were hitting below the charging enemy. Rick adjusted and the dirt erupting from bullets crawled up the hill and right into them. They rolled down the hill screaming in pain. Another wave of enemy came over the hill with no guns. They picked up the weapons of their dead and wounded comrades and rushed the positions.

Sergeant Mitchell ordered, "All positions fire at the group who are picking up weapons." In unison all machine guns fired at the last wave who were grabbing up the weapons. They dropped like a giant fly swatter slammed down on them and laid in big heaps not moving.

The battle continued for two more hours. Sergeant Mitchell yelled. "Don't let up. The worst is yet to come. They're regrouped behind those hills and are gonna come back full go. We're going to get some help from artillery. Keep your heads down because it's going to be coming in low."

The bugles blew again and a loud roar from men screaming behind the hill in front of the positions. Sergeant Mitchell screamed. "Here they come. Be ready to fire when they get in range." Flares again were bursting open high above, lighting the valley. Loud shrill, whistling sounds came from the rear and overhead as artillery shells made their way to explode into the charging mass of enemy. The men in the positions slid their hands under their metal helmets and pushed their fingers into their ears. Mike squinted and shook his head as he saw the enormous white flashes and the deafening sounds of the exploding shells. Bodies and body parts flew in all directions. The barrage continued, Mike tried to talk to Rick but it was useless. The noise was deafening. The enemy stopped firing on the positions. The forward observer must have told the artillery unit to stop shelling. An eerie silence came over the positions.

Men tried to talk to one another but their ears were still echoing the battle. They looked at one another and saw lips moving but their ears couldn't hear.

Two hours passed and the sun started to rise. Mike and Rick stared at one another. Finally Rick said. "Did last night really happen?"

"Yeah, it happened." Mike went to the front of the position and leaned on the sandbags which were riddled with holes. Rick came next to him and they both peered down at all the enemy bodies laying motionless. "You know, Rick, I didn't know one of them."

In a low voice Rick said, "You were introduced to them last night."

"Is this a conflict?" Mike wondered.

"Look it up in the dictionary. I did. This is WAR." Rick came back.

Sergeant Mitchell's voice pierced the silence. "Just because it's daylight doesn't mean a thing. They're still out there and as soon as you relax, they'll come again." Rick, and Mike, tired and wary, went back to the machine gun.

"Rick, they're probably behind that big hill to the right. That's where most of them came from last night."

"Yeah, I was thinking the same thing. They're probably regrouping and thinking how they can overrun us. Those bastards don't give up easy."

The Americans continued to wait. Mike looked at Rick's hand that was on the grip of the machine gun. He squeezed it so hard his knuckles turned white. No one was talking. They just stared.

The silence was shattered as loud roaring noises erupted above them that shook the ground. Everyone looked up. One jet plane after another with white stars on their wings skimmed the positions. An older soldier by the name of Meyers shouted.

"Ain't they beautiful. You guys watch now. We've got the greatest pilots in the world."

Rick's eyes were wide open. "Man they scared hell out of me. Those planes are so low I saw a pilot smiling. I never saw a plane fly so low." The planes flew over the large hill in front of the positions, banked to the left and gained altitude.

The older soldier shouted, "They wanted a look- see. Watch what happens when they come back."

Mike tapped Rick on the shoulder and pointed to tiny specks in the sky high to their left. Rick, looked up to where Mike was pointing. The tiny specks were now planes diving in single file. The first one came in low with guns strafing behind the large hill. The planes following released napalm bombs. When the bombs struck the ground, they exploded into large waves of fire burning everything in their path. Screams of men burning to death could be heard. The soldiers in the positions stared at the inferno, the bright flames reflected in their eyes.

Sergeant Mitchell yelled. "The fly boys are putting the finishing touch on them. It's like putting the frosting on the cake."

The planes made another pass behind the hills strafing and bombing. They gained altitude turned and dove straight at the American positions. One at a time they came over the positions, dipping their wings to the soldiers below. The soldiers in the positions waved and shouted to their brothers in the sky. Rick looked at Mike and smiled. "Don't say it, Rick, I know what you're going to say." "What?"

"You know. We adapted to the situation." Rick smiled and nodded.

Two hours passed and all was quiet. Dark black smoke still billowed from behind the hill. Sergeant Mitchell came into the positions and said. "I'm proud of the way you men fought." He pointed at Rick. "I watched you Miller. Where in the hell did you learn how to shoot like that? I've seen some good gunners but I never saw one as good as you. You and Mike are a hell of a team. Those Gooks got their fill of you two. Nice work, men. I'm glad you're on my team." Mike thanked him.

Rick's eyes watered and he turned away. "Okay, men, get down the hill and get something to eat. You deserve it."

Rick and Mike crawled out of the position and as soon as they got on the other side they stood up and stretched, then started down the hill. About half way they stopped and stared at the ground below. Wounded soldiers were on stretchers. Some had white bandages wrapped around their heads. Others had chests wounds with bandages stained red. Medics stood over others with plasma bottles, trying to drip life into them. Farther away, stretchers with blankets covered the dead.

Mike shook his head. "We took some losses too. I wonder how many guys we took basic training with got it." No more was said. They got their food and sat next to a group of men. Mike watched them eat. *They don't have any trouble eating after last night. I guess we're getting hard to it, seeing all that killing.*

Sergeant Mitchell came up. "You guys did a great job. I'd like to tell you to get some sleep but you know how serious this is. Go back to your positions. One of you stay awake and the other one catch a few winks. If the gooks attack, wake the man sleeping. We can't take any chances." No one said anything, not even Rick.

Back in the position Mike pointed to all the holes the exploding shells put in the side of the hill. "Rick, we were lucky. A couple of those mortars came close to dropping right in on us."

Rick stared at the deep craters. "Man, this place took a hell of a pounding. You're right. We're lucky to be alive. If you're praying, remember my name when you talk to the Lord."

Meyers, the older soldier in the next position, commented, "You guys notice how fast those gooks fired those mortars? They just sat down and started dropping those shells down the tube. They don't have any instruments on their mortars like ours. If a mortar shell drops in front of you, and then one drops behind you, you'd better get your ass out of there because the next one will land in your back pocket. I saw you guys last night firing that machine gun. You kept them off balance and they couldn't find the range. It's a pleasure fighting next to you." He crawled half way out of his position and extended his hand. Mike and Rick shook the older soldier's hand.

They both told him the feeling was mutual. They thanked him for his advice. Rick smiled. "We'll buy you a beer when we get on R and R."

142

"I'll take you up on that."

Rick had his hand on the handle of the machine gun casually swinging it back and forth. "Man, I don't know how in the hell anyone could survive in those hills after all that bullshit last night."

Myers spoke up, "Don't worry about those bastards over there. There's a lot still alive. We pounded a hill once for three days and thought no one could live through that barrage. We walked up on that hill and the damn thing came alive with gooks just like a disturbed ant hill. Those sons-of-bitches can dig in. They're over there right now looking, and thinking of a way to overrun us."

Captain Marko shouted through a bullhorn. "You men in the positions, don't waste time talking. Alternate getting sleep. Remember one of you stay awake. Don't both of you fall asleep at the same time. Be alert, if you get tired wake your partner."

"Rick, you go first. I'll wake you in a couple of hours."

"Okay Mike." Rick grabbed a heavy sand bag and dragged it to the front of the position to use as a pillow. They took turns getting sleep throughout the day. It was dusk now. Mike stared into the valley and the surrounding hills. His eyes were playing tricks on him. It was hard to see through the haze.

The older soldier saw Mike squinting. "Be ready, Mike. They like to attack at dusk or dawn when things are hard to see. If anything moves out there shoot it." Mike assured him he would.

The hours passed and still no activity from the hills. The silence was nerve wracking. There were a few stars out and it's wasn't as dark as it was last night. Suddenly a voice out in the darkness pierced the silence. In broken English it traveled through the valley and echoed off the walls of the hills. "Tonight you die, Americans."

Immediately an answer from the positions. "You come up this hill sucker, your mammy's going to cry tomorrow."

"You know who that was, don't you Mike?"

"Yeah, that's Leroy Johnson."

"Remember back at Captain Carson when he used to make fun of Captain Thimp on that bitch box? He had that man crazy."

"Yeah, he was almost as good as you were mocking that Captain."

"Naw, he was better than me. He knew how to talk that mother-talk. Rick cupped his hands around his mouth and shouted. "Hey Leroy, was that you talking shit to that gook?"

"Sure was. Is that you, crazy Miller?"

Rick was ready to yell back when the bugles started blowing that repetitious noise. Leroy yelled. "Hey Miller, tell Zug to get his horn going. Man, those Jive-Asses out there ain't hitting on shit. They need some good sounds."

Zug must have had his horn to his lips. The music started to flow immediately. Leroy clapped and shouted. "Go Zug, go. Work it baby. You're blowing those slope heads' cool. The bugles stopped and Zug was playing solo. Rick and Leroy encouraged him to keep playing.

Rick kept yelling. "Zug, play *Far Away In Africa.*"

Zug pulled the horn from his mouth. "Damn, Rick, I told you twenty times the name of that song is *Skokiaan.*"

"What the hell is the difference. *Far Away In Africa,* or whatever you want to call it. You know what I mean. Come on now, play it, will you? Tell him Hillbilly."

"Sure enough, Zug. I like that song too. Go ahead and play it."

"Listen to that Mike." That's the prettiest song I ever heard. Man I love that song."

Zug got done playing *Skokiaan* and Rick shouted. "Play it again Zug."

"Man, kiss my ass. That's enough *Skokiaan* for awhile." He played a few more songs before tiring. The valley was quiet except for some faint shouting in Korean from a distance.

Sergeant Mitchell came to each position and ordered. "I want you men to be as quiet as you can tonight. We got a surprise for the gooks. I don't want any of them deep in their holes."

Rick asked. "What's the surprise, Sergeant?

"The Battle Ship Missouri is sitting off the coast. She is going to fire her Sixteen inchers into those hills in front of us. Remember we want them out of their holes so hold your fire."

Incoming mortars started hitting the positions. Mike and Rick dove to the front of their position, huddled over and snuggled the sandbags. Incoming artillery shells were clobbering the positions. White flashes and loud explosions erupted all over. The ground trembled, some of the men yelled, "Let us fire back."

Sergeant Mitchell and Captain Marko kept shouting. "Don't fire men. We know they're out of their holes now, because they're firing their artillery. It won't be long now."

Rick looked at Mike with a serious expression. "Those gooks are firing their heavy stuff to weaken us up. If we don't fire back, sure as hell they're going to charge and overrun us." He crawled behind the machine gun.

"Stay down Rick, have faith. The captain, and the sergeant know what they're doing. Don't do anything that might screw up their plan."

Rick sat behind the gun with his finger on the trigger aiming the gun into the valley. A tremendous roar erupted above. All the men jumped and their heads whipped back and their eyes searched the sky. A mammoth explosion on the hill in front of them. "Mike, did that scare you?" I almost jumped out of my skin. I never heard anything so loud. That must of been from that battleship."

"That shook me too. It had to be from the battleship. Can you imagine how far away it is?"

"Mike, I don't care how far away it is. I just hope those sailors know how to aim that gun."

There was another roar over head and a gigantic explosion on the side of the hill in front of them. All heads in the positions were aimed at the large fire on the hill that was hit.

"Rick, did you see the hole that shell made? Man that was powerful."

"Like I said before, I hope those sailors know what they're doing when they fire that big gun. I don't want one of those shells exploding around me. The gooks sure don't like it. I haven't heard a shot coming from their hills."

Sergeant Mitchell shouted, "She was just firing for effect. Wait till she really opens up." Another round screamed overhead and struck a hill, taking the whole top off. Sergeant Mitchell yelled again, "She's found her range, now watch." It was quiet, everyone was straining their ears anticipating the barrage. The roaring noise again, only it was magnified ten times. Mike and Rick's heads went forward and they forced their fingers into their ears. Gigantic explosions were vibrating the ground. They both looked up. Enormous explosions were tearing the guts out of the hills. It looked like massive volcanoes erupting every time a shell hit. The bombardment continued and the men in the positions couldn't believe what was happening. The explosions were deafening.

The shelling finally stopped and not one soldier said anything. They just continued to stare at the pulverized hills.

Rick tried to talk to Mike but he didn't answer. The thunderous noise had momentarily deafened him. Rick saw Mike's lips move and he realized he couldn't hear either. Slowly their hearing returned. "Mike I can't believe what I saw. I never thought anything could be so loud and powerful. Man, I'm glad I wasn't on that hill when them shells went off. My ears are going to ring for a week."

"I know what you mean. It feels like the ground is still rumbling."

The sun had a strange color as it fought to pierce the dust and smoke. Heads were sticking up from the positions looking at the hills. A slight breeze moved the cloud of gray smoke like a stage curtain. Someone yelled, "Which hill were the gooks on?"

Another guy answered. "The one that ain't no more. The Missouri erased the damn thing."

"Rick, that whole hill is gone. It looks like someone stuck it in a grinder and ground it. The whole hill is pulverized.

There's no way anyone could live through that pounding."

The older soldier shook his head. "You wouldn't want to put some money on that would you?"

"Mike, I wonder what's going on here. We knocked wave after wave of them off. The air support came in and shot hell out of them. The big ship blasted them. Why are there so many of them in this area? It's just hills. What the hell is so important about this place, that they have all these men here?"

"I was thinking the same thing. Maybe they got so many men they want to get rid of some of them. I don't understand how they charge right into our guns. Some don't even have weapons."

Three days passed and no sign of the enemy. It felt good to sleep in the large bunker and not shake from the explosions. Sergeant Mitchell stuck his head in the tunnel leading to the bunker and yelled. "The following men report outside. Miller, Ryan, Johnson, and Keith.

Rick started cussing. "Son-of-a-bitch you finally get a chance to get a little rest and some fool wants a work detail. I didn't do a damn thing wrong." The men slowly came out of the bunker and Sergeant Mitchell met them. He pointed to a patch of grass. They walked to it.

"You've been picked to go on a reconnaissance patrol. We'll assemble here at 1800 hours. I want everyone to have his Ml. I'm hoping we won't have to use them. You will listen closely, because this is not going to be an easy assignment. We're going to find out where, and what the enemy is up to. For some of you this will be your first patrol. It is extremely important you pay attention. We're going behind enemy lines. We do not want to engage them in a fight. Our primary mission is to gain information and get back to our positions as soon as possible. Now remember we meet here at 1800 hrs. Are there any questions?" Everyone remained silent.

"Okay, we need a password. Anyone have a suggestion?"

The men looked at one another and no one said anything. Finally Rick yelled out. "Your mammy."

Everyone laughed and looked at Leroy Johnson. Leroy reached over and hit Rick on the back. "Man, don't you ever quit that bullshit?"

Sergeant Mitchell laughed. "That's a good one. We won't have a problem remembering it." He got serious again. "Don't say anything about this patrol to anyone. If there are questions, we'll discuss them when we meet later. Am I clear?"

The group replied they understood. Sergeant Mitchell walked away and the men stood, trying to figure out what was in store for them. Rick was the first to say something. "Shit, this isn't right. I haven't done a damn thing wrong since I've been here and he picked me for a suicide mission. I don't understand this crap."

Meyers, the older soldier, heard him. "Hey Miller, you weren't picked because you're a goof off and he wanted to punish you." Rick looked at him. "That sergeant picked you because he thinks you're a good soldier and he can depend on you."

Rick was confused. "You mean to say that Sergeant Mitchell thinks I'm a good soldier?"

"Yeah, that's just what I mean. He told you before. Think about it. Sergeant Mitchell is going on that patrol, too. Do you think he would take goof offs? His life depends on the men he picks."

Rick thought about it. "You're right, Meyers. If I was going behind that gook hill I'd want the best men I could find to go with me. It stands to reason." He looked at Mike. "Can you imagine that? Sergeant Mitchell thinks I'm a good soldier." Mike thought Rick was making fun of the conversation but Rick kept bragging he was told he was a good soldier. It seemed like no one had ever given him a compliment. Whenever he got recognition he was overwhelmed.

147

Mike realized what was happening to Rick "Sergeant Mitchell was right Rick. You are a good soldier. He watched you when we were attacked, and he knows you can handle yourself."

Rick nodded. "He thinks I'm a good soldier. And you, Meyers, think I'm good. I can't believe it. You know Mike I didn't cherish going behind those hills with those gooks. But now, I'm glad I was picked along with you good men."

At 1800 hours they assembled on the patch of grass. Sergeant Mitchell passed around jars of black cream. "Take this cream and put it on your faces and hands and any other place your skin is exposed."

Rick rubbed it on his skin. He turned around when he was done and started to hand it to another soldier. Leroy Johnson stood smiling. "Don't say nothing, Jive Ass." They both laughed and Rick handed it to another soldier. When they were done preparing themselves, Sergeant Mitchell motioned them to follow him. He made his way up the hill and stopped. The men gather around him.

"Okay, from now on it's going to be tricky. It's a dark night, so let's use it to our advantage. We keep low, and no more talking. Be as quiet as you can."

They hunched over holding their rifles at port arms and followed the sergeant down the hill. Soldiers in the positions reached out and patted them on the back. "Good luck gang, be careful, and the Lord be with you."

The men in the patrol mumbled, "Thanks."

When they got to the valley floor Mike thought, A few nights back there were thousands of enemy soldiers charging the positions on this same ground. How many of them got killed. If they decide to attack with their thousands of men, this patrol will be slaughtered. How many enemy soldiers are waiting for us on the other side of those hills.

His trance was broken when Sergeant Mitchell's hand went up. They huddled around him. He whispered, "I know it's dark, but it's important you see my hand signals. Remember this area is mined. Stay close and don't trip over one another." They made it to the base of the largest hill. Sergeant Mitchell pointed to the ground. Everyone dropped to his stomach. Mitchell crawled alone up the hill then waved for the patrol to come to him. They slowly inched their way up.

Mike's imagination was running wild. He pictured a flash from a rifle, a bullet piercing his body, and then rolling down the hill dead. *I've got to quit thinking these things. I got to pay attention to what we're doing. If I don't I won't be going home. How would my mother take it if I got killed? I must be alert. No more day dreaming.*

They made it to the top and stayed on their stomachs, squinting into the darkness. Mike tapped Sergeant Mitchell on the back and whispered, "Sergeant, I saw a faint flicker of light at one o'clock."

"I saw it too. It's too dark, and too far away to make out what it was."

The patrol continued to watch and no more lights or noise were seen or heard. The Sergeant motioned for them to get closer. He whispered, "They're definitely out there. We saw a flash and someone did it. We have to get closer to where that flash came from. It wouldn't be wise to risk the whole patrol. I'm asking for two men to volunteer and investigate that area."

Rick immediately replied. "Mike and I will go." Mike was startled. He never heard Rick volunteer for anything.

Sergeant Mitchell whispered. "Mike, did you hear what Miller said?"

"Yes, I heard him."

"He volunteered you. Will you go along with him?"

"Yes, Sergeant, I'll go."

"Okay it's settled. I don't want either of you to take any unnecessary risks. Just get close enough to determine how many men and what kind of equipment they have. Do not try to take them on. Get in and get out. Is that understood?"

They both nodded.

Mike and Rick carefully went down the hill and headed toward the direction the flash came from. After a half hour they climbed a high hill and started going down the other side. Rick grabbed Mike's arm and stopped him. He put his mouth close to Mike's ear. "Them bastards are down there, I can just make them out. You stay here Mike. I'll be back. There's no sense both of us going. If I get into a jam and they start chasing me, fire at them." Mike thought about it and nodded. Rick slowly slid down the hill. Mike watched till he disappeared in the darkness.

Mike strained his senses trying to know what was going on below him. There was no noise or movement. All at once he heard Rick's voice. "Damn it, Mike I told you to stay up there. What the hell's the matter with you? You crazy, get your hand off my helmet." Mike couldn't understand what was happening. He was tempted to yell to Rick, but he kept quiet. No more voices.

Mike was worried. He clutched his rifle and was about to go down the hill and look for him. Rick's voice came from the darkness. "Mike, it's me." Mike felt relieved when he saw him.

"We're in a heap of shit. That valley down there is wall to wall gooks. There must be thousands of them. I didn't see any tanks or heavy artillery. They must be waiting for the big stuff to come in and then they're going to attack."

"Rick, who were you talking to down there?"

"You're not going to believe this. I was about twenty yards away from the gooks and all at once I felt this hand rubbing the rim of my helmet, then it reached into my shirt and grabbed my dog tags. I thought it was you, then this voice said, 'Yank', real low and the guy disappeared. Man, it had to be one of those Turks."

When they crawled to the top of the hill Sergeant Mitchell reached out and grabbed the back of Mike's jacket and pulled him over the top. Other soldiers gripped Rick and pulled him up. Sergeant Mitchell whispered, "What did you see down there?"

Rick replied, "We didn't see any heavy equipment. There's so many men it looked like Coney Island on a hot day. There must be over a thousand of them down there."

"Anything else?"

"Oh, yeah. I was laying there watching these gooks when a hand rubbed my helmet. I almost crapped my pants till I heard him say, 'Yank'."

Sergeant Mitchell nodded. "It's a scary feeling. I had it happen a couple of times. You never get use to that. I'm glad you brought this to my attention. We'll send a man over to the Turks and compare information. Nice going you guys. Okay men, let's get back to where we belong." They silently made their way through the valley and started up the hill to the positions.

A voice shouted. "Halt who goes there. Identify yourself."

In unison the men in the patrol yelled. *"YOUR MAMMY."*

Laughing, the sentry said, "Come on in."

Sergeant Mitchell led them to the patch of grass where Captain Marko was waiting. He pointed to Rick. "Tell the Captain what you and Mike saw down there."

Captain Marko listened to everything Rick and Mike said. He asked. "Did you see any wounded?"

Rick shook his head. "No sir. It was really dark, and there were so many soldiers, I couldn't determine if any were wounded."

Captain Marko told them good work and released the patrol.. Mike and Rick went to the bunker and laid down. Hillbilly came to them. "Hey, how did it go?"

Rick shook his head. "It don't look good. There's a mess of them behind that hill. I can't believe they could survive that pounding the Missouri gave them." Hillbilly walked away shaking his head. Other soldiers who heard the conversation stared at each other.

The next two weeks were living hell in the positions. The enemy tried every tactic to overrun them but the Americans held. Every soldier slept, ate and fought in the positions. Mike and Rick's faces were as dirty as their clothes. Their drawn looks showed how exhausted they were. They didn't talk. Their squinted eyes looked like they were hypnotized as they glared at the hills waiting for another attack.

Chapter 14
The unwritten truce broken

The sun came up bright this morning and the day was warmer than it had been for a long time. Someone shouted. "A gook at one o'clock." Mike and Rick's tired eyes riveted on him. Rick grabbed the handle of the machine gun and aimed at the enemy soldier on the hill.

Mike looked through the field glasses. "Hold it Rick. That fool is washing his clothes and hanging them on a rope. Don't shoot him. Let's see what he's up to." Rick slowly eased up and looked at the man.

The enemy soldier stood on the hill in his undershorts waving a pair of pants. He was shouting. "Hey, Joe, don't shoot my ass."

Rick sat down again behind the gun. His finger was on the trigger and had the guy in the sights. "It's some kind of trick. I'm going to blow his gook ass right off that hill."

Meyer, the older soldier yelled. "Hold it, Miller. It's a truce signal They're tired of this killing and know we are too. A human can only take so much of this war. It'll be quiet for awhile."

Another North Korean came out of his hole waved his arms and shouted. "Hey, Joe no bullshit, okay."

Zug yelled. "Hey Rick, them fools are either drunk or crazy."

"Who cares. Just watch them. They're up to something."

The Americans stared at the enemy on the hill. They couldn't believe they were washing their clothes in plain sight. Rick continued to look down the sights, with his finger on the trigger. "I could get both them bastards with one burst."

Mike warned him. "Don't do anything till you get orders from the captain or Sergeant Mitchell. They probably experienced this before." Mike eased back and let the warm sun hit his body. It felt so peaceful not hearing guns and explosions. "Let's enjoy this peace. It feels like I'm a human being again." He thought how strange it was. Just yesterday everyone on this hill was so embedded with hate and fright they were killing those same soldiers on that hill. Today they're in plain view and no one fires a shot, it's like two boxers who pound each other throughout the fight, and when it's over, they hug one another. A human must have only so much hate and when it's exhausted, it takes time to replenish.

Captain Marko ordered. "Don't fire till we tell you." He and Sergeant Mitchell watched every move the North Koreans made. More North Koreans came out and lay in the sun. Every so often one yelled to the Americans. "Nice, hun, Joe? This good Joe."

Rick kept the machine gun aimed at them. Mike asked him. "I wonder how they got the first one to come out and wave his pants?"

"They probably told him if he didn't, they'd fix him up with Bertha."

"Man, you still haven't forgot about that woman. I think you're carrying a torch for her."

Rick spit. "Damn, I still think it was a nightmare. How in the hell can anyone look like that?"

Mike laughed hard. "Are you going to look her up when you get back?"

Rick just shook his head. He finally walked away from the gun and leaned on a sandbag and breathed deeply. "Boy, the air smells good without burned gun powder and smoke from burning bodies. We better enjoy this Mike, because I think they're trying to make us relax and then they're going to womp our asses with those damn mortars."

"I think you're right Rick, but it sure feels good. It's been days since we could look up and enjoy the sun. People don't realize how nice peace is. It's great to relax for a few minutes."

Darkness came and Sergeant Mitchell crawled around the positions warning his men. "Be ready, we don't know what to make of this." From the distant hills, music and laughter was heard.

A voice in broken English yelled. "Hey, Joe, you like. We like very well, Joe." No one answered.

"Rick, listen to that. They're really enjoying themselves."

"I know. This sure beats shooting the shit out of each other."

"You can say that again. I'll take all of this I can get."

Morning came and not a shot was fired. Another clear beautiful day and the North Koreans were walking all over their hill laughing and waving. Two more days and it was still peaceful.

"You know Mike, these pasts few weeks have been hell. A few times I didn't think we were going to make it. Look at those guys over there. Who the hell are they? They don't know us. And we don't know them. For some reason we were pushed together to kill one another. I bet they feel the same way. I wonder if they think about how many of their friends got killed. It's funny what's going on."

The soldiers in the positions looked to the rear when they heard a motor. A jeep approached with a dust cloud trailing it. It stopped at the base of their hill. A major in Class A uniform got out and started climbing the path to the top. "Hey, Mike, what the hell is he doing here?"

"I don't know and I really don't care."

When he got to the top of the hill Sergeant Mitchell met him. "Don't you salute an officer sergeant?"

"Sir this is a combat zone."

The major ignored the answer. "I'm from Head Quarters Company and I'm here to get information. He scanned the hills with his field glasses. He pointed to a group of men on a hill. He put the glasses down and said. "Those South Koreans are enjoying themselves over there."

Sergeant Mitchell shook his head. "Sir, they're not South Koreans. They're North Koreans."

The major dropped down and hid behind some sandbags. "North Koreans? What the hell's going on? We thought you people were catching hell up here. I never saw anything like this." The major put the field glasses to his eyes. "By God, they are North Koreans."

"Yes Sir. For the past two weeks we were really going at each other. I guess they felt they had enough. We're monitoring them closely to determine their strategy. We feel they just had enough. Our men need a rest too. We're going to wait and see what they do. We have no orders to advance."

Sergeant Mitchell noticed he didn't have any ribbons on his uniform which indicated he's never seen combat. "Major how long have you been in Korea?"

"One year, Sergeant." He rested the field glasses on the sandbags, stared at the North Koreans and mumbled to himself. He stepped back and laid the field glasses down. He yelled at a soldier in a foxhole. "Give me your rifle, soldier. I never killed a gook." The soldier reluctantly handed it to him. The major released the clip and pulled the slide back and the bullet in the chamber ejected. He went to a machine gun and took a tracer round from the belt. He replaced it with the one he took from the M 1. He seeded the tracer into the barrel then pushed the clip into the rifle, leaned the rifle on the sandbags and got into the ready position."

"Rick, you're not going to believe what that major is doing."

"Why that no good son-of-a-bitch."

The major gritted his teeth and mumbled. "Get them in my sights, hold my breath, and slowly squeeze the trigger." The rifle erupted with a loud report echoing through the valley. The tracer marked the projectile's path to the hill where the North Koreans were. Five more reports came from the rifle. The North Koreans dove into their holes.

A short silence, then someone shouted in broken English from the enemy hill. "Hey, Joe, you some-bitch." A barrage of mortar shells were now exploding on the American positions.

Rick jumped up and shouted. "You stupid asshole, are you satisfied?"

The Major instantly turned to Rick. His eyes glared and he started to walk toward Rick when a shell exploded about ten feet from him. He dove to a prone position and slithered to the backside of the hill. Rick started crawling out of the position. "Come back, you dirty yellow bastard."

Mike grabbed him by the waist and pulled him back into the foxhole. "Leave it alone, Rick. You'll get killed if you go up there."

"Let me go, Mike. I want to get that bastard and make him stay." Rick was out of control and Mike held him down.

The major crawled to the edge of the hill and pointed down at Rick shouting something but he couldn't be heard. Rick saw him and he broke free and grabbed his rifle and started aiming it at the major. Mike wrestled it away. The major saw this and quickly hunched over and started running down the other side of the hill. Rick grabbed a grenade, pulled the pin and lobbed it over the hill. It landed on the path making a clinking noise. The major turned and saw the grenade following him down the hill. He dove over a protruding rock and hugged it. The grenade exploded sending fragments in all directions. He hugged the rock for about five minutes then jumped up and started running down the hill. He lost his balance and rolled down next to the jeep. He dove inside, the wheels threw dirt and he sped off.

Mike shouted. "Rick, are you crazy? You should of never done that." Rick didn't say anything he just stared at the incoming explosions and mumbled to himself.

The bombardment kept up throughout the night. The rest period was over, thanks to the major. No one mentioned the incident, not even Sergeant Mitchell or Captain Marko.

After the shooting stopped Mike and Rick came off the hill to get breakfast. While they were eating a truck pulled up and the driver yelled, "Mail Call." All the soldiers put their mess kits down and ran to the truck. Rick continued to sit like he always did for mail call. He stared into his mess kit and moved the food around with his fork, not eating a bite. A soldier stood in the back of the truck. He yelled out a soldier's name and then sailed the envelope to the one with his hand up. Mike got his mail and walked back. He saw Rick sitting on the hill staring at the truck and wondered why he never got any mail.

Rick saw him come up the hill with a handful of letters. He knew Mike was going to ask questions. He shouted. "You did pretty good Mike. My mail will be coming. They're still trying to figure out where I am."

Mike knew this was an excuse. Ever since he met Rick, he never went to mail call. Mike didn't press the issue, "Yeah, this Korea is a big place."

Mike sat below Rick and looked at the envelopes. He quickly opened the one from his mother and hoped there wasn't any bad news. While reading it he sensed Rick looking over his shoulder. When Mike read the first page he held it up. Rick immediately grabbed it. Mike could hear him whisper, "Aw, man, wow," when he read the letter. Mike finished the second and third pages and held them up. When Rick got done reading, he became quiet. A choked up voice said. "Mike that is the most beautiful thing I have ever read. If I got a letter like this I would carry it over my heart forever. Man that is precious, it's worth more than all the money in the world." Mike turned around and looked at him. "Tell me, Mike does she wear an apron? And when she gets done cooking does she wipe her hands on the front of it? When you came home from school did she hug you?"

"Yes."

"When you were sick did she come in your room and feel your head to see if you had a fever? Did she pull the covers up around your neck and kiss your forehead?"

"Hey, what goes with all these questions?"

Rick shrugged his shoulders. "Oh, I was just wondering, that's all."

Hillbilly shouted. "Hey, you all, get your butts over here."

They walked to him. He had his hand in a large box containing several loaves of bread. "Look what my uncle sent me." He pulled out a large loaf.

Rick stared at it. "That shit ought to be stale."

"Miller, you all don't know nothing. This here is a large sandwich."

"Sandwich? What you talking about?"

Hillbilly pulled the loaf apart exposing a bottle filled with a clear liquid."

"What's in that bottle?"

Hillbilly kissed it. "This is good old moonshine. Of course, where you come from you never heard of the stuff."

"I heard of it, but never tasted it. Open it up, let's try it."

"No, man, we're going to drink it later. You don't want to mess with this firewater and go back to your position. It'll knock you out of your mind. This is powerful stuff."

Rick coaxed, but Hillbilly wouldn't open it. He hid that bottle and the other ones encased in the bread and they returned to their positions. Rick kept yelling at Zug and Hillbilly, "There's going to be a good time in the old town tonight." Hillbilly and Zug smiled back at him.

When they were relieved they quickly went down the hill. Rick tapped his canteen. "I've got the mix." Hillbilly wrapped the bottles in a shirt and they walked down the road to a clump of bushes. The four of them laid back and concealed themselves. Rick put out his hand. "Give me a bottle. I want to taste that stuff." He pulled the cork and raised the bottle to his lips. "Wow, that's like putting your mouth on the end of a flame thrower. That shit is hot."

Hillbilly grabbed the bottle and took a sip. "Oh, this is sweet nectar. Thank you Uncle Curtis" He handed it to Mike, who was reluctant, but he took the bottle. "Go ahead, Mike. Are you scared of it?"

"No, I want to make a toast." He raised the bottle. "Here's to Bertha back in the States. She misses her lover, Rick. He'll be home soon, and he'll jump up in your arms."

Hillbilly, slapped Zug on the back. "Man, we'll drink to that. Won't we, Zug?"

"Damn straight, she was some chick. I mean a big chick. Tell us about that scene in the motel, Rick"

"Knock off the bullshit you guys." They drank the first bottle and Rick threw the empty against a large rock. He reached down and peeled the bread away from another one.

Hillbilly yelled. "Hey take it easy on that stuff. It's powerful, it'll sneak up on you and kick your ass." Rick ignored him. Hillbilly looked at Mike and Zug. They didn't say anything, so he kept quiet.

Rick raised the bottle. "Now let's adapt to the situation. We're in the middle of Hell, so let's enjoy ourselves. Drink up, because tomorrow some gook might drop a mortar in your back pocket. Let's enjoy ourselves while we can." He handed the bottle to Zug who took a big swig.

Zug brought the bottle down and stamped his foot. "Damn, it's like drinking burning gasoline. That taste is the hottest I ever drank." He grabbed his canteen and took a big swig. "Come on baby, put out my fire."

Two more bottles were passed around and emptied. Rick grabbed another bottle. He clawed the bread away and threw chunks of it to the other guys. They caught it and munched on the stale bread. Hillbilly shouted, "Hey, y'all wait till tomorrow to drink the last one." They ignored him and drank it anyway.

The four of them lay in the grass slurring and reminiscing about the funny things that happened in basic training. One by one they fell asleep. Rick looked at them. "Come on, you guys, wake up. It's time to have some fun." No one responded. He tried to wake them, but it was no use. He staggered down the road and fell in some bushes and his knee struck something hard. He pulled branches away and uncovered a jeep. He slid behind the wheel and turned the ignition. The motor came alive. He slurred, "Don't you guys worry, I'm coming and I'll get you back to the bunker." He turned on the lights and swerved from side to side on the dusty road. He saw his three friends sleeping in the high grass. "Hey, you guys wake up. I got some wheels. Let's get some broads and have a real party."

Rick slammed on the brakes and the jeep swerved and stalled. The headlights illuminated the three drunken soldiers sleeping. Rick tried to shake them awake, but they wouldn't respond. He grabbed Zug and shook him. "Come on Zug, you're messing up the party."

Zug, garbled. "Shit man, I'm not messing up the party. The party messed me up. Man, my head is tore up."

Rick carried him to the jeep then went back and got Mike and Hillbilly. After falling a couple times he managed to get them into the jeep. Hillbilly and Zug were in the back. Mike was in the front. All three were sound asleep.

Rick rested his head on the steering wheel. He was exhausted and the White Lighting was raising havoc with his senses. He tried to clear his head but it didn't work. Mike slurred, "Hey, Rick, where we going?"

Rick blinked and squinted. "We need a drink. Hang on, you guys. We're going to have a ball." He started the jeep and drove down the dirt road away from the bunker. He went about two miles and made a sharp left turn. "The broads and the booze are this way, I know."

High on the hill overlooking the American positions, a soldier shouted. "Lights at three o'clock in the valley." The beams from the headlights were jumping up and down in the darkness as the jeep hit ruts and rocks. Rick did everything possible to control the vehicle, but he was off the road and drunk.

Captain Marko was summoned and he rushed to the top of the hill. Sergeant Mitchell handed him the field glasses. "Damn, what in the hell is it doing in the valley with its lights on. It doesn't seem to be going in any one direction. Let's watch and see where it's going. If it heads for our position we'll fire on it."

From the enemy hills white tracers were streaking at the headlights followed by artillery shells. Captain Marko shouted, "Fire at the flashes on those hills. They're giving their locations away." Immediately machine guns and heavy mortars erupted from the American positions. White explosions lit up the enemy hills.

Rick sang. "We're on the way to get some booze and find the broads. It won't be long now." Mike sat limp and held on to the bar on the dash. Bullets shattered the windshield and glass showered them. The familiar sound of machine guns brought everyone out of their stupor. Shells exploded all around them. The force of the barrage rocked the jeep from side to side. Rick shouted, "Hey, some son-of-a-bitch is shooting at us. Man, we're under attack."

The shocking word "attack" caused Mike to come fully awake. Both his hands gripped the bar on the dash board. His body came erect and he looked at Rick. "Where the hell are we?"

Rick's hands bounced on and off of the steering wheel as he tried to steer through the rocks and holes. "I don't know Mike. I think I made a wrong turn somewhere."

Hillbilly shouted. "That drunken fool has got us all in the valley. Oh, Lord, how we going to get out of this mess?"

Mike shouted. "Don't drive in circles. Go away from the shooting."

"How the hell can I go away? It's coming from all directions."

A shell exploded and the jeep turned over throwing the four of them out. Mike was on his knees and stunned. He shook his head and breathed hard. He saw the jeep on its side with its head lights still on. "You guys, get as far away from the jeep as you can. They got a still target to fire at now." He crawled as fast as he could to distance himself from the jeep. He kept calling out their names.

Zug's voice came out of the darkness. "Man, there is some crazy happening going on. I've been in some bad scenes before, but nothing like this. Ain't this a bitch."

Rick yelled. "Come on you guys. Help me upright this jeep. I think it will start."

Mike screamed, "Get away. They're going to shell it."

A bombardment hit all around the jeep. Mike hunched over and ran to a large boulder. Concentrated volleys were now making direct hits on the jeep. The headlights were blown out and parts of the jeep were flying in all directions. Mike had his hands over his head. Then the shelling stopped.

Hillbilly shouted, "Mike can you hear me? Are you all right?"

"I'm over here. I'll keep talking so you can find me."

Hillbilly crawled next to him. "Man, we're in a rash of shit. Where's Zug and Rick?"

"Zug is coming. He yelled to me. I don't know where Rick is."

"That crazy fool was going back to that damn jeep. I wonder if he got himself blown up. Man, there's nothing left of it. I hope he wasn't in it."

"Hey you guys, it's me. Zug, say something so I'll know where you're at. I can't see anything it's so dark."

They directed him to them. The three of them leaned against a boulder for about fifteen minutes trying to figure out how to find Rick. A low moan was heard. They crouched over and made their way to the sound. Mike saw him on the ground and turned him on his back. "Rick are you all right?"

Rick slowly shook his head and blinked his eyes. "Hey, Hillbilly, that shit was really potent. Do you think your uncle could send some more?"

Mike grabbed him by the shirt. "You damn fool, you got us in a mess. This is no time for jokes. We got to get out of here. I believe our positions are to the left but not sure. Either way we go, we have a problem. The gooks will shoot us if we go up their hill. Our guys will shoot us because we don't know the password. This valley is mined. Man I don't know why I let you get me into these problems."

"I'll tell you what we got to do. We adapt to the situation, an —"

Mike dove on him. "I told you I didn't want to hear that crap again." Mike was ready to punch him. Hillbilly and Zug grabbed his arm and pulled him off Rick.

"Man, y'all know this is no time to fight. We got to clear our heads and figure a way out of here. "Mike rolled over and sat up rubbing his fist, glaring at Rick.

"Listen Mike, I didn't say that to be wise. I meant we have to think this thing out. Now the way I look at it, all the shells hitting around us were coming from those hills over there. That must be where the gooks are. Our positions are the opposite way. Most of the mines exploded when the gooks tried to overrun us the other day."

Mike looked at Hillbilly. "What do you think?"

"Well, I was passed out when he drove us down here. It seemed like all the shooting did come from those hills. We have to make a decision and get out of here now."

Zug nodded. Mike thought for awhile. "Okay, we'll go the direction he thinks our positions are. The damn fool was the only one awake when he got us in this mess. I think the best thing to do is crawl. We'll take turns leading, and stay directly behind one another. That way we'll have less chance of setting off a mine."

Rick jumped up. "I'll be lead man all the way to our positions. I got you guys in this mess and I'm going to get you out. Stay far enough behind so if a mine goes off you won't get hit."

"I said we'll alternate the lead man and I mean it. We don't need any heroes. Okay let's go."

All four dropped to their knees and crawled. Zug asked. "Hey, Mike, wouldn't we make better time if we hunched over and walked?"

"No, we crawl. There's less chance of being seen, and if our guys see us crawling they'll think we're Turks and not fire at us."

"You're right, that's good thinking."

They slowly made it to the base of the hill. Mike whispered, "This is the hard part. Don't make a noise." Slowly they slithered up the hill. Half way up a loose rock rolled down the hill.

"Who goes there, mother fucker? What's the password sucker?"

The four of them froze and pushed their faces into the dirt.

"I said who goes there?" Rick pulled Mike's pant leg. "That's Leroy." Mike didn't say anything. He was sweating and waiting for the bullets to fly. Rick slowly lifted his head. "It's your mammy down here Leroy." It felt like eternity till Leroy answered.

"Jive Ass, Miller. I knew it was you, putting on that shit out there. Man, you've been straight too long."

Mike whispered. "Leroy, it's Mike. Zug and Hillbilly are with us."

"I got you, man, come on in."

Mike wiped the sweat from his face, took a deep breath and crawled up the hill. Leroy saw him, grabbed his arm and pulled him into the foxhole. "Man, Mike, why you run with a fool like Miller. That boy gonna get you killed."

"Yeah, I know what you mean."

The other three squirmed in. Leroy laughed. "Jive Ass, I knew it was you pulling them stunts. That was some trick'en you were doing out there. No wonder you cats didn't get tore up. Why in the hell you guys let that fool get you in so much trouble? I thought you cats were smart."

Rick looked at him. "I'm going next week again. Want to come along?"

"Listen, sucker, I wouldn't go to church with you. My mama didn't raise a fool."

Mike put his hand on Leroy's shoulder. "Keep it down Leroy. Does anyone besides you know that was us out there?"

"Hell no, but I knew right away. Most of these cats weren't in basic with Miller. I swear when I saw them lights jumping up and down and going around in circles, and them gooks shooting, I knew it was that fool. Man, Mike, I sure didn't think you'd go along with that kind of bullshit. Leroy pointed at Rick. "Hey, fool, where did you get that ride?"

"What ride? I don't know what your talking about."

"Man, you know, that ride that ain't no more. In other words the ride that's in a million pieces, Jive Ass."

The four crawled out of Leroy's position and started up the path. They heard soldiers talking about the commotion that happened in the valley. They tried not to draw any attention and quietly went into the bunker and laid down.

"That was my goddamn jeep that got blew up last night." Mike raised his head when he heard the Captain's voice. "Some son-of-a bitch stole my jeep, and if I find the bastard, I'll personally kick his ass."

Mike slid his head inside his sleeping bag. "Aw, shit."

Zug crawled over to Rick. "Man, did you hear that captain jawing out there about his jeep getting busted up?"

"Yeah, I heard him. Don't talk about it. Keep quiet and don't admit to anything. You got it?"

Yeah, man, I got it. But if he finds out who did it, there's going to be some terrible scenes."

Later the four of them went down to the mess truck for breakfast. They stood in line, and soldiers were talking about the captain's jeep. One of them looked at Rick.

"What do you think happened last night?"

"The captain probably got drunk and parked his jeep in the wrong place."

"Not Captain Marko. He don't drink. When he was on R & R he didn't touch a drop. He's a easy going guy, but when he finds the guy who did it, I pity him."

Mike changed the subject. "Man that sounds great. R & R Boy I can't wait. How did you guys like it when you were there?"

"Man, Japan was great. Wait till you see all the bars and Joesans. You won't want to leave."

Mike and Rick got their food and sat next to Hillbilly and Zug, away from the other soldiers. Leroy saw them and came over.

"What's happening, wheel man, Miller?"

"What's your problem, Leroy?"

"I ain't got a problem. I just wanted to tell you I saw the captain looking through field glasses at pieces of his jeep scattered all over that valley. He was looking for a body out there and hoping the crazy fool that stole his jeep was in pieces too. Beings there was no body he thinks some sneaky mother fucker from this company hustled it. I'd hate to be the cat he catches." Leroy pointed at Rick. "Now you, Miller, would have no problem if he caught you. You could get a Section Eight without any problem. Shit, man, all that crazy shit you pulled you could get an instant Section Eight."

Mike was concerned. "Tell me, Leroy, do you think he knows who took his jeep?"

"Hell no, he don't know. I heard him say he thinks a popasan ripped it off. I was just bullshitting old Jive Ass Miller."

"I don't know Leroy. I'm a little scared he'll find out. "

"I'll give you some good advice." He pointed at Rick. "You best get away from that sorry son-of-a-bitch or you'll end up dead or in the brig."

Rick jumped up. "I had enough of your jawing. Take your bullshit some place else."

"Be cool, Rick I'm just funning you, man. I got to split. If I hear anything, I'll let you know." Leroy walked away making motions like he was driving and making sounds like a motor and explosions.

Rick glared at him. "I'll get even with his silly ass."

Chapter 15
Big price for a hill

Days passed and the enemy slowed their attacks. Sergeant Mitchell came into the position. "Soldiers be ready in four hours. We're leaving these positions and going on the offensive. You see that large hill in front of us? We're going to take it."

Rick asked. "What the hell we going to do with it when we get it?"

"We know that's where they're regrouping. The hill is high and we want the advantage of high ground. If we attack now we'll have the element of surprise. Does that answer your question, Miller?"

"Yes Sergeant. But, I was just getting to like my dirt home."

Sergeant Mitchell laughed. "Be ready in four hours."

"Well here we go again, Mike. I was just getting comfortable and we have to move."

Mike detached the machine gun from the tripod. He handed it to Rick. He kissed it. "Baby, we'll be counting on you. You got us through some rough times. Please do it again. Those gooks over there are as thick as ants."

Artillery shells whistled over their heads blasting the hill. It no sooner stopped and the jets came in strafing and bombing. Momentarily it got quiet. Sergeant Mitchell shouted, "Okay, men let's take it." American soldiers climbed out of their foxholes with rifles firing charging the enemy hill. Incoming mortar shells were exploding among them. Sergeant Mitchell kept yelling, "Keep firing your weapons. We got to keep their heads down so they can't shoot at us."

Mike and Rick made it to the foot of the enemy hill. Mike quickly dropped to his stomach and set up the tripod. Rick was right behind and seeded the machine gun on top of the tripod and dropped behind the gun. Mike fed a belt of bullets into the gun and tapped Rick on the helmet. Fire was spitting out of the barrel. Mike pointed to a group of North Koreans rolling a small artillery piece to the edge of the hill. Rick fired burst after burst at them. He could tell he was hitting the area because a dust cloud formed where the bullets hit. He stopped firing and the dust cleared. One enemy soldier was draped over the gun, not moving. Two others were lying motionless on the ground next to the gun.

The fighting was fierce and the Americans were pinned down. Sergeant Mitchell shouted, "Our planes are coming back. After they bomb, the gooks will have their heads down. Get up and rush the top of the hill. Keep firing your weapons. Don't let them get their heads up and shoot down on us."

"Rick, we're in a jam here. We're sitting ducks for those gooks up there."

"I know, Mike. Keep your head down." Rick looked at Mike and saw his lips moving. "Mike, put my name in your prayers. Will ya?"

Just as Mike nodded the jets screamed over their heads strafing and bombing. Dirt, blood and pieces of enemy bodies rained down on the American soldiers. The jets made two more passes and left. Sergeant Mitchell shouted, "Now, get up and take this damn hill." Rick grabbed the machine gun and Mike picked up the tripod and the cans of bullets. They got three quarters up and Mike planted the tripod and Rick locked in the machine gun. He aimed at the top of the hill and fired back and forth. Seeing this, soldiers with their M1's firing ran past going for the top. One of them got hit and his rifle flew in the air and his limp body rolled down the hill. Rick saw the gook who fired the shot who now was hiding behind the hill. The guy stuck his head up again to fire. Rick had the sights on the spot. He squeezed the trigger. The guy's hat flew in the air. His head blew apart. Rick kept firing at the spot throwing up dirt. A soldier saw this and ran to where Rick was kicking up the dirt. When he got to the top, Rick stopped firing. The American soldier shot three more who were hiding. The soldier continued firing his M1 and at the same time waved for Mike and Rick to come up with the machine gun.

They ran to the top, set the gun up and aimed downhill on the other side. Enemy soldiers were running away, trying to escape. Mike threw a couple of grenades at a group. Rick let loose with the machine gun. The enemy got hit in the backs. Their bodies arched as the bullets tore into them.

"We did it, Mike, we took the hill."

Mike patted him on the back. "We sure did. We got to keep alert and watch those guys down there. They might be faking they're hit."

They heard Zug's shouting, "Mike, Rick, help." They looked back down the hill they just came up. Zug was standing with his arms in the air screaming.

They yelled, "Get down Zug. Don't stand up. Crawl, Zug, get up here with us."

Zug stood screaming. Rick saw dirt flying up by Zug's feet. He looked to his right about fifty feet away. A gook was in the prone position firing at Zug. Rick swung the machine gun and fired. The bullets struck the guy in the side rolling him over. Mike ran down the hill shouting for Zug to get down. Zug just stood there shaking. It was like he couldn't hear. Mike dove and tackled him to the ground. "What's the matter with you Zug? Answer me." Zug just mumbled. Mike struck him in the face. "Tell me what's the matter Zug?"

"They got him. They got him."

"Who Zug? Who are you talking about? He grabbed Zug by his shirt and pulled his face close to his. "Tell me Zug."

Zug had a look on his face that Mike will remember the rest of his life. Tears were streaming down his face. "Hillbilly is dead. They got him."

"You're wrong Zug. Where's Hillbilly? Do you hear me Zug? Where's Hillbilly?"

Zug was trembling so bad he couldn't talk. He pointed a shaking finger down the hill where a soldier in an olive drab uniform was lying face down, not moving.

Mike yelled to Rick, "Hillbilly is hit. I'm bringing Zug to you. He's out of it. Cover us."

Mike dragged Zug up the hill. Rick grabbed Zug with one hand and kept his other hand on the machine gun firing.

"I'm going back down to Hillbilly."

"Go ahead I'll cover you." He started shooting across the top of the hill.

Mike ran down the hill half falling and shouting "Hillbilly, Hillbilly." There was no movement from the soldier laying on the ground. The closer he got he could see the blood on the clothing and ground. He knelt next to him and turned him over on his back. Hillbilly's limp head slumped on his shoulder. Mike saw his face and quickly turned away. "Aw, my God, aw my God!" He could feel this horrible sight being carved in his mind. He grabbed Hillbilly by his shoulders and held him. Tears were streaming down Mike's face and he shouted. "Oh my God, Oh my God!"

Sergeant Mitchell saw Mike and quickly ran to him. He pulled him down and looked at Hillbilly. "Mike, there's nothing we can do for him now.

You pull yourself together." The sergeant removed Hillbilly's fatigue jacket and put it over his face. Mike turned his head and bit his lip.

Sergeant Mitchell put his arm on Mike's shoulder. "It's hard, but you got to forget it. You got to get out of this mess alive and if you don't straighten up you'll be the same way. Your buddy Hillbilly would want you to make the best of it, and you know it. Now get back up that hill to your weapon."

Mike breathed deeply, got up and started up the hill hunched over. He felt like every bit of energy was drained out of him. He could hardly make it up the hill. Rick saw him coming and knew something was really wrong. He ran down and grabbed him. "Hurry get to the top." Rick pulled him next to the machine gun. "Mike what happened?"

"Hillbilly got it bad in the face and he's dead."

Rick shouted. "Son-of-a-bitch. Son-of-a-bitch. For a stinking fuck'in hill." He started firing the machine gun. I'll give them their goddamn hill. He lifted the machine gun up and started down the hill. I'll kill every goddamn gook over here."

Mike grabbed the tripod and ammo cans. "Wait for me Rick we'll do it together."

Zug quit mumbling when he saw Rick and Mike going down the hill. He looked for his weapon but couldn't find it. He ran to a dead North Korean whose body covered his rifle. Zug kicked him till he rolled over. He took the Korean's gun and ammunition belt. He yelled at Mike and Rick. "Wait for me, you guys."

Sergeant Mitchell saw what they were doing. "Oh, no. Hold it you guys. I mean it. Don't go any further that's an order." He grabbed Rick by the collar. "You listen to me. Do you hear me?"

Rick just glared and gritted his teeth. He was burning with hate. "We got you the goddamn hill. Now what the fuck you going to do with it. Give us the order to go after those gooks who killed Hillbilly. We've been doing everything you wanted us to do. Now do something we want to do."

Sergeant Mitchell spoke in a low voice. "I can understand what you're saying. We'll get even but we got to have a plan. I know what you're going through. It happened to me three times. Every time I had a close friend he got knocked off. I try not to make friends because of that. Believe me, what you're doing is crazy. You know those bastards will come again. When they do we'll knock their asses off. Please listen to me, men. Mike did you hear what I said?"

"Yes. Sergeant, you're right, I'm in control."

"Rick, what about you."

"Yeah, we'll get another crack at them." The sergeant looked at Zug. Zug nodded his head.

The Americans stayed on the high hill for three days and no sign of the enemy. They were ordered back to the positions. The soldiers were happy to once again sleep in the large bunker. Sergeant Mitchell had a meeting with his squad. "Men, I'm going on a patrol and I need four volunteers. Before he even completed the sentence Mike, Rick and Zug threw up their arms. The older soldier raised his. "Very well I'll get with you four later." He walked out of the room and the older soldier followed him.

"Sergeant, can I talk with you?"

Sergeant Mitchell stopped and turned around. "Sure, go ahead."

"Do you think it's wise to take those three guys on this patrol? They're still mad at what happened to their friend. They may be a little trigger happy if we see gooks."

"Yeah, I know what you're talking about. I knew when I asked for volunteers they'd want to go. They're good soldiers and I believe they'll follow orders."

Before leaving the positions Sergeant Mitchell explained the purpose of the mission. "I want it understood. There will be no shooting unless we have to defend ourselves. We're going behind enemy lines to find out what they're up to. We will take the information we gain so we can plan an attack against them and give them maximum casualties. Keep this in mind. Am I clear?"

"Yes Sir."

Under cover of night they left the positions. Rick kept rubbing the knife he conned off a Turk. They were out for five hours and no enemy was observed. Sergeant Mitchell motioned for them to get close to him. They were lying on the ground on a hill and the sergeant explained it was time to go back because the sun was starting to come up. The older soldier tapped the sergeant on the shoulder and pointed below. Everyone looked. An enemy patrol was at the bottom of the hill walking in single file. The Americans watched the patrol slowly walk below them. They'd almost passed when one of them sneezed. He wiped his nose on his sleeve and he saw the Americans. He pointed up and shouted.

Sergeant Mitchell didn't hesitate. He shouted, "Fire."

The three young soldiers jumped up cursing and ran down the hill shooting. Sergeant Mitchell and the older soldier kept in the prone position taking careful aim at the enemy. It was a short fight because the Americans caught them off guard. Sergeant Mitchell and the older soldier ran down the hill. One of the downed soldiers started to move. Rick dove on him with the Turk knife. Sergeant Mitchell grabbed him. "Don't kill him. A wounded man slows down the main force. You hear me, Miller?" Rick slowly got up, glaring at the man.

Zug yelled. "Watch out Mike, grenade."

Mike looked down. Another wounded Korean was pulling the pin on a grenade. Mike dove on him and grabbed the live grenade and shoved it under the downed man's back. Mike was on top of the soldier squeezing his throat. The man had a terrified look on his face when he felt the grenade under his back. A muffled explosion and Mike felt the concussion go through the man's body into his.

Mike didn't remember anything till he heard Rick shouting. "Mike, Mike, are you all right? Please be all right." Mike slowly opened his eyes. His body ached. He was stunned and couldn't talk.

Sergeant Mitchell knelt next to him. "Mike, lay still. I want to examine you, to see if anything is broken."

Mike slowly came to his senses. "I'm, I'm, all right." He got to his knees and stared at the dead enemy soldier and shook his head. Rick grabbed him and lifted him to his feet.

"Aw, Mike, it's so good seeing you're all right. Man, you saved our lives. Aw, man, I was worried."

Sergeant Mitchell shouted. "We gotta get out of here. That shooting will bring every gook within miles."

Rick still had the knife in his hand glaring at the wounded enemy soldier on the ground.

Sergeant Mitchell yelled. "I said let him alone. Now let's get the hell out of here."

They hurriedly made their way back to the positions. Men in the fox holes shouted questions. "What was the shooting about?"

"Are there many gooks out there?" "How many gooks did you get? We heard the shooting."

Sergeant Mitchell yelled. "Knock off the questions. These men are tired. We'll fill you in later."

The patrol was taken to Captain Marko's quarters. Sergeant Mitchell explained the mission. He told how Mike saved the lives of the patrol. Captain Marko immediately walked to Mike and shook his hand. "I'm writing a commendation for you, Mike. It's great to have men like you and the rest of this patrol in my company. I'm proud of you. Get yourself something to eat and some rest. Again, good work."

Mike, Zug, and Rick went to the mess truck and got some food. They sat by a large rock. The older soldier had his food and walked to them. "Is it all right if I sit next to you guys?"

Mike smiled. "You're always welcome, Meyer. You know, you don't have to ask."

"I want to tell you guys something. What the captain said goes for me too. I'm glad you were on that patrol. I'm sorry about your friend Hillbilly. I went through it too. It's a hard pill to swallow. You'll never completely get over it. A lot of us who have been in for a few years have gone through it. If I can be of any help just ask."

They looked at him and said. "Thanks."

Chapter 16
R & R - Watch out Japan

Captain Marko and Sergeant Mitchell watched as the soldiers came out of the bunker and climbed onto a flatbed truck. They were both smiling. Sergeant Mitchell, shook his head. "Watch out Japan, here they come."

Captain Marko walked to the loaded truck. "Have fun on R and R. men. You deserve it. You're great soldiers. We'll hold the fort till you get back." He and Sergeant Mitchell watched as the truck faded away on the dusty road. The captain looked at Sergeant Mitchell. "It's not a day too early. Did you see those tired looks on their faces? Them boys really need it."

The truck pulled up to the same Quonset hut they had left their duffle bags when they came to Korea. They cleaned up and put on fresh uniforms. Back pay was given out and they were taken to the airport. One soldier kissed his money and shouted. "I'm going to find me a nymphomaniac who owns a bar."

The soldiers slowly climbed the steps and entered the plane. Rick saw an empty seat by a window. Leroy was sitting next to it. Rick pointed to the window seat. "Hey Leroy, move over. You can have the window seat."

Leroy looked up. "Aw, shit, man. Not you Miller. Can't you find another seat? I don't need all that bullshit you put out. This is no time to play, man."

"Well, move your ass over so I can sit down."

"Man, if you want to sit here, carry your ass, next to that window."

Rick squirmed past Leroy and sat in the window seat. He noticed Leroy was nervous. "Hey, man what goes with you? Shit, you're whiter than I am."

"I don't like this flying shit. I don't need it."

"Aw man, there's nothing to flying. After all that crap we went through back at the positions, this is like heaven."

"Man, I'm scared of this bird. I want my damn feet on the ground. I can control myself on the ground. I don't want any part of this shit."

A bell rung in the front of the plane. A stewardess stood in the aisle holding a yellow rubber life jacket. She explained that every time a military plane takes off over water the personnel on board will wear life jackets. She instructed the men to get one from the racks above their heads and she would show them step by step on how to put them on. After they were wearing the life jackets, she showed how to inflate them. "Now, men, you will continue wearing your life jackets until we reach a certain altitude. The pilot will advise you when to take them off and store them in the rack." She thanked them and they gave her a loud cheer.

The engines screamed and the propellers were spinning so fast they disappeared. The plane bolted forward and raced down the runway. The front of the plane lifted and they were airborne. A banging noise sounded as the wheels were drawn in. Rick looked at Leroy. His eyes were wide, staring at the floor. He had his hands folded together.

"Hey, Leroy, lean over and look out this window and see how small those houses down there are getting."

"Man, shut the fuck up. I don't give a damn about that window or them houses."

"Oh, look down there. Remember that big ship we came to Korea on. There's one down there just like it. We're so high it looks like a piece of fly shit."

"I'm telling you, Miller. Knock off the bullshit. I'm scared of this flying and I don't need what you're putting out. Man, go sit next to some fool who appreciates your off the wall shit."

Rick stared at him. Leroy rolled his eyes to see Rick, but he didn't move his head. Sweat was forming on Leroy's forehead. Rick sensed he was scared and he left him alone.

The bell in the front of the plane rang. "This is the pilot. We have reached the altitude where you can remove your life jackets. Please store them in the overhead racks."

Rick, like the rest of the soldiers, took off his jacket and put it in the rack. He sat back down and looked at Leroy who still had his jacket on.

"Hey, Leroy, the pilot said we could take off the jackets. Take yours off and I'll put it in the rack for you."

"Man, I don't care what that pilot said. I'm leaving it on till I put my feet on dry land. If this sucker goes down I'll be ready. I can't swim a damn lick. Now why don't you keep your silly ass next to that window and don't fuck with me."

Rick put his head back and fell asleep for a couple of hours. He woke up and looked at Leroy, whose face was still aimed at the floor. His hands were clenched together. He fell asleep in this position. His life jacket was still on. Rick leaned over and read the dark writing on the jacket. **PULL TAB TO INFLATE.** He looked at Leroy sleeping, and slowly took the tab between his thumb and finger. He rubbed it a couple of times and smiled. He looked around to see if anyone was looking at him. Everyone seemed to be sleeping. He turned his head and looked out the window and at the same time he jerked the tab.

A loud gushing noise erupted as air blasted into the life jacket. A belching sound pierced the quietness as air ballooned the rubber. Leroy shot out of his seat with the puffed up jacket surrounding his ears. His eyes showed fright. He shouted "Mother fucker." He flew into the aisle and was jumping up and down like a bloated frog.

The sleeping soldiers woke up. At first they stared at him, then broke out laughing. The stewardess rushed to him. "What's the matter? What happened?"

Leroy tried to talk but all he could do was stutter. She calmed him down. "Lady, I was sleeping and this sap sucker popped."

Rick looked up and laughed when he saw Leroy's head surrounded by the yellow blown-up life jacket. "Leroy, why didn't you listen when the stewardess told us when to inflate our life jackets? She said only inflate it when we get in the water."

Fright left Leroy face and anger appeared. "You smart jive ass mother fucker you had something to do with this bullshit."He dove at Rick with his fists clenched. Rick saw him coming and stood up. Both of them were fighting on top of the seats.

Two soldiers grabbed them and pulled them apart. One of them yelled. "Hey you guys, keep the fighting for the gooks." They broke loose from the two soldiers, and glared at one another for a short time, then they busted out laughing. The stewardess got between them and deflated the jacket. Leroy took it off and handed it to her

Leroy looked at Rick. "What you gonna do now jive?"

174

"Well I'm going to be a good sport. You can have the window."

"Aw, man, shit, don't you ever quit this crazy carrying on?"

"Just a thought, Leroy. Remember when you were calling me 'wheel man?' Well, we're even now." They laughed, and shook hands.

The plane landed at Tokyo International Airport and the men were taken to Camp Drake. They were instructed to wear their Class A uniforms while on R and R. A captain ordered, "Be back in ten days. If there's anyone who doesn't want to go on R&R, he can leave on the next flight back to Korea." No one took him up on that offer. Everyone laughed, and he said, "Okay, men you're free to go. We'll see you in ten."

Mike, Rick and Zug ran out the main gate. It seemed strange seeing buildings standing without bullet holes in them. A small cab was driving by slowly. Rick threw up his hand. The cab stopped and the driver stuck his head out the window. "Hey Joe, good time shit happening." The three of them got in. The driver turned around. "Where to, Joe?"

Rick pulled out the Japanese Yen roll he had changed for American money and showed it to the driver.

"That good time shit, Joe."

Rick pointed to himself. "No Joe. I'm Rick. Rick you understand?'

The driver shrugged his shoulders. "Joe, Rick, give fuck."

"Okay, we want to go to a nice quiet bar with lots of broads." He showed the driver a large bill. "If you go extra fast, I'll give it to you."

"I, number one fuck'in race driver. I get you quick."

The cab leaped forward and accelerated dodging in and out of traffic with the driver constantly applying his breaks and blowing the horn. Mike and Zug moved their bodies and shut their eyes as he narrowly missed other cars and people. Rick was leaning forward encouraging him to go faster. Rick saw a traffic jam in front of them. "What you going to do now?"

"No fuck'en problem Joe, er Rick. I get you there early." He swung the wheel to the right and the cab jumped the curb and now was going down the sidewalk with the horn blaring. People cussed and dove into doorways. The driver cussed back at them.

Mike and Zug shielded their eyes with their arms. Mike shouted. "Rick tell him to get off the sidewalk and slow down. He's going to kill someone."

"Naw, he's doing a great job."

The driver looked back at Mike. "No sweat, Joe I can handle."

The cab came to the intersection where the beginning of the traffic jam was. The driver drove off the curb and back onto the street and ran a red light.

Rick tapped him on the back and yelled. "Nice work."

The driver laughed. "That's okay, huh. I use to be Kamikaze pilot." He slammed on the breaks and the cab slid sideways into a parking space in front of a bar. A large picture of a woman with a low cut dress was painted on the window. Above the door a speaker was playing loud American songs. The driver looked back, and grinned. "This number one bar. Raise a lot of hell. Good time."

They got out and Rick threw the driver the big bill. The driver bowed and said. "Doe-ma-te got toe. The three soldiers stared at him. "That mean, thank a fuck'in lot. Hey, Ricksan, maybe I wait. Maybe you go to another place. I drive faster."

"No, we just want some quiet joint with drinks, and broads. We'll stay here."

He pointed at the bar and shouted. "That place. Raise plenty hell. Have good time. He squealed the tires and drove off. '

Mike shook his head. "You can tell he's been around G.I.'s.

Mike looked at Rick. "How much did you give him? He sure was happy."

"Hell I don't know. Just look at all this money. When I changed my American scrip to Yen, they gave me enough to put in a suitcase. Hey, the cab driver is happy, and I'm happy I made it here alive. What good is money if we go back and some gook blows us apart with them damn mortars." They stared at the bar for a moment and went inside. It was dark but neon lights flickered and gave the place atmosphere. No sooner did they sit down and three young ladies came to the table.

One pointed to her friends then to the empty chairs at the table. "Joe, okay."

Mike stood up and nodded. He pointed to the chairs. "Yes, please sit down."

Rick smiled. "Oh, baby, this is what I heard about. Come on you pretty things you can sit on my lap, or where ever else you want to sit."

The girls just stared at Rick. "No speakie English, Joe."

"Hey, knock off the Joe shit." He pointed to himself. "Rick-Rick-Rick. No more Joe."

The girls laughed, and pointed at him. "Rick, Rick."

"Yeah, that's me, Rick."

Zug looked at Mike. "Man, here we go with the name scene."

A smiling waitress came to the table and looked at Rick. "What you want Joe?" Mike closed his eyes and shook his head. Rick looked disgusted. "Man, where do they get this Joe shit?"

Mike laughed. Ignore it Rick. They call all soldiers Joe. They can't speak English and that's what they know us by." Mike told the waitress beer for them. He pointed to the girls. "Get them whatever they want."

Rick said. "Hey, wait a minute. What are we drinking beer for, when we can have whiskey?"

Mike threw up his hands. "Oh, no, if you're starting on hard stuff, I'm getting out of here. I intend to have a good time and I'm not going to jail."

Rick pointed to himself and told the waitress. "Beer for me too."

Zug, laughed. "Man after that jeep ride you gave us it ought to be soda."

"Hey, Zug I thought we were going to forget about that. Don't even think about that hell hole. It's bad enough we have to go back in ten days. No more talk about Korea."

The girls ordered in Japanese. Mike asked Zug what they ordered? "Man, how do I know. I don't speak their lingo. They're playing a different song than we are."

Rick said, "I'll tell you guys what they're drinking. It's tea. They make you think they're drinking booze. You keep buying them drinks to get them drunk. But it never happens. I seen broads do it back in the States."

Mike took a handful of coins from his pocket. He showed them to the girl sitting next to him, and pointed at the juke-box. She smiled and blushed. They got up and went to the juke-box. Mike put the money in and she picked the songs. Every song was a popular American one. Mike nodded and smiled every time she picked a tune. She pointed at him and motioned for him to pick some songs. He shook his head. "No, you number one song picker."

Back at the table Rick had his chair turned so he could look directly into the girl's eyes. He glanced up at Mike and the girl who came back to the table. "Mike, these girls are pretty and built like brick shit-houses."

The girls blushed and put their hands over their mouths and laughed. Zug stared at them. "Man, these broads have been around G.I's before."

Mike looked at Zug. "What's Rick up too?"

"Aw, man, the cat's trying to talk do-do, you know, lie. The chick don't understand that off the wall talk. The fool is going to blow his mind trying to make her understand."

Rick looked disgusted. "Man, how in the hell do you make out, if she don't know what you're talking about. She just blushes, and laughs. I've been talking for ten minutes and she hasn't said a word. I think I'll pull down my pants and show her my tattoo."

Both Mike and Zug yelled. "No."

The popular songs continued to play. Mike stared. *It was last year those songs were playing after the football games. The wonderful prom night. I didn't realize how great those times were. Will I ever get back to those peaceful times?*

Rick knew Mike was thinking of home. "Come on Mike, the hell with the past. We got these beautiful broads, drinks, music and this nice quiet place. Isn't it great not having some son-of-a-bitch trying to slice your throat, or a machine gun cutting you in half. Man, this is great. Let's enjoy it. Live for today. Come on, get these broads on the dance floor."

Rick took the girl's hand. "Come on Babysan let's dance." Mike and Zug went to the dance floor with the girls who were sitting next to them. Mike looked at her face when they danced. She was pretty and felt so warm and soft. Back in Korea everything was cold, hard, mean and ugly. While dancing the girl sang in English the words to the song. He thought she must have heard those songs a thousand times to be able to sing them so good.

Rick was the last to come back to the table with his girl. "Ain't this nice being able to sit down and not have some gook yelling how he's going to kill us. No more of those damn bugles. Man, this is the way life should be."

Zug raised his glass. "I'll drink to that."

They were so engrossed in the tranquility and the nice looking young ladies they didn't notice a group of Marines who came in and sat down at a large table behind them. It appeared they had been drinking all day. The other hostess girls sensed this and were reluctant to go to their table. The drinks were flowing fast at the Marines' table. One of the Marines yelled. "Hey these broads are drinking tea."

Someone else answered. "Who gives a damn. I'm drinking whiskey and that's all that matters."

The noise from the Marines' caused Mike to look at them. "Hey, Rick, this place is starting to get crowded."

"Man, I don't care how crowded it gets. We got our table. We got our broads and that's all that matters."

Rick, Mike and Zug felt like they were in heaven. It was so peaceful looking at the pretty girls and hearing the nice slow soothing music. They didn't pay attention when a group of British soldiers came in and took a table parallel to the Marines. The Marines elbowed each other and pointed at the British soldiers. The British soldiers stared at the Marines.

Rick had his arm around the girl and his head was on her shoulder. "Babysan, I know you're getting paid to sit here with me. But it don't matter, this is the greatest. If only you could understand English I'd tell you so much. It's so peaceful here I don't think I'll go back to Korea. I'm going to stay with you, here in paradise."

The girl smiled. She probably heard it a million times by other soldiers. Mike and Zug were slowly rocking their heads and tapping their hands on the table with the beat of the slow music. The girls smiled at them.

"Mike, this is great. My nerves are completely settled down. The only problem I got is how to get this fine thing into bed."

The three young men looked at the pretty ladies. They couldn't speak each other's language but they still managed to enjoy one another.

The peaceful atmosphere was broken by a loud yell from the Marines' table. "I had the Queen out last night and she ain't no better then these street walking whores over here."

The bar became quiet then another shout with a British accent. "Babe Ruth sucks."

Mike looked at Rick and Zug. "There's going to be trouble, let's get out of here."

Rick shook his head. "Yeah, I know what you mean, those ass holes are gonna wreck everything."

Mike pointed to the girl sitting next to him then pointed to the door. "We, go okay."

She became very serious. "No can do. Honcho get mad." Rick and Zug tried to convince the girls next to them, but they wouldn't go either."

The Marines and British soldiers were standing shouting profanities at each other. Rick looked at the pretty girls. "Mike this is too good to leave." He walked between the Marine and British tables, "Hey, you guys knock off this bullshit, are you crazy? You've been fighting for six months in Korea and then you come here and start a damn fight. What goes with you people?"

They ignored him, and a Marine yelled. "I got a dose of clap off the Queen."

An English voice answered. "Eisenhower is a queer."

Rick's arms went up in the air and he shouted. "Quit this bullshit. Both of you shut up." Someone threw a chair and hit Rick in the head knocking him to the floor. The Marines and British soldiers were now in hand to hand combat. They grabbed each other and started punching. Others dove from one table to another. It looked like an old pirate movie when the pirates use to leap from one ship to another. Mike saw Rick get hit with the chair and ran to him. He started to pick him up when someone hit him across the back with a chair and knocked him on top of Rick. Zug grabbed Mike and pulled him away from the fight. He ran back and helped Rick get up. "Zug, which one of those bastards hit me with that chair?" Zug pointed at the guy. Rick ran and punched him in the ear. The guy went limp and was going down. Rick swung again hitting him in the forehead. He stood over him to make sure he wouldn't get up. Mike saw a British soldier getting ready to swing at Rick's blind side. Mike dove and landed on the guy's shoulders knocking him to the floor.

The fight was at its peak. A lot of name calling, bottles breaking, and chairs flew through the air. The hostess girls ran behind the bar and watched the brawl. The owner, an old Popasan, was standing on a chair with a pencil and pad. Every time something got broken he wrote it down. The fight roared on, mixed with the sounds of broken glass, splintered wood, meat hitting meat, and name calling. "You, Yank bastard."

"You no good Limie son-of-a-bitch."

The front door flew open and helmeted military police rushed in with their whistles blowing and their clubs swinging.

The bar quieted down. The Marines slowly walked back to their table. The British soldiers did the same.

Rick grabbed Mike and Zug. "Let's get out of here. Act like nothing happened."

They slowly walked toward the door and an MP shouted. "Where do you guys think you're going?"

Rick pointed to his army uniform. "We weren't involved in that mess. It was the Marines against the British. "You see, we're army and our uniforms are different."

The owner, old Popasan yelled. "They fight, they fight."

Rick yelled back. "You old lying son-of-a-."

The MP threw up his hands. "You better not say it and you best keep quiet."

"Just hear me out. We didn't have anything to do with that fight. I tried to break the damn thing up."

A military police sergeant walked up to Rick. "You three go over there with the rest of the fighters. I don't want to hear anymore talk." He went to Popasan who handed him the pad with the damages written on it. The sergeant looked at the figures, then at the men in the bar. "The way I see it, you guys had a fight here and tore up Popasan's bar. Popasan says there's two hundred and forty dollars worth of damage. In order for Popasan to fix up his joint each one of you will pay him ten dollars in yen."

Rick shouted. "Hey, that's a bunch of shit. We didn't have anything to do with starting this fight. I tried to break the damn thing up." He pointed to the Marines and British soldiers. "Those damn fools did it. I had enough of that fighting in Korea."

The sergeant stared at him. "Whoever don't want to pay Popasan the ten bucks will find his ass in jail, and will probably stay there all the time you're on R& R."

Rick was ready to say something, but Mike grabbed his arm. "Don't argue with him. Let's pay the ten dollars and get out of here."

"Wait Mike, that ain't the point. This is one time we didn't do anything wrong. We got to stick up for what is right."

"Yeah, I know what you mean. But look at it this way. If we go to jail for ten bucks we'll probably have to wait a few days till we go to court. Let's pay the money. Think of all the fights you started and never got blamed."

Rick laughed, "You're right." They got in line behind the British and the Marines. As they went out the door Popasan had his hand out and took the ten dollars.

When the Marines reached the sidewalk they mingled with the British soldiers. They were talking, and laughing. One of the Marines shook the hand of a British soldier. "You guys are all right. We didn't mean what we said about the old girl. She's a nice lady."

"We know, and we apologize for saying the things we said about Babe Ruth and Eisenhower. It was a jolly fight and we enjoyed the go."

Everyone was laughing and putting their arms on each other's shoulders. The English invited the Marines to a party. Rick, Mike and Zug started to walk away. A British soldier ran up to them. "Hey, Yanks, you're invited too."

Rick looked at Mike and Zug. "What do you guys think?"

Mike nodded his head. "Might as well. We don't have any other place to go. What about it Zug?"

"Count me in."

Talking to the Marines and British soldiers on the way to the party, Mike found out their units were only about thirty miles from them in Korea. They exchanged stories about the waves of men the enemy were throwing at them. They too, couldn't understand how the enemy could take so many causalities and keep sending more men.

They entered a large hotel and heard British soldiers singing songs from their homeland. The Marines, Rick, Mike and Zug sat down with their new friends. Large mugs and pitchers of beer were brought to the table. A British soldier raised his drink and yelled. "Here's to the Yanks. We had a go with them and it was a good one." A loud clunking noise and the mugs were brought to their mouths.

Rick took a mouth full of the beer. He made a face and swallowed. The British saw the look and shouted, "What's the matter, Yank?"

Rick shook his head. "That beer is warm as piss."

They laughed. "That's the way we drink it."

Even though the Americans didn't like the warm beer at first, it didn't take long for them to adjust to it. Mike watched Rick drink one mug full after another. "What you looking at?" Said Rick.

Mike pointed to the mugs. "I guess you adapted to the situation."

Rick smiled and raised the mug. He shouted to the Marines. "We adapted to the situation." They all raised their mugs. Some knew what he meant, the others didn't care.

After a few more drinks, Rick, Mike and Zug shook hands with their new friends and left. They walked down the business section of the city. Zug pointed to a large department store. "Hey, man, we ought to get some civilian rags."

Rick nodded his head. "You, know Zug that is the first sane thing I ever heard come out of your mouth."

"What you talking about? What about *Skokiaan?* Man, you keep putting me down and I'll never play that song again."

"You're right Zug. I'm sorry."

When they came out of the store they had on new pants, shirts, and jackets. Rick sang, "I feel like a million bucks!" Every window he passed he'd stop, look at his reflection and comb his hair and say, "Man, you sure are a good looking son of a gun in civilian clothes. I'm going to have to beat the broads off me." The people passing him on the sidewalk laughed at him. He didn't care. He tipped his comb, smiled, and winked at them. They smiled back at him. They walked into a beautiful park with well-kept grass and large trees. They sat on a bench and watched the people go by. Every time a pretty girl passed, Rick would wave and say, "Look beautiful, I got my best on, let's go out on the town."

They'd blush and say. "Sorry, no speekie."

Rick looked disgusted. "Man, I got to do something about this language barrier."

The three of them sat and enjoyed the peaceful park. A man came by pulling a rickshaw with a man and woman. There was a small hill and the man struggled to get up it. The rickshaw gained speed going down the decline and the guy coasted with his legs suspended in the air till the rickshaw slowed down. When his feet came back to the ground he pulled again. Mike and Zug were amazed when they saw this. Rick didn't say anything. Mike said. "Man, that fellow pulling that cart has to be in excellent shape."

Rick was concerned. "I don't know about being in shape. How would you like to get up every day and have to do that shit?"

Zug shrugged his shoulders. "Man, if that's his bag let him do it. It puts three squares on his table every day."

Rick's voice grew serious, and louder. He felt sorry for the man who had to pull the rickshaw. "I'm telling you guys, this government shouldn't allow this. These poor guys are working their asses off. It's not fair."

Mike stood up. "Come on Zug, Let's go, the next thing he'll be out in the street trying to organize a union for them."

Zug looked at Rick. "Hey, man, why don't you tell him to adapt to the situation."

Rick didn't laugh. He followed Mike and Zug about ten feet behind. He stared at the little guys pulling the big carts. As they started to exit the park another rickshaw came by and an older man was straining to pull two fat men up a hill. Rick glared at them. They passed a bottle of wine to each other. Both were drunk. One was yelling at the old man and pretending he was hitting him with a whip. Rick yelled. "You, fat sons-of-bitches." He ran to the rickshaw. The surprised old man looked at him. Rick handed him a handful of Yen. The old man let go of one of the poles to put the money in his pocket. Rick got between the poles and released the old man's hand on the other pole. He gently pushed the old man clear and now he was in control of the rickshaw. "I just want to help you, for a little while, pop."

The old man was shouting in Japanese. Mike saw what was happening. "Oh, no." He ran after Rick and the rickshaw. "Rick, what the hell is the matter with you? Are you crazy? Stop this."

"Hell no, I'm not crazy, I'm going to give these fat bastards a good ride."

The rickshaw was now going downhill. Rick could feel it gaining speed. The fat guys screamed and cussed in a language Rick didn't understand. Mike was running next to the rickshaw and pleaded for Rick to stop it. The speed of the rickshaw increased and Rick's legs couldn't keep up. He jumped up and his feet left the ground and now he was dangling from the poles. The weight from the two fat men were sending him higher. He shouted, "Mike, grab it I'm losing it." Mike couldn't reach the pole in time and Rick started going higher. Rick shouted, "Screw it." And let go. The two parallel poles shot up and went over the rickshaw. The two fat guys were slammed to the street on the back of their heads.

The empty rickshaw continued to roll upside down into a grassy area and the old man chased it. When it stopped he quickly grabbed it and ran off. The two fat guys got up from the pavement rubbing their heads. They both cussed, and pulled out curved knives and pointed them at Rick. Rick saw them coming. He looked on the ground for a weapon. "Mike, find me a rock or a stick."

Mike grabbed him. "Oh, no, were getting out of here. He pushed Rick. "Now run you damn fool. No more fighting."

They ran to the business district and looked back. The fat guys weren't following. Rick leaned over with his hands on his knees breathing hard. Mike yelled, "Why did you do that? Are you crazy? What is the matter with you?"

Rick was still trying to catch his breath, he glanced at Mike. "I really don't know other than I felt sorry for the old man straining to pull those fat slobs up that hill. I couldn't take seeing them fat ass drunks making fun of him."

Mike was mad. "Don't you understand, that's how that man makes his living. You almost broke up his rickshaw."

"Yeah, Mike, you're right. I screwed up again. But at the time I thought I was helping the guy. Hell, those fat bastards were drunk and making fun of him. They should of never put their big asses in his cart. The old guy could hardly pull all their weight and they didn't care."

Zug smiled. "Man, you should of seen those fat cat's eyes when you hijacked their rickshaw. Man, that was a scene when it did a somersault."

Mike shouted at Zug. "You think that stuff is funny? I don't. You don't know what he's going to do next. We've only been here for a short time and already we've been involved in a big fight, and now this. Man, I want to enjoy the few days we got left over here. I don't need any more trouble."

Rick didn't say anything for awhile. "I'm sorry Mike, I won't do anything wrong again, I promise."

Mike waved his hand and shook his head. "I heard that so many times before."

"No, Mike, I mean it this time. A guy could come up and punch me in the face and I would walk away. You're right, we only got a few days. It will be peaceful, I promise."

"I know you too well Rick you can't leave well enough alone." He looked at Zug. "Do you believe him?"

"Hell, no, I don't believe him."

Rick got mad. "Why do you want to say something like that for?"

"Because you're the best liar, and con man I ever met."

Mike started walking and Rick was right behind. "Where you going Mike?"

"I'm going back to camp. I've had enough excitement for today."

"Back to camp, are you out of your mind? What the hell is back there?"

"There's a nice quiet bed and I heard they have a good U.S.O show tonight."

"Aw, come on Mike. I gave you my word. There aint going to be any more problems."

Mike didn't answer He hailed a cab. Rick looked at Zug. "What do you think?"

"I heard those U.S.O. shows are pretty good. Let's go back with Mike."

All three went back to camp.

The show had good comedians and they enjoyed it. Rick said to Mike. "I told you there wouldn't be any more trouble out of me. You're my best friend Mike. If I promise something, I mean it."

"Like Zug said. You're the biggest con man I ever met, or ever will meet. I never saw a man lie with such an innocent look. You must of really practiced to get that good."

Rick tried to keep a straight face but he busted out laughing. "You know, Mike, you got me all wrong. I don't try to get in trouble. It just comes to me. I can't help it."

"Well, I'll tell you something. When that trouble comes to you, let me know because I had my fill of it, and I don't want to be around it."

186

Chapter 17
Zug brings the house down

The next day they made their plans. Zug talked to some soldiers who were stationed at Camp Drake and they told him about a nice nightclub on the Ginza in the heart of the city. They explained it had great entertainment, but was expensive. They never saw any trouble there.

Rick pulled out his wad of Yen. "Look at this, we're rich, let's go. There's no place to spend this stuff in Korea."

Mike agreed. He might behave in a rich place. There's less chance to get in a fight in a place like that. They waved down a cab and told the driver to take them to Club Elegant on the Ginza. The Ginza was crowded. Cars were bumper to bumper. It seemed like everyone was blowing their car horns. People lined the sidewalks. Large neon signs flashed on and off. Rick pointed at one. A large ball worked its way to the top of a high sign. Then lights exploded in all directions. It looked like a sky rocket. The ball went down and repeated its upward course.

Rick shouted, "That's the place. Club Elegant. It sure looks like a classy joint." The driver pulled up in front and Mike threw him some Yen. The driver's eyes got wide and he bowed his head and said something in Japanese.

They entered through large stained glass doors where a beautiful lady in an evening dress collected the cover charge. Another girl, just as pretty, escorted them over a thick red carpet to a table. One wall was covered by a lighted stained glass picture of men on white horses. The bar was round and made out of clear glass. Goldfish swam inside. It rotated like a slow moving merry-go-round. On top was a bandstand. On each side was a giant sized dance floor with two more bandstands. The three of them sat wide-eyed. Zug smiled. "I'll take this over the positions." Rick and Mike laughed.

An attractive waitress came to the table wearing a beautiful formal dress. Rick tried to convince Mike and Zug not to drink beer here in this classy place. Mike and Zug both shook their heads. Mike said to Rick. "Now, there you go, trying to con us. Let's drink beer. There's less chance for trouble. Let's have a good time."

"Okay, you guys win. Beer it will be."

Zug pointed at a group of young women dressed in beautiful gowns. "Man what a scene that is. I think I'll get one of those fine chicks to come over here and pour my beer."

Mike cautioned him. "Zug, you better find out how much that will cost. The prices in here are probably high. Let's wait till we find out before inviting them to our table."

A group of men in black tuxedos took their places in the bandstand above the bar. As the bandstand rotated, they played slow classical music. The drinks were expensive but worth every penny being in this magnificent place with the nice music. After ten songs the band came down, and another band started at one of the bandstands on the dance floor. The men were dressed in open necked shirts and sport jackets. Their first song was jazz. Zug's eyes got big. He tapped the table with the beat and shouted. "All right, let it flow."

Mike asked. "Are they any good Zug?"

"They're pretty good but they're playing right off the sheet. If you're going to play jazz you throw the sheet away and ad-lib, then you get with it, baby. Go wherever the music takes you."

Rick wasn't paying attention to Mike and Zug's conversation. He was fascinated by a man in a tux holding a gold cigarette lighter. Every time someone put a cigarette to his lips, the guy would run to that table and light it for them. Mike noticed Rick laughing. "What's so funny?"

He pointed at the guy with the cigarette lighter. "Watch that guy. Man, he's really quick. I haven't seen anyone put a cigarette to their mouth and light it themselves. Watch him run to the tables with that lighter." The man in the tux stood straight as a pin and his head was going back and forth looking for a cigarette to light. He spotted a man taking a cigarette out of the pack. He ran, lit it and ran back to his observation spot. Some woman on the far side of the room started to put a cigarette to her lips. The guy in the tux got to her before she lit her lighter.

The three of them couldn't believe how fast he was. Zug said, "He looks like a spider going for a bug. That cat is quick."

Mike laughed. "I don't believe anyone in here could light his own cigarette."

Zug smiled. Yea, I know what you mean. He's a fast cat."

Rick motioned for the hostess who had a tray of cigarettes draped over her shoulders. She came to the table and he bought a pack.

Mike asked. "Why did you buy those cigarettes? You don't smoke."

"I always wanted to and this is a good time to start." He unraveled the cellophane and tore open the pack. He looked out the side of his eye and saw the guy in the tux had spotted him. He slowly pulled out a cigarette then quickly put it between his lips and grabbed a box of matches. Before he could light the match, the flame of the lighter touched the tip of his cigarette. Rick puffed and it was lit. The man bowed, Rick nodded and thanked him. The man walked back to his spot. Rick quickly smashed his cigarette in the ashtray and put another one in his lips. He went to strike a match and the guy beat him with the lighter. He bowed again and started to walk away all the time looking over his shoulder. Rick quickly smashed out the second cigarette. He grabbed another cigarette, lit a match and raised the cigarette to his mouth.

The guy in the tux dove with the lit lighter in front of him. He pushed it to the cigarette before Rick could get the match to it. The guy laughed and whispered, "Fuck you, Joe. I'm faster"

Rick laughed. "Hey I like that." He handed the guy some money." The guy patted Rick on the back and thanked him. Rick asked, "Hey, man, where did you learn such good English?"

"I used to be a house boy for the G.I's till I took this chicken shit job."

Rick was breaking up laughing. "Hey, what's the chance for my friend here to play the sax in the band?"

"He any fuck'in good?"

"Yeah, he's number one."

He stared at Rick and shook his head. "You mean he's number fuck'in, itchie bonn, number one. What the hell you guys fuck'in, farm boys?"

Rick got serious. "What do you mean farm boys?"

"You guys on R&R from Korea?"

"Yeah we're on R&R"

"Well, that's what they call you over here. You don't know what the fuck is happening. You get shit faced and throw money all over the place. You had me fooled wearing those civies. The guys stationed over here wear their civilian clothes all the time. Not like you farm boys."

"Okay, let's skip the bullshit. Can you get my friend up in that bandstand so he can play?"

"Don't worry, Joe. I can handle it."

That name Joe hit a sensitive nerve with Rick. He started to tell the guy but he'd already left and was walking to the bandstand

The band played a few more songs and the guy in the tux came back. "The bandleader said for your friend to come up and talk with him."

Zug walked across the dance floor and shook the bandleader's hand. The guys at the table couldn't tell what they were talking about, but felt good when the leader walked over to one of the band members and spoke with him. The man stood up and handed Zug his sax. Zug sort of bowed and shook the man's hand. Zug took the man's chair. He studied the horn and fingered the movable parts.

The band begun playing Night Train. Zug moved his head with the rhythm of the song and played from the music sheet like the other band members. Rick yelled to Mike. "Old Zug, wants to get with it, but those guys are just playing off the music sheet." Rick jumped up.

Mike shouted at him. "Don't do anything nuts or I'm leaving. You promised."

Rick went to the middle of the dance floor clapped, and shouted. "Go, Zug, go. Go, Zug, go."

The customers were mostly Japanese and they stared at Rick. Mike felt uncomfortable but there was nothing he could do. Rick kept it up, only louder. Zug's, body was swaying, his foot was thumping the floor. The sax was rocking back and forth. He couldn't take it any longer. He jumped up, threw his head back and arched his back. He wasn't playing off the music sheet anymore. The guy who lights cigarettes ran next to Rick and started clapping and yelling, Go, Zug go. Go, Zug, go."

Zug could feel the momentum building up inside him. He walked out onto the dance floor and let the music come out of the horn naturally. The other members of the band were wide-eyed and being influenced. They stood up and swayed with the music. Zug felt that wonderful feeling he used to get back home when he played at jam sessions. This sensation had every part of his body radiating rhythm. The band was backing him up with their instruments, encouraging him. The people at the tables were no longer sitting. They were on their feet, swaying, clapping and chanting. "Go, Zug, go. Go, Zug, go"

Zug was gyrating now. He dropped to his knees and bent backwards till the back of his head touched the floor. Everyone in the place stood and cheered.

Zug jumped up and pranced to the bandstand all the time playing. He motioned for another sax man to give him his horn. The man handed him the sax. Zug brought that horn to his lips and now was playing two horns at once. The music was coming out of those horns fast and furious. The customers stared in disbelief. All the hostess girls moved to the edge of the dance floor to get a better look at this amazing performer.

He strutted in front of the girls and motioned for one of them to put her hands on his hips. She did. The other girls got the idea and they formed a snake dance. He wove in and out of the tables encouraging people to hook on. They did. When Zug leaned right the whole line leaned right. When he leaned left they did the same. They were caught up in the rhythm and Zug led them to the back of the room, then onto the dance floor. When he passed the band-stand he handed one of the horns back. Every person in line was laughing, and enjoying themselves. They cheered for him to continue. He lead them once more through the tables and back onto the dance floor. He stopped playing and the line broke apart. Everyone gathered around him. He lifted the sax above his head and shouted. "I'm going to get with it now, baby. I'll blow you right to the ceiling." He brought the sax back to his lips. His cheeks blew up like balloons, his eyes bulged and his face turned red. The music blared out of that sax and the people loved it. They never heard Night Train played that way. The band stopped and let Zug play solo He didn't miss a beat. The band again joined in and the song ended. A hostess girl brought him a towel. He thanked her and wiped his face and head. He shouted. "Wow, I love it." He took a bow and everyone cheered. He took the sax back to the man who loaned it to him. He thanked him and the man shook his hand.

The people were still standing on the dance floor. They began shouting. "More Zug. More Zug. The band leader grabbed Zug's arm and talked him into playing again. It didn't take too much talking. The sax was handed back to Zug. The people on the dance floor and the ones at the tables responded with a loud cheer.

Zug talked to the bandleader and was handed the microphone. The room became very quiet. "Ladies and Gentlemen, thank you for being so kind to me. I want to thank the man who loaned me his sax, the bandleader, and the rest of the fellows. I would like to dedicate a song to a friend of mine and those two soldiers sitting at that table. He pointed at Mike and Rick. As you probably already know, we're American soldiers who have been in Korea. A great friend

191

of ours was not as lucky as us. He didn't make it." He looked up and said. "This is for you Hillbilly. We miss you."

People looked at each other and whispered. The ones who understood English explained what Zug had said. Zug looked at Mike and Rick. "The four of us got close over the past months and as strange as it may seem, this is our theme song-Skokiaan. I hope wherever you're at Hillbilly you enjoy it."

Rick tried to say something but he choked up. He turned away from Mike and wiped his eyes on his shirt sleeve. Mike didn't say anything. He looked down at the table.

Zug stood and took a deep breath, and began to play Skokiaan. The band slowly accompanied him. Zug picked up the tempo. The people started chanting, "Go, Zug go."

He got caught up in the song and wanted it to be the best he ever played. He put the sax down and reached over and grabbed the clarinet from the man next to him and continued to play the song. He was determined and tears streamed down his face. The people were amazed seeing him play the clarinet perfectly. They cheered and clapped louder. They knew he was doing this for his friend. He played the trumpet, and then the piano. The more he played the more intense he became.

He pointed at the drummer who got up and Zug grabbed the sticks and took his place. Zug threw his head back in an attempt to stop the tears. He shook his head a couple times and took a deep breath. The sticks hit the drums and the beat was perfect. Again, the band let him solo. People left their seats and crowded in front of the bandstand to get a better look at this young American perform. Every time Zug changed instruments the band leader encouraged the people to cheer.

Rick wormed his way to the front of the crowd. He shouted. "Take them where they never been." Zug nodded. He played the rest of the instruments and worked his way back to the sax where he finished. The people cheered. The hostess brought him another towel. He thanked her, wiped off his face and handed it back to her. Zug smiled and bowed.

The band leader put his arm around Zug's shoulder and shook his hand. "I have never seen a man do what you did. I'm proud to have met you. Someday we'll be reading about you." The other members of the band walked up and shook Zug's hand. Everyone on the dance floor continued to applaud. Zug walked back to the table. People patted him on the back and shook his hand.

They spoke in Japanese and he didn't understand, but he knew it was praise from their expressions and smiles.

Rick reached across the table and shook Zug's hand. "I knew you were good, Zug, but seeing you tonight was something else. You got real talent. Where did you learn how to play all those instruments?"

"Oh, I picked it up along the way. Man, that sure felt good. After all those bad scenes in Korea it built up in me. It had to come out. I feel great."

Mike nodded. "You ought to. You are great Zug. I just wish I could play just one instrument like you. That was unbelievable."

The waitress came to the table and pointed at Zug. "G.I. you number one, itch-boon, honcho. She was going to say something else but she saw a stocky man walking toward the table. She quickly stepped aside. The man asked if he could sit down. They nodded and he sat and extended his hand to them. He said his name in Japanese and it was a long one. He laughed when he saw the expressions on the three soldiers' faces. "Don't worry about the long name. My friends call me, Mike."

Rick said. "I'm Rick, and that's Mike and Zug. The man pointed to Mike. "Hey, I'm Mike also."

The man spoke to Zug. "I'm the owner of this night club. I have had a lot of entertainers perform here, but you are the best. I never saw my customers act this way before. I want to thank you for giving us a fine treat."

Zug smiled and shook his head. "Oh no, the pleasure was mine. It felt so good to get back with it, after these past few months. I really appreciate the opportunity."

The waitress was still standing next to the table and Rick started to order. The owner put up his hand. "Bring us the best champagne and it's on me." She bowed her head and walked away.

Rick got everyone's attention. "I have to straighten something out. Beings as we have two Mikes, from now on were going to call you Owner Mike." He pointed at Mike. "You're just going to be Mike."

The owner looked at Mike. "Is that all right with you Mike?"

Mike laughed. "Sure it's all right with me."

Owner Mike asked Zug if he was stationed at Camp Drake. Zug explained they were from Korea and were on R&R.

"That's too bad. I was hoping we could see more of you, we really liked the way you play. You are a gifted man. Now listen, Zug. Any time you are in the area, you are welcome to play. Anything you or friends want is free. Do you understand? It is very rare when we see someone with so much talent." Zug said he understood and thanked him.

The waitress came back with the champagne and the owner motioned for her to come next to him. He whispered, she giggled and left. In a short time she came back accompanied with three beautiful hostesses. Owner Mike motioned for them to get chairs and sit next to the men. Rick eyed them, and shouted, "All right." He jumped up and helped them bring the chairs to the table. Each girl sat next to a soldier.

Owner Mike looked at Zug. "Would you play some more tonight? The people and I would appreciate it. Most of them are staying in hopes you perform again."

Rick looked at the girls. "Sure, he'll play. Won't you Zug?"

Zug had a concerned look. "Hey man, wait a minute. I don't want to put the cat out in the cold with the sax. He was nice enough to loan it to me once."

Owner Mike talked to one of the hostesses. She left the table. When she came back she was carrying a musical case. She handed it to Zug. Owner Mike said, "Open it Zug, I think it will solve the sax problem."

Zug opened it and his eyes widened. There was a new gold shiny saxophone inside. He slowly took it out. "Man, this is some piece." He held it up in admiration. "Man this is beautiful. Yes sir, this is a piece. It would be a privilege to play this horn."

People who saw him with the horn started chanting. "Go, Zug, go."

Waitresses were bringing drinks to the table. Rick looked at Owner Mike. "Hey, where are all these drinks coming from?"

The owner pointed to the people sitting at the surrounding tables. "They are buying them. Your friend Zug has made many friends for you guys."

Zug, Rick and Mike stood up and raised their drinks. The people at the tables raised their drinks. The three drank and the people did the same, then cheered. Zug walked to the bandstand with the sax. The band stopped playing and clapped. He raised the shiny sax over his head and golden rays reflected from the spotlights. The people again gathered in front of the bandstand.

Owner Mike, looked at Rick and Mike. "It's too bad we have to have wars and men have to die. So much talent destroyed." Mike and Rick both nodded.

Zug was playing again and all eyes were on him. Owner Mike smiled. "Usually at this time of night the crowd is thinning out. Not tonight, Zug knows how to entertain."

Rick said. "Hey you ain't heard nothing yet."

"What do you mean Rick?"

"Well, I'm going to get up there and play the trumpet."

"That's great, go up and tell the bandleader."

Mike didn't know what to think. He watched Rick walk to the bandstand.

Owner Mike looked at Mike. "How good is he on the trumpet?"

"I never heard him play. He never mentioned he could play a musical instrument. I really don't put anything pass him. You don't know what he's going to do next."

Rick motioned for the bandleader. "Hey Popasan."

The leader walked over to Rick. "Can I help you?"

Rick pointed at a trumpet player and motioned with his hands. The leader said. "There's no need for that, I speak English." He went to the trumpet player and said something and the man handed him his horn. He came back to Rick and gave him the trumpet and asked what he'd like to play?"

"I would like to start out with Tenderly, if that's all right with you?"

"It's all right with me. Would you like to sit down or would you rather stand in front of the band?"

"I'll stand in front."

Zug saw Rick with the trumpet. Oh, man, what's he up too now. This probably will be the last song we'll be playing in this place. Rick looked real professional. He moved his fingers up and down on the valves and started to tap his foot.

Mike stared at him with the trumpet in his hand. He got that uncomfortable feeling whenever Rick was going to do something crazy. Owner Mike had turned his chair toward the band. His elbows were on his knees and his hands were under his chin, his eyes on Rick. The hostess girls at the table were excited. People at the other tables clapped even though he hadn't played a note.

The band started the song and then lowered the tone so Rick could come in with the trumpet. Rick didn't join in. He turned to the bandleader. "I'm sorry I missed my cue. Will you start from the beginning again."

The director nodded and raised his arms. The band started. Rick got ready to join in. The horn was on his lips. His cheeks were puffed, and his eyes were opened wide. It was his time. He let out a blast that sounded like a semi truck horn. The band director was startled. Owner Mike had just taken a drink. He laughed so hard it sprayed out. Rick made two more loud blasts. The director looked at the audience, shrugged his shoulders and had his palms up. The band stopped playing. Rick walked to the trumpet player and gave back his horn. He took a bow and walked back to the table. Owner Mike stood up and was laughing so hard it looked like he was going to lose his breath. He shook Rick's hand. "You were great. Where did you learn how to play like that?"

"Well, I'll tell you. I learned from the North Koreans. Every time they attacked I got a lesson from their horn blowers. They ain't worth a shit either."

Owner Mike looked at Rick. He never met a guy like him. Everything Rick said or did, he'd laugh. He asked Mike. "Does he act this way all the time? Mike sort of bent his head to the side, opened his eyes wide and nodded. Owner Mike laughed again.

People kept sending drinks to the table. Mike looked at the owner. "I think we better slow up on the drinking. We have to find a place to stay tonight."

"Hey Mike, don't worry. Like the G.I's say, no sweat. I got a hotel in back of the club. You guys are my guests."

"If we stay, we pay. You've been great to us and we don't want to take advantage of you."

Owner Mike threw up his hands. "No way, you guys made my customers happy and that makes me happy. And when my customers are happy they make me money. You guys are my guests and can stay here all the time you're on R&R." He winked. "Now, maybe if you stay here, Zug will play again."

Mike laughed. "What about Rick, can he play the trumpet?"

"Sure, I have no problem with that." He looked over at Rick and started laughing. Rick was using the cigarette guy for an interpreter to talk to the hostess. Owner Mike leaned over to hear the conversation. Rick said something to the cigarette guy and he shook his head.

"Hey man, you don't want to say something like that. She'll get pissed off at me."

"It's all right, she'll understand."

196

The guy hesitated then whispered to the girl."

She pointed at Rick and shouted. "Skibbie Honcho."

Owner Mike heard this and laughed so hard he almost fell out of his chair.

Mike asked, "What does Skibbie Honcho mean?"

Owner Mike finally stopped laughing. "It means he's a number one sex maniac."

Mike yelled to Rick. "You promised, and see what you're doing. You're going to embarrass us."

Rick shrugged his shoulders and squinted. Owner Mike saw the way Rick looked and started laughing again. "You are something, Rick."

Mike smiled. "Yes, you don't know what he's going to do next. He told Owner Mike some of the stunts Rick pulled in basic training. Then about the big fight between the marines and British soldiers and also the rickshaw. "Zug, and I try to keep him out of trouble but it's impossible."

Owner Mike was fascinated by Rick. He never saw anyone act this way. He shouted over the music to him. "Hey, Skibbie Honcho, how would you like to go for a rickshaw ride?"

"Yeah I'll go if you get one with a motor on it. You can call me Skibbie Honcho. I like that name. Skibbie Honcho, yeah"

The hostess girl next to Rick put her hand over her mouth and blushed The cigarette lighter guy looked serious. The owner laughed, then both the hostess and the cigarette lighter guy busted out laughing.

There was an intermission and Zug came back. Everyone at the table stood up and congratulated him. Owner Mike said. "Men, I'm sorry in all this fun I failed to introduce you. Mike this is Mitzko." Mike stood up and nodded. The owner looked at the girl and said something in Japanese and the only thing Mike understood was his name. She bowed and smiled. Owner Mike looked at Rick and started to laugh. "Rick this is Kimeko." He looked at Kimeko and spoke in Japanese. Rick assumed he was introducing her to him. They both smiled at each other.

Rick pointed to himself. "Rick, Number one Skibbie." Owner Mike and Kimeko shook their heads. He introduced Zug to Susie.

Rick pointed to the young guy dressed in the tux. "Owner Mike, what's this guy's name? He's great."

"His name is Jimmiesan." Jimmiesan stood and they shook his hand.

After the introductions Rick reached across the table and shook Owner Mike's hand. "Mister, you don't know how much me and my friends appreciate how you are treating us. I have never been this happy in all my life."

Owner Mike looked at him strangely. "You don't really mean that do you Rick?"

"Yes I do. I mean every word. When I'm done over there in the frozen chosen, I think I'll come over here and go in business with you."

Owner Mike smiled. "I would like to have you Rick."

Mike threw up his hands. "Hey wait a minute, you don't know what you're getting into. You don't know him like Zug and I do. Right, Zug?"

"Damn straight. That cat is from a different planet."

Again Owner Mike erupted into laughter. The drinks kept coming, Zug went back to playing. Rick took Kimiko to the dance floor and danced very close.

Mike saw Jimmiesan smiling watching Rick dancing. "What do you think he's saying to her Jimmiesan?"

He laughed out loud. "I know what he's saying is no good."

Customers started to leave. Zug came back to the table. He grabbed his drink and raised it to the men in the band. "To some great cats who know how to wail." Everyone at the table raised their glasses. The men in the band waved and smiled.

Rick asked Zug. "What are we going to do later?"

"Well, I was talking to the guys in the band and I told them about jam sessions after the bars closed in the States. They thought it would be cool to do it here tonight. It'll probably last all night. Did you guys have something else in mind?"

Rick pointed at the three girls. "Yea, I think we could have more fun with them than listening to music all night."

Zug looked at the girls and sort of nodded. "I see what you mean, but man, I gotta go with the session."

"Are, you crazy? You can blow that damn horn anytime. You can't have women like this every day." Rick tried to convince him to cancel the jam session and stay with the girls.

Mike threw up his hands. "Hold it. We're on R&R. Let Zug do what he wants to do. If you remember, he didn't interfere with you when you pulled that rickshaw." Rick shook his head, and looked disgusted.

Owner Mike stood up. "Men, I have to bid my customers farewell. Like they say in the army, I got to hit the sack." He called the three girls to him and talked to them in Japanese. He looked back at Mike, Rick, and Zug. I told them you guys were welcomed to stay all night and drink anything you want, and listen to the jam session. Is that what you call it Zug?" Zug nodded. "I believe my band will learn a lot tonight. When you get tired, the girls and Jimmiesan will show you to your rooms. In the morning go to the kitchen. The cooks will make you breakfast."

The three got up and shook his hand. Mike pulled out his wallet as did Rick and Zug. Owner Mike shouted. "You are my guests. If you try to pay me, I'll be insulted. I have only known you for a short time. I feel like you have been my friends for a long time. So from now on, my friends, I do not wish to hear anything about money." He waved and went to the door where his customers were leaving.

Rick looked at Jimmiesan. "What's the chances of getting these broads into bed?"

"Chances are no good. These girls not whores. They are hostess girls only. You can try but I don't think it will happen."

Rick turned to Kimeko. "Well, Babysan, what do you think? Is there going to be any action tonight?"

She couldn't understand English but she could sense what he was up to. She blushed and put her hand over her mouth. Mike overheard the conversation. "Knock it off, Rick. You heard what Jimmiesan said."

Rick looked back at the girl. "Oh, if only you could speak English. There wouldn't be any problem. You could tell me what you want to do."

Mike warned him again.

"Aw, Mike, what's the matter with you? Owner Mike said we were his guests and to enjoy ourselves. He even gave us a room."

"I realize that, but he didn't say to shack up with his hostess girls. Jimmiesan told you they were hostess girls and not prostitutes."

The argument continued till Jimmiesan interrupted. He looked at Rick. "Listen Joe, I know a good time house in Yokohama, it's a sure thing and no one will get in trouble. The girls there are just what you're looking for."

Rick got serious. Jimmiesan, I have a name and it's Rick. Will you please call me that?"

"Sure, Rick, no problem."

The customers left. Jimmiesan went behind the bar and brought back a fifth of whiskey. He unscrewed the cap and filled their glasses. He explained about the good-time house in Yokohama. Mike was a little leery. "You know Rick, we had a lot to drink. Yokohama is pretty far away and it's getting late."

"Aw, Hell, come on. It won't be no time and we'll be there, right Jimmiesan?"

"Yes, it won't take long. Train very fast." Mike didn't say anything, he shrugged his shoulders. Rick again asked. "Well, are you going to come?"

"Why don't we stay here and listen to Zug and the band play?"

"I heard enough music. I don't know what the hell goes with these broads. You try to talk to them and they giggle. I might grab one by the ass and see what she does."

"Hold it, Rick, you've been drinking pretty heavy and this isn't the place to try something like that. The owner of this place treated us good and I don't want any problems. Do you hear me?"

"I understand what you're saying, but in a few days we're going to be back in that hole. If we stay here, I know there's going to be trouble. I got to get the hell out of here." He gave Jimmiesan some money and told him to get a couple bottles of whiskey and to leave the money on the back bar. Jimmiesan came back with the bottles. "Come on Jimmiesan, let's make it to Yokohama. See you in a couple of days, Mike."

Mike watched him stagger to the door. The girls said. "Ricksan, sayonara?"

Mike looked at Zug in the bandstand then to Mitzko. She looked concerned, like, what happened? Mike stared at the beautiful girl. Maybe Rick was right. This girl seems innocent and with the drinking and the room something might happen that I'll feel bad about later. He hated to leave but got up and went to the bandstand. "Zug, I'm leaving. Rick was feeling good when he left. He's got two bottles of whiskey. They'll be a problem for sure. Will you tell Mitzko what happened and I'm sorry?"

"Sure thing, Mike, I'll get the message to her. I'll be here when you guys get back."

When Mike walked to the door he waved at Mitzko and she slowly waved at him till he went out. He saw Rick and Jimmiesan in the distance. He yelled for them to wait. The three walked to the train station. Rick handed Jimmiesan a handful of Yen and in a short time he returned with the tickets.

The train announcer shouted in Japanese over the P.A. system. Mike asked Jimmiesan what he said. Jimmiesan told him the train for Yokohama would be arriving in a couple of minutes. A white light pierced the darkness. The train screeched to a stop next to the platform. The doors slid open and people rushed in. The guys took a seat on a long padded bench. Another bench was directly across from them and people quickly sat down. Rick asked Jimmiesan how to say good morning in Japanese. He told him Ohio-go-za-ne-ma.

Rick looked at the people across from him and smiled. He nodded and said "Ohio-go-za-ne-ma." The people all bowed, smiled and said the same thing. Rick nudged Jimmiesan. "Give me one of those bottles."

Jimmiesan reached inside his coat and reluctantly brought it out. Rick grabbed it. The passengers across the aisle became silent, their eyes opened wide. Rick unscrewed the cap and took a big drink. He pulled the bottle from his lips and exhaled saying. "Ha, ha, hot." He rubbed his stomach and said, "Good." An old man smiled and stared at the bottle. Rick grinned at him. He knew what the old man wanted. He held the bottle up and the old man nodded several times. "What's the matter Popasan you got the bends and you need some medicine?" He offered the bottle to him. The old man snatched the bottle and put it to his lips. His head leaned back and large bubbles shot up in the bottle as whiskey drained from it. Rick grabbed the bottle. "Damn, Popasan, hold up. Rick examined the bottle and saw how much was gone. Everyone laughed. "If I give you another drink Popasan, I'm going to put a nipple on it."

Mike wasn't aware what Rick was doing. He saw him standing in the middle of the aisle with the whiskey bottle. "Aw, Rick put that away."

Rick came back and sat next to Mike. "Don't worry, Mike, we won't get in any trouble. Don't be scared."

Mike asked Jimmiesan. "What happens if you get caught drinking that stuff on the train?"

"I don't know. I never saw it done before."

Rick shouted. "Don't worry about it Mike. If old Hillbilly was here, you know he would be putting it away. Shit we'll be back in that hell hole in a few days and maybe we won't ever have the chance to drink any more. If Hillbilly was here. He'd be having a ball. Come on, let's have a good time for him."

Mike thought back to Korea. He saw Hillbilly smiling. Then he was lying on the ground with that terrible wound to his face. He grabbed the bottle from Rick and took a big drink. He brought the bottle down, and remembered Hillbilly's body lying motionless on the ground with his field jacket covering his face. He raised the bottle again and took another drink. When he brought the bottle back down he shut his eyes and shook his head. Mike started raising the bottle to his lips again. Rick knew Mike never drank this way and that something was bothering him. "Hey Mike, let me have that bottle." He took the bottle and Mike just looked at the floor. Rick handed the bottle to Jimmiesan. "Hey, Mike, shake it man, we're going to have a ball. Come on let's have fun."

Jimmiesan took a drink and passed it back. The old man across the aisle clapped, and put out his hand. Rick looked at Jimmiesan. "Hey, how do you say little."

"Skoshie."

Rick got up and walked to the old man. He pointed at the bottle. "Skoshie, skoshie." Rick formed a small space between his fingers and thumb. "Skoshie." He handed him the bottle. The old man didn't hesitate. He grabbed the bottle and chugged the whiskey. "Hey, Popasan, I said skoshie. Skoshie, what the hell's the matter with you?" Rick grabbed it before he emptied it. Rick examined the bottle and saw how much the old man drank. He shook his finger at the old guy. "I said skoshie, you take too much. No more for you." The old man smiled and rubbed his stomach. Rick looked at him. "Wait till Momasan finds out you've been tipping the bottle. She'll kick your ass."

Everyone laughed. Rich heard the announcer talk in Japanese and the only word he understood was Yokohama. "Hey Jimmiesan, what did he say?"

"He said, next stop is Yokohama. That's where we get off."

Rick elbowed Mike and told him they're getting off pretty soon. Mike was in a stupor and didn't answer. The three of them got off the train and everyone who was in their car waved at them through the windows. Jimmiesan, and Rick waved back. Mike kept walking. The streets were jammed with bars. Rick looked in the windows and couldn't believe all the women inside. He wanted to go in every one of them but Jimmiesan told him to keep going, the place he was taking them to was better.

Rick was concerned about Mike. "Hey, Mike forget about that shit in Korea. We're here and everything is going to be happy times." He took out the other bottle. Mike didn't hesitate. He grabbed it and drank. He brought the bottle down, took a deep breath and immediately brought it back to his mouth.

Rick grabbed the bottle. "Mike take it easy. You're drinking too fast. Slow down. Jimmiesan is taking us to a nice place. We're going to have a good time. Don't get crazy."

Jimmiesan tapped Rick on the shoulder. "The place we're going doesn't sell alcohol and if you want some we should buy it before we go to the good-time house." Rick agreed and Jimmiesan led them down a narrow side street. The buildings were small and made of raw wood. Rick tried to talk to Mike but the drinking got the best of him. He thought he should have never mentioned Hillbilly. He tried to cheer him up but Mike was in a trance and his eyes were watering. Rick felt the best thing to do was leave him alone.

"Jimmiesan, here's some money. I'll stay here with Mike. You go get the whiskey."

Mike didn't say anything. He awkwardly pulled out a roll of Yen and handed it to Jimmiesan.

"Hey, toxsan money, Mike, Too much." He handed it to Rick. Rick took a couple of bills and gave it to Jimmiesan. He then sunk the wad deep in Mike's pocket. He watched Jimmiesan disappear into the darkness then reappeared under a light He knocked on a door. Someone slid it open and Jimmiesan walked in.

Twenty minutes passed and Jimmiesan didn't come out. Rick was concerned. He heard a lot of yelling in Japanese and the door slid open. A large man hurled Jimmiesan into the street. Jimmiesan didn't move and the door slid shut. Rick ran to Jimmiesan. His eye was swollen and his lips were bleeding. Rick shook him a couple of times and Jimmiesan looked at him. Rick lifted him to his feet. "Are you all right? What happened in there?"

"Honcho, is a slickie. He charged me too much, I complain. He mean, man. He punch me and tell me to leave. I start out the door with the bottles. A soldier grab bottle. I pull away and Honcho grab me and punch again. He push me out the door and say. You come back, I kill you. I still hang onto bottles."

"We'll fix that rotten son-of-a-bitch."

"No Rick. Bad people in there. Like gangsters in States. No one to fool with. Many soldiers drunk in there."

Rick took Jimmiesan back to Mike. "You stay with him. I'll be right back."

"Rick, best we leave. Too many bad people. You get hurt."

203

Mike scowled and started to follow Rick. "You're going to mess me up Mike. Let me check out the place and we'll go back together and kick hell out of them."

Rick slid the door open a crack and peeked in. He could hear laughing in another room. There were many combat boots neatly lined on the floor. Silently, he went inside and took off a bed sheet that was protecting a davenport. He stretched it out on the floor and quietly placed the combat boots on it. He noticed these were not ordinary combat boots like he had in Korea. These were Airborne boots. He grabbed the four corners of the sheet and pulled up forming a large sack with the boots inside. He looked like Santa Claus with the sack draped over his shoulder when he went out the door. Jimmiesan and Mike watched him struggling with the large sack. Rick dropped it in front of them. Jimmiesan shouted. "Man, those are paratroopers boots. Them guys are tough. You better put them back."

"Hell, no, we're going to do something with them. Give me one of those bottles." He opened it and took a drink. He spit it out and looked at the label. "This piss is wine. That no good bastard switched bottles on you."

Mike took a drink and smiled. "That-a-boy Mike. You like that wine. That's good, now let's have a good time."

Mike awkwardly picked up the sheet with the combat boots in it. They walked for about fifty yards and were going over a bridge. Mike didn't hesitate, he threw the sheet full of boots over the side. All three looked down and saw the boots floating on the water being carried away by the current. Jimmiesan screamed. "Let me out of here. Them paratroopers will kill you."

Rick grabbed Mike's arm. "Come on, let's get the hell out of here. If those paratroopers see their boots traveling down the river, there'll be a riot."

Mike slurred. "Let them come I'm ready."

Rick convinced him there wasn't going to be a fight and they had to go with Jimmiesan. They caught up with Jimmiesan who was about a hundred yards ahead. His head was sticking out of an alley watching them. "Hey Rick, I'm never going back to that place. Man there is going to be a real problem when those paratroopers find out their boots are gone."

"Serves that son-of-a-bitch slick-bastard right. He'll think twice before he cheats and beats up somebody."

Mike continued to drink the wine. Jimmiesan warned Rick. "Mike, maybe drinking too much. Trouble come sure as hell."

"Don't worry about it. Mike is a big boy. He can take care of himself."
He tapped Mike on the shoulder. "Ain't that right, Mike?" Mike didn't answer.
His eyes were almost closed and he was staggering. "Maybe you're right
Jimmiesan." He took the bottle from Mike and put it back in the bag. "Come
on, Jimmiesan get us to the place."

Jimmiesan pointed. "There it is. Pretty nice, huh?"

Rick nodded. "Not bad, not bad at all."

Jimmiesan knocked on the door. A man's voice spoke in Japanese, and
Jimmiesan answered. The door slid open and they walked in. The man directed
them to a room and pointed to some chairs. He said something to Jimmiesan
and left the room. Rick and Jimmiesan sat down. Mike stood. Rick said, "Come
on Mike sit down. Get comfortable. This is the place where we're going to have
fun."

Mike acted like he didn't hear him. Rick took a bottle out of the bag and
took a big swig. "Come on Mike this will cheer you up. Drink and get that
bullshit about Korea out of your head." Mike took the bottle. His expression
didn't change. Rick did everything possible to change Mike's mood. He yelled.
"Hey Popasan, pass those whores in review." Mike, wouldn't Captain Thimp be
proud of his two fighting machines in a whore house?" Mike didn't smile.

Jimmiesan put his finger to his lips. "Hey Rick, not so loud. Hold it
down." Rick ignored him. He looked at the walls in the room. They were made
out of grass and plaster.

"You know Mike, I heard how good of a football player you are. I
would have liked to of seen you play. Man, you must of been fast and powerful.
Shit, I bet if you wanted to, you could run right through that wall."

Mike smiled. He bent over and put his hands on his knees like a
halfback. He mumbled some numbers as if a quarterback was calling signals.
When he got to five he put his head down and ran. He hit the wall at full speed.
A large hole exploded and pieces of plaster showered the room. A woman
screamed and a soldier shouted from the room, "What the fuck is going on."

Another crunching noise and the other wall in the bedroom came down.
Jimmiesan shouted, "Man, I'm getting out of here."

Rick laughed. "Come on back, Jimmiesan, the party's just beginning."

"No way, I don't want no more trouble." He ran out the door.

Rick walked through the holes. A soldier was quickly putting on his
clothes. A Japanese girl with a startled look was covering herself with a

blanket. Rick walked through the second hole and into the next room. A soldier and a girl were lying on their backs with a sheet up around their necks. Rick asked. "Did you see Superman?" Neither one said a word. They just stared, wide eyed.

Rick could hear other walls being knocked down and people yelling. He followed the holes in the bedrooms. One soldier yelled. "We better get the hell out of here. Some damn fool is diving through the walls."

Rick walked through the holes counting as he went. There were eight walls with gaping holes in them. The last hole led into a hallway. Rick could hear banging metal hitting the floor. He followed the noise and saw plaster all over the hallway floor. The wall had a huge hole. Rick looked in and it was the kitchen. Pots and pans were strewn all over the floor. Mike was in it fighting three guys. Rick grabbed the one on Mike's back and threw him to the floor. Mike screamed. "Hurry Rick get the gun working or we'll be overrun."

"No Mike, snap out of it. We're not in Korea. Stop fighting. We got to get out of here."

A group of Japanese Police officers came through the hole. Mike saw them and shouted. "Rick, shoot, shoot. We don't want to die here. Fire Rick, fire."

Rick saw Mike was rushing toward the police. He tried to hold him, but it was no use. One of the police saw Mike coming at him. He raised his large stick. Mike grabbed it and pulled it away from him and aimed it like it was a rifle at the policeman. Other police surrounded Mike and swarmed on top of him. Rick pulled them off. "Let him go. I can handle him." The police didn't understand and they again jumped on Mike. Rick grabbed them by the necks and pulled them off. Rick felt a thump to his head and everything went black.

A cool feeling to his head and Mike regained consciousness. He slowly opened his eyes. Sharp pain made him blink a couple of times. A Japanese girl was putting a damp cloth on his head. His eyes explored the surroundings. The walls and floor were concrete. Bars were over the windows. He looked at the girl but she didn't smile. She kept putting the cool wet cloth on his head. "Where am I?"

"You're in the congokoo."

He sat up and took a better look at the room. "Oh, wow, I'm in jail." He tried to get up but the pain was too intense. He rubbed his head and felt bumps.

He tried to think but nothing seemed to register. The only thing he knew was, he's in jail and in pain.

The girl pointed and said. "Your comadotchie." (friend) Mike looked over at Rick who was sleeping on the floor with his back against the wall. He staggered to him.

"Rick, wake up." He shook his shoulder. "Rick, Rick, wake up we're in some trouble."

Rick's head wobbled and his eyes opened. "We're just in a little trouble. We tore up a whore house, and fought half the police department."

"We did what?"

"Don't you remember getting blind-ass drunk and running through those bedroom walls in that whore house, and all those people yelling and running for their clothes?"

"Oh, no, I don't remember doing that. Are you sure, Rick?"

Rick sat up and reached into Mike's hair. He showed him a piece of plaster. Mike quickly ran his hand through his hair and found more pieces. "Oh, we're in a mess."

"Yeah, I guess we are. Do you remember when the Japanese police came and you thought they were North Koreans trying to overrun us and had a big fight with them?"

Mike sat next to him on the floor and looked up at the ceiling. "How we going to get out of this trouble? Are they holding us for the MPs?"

"Hell, I don't know. I've never been in a Japanese jail. Do you remember those paratroopers boots?"

"Paratroopers boots? What about the paratroopers boots?"

"Well, you threw them in the river and they floated away. I imagine right about now there are some unhappy paratroopers."

"Don't tell me anymore. I never want to drink again."

The girl who had been rubbing Mike's head with the damp cloth came over and knelt in front of him. She sat back on her legs and stared at him and then smiled. "You look like my Joe who went back to Chosen and never come back no more."

Rick looked at her. "Who is she Mike? What the hell is she talking about?"

"Some soldier must of came over here on R&R and jilted her."

Her voice quivered and tears came to her eyes. "No way, not my Joe. My Joe get killed in Chosen." Rick was going to say something but Mike told him to listen to her. They watched her reach into her pocket and pull out a worn, pig-eared photograph. She handed it to Mike. "My Joe - he no more." Mike looked at the picture and Rick leaned over his shoulder so he could see. The photo was of an American soldier dressed in fatigues with his helmet on. On the back was written. Killed in action.

Mike slowly handed it back to her. "I'm sorry." She pulled another picture from her pocket. It was of a beautiful little girl with features of Japanese and American.

She pointed at the picture of the soldier. "He is daddy. He was my Joe."

Mike handed the picture of the little girl to Rick who studied it and didn't say anything, then handed it back to her. Mike asked. "Were you married to this soldier?"

"No, he stay with me when he on R&R. Two R&R times. When babysan come he send money. He try to stay in army and come to Japan to work so we can get married and have good time. No come, my Joe get killed."

Mike asked. "How do you support yourself and the baby?"

"What you mean support?"

Mike thought a minute than asked. "How do you make money for you and the baby to eat?"

She took a deep breath and slowly let it out. She stared at Mike for a moment. "Many times, no eat. Sometimes I do bad things to get money."

"What you mean bad things? What do you do bad?"

She hesitated then said. "Bar girl, slickey Joes when they get drunk."

Mike looked at Rick. "What does she mean?"

Rick blurted out. "She's a whore who rolls drunks."

"Naw, you're wrong Rick. I don't think she's like that."

"Then what the hell is she doing locked up in this jail?"

She nodded. "It is true what he say. It is very hard to make money when baby Joesan is half Japanese and half American." She bowed and took out the pictures again. Tears streamed down her cheeks.

Mike shook his head and squinted. He saw how worn the picture of the dead soldier was and though She must of held that picture many times. It's got to be rough having to work the streets and having a small child. Her face shows signs of toughness but she seems to be a nice girl caught up in a terrible situation. I feel sorry for her but I don't know how to help her.

The three sat in silence till she put her hand on Mike's cheek. "I am sorry but you look like my Joe." Her hand dropped into her lap and she bowed. She turned to the side trying to hide the tears. Mike looked at Rick and Rick just shrugged his shoulders.

Mike patted her on the back. "Don't worry, something will happen that will make your life better." He reached for words to cheer her up but couldn't think of anything to say. He felt helpless. He glanced at Rick for help. Rick looked at the ceiling and slowly shook his head. "What did you do to get arrested?"

"I was working the street and had a problem. The man called the Montesans. (police).

Mike stood up and wanted to say more. He felt awkward. He jammed his hands into his pockets and felt the roll of Yen. He pulled it out and dropped to one knee next to the girl. He grabbed her hand and put the money in it and wrapped her fingers around it.

She looked at the money. "I can no take." She tried to put it back in Mike's hand.

"I will be insulted if you don't take this money. It will make me happy if you buy food and clothes for yourself and your baby. I'll just buy drinks and get in more trouble. I want you to have it."

She put the money in the lap of her dress. Another wad of Yen dropped into her lap. Mike looked up. Rick was walking away. "Don't say anything. I was there myself. I know what she's going through and I don't want to talk about it." The girl hugged Mike and kissed him on the cheek. She wanted to do the same to Rick but he put up his hands.

"Save it for another Joe."

She bowed and said. "Do mo ar ga to. " (thank you) "Mike what does that mean?"

A voice behind them said through the bars. "She said, "Thank you very much." He was a policeman. He opened the door and motioned for them to come out.

They looked at the girl and she waved. "You good G. I's ." They waved back at her and left with the policeman.

Mike asked the policeman. "Sir, what do you think is going to happen to us?"

"Don't know. You will find out very soon." They entered the court room.

"Rick, no matter what happens, don't get wise in here."

"You don't have to worry about that. I went through this before."

The policeman pointed to a spot in front of a highly polished wooden railing where a judge looked down at them from an elevated desk. He was an older man with a decorated gown and a triangular hat. The policeman who escorted them into the courtroom carried on an extended conversation with the older man. Mike and Rick strained their ears trying to hear what they were talking about. They made out a couple of words like Yen, and do mo ar ga to. Every once in awhile the older man would nod his head and say, "Ah, so."

They stopped talking and the judge looked down at Rick. "What were you doing in that place?"

Rick started to say something but Mike quickly answered. "Sir, we're here from Korea. They gave us some time to get away from that terrible war going on. We drank more then we should. We were completely wrong for what we did. We are sorry for what happened."

The judge looked down at some papers on his desk. He looked up. "Do either of you know that woman who was in the room with you?"

Mike and Rick shook their heads. Mike said, "No, Sir, we never saw her before we were placed in that room."

"Why did you give her all your money?"

Mike grimaced, hesitated, then said. "Sir, she and her baby need the money more than we do."

The policeman again started talking Japanese to the older man who listened to every word the policeman said. Silence again. Mike and Rick expected the judge was going to turn them over to the Military Police. The judge spoke again. "Are you going to get drunk and act that way again?"

They immediately shook their heads and said. "No Sir."

"You men be careful when you get back to Korea. I'm taking you for your word. You may leave."

Mike looked at Rick and they just stood there. The Judge pointed to a door. "You may leave."

They slowly turned and walked a few steps, then almost broke into a run. When they got closer to the door they saw Jimmiesan sitting in one of the seats in the back. They didn't acknowledge him and kept going for the door. Once outside, Rick yelled, "Run Mike, I think that judge made a mistake. Let's get as far away from here as we can."

Jimmiesan chased them. "Hey, Mike, Rick wait up." About two blocks away from the courthouse they stopped and waited for Jimmiesan. "It's okay you guys, you don't have to run."

They looked behind him to see if any police were following. Mike asked Jimmiesan, "What happened back there? I thought we were going to jail. What was that policeman and the judge talking about."

Jimmiesan caught his breath. "How did you two become such good friends with that montesan?" Mike and Rick looked puzzled. "That man spoke good of you two. He said that you gave all your money to a down and out woman. He also said the whore house you wrecked was nothing but a trouble place. The judge liked what the montesan said and he let you go."

Jimmiesan reassured them they didn't have anything to worry about. Mike put his hand in his pocket and remembered he gave all his money to the woman. "Hey, how are we going to get back to Tokyo I don't have any money."

"You're right, Mike. We don't have any money."

Jimmiesan asked what happened to all their money.

Rick shrugged his shoulders. She needs it worse then we do."

"You mean to say you guys gave her all your money? You didn't keep any for yourselves? Shit, I know now why they call you guys farm boys." He reached in his pocket and pulled out some Yen. "This is what I have left after that guy punched me. It's enough to get train tickets."

On the way to the train station they passed the place where Jimmiesan got beat up. Rick pointed at it. "Hey Jimmiesan, Want to go in and get even with the guy who worked you over?"

"Hell, no. If you start something I'm running again. I don't want any part of that place." They got on the train and sat on the bench seat. Most of the passengers were Japanese. A group of American soldiers got on and sat across from Mike, Rick, and Jimmiesan. They noticed the patch on the soldiers' caps. Mike said. "They're Airborne."

"I know. Look what they're wearing for shoes."

Mike and Jimmiesan looked and the paratroopers were wearing shower shoes instead of shiny jump boots. Jimmiesan got up and took a seat in the front of the next car.

One of the paratroopers saw Rick looking at the shower shoes. "What the fuck you gawking at?"

Mike felt the tension. He tried to warn Rick not to say anything. It was too late. Rick was standing over the paratrooper. "Yes, I've got something to say. "I'm Lieutenant Miller from the Hundred and Ninth Military Police. Don't let these civilian clothes fool you." He pointed to the shower shoes. "Why are you out of uniform? Where are your boots? You are a disgrace to your outfit. Look at these people staring at you. I've got a good notion to contact the Military Police in Tokyo and have them wait for this train and show them how you look. Explain yourself, soldier."

The soldier got to his feet, as did the rest of the group and came to attention. "Sir, there is an explanation."

Rick glared into his eyes. "Let's hear it."

He stuttered for a moment. "Sir, we stayed overnight in a hotel and didn't know it was run by a crook." He hesitated.

"Go ahead soldier."

"Well Sir, some slick stole our boots."

"Stole your boots? Soldier, you know how important your boots are. Sometimes they're as important as your weapon. Do you understand what I'm saying?"

The paratrooper's face was red. "Yes, Sir, I'm very aware of that."

"You let a damn slick steal your boots in a cat house and you didn't do anything to get them back?"

"We didn't get our boots back but we got even. That thief will never do it again. As soon as we get back to camp we'll buy new boots."

Mike got up and whispered in Rick's ear. "That's enough. If these guys get wise to you there will be hell to pay."

Rick came to attention. "Yes Sir." He looked back at the paratroopers. "When you get back to camp the first thing you do is get reissue slips for new shoes. Do you hear me?"

"Yes, Sir,"

Rick smartly turned around and sat next to Mike. The paratroopers sat and tried not to make eye contact with them. Jimmiesan stared from the other car. He saw everything was quiet. He made his way back and sat next to Mike. He whispered. "Mike, how did Rick get this way? Was he always crazy, or did combat make him this way?"

"He's been like that from the first time I met him in the States."

The wheels screeched and the train came to a halt in Tokyo. The aisles immediately filled with people getting ready to exit. The paratroopers were the first at the door waiting for it to open. Mike laughed when he heard one of them complaining. "Get your damn boots stolen and some chicken shit lieutenant gives us a sermon. If I knew I could get away with it, I'd knock him on his ass." The door slid opened and the people poured out. The paratroopers went one way and Mike, Rick and Jimmiesan went the other. When they were about twenty five yards apart Rick stopped and turned around. He cupped his hands around him mouth. He started to yell something to the paratroopers. Mike quickly put his hand over Rick's mouth and muffled what he was yelling.

Rick shook away from Mike. "What's the matter with you, Mike?"

"I'm wise to you. I don't want any more trouble. I knew you were going to yell something smart and get them mad."

"Don't worry about it, Mike. It will be fun to see their faces when I tell them I'm not an officer. If they get mad, we'll run. They're wearing those shower shoes and won't be able to catch us."

"I said don't do it."

They wandered the streets of Tokyo trying to think of a way to get money. Rick's eyes focused on an American flag across the street. He crossed and looked at a bronze plaque that read. The Embassy Of The United States. He pointed at the plaque and waved for Mike and Jimmiesan to come over. They crossed the street to him. "Look here you guys. The Ambassador is in that building. He ought to be good for a couple of bucks. Come on. Let's go see him."

Mike shook his head. "No, I think I'll pass on that."

"Suit yourself, I'm going in to see the guy."

Mike couldn't believe the way Rick walked up to the American Marine standing in front of the door. Rick talked a short time and went inside. Jimmiesan said. "Mike, should we wait or walk?"

"We'll wait. Let's see what happens."

Time passed and the two paced the sidewalk with their hands in their pockets staring at the front door. "Jimmiesan, I sure hope he doesn't do anything nuts. They'd court martial him for sure if he messed up in there."

"Don't worry about it till that Marine guard runs inside." Mike gave a sigh of relief when he saw Rick strut out the front door. He said something to the guard and the guard laughed. Rick walked up to Mike and Jimmiesan waving a handful of money.

He slapped the money in his hand and yelled. "Here we go again. Let's celebrate."

Mike stared at the money. "How did you get it?"

"Well, I told him what happened back in Yokohama. I said there was an American in jail and I had to use all the money I had to get him out."

"And who did you say that American was?"

Rick looked concerned. "Well, I couldn't think of a name and the ambassador was staring at me. So I gave him your name."

"You gave him my name? Are you crazy? Why would you do that? What if he has someone go to that jail and check their records and they find out what we did?"

"He kept asking questions and your name was the only one I could think of."

Mike clenched his fist. "Why you damn fool. I ought to punch you out."

"Now, wait a minute. There's a lot of guys with the same name as you. Hell, I knew at least twenty guys with the name Mike Ryan. Besides he didn't write anything down." Rick knew Mike was mad. Mike turned and walked away. Rick caught up with him pushing money into Mike's hand. "Come on, Mike, take this money. He probably already forgot your name. I told you he didn't write it down. The guy was a nice man."

Mike pushed Rick's hand and walked away. Rick looked at Jimmiesan and winked. "He's a good guy and he'll only stay mad for a short time. He's my best friend. You watch Jimmiesan before we get another mile he'll be talking to me and everything will be all right."

"Mike is a good man, Rick. I would give him a lot of time to cool off. He can fight and I sure would hate to have him mad at me." The two of them followed Mike at a safe distance.

Back in the downtown section of Tokyo, Mike was still walking in front of Jimmiesan and Rick. He hadn't said a word to either of them. Rick ran up to him. "Aw, come on Mike everything turned out all right. We helped that girl with the baby. We didn't have to stay in jail and they didn't report us to the MP's. We got money again, let's enjoy ourselves." Mike still didn't say anything. Rick continued to follow him closely all the time telling him how sorry he was that he used his name.

"I'm going back to Camp Drake and watch movies, and see the USO shows. I'm staying there till it's time to go back to Korea. I've had enough of this trouble. Everywhere we go there's a problem."

"Yeah, you're right. We'll go back to Camp Drake and watch movies and go to the USO shows. We'll stay out of trouble that way. You're my best friend. If it wasn't for you I'd be serving time in jail. You saved me so many times I will never be able to repay you."

Mike stopped and stared at Rick's eyes. "Don't go giving me that bullshit. It's not going to work this time. I heard enough of it."

"Yeah, you're right. I never treated you like a friend. I always got in trouble even when I promised. That's no way for a friend to treat a buddy. The only thing I can say is I'm sorry."

Mike turned and started walking again only not as fast. Rick sensed Mike was starting to cool off. He turned to Jimmiesan, and smiled and winked. "Hey, Mike, before we go back we better stop at the club and see how Zug is doing. He might want to come back with us." Mike didn't answer. It's only a short distance from here."

Mike stopped. "How far is it Jimmiesan?"

"It's about four blocks."

"Okay, we'll talk with Zug and see what he wants to do." He turned and continued to walk in front of Rick and Jimmiesan.

Rick looked at Jimmiesan and opened his eyes wide, nodded yes and smiled. "He'll be all right. We're not going back to no army camp."

Jimmiesan directed them down the Ginza and when they saw the club, there was a long line waiting to get in. Jimmiesan squinted. "I wonder what's going on?" They walked to the front of the line where the girl collecting cover charge was standing. She recognized them and waved them through. Jimmiesan asked. "What's going on?"

"Zug, GI very good with sax. Many people want to hear him."

215

Inside, they saw Zug playing in the band and he was enjoying every minute of it. Rick said to Mike. "Let's stay till Zug goes on break. Mike agreed. "Mike, let's get the same table we had the other night. We had a lot of fun there." Again, Mike agreed.

They sat down and immediately a waitress came to take their order. Two of the hostesses waved at them. They waved back and Rick looked at Mike. "You know we should have stayed here instead of going to that cat house." Mike glared at him but didn't say anything.

At intermission Zug came to the table. "Well, did you studs go and sow your wild oats?" They didn't answer. "Man, that must of been some cat house the way you guys look. They took the wind out of your sails." Again they didn't answer. "Hey you guys, you can lay it on old Zug. You're my friends. Give me the happenings." He stared at them.

Rick blurted out. "We tore up a whore house and got thrown in jail."

Zug busted out laughing, grabbed a chair and sat facing Rick. "You tore up a cat house and they jailed you? What about you Jimmiesan?"

"No sir, I ran when that mess started up."

Zug kept asking questions and Rick filled him in on the whole thing. He looked at Mike. "Man, what did those cats do who were working out with their broads? That sure would of scared hell out of me, if I was in a room with a squeeze and some dude crashed out the wall with his head and then got on the bed and dove through another wall. Man, that is a crazy scene."

Mike shrugged his shoulders.

"You sure that was you diving through those walls and not Rick? Man, I can see him doing something crazy like that, but not you."

"Yes, it was me, and I'm not proud of it." Zug laughed. "How's it going Zug?" Asked Mike We're on our way back to Camp Drake. We wanted to check with you before we went back."

"Man, everything is cool here. I think I'm in heaven. These cats catch on pretty quick and we're making some way out sounds. I never been so happy in all my life. These people have been great to me. I'm going to stay till it's time to go back to Korea."

Mike looked at Rick. "Well, are you going back to Camp Drake with me or do you want to stay here?"

Before Rick could answer, the two hostess girls, Mitzko and Kimeko walked up to the table. They bowed and smiled. Rick immediately jumped up and pulled two chairs away from the table and motioned for them to sit. "I'm never going to leave you beautiful Joesans. You're number one. Skibby honcho has returned."

Both girls put their hands over their mouths and blushed. They slowly looked around to see if the people at the other tables heard him. Both were attractive in their beautiful formals. Mitzko stared at Mike with her dark eyes. He looked at her and thought, She's the most attractive girl I ever met. She makes me feel good being around her. No girl ever made me feel this way. I know I don't want to go back to Camp. I want to be with her the rest of my time. Even though they are not talking, he could feel what this girl was thinking through her dark eyes. He sensed she was understanding him also. Slowly she took his hand and squeezed it. He put his other hand on top of hers. She felt so soft. Everything about her was right and peaceful.

Kimeko stood up and started to walk away. Rick asked, "Hey, where you going?"

She turned and said, "Comadotchie." Then walked to the office door.

Rick asked Jimmiesan. "What did she say? Where is she going?"

"She's going to get your friend, Owner Mike."

She walked inside of the office and in a few minutes she came out and Owner Mike was right behind her. When he got to the table he quickly pulled a chair up and sat next to Rick. He was laughing already and Rick hadn't said a word. "Did you have a good time in Yokohama? What did you do there Rick?"

"We went to the museum and then to the zoo. Later we went to the opera. We had an educational time."

Owner Mike stared. "Oh, that's great. They have a nice museum in Yokohama."

Jimmiesan broke out laughing. Owner Mike started laughing too. He realized Rick was not telling the truth. "Come on, tell me what you guys really did?"

"Okay, you want the truth? We got in a mess in a skibby house. We met the montesans. We went to the kongoku and then met a judge."

Owner Mike laughed so hard he almost fell out of his chair. When he got control he coaxed Rick for the details. Rick looked at Mike and he didn't say anything. Rick explained how Mike got drunk and dove through the whorehouse walls and people were running out of the rooms trying to put their clothes on. Mike's face was red. He was embarrassed till he saw Owner Mike hit his knee and start to laugh again. Owner Mike motioned to a waitress. "Bring us drinks. My friends are back."

Mike put up his hands. "Please, skip me for drinks. I had my fill of that stuff for awhile. I never want to act that way again."

"Don't worry, Mike. I have the hotel in the back. Like I told you the other night, after you're done having a good time here, just walk back there and go to sleep."

The waitresses came with drinks and food. Rick threw money on the table. Owner Mike became serious. "Like I said the other night, you don't pay for nothing. Look at this crowd your friend Zug has brought into my club. I have never seen so much business." He pushed the money back to Rick. "Look at all these people, Rick."

Rick saw the people and then turned back to Owner Mike. "Well thanks for being a nice guy. I didn't meet too many in my life."

Rick took Kimeko's hand and went to the dance floor. He looked at her and said. "Gosh, I missed you. You were on my mind all the time I was gone. Your skibby honcho is back."

She giggled and said. "Koddie, koddie pie."

He laughed out loud. "Hey, that means crazy. I'm getting pretty good at Japanese." He dropped his head on her shoulder and held her tight and continued to whisper in her ear. She smiled and enjoyed it.

Mitzko watched every move Mike made as he talked with Owner Mike. Owner Mike said Mitzko was very concerned when he left with Rick and Jimmiesan. Mike looked at her, felt the hot blood rush to his face and knew he was blushing. He told Owner Mike she was very beautiful and he had a lot of respect for her. He and Rick feared if they had stayed around and kept drinking, something would of happened between them and the girls.

"Don't worry about that, Mike. These girls are very nice and they are attending college. They would not do anything like that, I can assure you."

Mike felt very uncomfortable talking about Mitzko when she was sitting next to him. He stood up and grabbed her hand. "Excuse us, Owner Mike. I would like to dance with Mitzko."

"Go ahead, Mike, enjoy yourself."

The music was slow and soft. He put his arms around her and she pulled him close. He sensed through her actions she was telling him something even though she didn't say anything. He looked down into her sparkling dark eyes that were radiating messages no words could say. They continued to dance and gaze into each others' eyes. He felt love and peace. He wished the night would never end. It will only be a few more days and he'll be in the mist of killing and maiming again. A cold chill ran through his body. Hillbilly's face flashed in his head. He shuddered and pulled Mitzko closer. She sensed something was wrong and grabbed his hand and led him back to the table. She told Jimmiesan what happened. He went to Rick on the dance floor. Rick hurried to the table and recognized the look on Mike's face. He went to the bandstand and motioned for Zug to come to him. Zug came over and Rick explained what happened. He asked him to play Far Away In Africa. Zug didn't tell him the name of the song was Skokiaan like he normally did. He said he'd do it right away.

Zug tapped Mike on the back. "I want to dedicate this song to a real jerk. The jerk liked this song when I played it for him back in the States, and I'm sure he would like to hear it tonight. This is for you, Captain Thimp.

The song started and Rick put his arm over Mike's shoulder. "Remember when we played that song back in those mountains and the captain thought those companies found us. That chicken shit son-of-bitch crapped his pants."

Mike smiled. "Yeah, those were the happy times. We didn't realize it back then. We had Hillbilly with us. Those days are gone. We'll never have fun like that again."

Rick reminded him of other funny things that happened. Mike started reminiscing and told stories and laughed. Mitzko smiled again. She took Mike's hands into hers and stared into his eyes. "He nodded, "I'm sorry for acting that way." She squeezed his hand.

The rest of the night was happy and peaceful. The club closed and the customers left. Mike, Rick, Zug, Jimmiesan and the girls continued to party with Owner Mike. After a couple of hours Owner Mike stood up. "I'm going to show you guys to your rooms. You can come back here if you like."

Mike shook his head. "No, I'm ready to hit the sack, after the last couple of days. It will feel good to get some peaceful sleep."

Owner Mike looked at Rick and laughed. "Are you ready to settle down for the night, Skibbie boy?"

Rick looked at Kimeko. "What about you, Babysan?"

Mike quickly took over the conversation. "We're tired, aren't we Rick?" He emphasized Rick's name so he would get the message to not say any more. Owner Mike led them down a hall to the hotel. He pointed out rooms for each of them.

Rick asked, "Hey Owner Mike. What about the girls, can they come into the rooms?"

"They're old enough to make that decision. I'm going to bed."

Rick smiled at Kimeko and took her hand and tried to lead her into his room. She hesitated and her face turned red. She didn't know what Rick said to Owner Mike but from his actions she understood his intentions. She slowly withdrew from him and shook her head. Rick tried to persuade her to go inside but she wouldn't go. She quickly kissed him and walked slowly down the hall. Every once in awhile she'd turn and seem like she was going to come back only to turn again and continue to walk. Rick stared at her.

Mike had Mitzko's hand and was looking into her eyes. He slowly bent over and kissed her on the cheek and said. "Good night, pretty girl."

Mitzko stood on her tiptoes and put her arms around Mike's neck and kissed him on the lips. Mike held her tight. They kissed for a long time. She slowly released her arms and looked at him. Mike just stood there. He had never felt this way. He didn't want this girl to ever leave him.

Kimeko was at the end of the hallway shouting Mitzko's name. Mitzko slowly walked backwards away from Mike never losing eye contact. He watched her until she got next to Kimeko and they turned the corner. He stared at the empty hallway, feeling he lost something very valuable.

Mike saw Rick in his room. He had his shirt and pants off and was sitting on the edge of the bed slamming his fist in his hand and yelling. "Shit! another night and we strike out again." Mike laughed at him and went to his room. Long strands of beads were hanging in the doorway to the bedroom. He formed his hands like he was going to dive and separated them. He took his clothes off and dropped in bed. It was a lot softer than the concrete floor he slept on the night before. He listened to Rick cussing in the other room.

Sleep came immediately for Mike but the dark calm was mixed with dreams of home and Korea. The peaceful tranquility was interrupted by a slight noise that only a combat soldier would hear in his sleep. His eyes came open and he lay motionless. His ears strained to hear any noise. The room was quiet again. Then another sound and Mike tried to determine what it was. It sounded like clothing being taken off, then a dull soft noise as if it dropped to the floor. He sat up in the bed and squinted his eyes, but couldn't see anything. The beads in the doorway rattled. He got into a defensive position ready to defend himself. He started to shout for Rick when a soft low voice said. "Mike, Mike." The room was dark and the voice spoke in a whisper but he didn't have trouble identifying that voice.

"Yes Mitzko." He sensed her coming closer. Her hands slid across his shoulders and then wrapped around his neck. She kissed him hard on the lips then forced him onto his back. Mike slid his hands up her warm soft back. Her body smelled like she just bathed.

She pulled him closer, saying, "Mike, Mike, Mike."

Hot pulsating sensations exploded in his body. Never had he experienced anything like this. All other thoughts left his head. The wonderful feeling of this soft warm loving girl engulfed him. I hope this wonderful feeling will stay with me the rest of my life.

They fell asleep holding each other in a tight embrace. Dawn came and light sneaked in waking them. She kissed him and slowly got up. The beads rattled again when she went into the other room. He raised up and watched as she put her clothes over her small well developed body. He beckoned her to come back to him. She smiled. "Sayonara, Mike." Mike watched her leave and continued to stare at the beads swinging. Why couldn't life always be like last night. To live in a warm world with people loving each other. What a contrast to the cold hatred of war in Korea. It's going to be difficult to go back.

The sun lit up the room and he continued to lay and think of Mitzko till he heard Rick shouting from the other room. "Son-of-a-bitch, I'm going to get me one of those damn books that interprets Japanese. I get a fine looking woman and I ain't getting shit." The beads exploded and Rick entered. "Come on Mike get up." Mike was still thinking of Mitzko and just stared at Rick. "Damn it, You're thinking of that Korean shit again. Get that crap out of your mind. It'll be there when we get back. Now knock it off and have some fun."

"I'm not thinking about Korea. It left my mind."

"Well, hell, don't just lay there. Let's get out of here. "

Mike stayed there with his hands behind his head. Rick jumped on the bed feet first and jumped up and down like it was a trampoline. Mike was bouncing. "Okay, I'm getting up."

"Mike, you get dressed and I'll get Zug up. Now don't go back to sleep."

"I told you I was getting up." Rick waited till he saw Mike out of the bed and started to put his clothes on.

Mike, heard Rick yelling. "Get up, Zug, we've got things to do. Do you hear me Zug? Get your ass out of bed."

"Aw, man come back in a year. I just got in bed. I ain't got time for them scenes you make."

"What you talking about? Get out of bed." "I'm talking about the last time we made that scene with them big broads. We almost went to jail."

"I'm not worried about jail. Now get up. Are you up, Zug?"

"Yeah man, I'm up. Do I have a choice?" Mike watched Rick come through the beads. "Well, Zug wants to go. He's getting dressed."

"Yeah, I heard him. He sounded like he was really excited about it."

The three of them walked through the empty night club and into the restaurant. Owner Mike was sitting with Mitzko, Kimeko, and Susie. He shouted for them to sit at his table. Mike took a chair next to Mitzko. She smiled the same way she did last night. He nodded and tapped her on the back. He thought, she's the prettiest girl I have ever met. Just being close to her makes me feel so good. They ate a delicious breakfast and Owner Mike suggested that the girls take the young soldiers for a walk in the park. He looked at Rick. "I got some tickets for rides in rickshaws. Do you want them?"

"Man, it's too early for your bullshit, Owner Mike. I get enough of that in the army."

Owner Mike laughed out loud. "Just kidding you Rick." He looked at Zug. "You going to come back for tonight? You would disappoint a lot of people if you didn't show up."

"You don't have to worry about that. I'll be here."

The city had a different meaning to Mike now that Mitzko was next to him. Everything seemed so alive and happy. The three couples were laughing and having a good time. On the way to the park there was a group of small stores and they looked in the windows. Rick saw a book store and immediately went in. The rest followed. Rick asked the clerk if he spoke English? The clerk nodded. Rick said, "I want a book that translates Japanese to English."

The man left and returned with four pocket sized books. Rick pointed at them. "Which book has the most swear words?"

The man smiled and shrugged his shoulders. He handed Rick one of the books. "This is a very popular one. I never counted the swear words, though."

Rick bought the book and handed it to Mike. Mike flipped through the pages and read some of the definitions. He gave it to Zug who did the same thing. Both of them bought books.

Entering the park they sat on a wooden bench surrounded by a beautiful landscaped lawn. Everyone pointed at words in the books and tried to express themselves. When Rick picked out a word the girls giggled and blushed. "Hey you guys I'm finally reaching them. Hell, this book is worth a million dollars."

They were laughing and enjoying themselves. A rickshaw passed in front of them. Zug pointed at it. "Hey, Rick, does that scene look familiar to you?"

"Never mind those guys. I got Kimeko and that's all that matters. We only got a couple more days and I'm not wasting them on trouble. Those days are over."

Hearing this Mike shook his head and took Mitzko's hand. They broke from the group and walked down a path lined with flowers and beautiful trees. He pointed to words in the book and made sentences. She acknowledged, she understood and squeezed his arm and looked up at him and smiled. They sat on the soft grass and with the book he learned that Mitzko was from a small town and just recently came to Tokyo to attend college. He watched her manipulate the book and he could tell she was an intelligent girl. She told him he was a very special person. She had never felt this way about a man before. She worried that something bad might happen when he returned to Korea.

Mike quickly shook his head. "No, nothing is going to happen." He grabbed the book and pointed out the words that explained he would be all right. Mitzko looked worried. He thought back to the girl in jail. Her Joe was dead and how terrible her life was with her young child. He stared into Mitzko beautiful face. Wouldn't it be a shame to put this wonderful girl through that. A feeling of guilt came over him. Mitzko sensed something was wrong and she blamed herself for Mike's change. She grabbed the book and fingered through the pages picking out the right words to tell him she was sorry. Mike assured her that she was not at fault. He slowly stood and took her hand and pulled her up. She hugged him hard and kissed him.

Mike held her close then gently broke away. "Sorry Mitzko we must go back." She bowed her head, took his hand and they slowly walked to where the other couples were. Rick was still talking Japanese from the book and everyone was laughing. He looked up at Mike and Mitzko.

"Man this is the greatest thing I have ever got. We should of bought one of these books when we first got here. Mike shook his head and smiled. Rick leaned over and kissed Kimeko on the cheek. "Babysan, I'm going to fill you so full of bullshit you'll think I'm the greatest. I'm going to be irresistible. You won't be able to help yourself."

Kimeko stared at him. "Bullshit? Bullshit? mean?"

Mike said. "Hey, Rick, she wants to know what bullshit means?"

Rick put up his hands and shook his head. "Never mind, she don't want to know."

Zug tapped her on the shoulder. "I'll translate that for you Kimiko."

Rick shouted. "Never mind Zug, you take care of your own business, and I'll take care of mine."

Rick looked at Mike. "Hey man, I've been watching that chick you got there. She's got moon eyes over you. Shit, you don't need a book. You're in like Flynn."

Mike didn't say anything for awhile, then, "Rick, I think we ought to talk about what's happening here."

"There's nothing to talk about. You see I'm a man and she's a good looking woman. I'm going to let East meet West and nature will take its course. We only got a couple more days then we'll be back in that mess over there. I'm going to have a ball with this girl. I advise you to do the same."

Mike continued to stand next to Mitzko. He tried not to think about it and just have fun, but things were bothering him. So much had happened the last few months. It seemed like a million years pressed into one. Things he never dreamed of, killing, wounding, getting shot at. Drinking and now, women. Everything was going so fast it was confusing. A whole new world was being shoved on him. He shook his head and walked away from the group.

Rick saw the look on Mike's face. He got to his feet. "Aw, shit, he's thinking of that damn war. He ran and caught up with him. "Mike, what the hell is going on with you. Straighten up. Forget about that shit."

Mike turned to him. "I'm sorry I don't know what's causing me to act this way. Life used to be easy. But now everything is complicated. I can't figure it out."

"You're thinking too much. Ever since you met that broad you've been acting goofy. I think you're falling for her. Am I right Mike? You got the hots for her?"

"To be truthful, she is something special to me."

"Well then take that special girl and get in bed with her and get the shit out of your system. You got to quit this bullshit."

"No, that girl is not a street walker or someone you just take to bed. She's intelligent and going to college."

"Well take that intelligent girl to bed then forget about her. She wants to get tickled just like you do. Shit, you'll kick yourself in the ass when you get back to that hell-hole and think back for not knocking it out. Some other guy will come along and ring her bell and not blink an eye. Quit all this good time shit and do what comes naturally. Man, adapt to the situation."

"You know Rick, I just wish it was that simple. I keep thinking of that girl that was in jail with us and all the trouble she has. Man, I sure don't want to get this girl into a predicament like that."

They continued to stare at one another. Rick blurted out. "It's not going to happen to us. You know what to do. Hell, I'm not going to worry about it. I never worried about it before and I sure as hell ain't going to start now. We might get back to Korea and some gook could snuff us out and then you'll never have to worry. Hell, who knows, some gook might be carrying the bullet that is going to do you in and is waiting for you to get back. You go and worry about things, but I know what I'm going to do. I'm going to adapt to the situation. And the situation is getting that broad in bed. End of story."

Mike looked at the other people and he felt like a fool. They stared at him. "I'm sorry it won't happen again. He stared at Mitzko and wished he could express himself to her. Why, one minute I have this wonderful warm feeling and the next minute my conscience takes over and I feel guilty. I'm making an ass out of myself in front of my friends. I'm going to get rid of these hang ups and quit wrecking the good times for everybody.

Back at the club Zug was in the bandstand playing. Mike and Mitzko didn't miss a dance. They held each other close and felt the impulses reacting between them. The evening came to an end and Rick took Kimeko out of the club. Mitzko stared at Mike. He stood up and pulled her chair so she could get up. Mike stuttered. "I'm going to bed." Mitzko just stood. Mike didn't know how to explain he wanted her to come to his room. She started to walk away.

He walked with her to her room with intentions of going in. He heard other girls voices inside and knew he couldn't go in with the other girls there. He didn't know how to ask her to come to his room. She looked up at him and they kissed. He slowly walked to his room.

Mike sat on the edge of the bed and tried to figure out what he should have done. He knew his time in Japan was short and wanted Mitzko to be with him all the time. He figured it was an awkward situation tonight and the best thing was to go to sleep. He waited in the dark for the sound of the door and Mitzko would walk through the beads to him. She never came. She must think I'm crazy the way I've been acting. Yet, this afternoon in the park she was happy even after I made a scene. He shook his head. Maybe it's best that it ends this way, even though I love her.

In the morning Mike put his clothes on and went through the empty nightclub out onto the sidewalk. He walked about a half block and he heard Mitzko calling him. He turned around and she ran up to him crying and handed him a note. She bowed her head as Mike read it. He could tell she used the translation book

Mike, I am sorry for coming into your room and doing what I did. I have never did that before but I never felt about a man the way I do about you. I know you have been going through a lot and I am making more problems for you. I am sorry and I hope very much you will be safe in Korea. I will not bother you again. I love you Mike.

Mitzko

She turned and started to walk away. Mike quickly grabbed her by the shoulders and turned her around. He shook his head and pointed at her. "No, no, not your fault Mitzko. It's no one's fault. No one is to blame. This is the way life is and it always will be. We cannot change it no matter how we try. When two people love each other these things happen. It's the way the world is. These emotions are for a purpose and no matter how we try we can't control them." He knew she couldn't understand English but somehow she seemed to. He wiped the tears from her cheeks and kissed her. He stared into her beautiful smiling face. He thought, I'm not confused any more. This is growing up and the part of life that has to be lived. I have a strong feeling for this wonderful girl. No more am I going to think of other things that might upset her or me. What is happening is right.

The remaining days and nights they spent together. They made memories that will never die. No matter what happens.

Chapter 18
Back to Hell

Owner Mike, Mitzko, Kimeko and Susie were waiting at a table in the restaurant. Today was the day the three soldiers had to go back to Korea. Mike, Zug and Rick walked in with somber faces. They sat at the table and the girls had faint smiles. Owner Mike appeared sad. Rick patted him on the back. "What you say skibbie honcho?"

Owner Mike started to laugh, then became serious. "You know my place will never be the same. It feels like I have known you guys for a long time. My friends, I'm going to miss you."

They nodded their heads. Mike put his hand on Owner Mike's shoulder. "We were very fortunate to of met you. I'm sure I can speak for Rick and Zug. After being in hell, we came to heaven meeting you. We will never forget you."

Zug looked at Owner Mike. "Mike pretty well covered it. You made some great scenes. I love this place and I will be thinking of it every day."

Rick just stared at Owner Mike. Owner Mike started laughing. Rick tapped him on the back.

Owner Mike led them to his car. On the way to Camp Drake he kept pointing out things of interest so he could get their minds off of leaving. Mike shouted, "Hey, Owner Mike, that's the park that Rick drove that Rickshaw. I mean crashed it."

Owner Mike laughed. "I don't know what I'm going to laugh at when you leave, Rick."

The MP's stopped the car as it drove up to the gate. Owner Mike told the guys he would follow their bus to the airport when it came out from the camp. That way the girls could be with them a little longer and say good bye. He explained this to the girls in Japanese. Mike squeezed Mitzko's hand as he left the car. The three of them blended in with other soldiers going into camp.

All civilian clothes were off now and was strictly military uniforms. Rick shook his head as he put his civvies back in his bag. "Boy, I wish I could put you back on and never have to take you off again."

Another soldier close by said, "Amen."

After the men returning to Korea were processed they were herded onto a bus. As the bus left the camp Mike saw Owner Mike's car parked on the side of the road. As soon as the bus passed, the car followed. When they approached the airport a master sergeant stood up in the front of the bus. "Men, I want everyone to stay together. The plane might not be at the field and we may have to wait a short time. I don't want anyone to wander off. Am I heard?"

The group acknowledged, "Yes, sir."

Owner Mike and the three girls came up to the guys. "Again guys, we had a good time. I will be looking forward to your return in six months. Please be careful, and good luck. That's all I got to say. I'm sure you want some time with the girls, so good bye." They said good bye and Owner Mike, walked to his car.

Mike took out the translation book and started to leaf through the pages. Mitzko shut the book and put her finger to her lips. She stood on her tip toes and wrapped her arms around his neck and kissed him. Her eyes were watering. "Sayonara, my Mike."

"Sayonara, my Mitzko." They held each other till the master sergeant shouted, "Kiss'em and weep. We got to get the hell out of here."

Mike release his arms from Mitzko and he squeezed her hands. "Good bye, Mitzko."

"Good bye, Mike."

Zug came down the aisle and sat next to Mike who had the window seat. Zug leaned over and looked out to see if he could see the girls. "Hey, Mike look out there. That fool Rick is still with Kimeko."

"I see him and so does the master sergeant." Rick saw the master sergeant coming and he gave Kimeko another kiss. Mike and Zug saw the master sergeant yelling. Rick broke the kiss off and patted Kimeko on the back as she walked away. Rick turned and started walking to the plane. The master sergeant was right behind him, yelling. Rick looked unconcerned He got on the plane and walked down the aisle. Everyone was laughing and joking him for getting chewed out.

He shrugged his shoulders. "Screw you guys." Leroy was sitting by the aisle. Rick looked down at him. "Hey, Fly Boy, I want to be fair with you. I had the window on the way over. You can have it on the way back."

"Aw, goddamn man, you ain't going to start that shit up again. Get your sorry ass next to that damn window."

Rick squeezed in front of him and took the window seat. "Hey, Leroy, did you get your head bad while you were on R&R?"

"Damn straight I did. Man I had a ball. What did you do?"

"Well, I went to the museums, the cathedrals, and the university."

"You shit did."

The plane made a smooth landing and came to a stop. No one jumped up to rush off. The olive drabbed colored trucks were waiting for them. The sky had a dirty gray overcast. The wind was cold. What a contrast to the place they left. Mike wished he was back in Japan with Mitzko. They climbed onto the open bed trucks. No one spoke. Their heads bobbed up and down as the truck made its way on the dusty pot-holed road. Faint sounds of explosions could be heard as they got closer to the positions. The smell of burnt gun powder was in the air. Everyone looked depressed and must have been thinking the same thing. Rick jumped up. "Hot damn, I missed that sound of bombs and guns going off. The sight of millions of gooks running at you blowing their bugles. I missed that. It's great to be back. No place like home."

Leroy shook his head. "Crazy fuck"

The trucks stopped in front of the large Quonset hut and they changed back into fatigues. The sergeant took roll call and everyone was accounted for. Mike looked at the soldier dressed in fatigues and thought, It's now back to team work. No more civilian life where a person can be an individual. It's going to be hard, but I got to work my way out of this mess. They boarded the trucks again and sat on the floor trying to shield themselves from the cold wind and dust. They traveled many miles before the trucks stopped. A sergeant came to the back of the truck. "Okay, men you've gone this route before. We got to hoof it in now. The vacation is over."

Two lines of soldiers on both sides of the road, six feet apart now were walking their way to the positions. Three hours later the large bunker with the holes in the side of the hill came into sight. No one said a word. Mike thought, six more months of hell.

They dropped their packs in the big bunker and immediately relieved the men in the positions. Mike and Rick checked out the equipment. Mike looked up at the hill they attacked before they went on R&R. Hillbilly's disfigured face flashed in his head. I wonder where Hillbilly is now. How did his family take it. When I get back I'm going to visit his family.

Rick noticed Mike looked depressed. Rick crawled from behind the machine gun and went to the sand bags in front of the position. He cupped his hands and shouted. "Hey, you gook sons-of-bitches. The bad asses are back and we're going to kick your asses. Come up this hill, you mealy mouth mother fuckers, let's play King of the Hill."

He got the enemy reply when a volley of bullets hit above showering dirt and rocks down on him and Mike. They dove to the floor of the position and locked their arms over their heads. Mike yelled. "Well you got your answer, you damn fool." They slowly sat up and brushed themselves off.

Leroy yelled. "Hey Jive Ass, Miller, act a fool again and stick your head up so I can get that gook in my sights."

"Give me about ten minutes fly boy and I will."

Sergeant Mitchell yelled. "Knock off the bullshit, Miller. There's a gook sniper out there and he's a good shot. He picked off five guys in the last week. You better stay down."

Rick stood up and was ready to yell back to the sergeant when a bullet grazed the side of his helmet, spun him around and slammed him to the ground. Mike crawled to him. "Rick, Rick are you okay?"

"The-son-of-a-bitch, I hardly had my head exposed and he hit part of my helmet. He took it off and examined the dent and scratch the bullet made. He kissed the scarred helmet. "We got to do something about that bastard." He leaned back and took out his canteen and gulped water. He turned the canteen upside down to indicate it was empty. "Mike give me your canteen. I need a drink. "

"How can you drink more water when you just emptied yours?"

"Never mind, I'm thirsty, give me your canteen."

Mike threw him his canteen and asked. "How can you drink so much water? What are you up too?" Rick didn't answer, he kept drinking the water. After he emptied Mike's canteen he threw it back to him.

Rick rubbed his stomach and said. "We wait for about ten minutes for nature to take its course. Then we'll deal with that sniper."

Mike sat behind the machine gun peering through the sights and scanning the hill for the sniper. "I know he's on the hill but he sure is concealed.

He's probably looking through his scope waiting for one of us to expose ourselves. What do you think Rick."

Rick didn't answer. Mike quickly turned around and saw Rick crawling up to a large protruding boulder on the side of the hill.

Rick shouted, "Hey, Leroy, do you hear me?"

"I hear you Jive Ass. What you gonna do crazy, now?"

"You ready to get that sniper?"

"Yeah, show me the sucker. My gun is loaded."

"Okay, now watch the hill and when you see that son-of-a-bitch shooting, blow his ass away. Tell the other guys to watch for the sniper's flash when he fires."

"Okay, I got you, Jive Ass. Don't get wasted."

"Rick, get back down." Mike yelled. "You're going to get shot."

"Don't worry. I'm going to give that sniper a golden, squirting target. I can guarantee he'll take a shot at it." Rick stood up behind the large rock and dropped his pants and shorts.

Leroy looked at Rick's bare ass. "Boy, I seen some crazy shit, but nothing like this. Hey Jive Ass what you going to do, moon those gooks?"

"Shut up, Leroy. Just watch that hill for a flash. Mike, are you ready?"

"I'm ready. Be careful."

Rick had his hands in front of his groin area and an arched stream of water squirted.

On the enemy hill a North Korean was scanning the American positions with his scope looking for a target. The rifle stopped when he saw the stream of water. He knew from the way the water was squirting where it came from. He aimed as close to the rock as he could in hopes of getting the source of it.

The bullets hit the rock right in front of Rick, shattering fragments of it in all directions. Rick squinted his eyes and managed to keep the stream going. He shouted, "Do you guys see a flash?"

Someone yelled. "He's at one o'clock." Mike saw the flash come from a clump of bushes. He squeezed the trigger and watched the tracers fly to the target. Other machine guns opened up. The clump of bushes where the flash came from was engulfed in a dust cloud.

The machine guns kept firing till Sergeant Mitchell yelled, "Cease fire."

The dust cloud slowly cleared. The clump of bushes was blown away. An enemy soldier was slumped over. His rifle with a scope propped up his motionless body. A loud cheer erupted from the American positions. Rick pulled up his pants and raised his hands in the air like a prize fighter who had just won the championship. He crawled into the foxhole with Mike.

"That was great, Rick We got him because of you. That gook couldn't pass up the target you showed him."

"Like I always said, Mike. You just adapt to the situation."

"Hey, Jive Ass Miller. If you would of stuck out an inch of that thing you were pissing through, that gook would of shot it off. You would of had another belly button."

Everyone laughed and when they quieted down, Rick shouted. "If that had happened, women from all over the world would be crying."

"Jive Ass, you're a dreamer."

The days were getting shorter and colder. The wind kicked up the dust from the treeless hills. The soldiers hunched over with their hands in their pockets. The collars on their coats were turned up and buttoned close to their necks. They hardly talked, it was so cold. The first snow came covering the hills giving them an eerie glow at night. Every morning when the sun came up the Americans scanned the hills in front of them looking for footprints the enemy might have made during the night. Two weeks passed and no sign of the North Koreans. Everyone was fidgety trying to figure out what was going on.

Sergeant Mitchell came to each position and informed them they were going to pull out and head farther north. For some reason the enemy had gone. They had orders and tomorrow morning they'd be furnished transportation to take them to their new destination. Rick looked at Mike. "You know what that means. We're going to be sleeping in those cold ass pup tents. It's going to be colder than shit. If them damn gooks want to let up for awhile let them. They know where we're at. Let the bastards come to us."

Soldiers were stuffing their belonging into packs and bitching. "Man, we were just getting this place comfortable and what the hell do they do? Tell us to pack up. We're going some other place. Hell, I was just getting to like it here."

They continued to complain and Rick was right in the middle of it. In fact, he agitated the ones who weren't. The two and a half ton trucks were parked at the base of the hill with their motors running. Zug took a deep breath. "Man, I love the smell of diesel fuel burning."

Rick tapped him on the shoulder. "Is it because it smells like Marijuana smoke?"

"Man, why you got to be a wise ass?"

They grabbed their packs and rifles and made their way down the hill.

Sergeant Mitchel watched as they got on the trucks.

Mike could tell the sergeant wasn't pleased with the move, either. Rick looked at him. "Hey, Sarge, it's going to be cold not living in that bunker."

"I know. We don't have to worry about that. The gooks will warm it up for us."

The monotonous rumble of the trucks made it hard to talk. Soldiers sat and leaned on their rifles. Dust filtered in from the dirt road. Every once in awhile a soldier jumped up and slapped his clothes making him look like a giant powder puff. The guys sitting next to him waved their hands in front of their faces and shouted, "Knock it off."

The journey continued for a few more hours and one by one the men leaned their heads back on the canvas and dozed. When the truck hit a bump they'd all wake and shake their heads and cuss the driver. The driver, hearing this, intentionally hit more bumps in the road. The cussing from the rear of the truck turned into threats. The driver shouted four-letter words back at them.

Dawn broke and the trucks came to a halt. The soldiers hunched over and jumped from the trucks. As soon as they landed they stretched and yawned. The driver leaned on his forearm and looked out the window, smoking a cigar. A soldier shouted, probably, Rick. "I ought to come up there and pull you out of that cab and kick your ass for driving like that."

The door flew open and the driver was now standing on the running board. He pulled the cigar stub from his mouth and threw it at the soldiers in the back. "Whose ass are you going to kick? Come up here and we'll see how bad you are, big mouth." A lieutenant saw what was going on. He told the driver to move on. The driver slowly got back in, all the time staring at the guys at the rear of the truck. He waited a couple minutes to see if there were any takers then drove off.

After they dug in and had the machine gun set up, Mike and Rick reached into their packs and pulled out their halves of the tent. They buttoned the halves together and in no time the tent was standing. They threw their sleeping bags inside. Captain Marko had a meeting with the men and explained what to expect. He told them the higher command felt that this area was where the enemy would come to regroup and how important it was not to let them. After he was done he told them to go to their tents and get some sleep because he knew how exhausted they were.

Mike was first to get in. He dropped on his sleeping bag fully clothed. Rick crawled in later. He saw Mike, fully dressed, sleeping. "Hey, Mike, you should take off your pants and boots before you sleep." Mike sort of raised up then dropped back down and fell asleep without saying anything. Rick took his time and untied his boots and placed them neatly in the back of the tent. He removed his pants and skillfully folded them and placed them under his sleeping bag all the time talking to Mike. "Yes, sir, tomorrow I'm going to look neat. You're going to wake up and be all wrinkled. The army taught me to do it their way. It's not always the right way but it's the army way."

Mike raised up. "Shut up and go to sleep."

Rick finally got quiet and fell asleep. It was short-lived. He shouted. "Mike, wake up. Mike, wake up." Mike heard him and thought they were under attack. He grabbed his M1.

"What's going on?"

"Some son-of-a-bitch is stealing my pants and I got him by the arm." Mike looked and sure enough, Rick had someone by the wrist. He quickly unbuttoned the flap of the tent and went outside. There at the side of the tent was a person on his knees struggling to free his arm from inside the tent. Mike stuck the barrel of the M1 into his side.

"I got him, Rick, let him go." From his short size Mike determined he was a Korean. The guy straightened up and Rick's pants dropped from his hands.

Rick crawled out barefooted and in undershorts. "Where is that thieve'n bastard?" He pulled the guy's hat off and long hair dropped down to his shoulders. "I'm going to kick your—."

"What's the matter Rick?"

"This ain't a man. It's a goddamn broad."

Mike squinted and took a better look. "You're right. What's she doing in the middle of a combat zone?"

235

"The bitch was stealing my pants, that's what she was doing." He looked down and saw she was wearing his combat boots. "The bitch is wearing my boots. Why the hell did she pick me?"

"Well, I guess, she knew you do things the army way."

"Aw, shut up, Mike."

Rick continued to shout and other soldiers came running with their rifles. One of them yelled. "What the hell is going on?"

Rick pointed at the girl. "She was reaching under the tent stealing my pants and boots."

They laughed. One of them said, "That ain't nothing. If you got gold teeth you better keep your mouth shut, or you won't have them long around here." The other soldiers went back to their tents.

Rick continued to hold her by the collar. "What we going to do with this thief, Mike?"

Zug laughed. "Hey, Rick, let her be your maid. She could really do a nice job in that pup tent."

Mike looked at Zug and shook his head letting him know Rick was mad and not to tease him. Mike eased up to Rick and released his hand from her coat. "Aw, let her go Rick. You'd probably do the same thing if you were in her shoes."

"Man, what you talking about. She's in my shoes. What the hell would I have done if she got away with my boots?"

Mike took her aside and talked softly. "Why don't you get out of here real quick before something happens." She didn't understand the words, but got the message. She bowed a couple of times, took off Rick's boots and ran.

Mike crawled back in the tent. Rick picked up his pants and boots and swore. Mike laughed. "Hey, Rick, do you still think the army way is the best way. Are you going to put your pants under your sleeping bag again?"

"Aw, shut up Mike. Man, I read that crap in one of those army manuals. The damn fool who wrote it, must never of been in Korea. If he came here believing that shit he'd be running around naked with all these thieves over here."

"What would of happened if the gooks attacked and you were in the sleeping bag with only your shorts on?"

Rick slid into the sleeping bag and pulled it over his head. "I'll tell you what I would of done. I'd adapted to the situation. Now go to sleep and knock off the bullshit."

The sun lit up the tent. Sergeant Mitchel was outside. "Okay, men get up. Come on let's make it."

Mike sat up and looked over at Rick who had slid deeper into his sleeping bag. Mike unbuttoned the flaps of the tent and stuck his head out. The ground was covered with snow. He took a deep breath and exhaled steam. "Wow, it's cold out there. Come on, Rick, get up." Rick just mumbled something.

Sergeant Mitchel heard them. "I said get up Miller."

Rick sat up and yawned. "Hey, Sergeant, what's the chance of some one bringing me my breakfast? If they do I'll go back to the States and lie and tell those young men how nice this army is and they'll join up."

"In a minute, I'll reach in there and pull you and that sleeping bag out."

Rick slowly unzipped the sleeping bag. He looked like a butterfly coming out of its cocoon. He stared at his breath which had turned into vapor. "Ain't this a bitch waking up to a place like this. People sleep in tents when they go camping in the summer. Man, I'm glad I only got another year of this shit."

They walked to the mess truck hunched over with their collars turned up, "I've never been so cold in all my life, Mike. Now we know why they call it the frozen chosen. " At the mess truck they were given small boxes of cereal and a cup full of milk. Rick was ready to take a spoonful when Sergeant Mitchel called him.

"Hey, Miller, come here a minute. I want to talk with you." Rick put his mess kit down and walked to him. "What was all that commotion by your tent last night?"

Rick explained about the girl trying to steal his pants and boots. Sergeant Mitchel laughed and told him to go back to his food. Rick tried to pull the spoon from the milk and cereal. It was frozen solid. "Well, I'll be goddamn." He got up and went to the garbage can. He slammed it three times before the spoon broke loose from the mess kit.

Leroy was laughing. "Hey, Jive Ass, don't throw that away. You lick it like it's a popsicle." Rick ignored him and mumbled to himself.

Someone shouted, "Mail call." Soldiers ran to the road where a jeep was parked. A corporal broke the brown twine holding the letters together. Rick stayed back as he always did. Mike got his mail and started to walk away from the jeep.

The corporal yelled. "Miller, Rick Miller."

Mike ran to Rick. "Hurry Rick, you got mail. Hurry up and get it."

Rick didn't believe him but still slowly walked to the jeep. The corporal was holding a white envelope. "Are you Rick Miller?"

"Yeah."

"You don't seem too excited."

"It's probably a bill."

Mike watched him walk back. Rick didn't take his eyes from the letter. Mike felt glad for him. "Hurry up and open it, you damn fool." Mike read his mail and occasionally glanced over at Rick. He noticed Rick's letter was only two pages long and when he finished reading it, he started over again.

"Is it good news, Rick?"

Rick, looked at him and slowly said. "Yeah, yeah, I guess so. It's good news."

"Who's it from?"

"It's from Sergeant Doyle." He continued to stare at his name on the envelope. "You know, Mike, this is the first letter I ever got in my life."

"Aw, you're kidding, Rick. You don't really mean it do you?"

"No, I'm not kidding." He stuttered and was going to say more when an explosion erupted about fifty yards from them.

Someone shouted. "Incoming mortars! Incoming mortars!"

Soldiers hunched over and ran to their positions. More shells exploded, throwing dirt in all directions. Rick grabbed the grip of the machine gun and aimed in the direction he thought the mortars were being fired from. A loud roar of men screaming and the ground in front of the positions was covered with enemy soldiers dressed in quilted jackets carrying small arms. It looked like someone disturbed an ant hill, there were so many of them. Captain Marko, shouted, "Fire. Fire at will." The Americans let loose with everything they had. The ones leading the wave were struck and slammed to the ground. The ones behind kept coming,

Rick shouted, "If they would of asked, I'd of given them this frozen armpit." He kept squeezing the trigger swinging the gun back and forth. The enemy who were hit, laid on the ground and the ones behind ran over them and continued their charge. "Mike, the barrel is hot. Sure as hell it's going to melt."

Mike scooped up handfuls of snow and squeezed it on the hot barrel. Immediately the snow turned to water. He quickly grabbed more snow and packed it around the barrel.

"Mike, stay low. You're going to get hit."

"Keep firing the gun or we'll both be dead."

A mortar shell exploded in front of them. Mike was thrown backwards. Rick left the gun and grabbed him "I'm all right Rick, get back to the gun."

The American artillery opened up into the charging enemy. Every time a projectile hit enemy soldiers squirmed on the ground screaming in pain. "Mike, the artillery are finding the range. Some forward observer knows what he's doing." The wave kept coming, even though there were large empty spots where the artillery exploded in their ranks.

Mike and Rick noticed the enemy looking up and pointing. Mike turned and saw jets very low screaming overhead meeting the enemy head on. As soon as the jets cleared the positions, they strafed and dropped napalm. About fifty yards from Mike and Rick a napalm bomb exploded and a wave of fire engulfed the enemy. The heat was so intense Mike and Rick dropped to their stomachs. They looked up and saw enemy soldiers on fire, running, screaming and thrashing their arms. They were human torches. The ones that weren't burning kept charging. Rick got back behind the gun, shouting. "They just keep coming. There's no end to the bastards."

The jets passed a couple more times exploding blazing gaps in the enemy ranks. Finally the stubborn enemy retreated. Sergeant Mitchel shouted Mike and Rick's names along with three other men's. They slowly walked to him. "Men, we're going to escort Lieutenant Williams to the dead gooks. He wants to see if any of them are carrying information. You watch and make sure none of them are faking in order to ambush us."

Sergeant Mitchel, cautiously led them to the bodies. "Remember men, be alert. One of them might jump up and start firing." The sight and smell of the burned bodies made them gasp and turn their heads.

Lieutenant Williams shouted. "Come here, I want to show you something." He pointed to a dead enemy soldier then reached down and removed a metal insignia from the his collar. "This man is a Chinese soldier. Let's get out of here, I found out what I wanted to know."

Rick was quick to ask. "Sir, you mean we're now fighting the Chinese, too?"

"I'm afraid so, soldier."

"Man, that means we got to fight a zillion more of them."

The other soldiers in the group mumbled and looked at each other with concern. Mike asked. "Sir, being, Chinese were in those waves, is that why they didn't blow their horns?"

"No, the Chinese like to blow them damn things too. I can't figure out why they didn't blow them due to the large size of the attack."

Rick laughed. "They couldn't blow their horns because it was so cold their lips would of stuck to the mouthpiece."

Lieutenant Williams smiled. "Maybe you're right. Okay, men, thanks for coming with me. Let's get back so I can send this information to headquarters."

Word spread fast through the positions about the Chinese. It was extremely quiet. Solders didn't talk. They just watched the openness in front of them. Rick looked at Mike. "Well, what do you think about the situation now?"

"I guess we just got to adapt to it."

Rick smiled. "Yeah, you're right."

Mike reached into his pocket and took out one of the letters he didn't get to read. It was from his mother.

Dear Michael:

I haven't heard from you in awhile. I've been worried and I hope everything is okay. Your Uncle Tim was over and he told me that they keep you pretty busy and that the mail travels very slow when it has to cross the ocean. The newspapers said that the fighting was pretty bad in Korea. I pray every day that you are going to be alright.

I saw a couple of your friends who were home for Christmas vacation from college. They asked how you were. Everything is good here at home, so don't worry. Thanks for sending the money. I don't need it Michael. Why don't you keep it? If you don't, I'll save it for you when you get home.

Please write and tell me you're okay. I know you're very busy, so I'll stop for now. Michael, please be careful.

Love, Mother

Rick watched as Mike continued to stare at the letter. "Is everything all right?"

"Yeah, in all the excitement I didn't write my mother. She's concerned because I haven't been writing. I'm going to send her a letter." He went back to the tent and got out his pen and writing pad.

Dear Mom:

I received your letter and I'm sorry for not writing more.

This Korea isn't such a bad place, but of course, I've got it made. I'm with an outfit that supplies the men doing the fighting. We take the equipment off the boats and that is about all we do. We eat real good and everything is going well. Like Uncle Tim told you, we get real busy and it takes time for our letters to get back to the States. I sort of feel guilty having such a plush job when some of my friends are in the combat zone fighting. I had a talk about this with my captain and told him how I felt. He said I was doing my part by keeping the soldiers supplied on the front. He told me I was doing a good job, I'd be doing it the rest of the time I'm here. I should mess up so they would send me to where the action is. I'd like to see what it's like. After I thought about it, I think I'll continue doing a good job for the guys up front.

A couple of weeks ago I went on R&R (Rest and Recuperation) to Japan with a couple friends. We saw some beautiful sights there. Japan is a nice country. Some of the churches are built just like ours at home. We ate Japanese food and it was delicious.

Everything is going perfect over here. It'll just be a short time and I'll be back.

I'm glad everything is going all right at home. Tell Uncle Tim I said hello and I'll drop him a letter as soon as things slow down.

Well, I see some more trucks coming through the gate and we'll have to load them. I'll write whenever I get a chance. Take care of yourself.

Love, Mike

Mike came back to the position and Rick turned. "Did you get the letter done?" Did you tell her what a wonderful place this is?"

"Yeah, I mentioned you, and what we did on R&R."

"You what? You told her everything?"

"Sure."

Rick shook his head. He was about to say something when Sergeant Mitchel shouted. "Attention, men, we're now on full alert. It's official. The

241

Chinese have joined forces with the North Koreans. We'll have to be at our best. We were informed their intentions are to push us down through South Korea and into the sea. We got a sample of them last night and got a taste of what to expect. I want all weapons to be cleaned and well oiled. We're going to be catching hell, so let's be ready for them."

No one bitched. They worked on their weapons and reinforced the foxholes. It was clear to them that their weapons were the only thing that were going to get them out of there alive. Mike gathered snow and packed it by the front of the machine gun. "That's a good idea, Mike. If it wasn't for the snow that barrel would of melted last night."

Mike didn't answer. He was squinting into the openness in front of him. He thought how his mother would react if she got a telegram telling her he was dead. Unconsciously, he started to pray. At the end of the prayer he accidently said out loud, "Only for her sake, Lord let me go back alive.' He realized he said it out loud and he glanced at Rick who was staring into the darkness holding the handle of the machine gun.

Rick didn't look at Mike when he said. "Mike, would you mention something for me?"

"Why don't you say your own prayer and ask Him yourself?"

"Naw, it wouldn't work, after all the stuff I did in my life. I don't believe that just because I'm in a bind now, I should ask Him. It wouldn't feel right. Besides He might get mad."

"You're wrong, Rick, it's never too late." Mike was ready to say more but Rick interrupted.

"No, Mike, I see these guys pray like mad when they're in combat because they're scared they're going to die and meet their maker. As soon as they get on R& R and shacked up, or all other kinds of sinning they forget about praying. That is what I call a chicken shit hypocrite. No, Mike, I can't be that way, and besides I never learned to pray. Just do me a favor. The next time you say a prayer, just mention my name to Him. Maybe something good will come of it."

"Okay, Rick, I will."

Hours passed and it got colder. Wind blew dust and snow. The soldiers put their heads down to protect them from the sting of it. Rick was sleeping huddled up with his gloved hands in his pockets and his helmet over his face. Mike looked at him. I wonder why he never talks about his family? He never gets mail. Why he gets so mad when someone calls him a name? The guy don't even know how to pray. The tension of the enemy ready to attack and the way Rick acted, caused Mike to shout. "What happens if you get killed?"

Rick didn't answer.

Mike shouted it again. "What happens if you get killed?"

"I'd be dead and then I'd adapt to the situation."

"I don't want to hear that pat answer. How would your mother act if you got killed?"

Rick lifted his helmet from his face and glared at Mike. "The bitch wouldn't give shit one."

Mike was baffled by the answer and regretted he asked. Rick continued to look at Mike and waited for him to say something else. Mike walked back to the machine gun. Rick leaned back and pulled his helmet over his eyes.

The night went on and the only noise was the wind. Objects sticking up from the snow took on the forms of humans. A small boulder resembled a man hunched over ready to run. Everyone was edgy.

A voice from the distance shouted. "Hey, Joe." Rick woke and crawled to the gun.

"Well here we go again Mike."

"Hey, Joe, do you hear me?"

Leroy shouted, "Joe Momma."

Rick yelled. "Tell him Sky King."

"Hey, Joe, wouldn't you rather be home with your girlfriend instead of waiting to get killed? She's probably getting ready for her date with a guy who paid his way out of the army. Just think, if you'd of had money, you would be with her."

"Hey gook I'm over here pedaling your old lady's booty. Most of your broads are over here with us. They like real men. You dig, Punk?"

It got quiet and then the enemy voice again. "Hey, Joe."

This time all the Americans shouted. "Yes, Punk."

No more talking for the rest of the night. Dawn broke and everyone turned to the rear when they heard loud rumbling the ground shook. At least ten tanks with white stars on their turrets took their placements behind the positions. Mike shouted over the motors. "You can bet there's a lot of gooks out there, to reinforce us with that many tanks."

"I don't care how many gooks are out there. I'm glad to see those tanks. I just wish one more thing."

"What's that?"

"Turks in front of us. We could really adapt to the situation then."

Chapter 19
Transferred

Sergeant Mitchel came running and yelling for Mike. Mike watched him jump into the position. "Mike, the captain wants to see you right away. I don't know what it's about, but get going. I'll take your place till you get back." Mike immediately crawled out, ran to the Captain's tent and rapped on the flap.

"Sir, Private Ryan reporting as ordered." "Come in Mike."

Mike saluted and the captain returned it. "Sit down." Mike was scared it was bad news about his mother. "Mike, you've been transferred to Japan. I don't know the reason. I received these orders and you're to leave here as soon as possible. I don't know the details about this matter. The army works in funny ways and we don't question. We just obey orders." Mike still had the puzzled look. "I explained everything I know Mike. I'm sorry I can't tell you anymore. I want you to know, you were one of the best men I ever commanded. It's going to be hard to replace you. The captain stood up, as did Mike. They shook hands. "Good luck."

"Thank you, Sir. You were a great company commander. I'll miss you and the rest of the men."

"Round up your equipment and get packed. A jeep will pick you up shortly. When it comes we'll contact you. Again, good luck, Son." Mike saluted and left.

Mike went to his tent, packed his few belongings and went to the position. Rick and Sergeant Mitchell both stared at him when he slid in. Mike lowered his head. "They're transferring me to Japan."

Rick shouted. "They're what?"

"I got to leave. The captain didn't tell me why. They got a jeep coming for me."

Rick didn't say anything, he turned and walked to the front of the position and remained silent. Sergeant Mitchell shook Mike's hand. "We're going to miss you, Mike. You're a good soldier. Good luck in your new assignment." He tapped Mike on the shoulder and crawled out of the foxhole.

Rick turned and walked to Mike with his hand extended. Mike grabbed his hand and they shook. Rick put his hand on Mike's shoulder. "It's going to be rough not having you with me, Mike. You're the closest friend I ever had and the only person I ever trusted. This will be the first time we've been apart since we met. I hope it's a good deal for you, Mike. You can thank your mother's prayers for the break. You deserve it."

While they were talking Zug crawled in. "I heard the good news, Mike. I'm very glad for you. When we get on R&R we'll get together again. Good luck, man."

Mike choked up. He got the same feeling he had when he left his mother at the bus station. "Man, I'll miss you guys. If I had my choice I'd stay with you. I don't know what this transfer is about, but as soon as I find out I'll write." He wanted to say more but the words wouldn't come. He started to say good-bye but Rick put up his hand.

"Please don't say that. Say, I'll see you."

Sergeant Mitchell shouted. "Mike, snap it up the jeep is waiting."

Mike stared at the two of them and felt the tears fighting to come down his face. He hugged them, turned and shouted. "I'll see you." He crawled out and picked up his pack. He ran about twenty five yards and turned around. Rick and Zug were still staring at him. They gave a weak wave. He waved back and ran to the jeep.

The driver, an older soldier, shouted. "You Mike Ryan?"

"Yes."

"Well, get in. We're going to get out of here as fast as we can. This is going to be a hot spot. I don't know what the hell I'm doing up here with this jeep. They ordered me to pick you up. You must be pretty important."

"No, I'm not important at all. I don't know what this is all about."

Mike kept the conversation short. He didn't want to talk about it. They stopped at the large Quonset hut and he got his duffel bag.

After a couple hours they were getting close to Seoul. Mike noticed all the ambulances carrying wounded from the front. He assumed the wounded were being flown to Japan. The driver stopped at the airfield and left him off. He pointed to a two-engine prop plane. "That's the one you're flying out of here on. I wish you luck." Mike thanked him and walked to the temporary steps set up next to the plane. He climbed aboard and the pilot asked him his name. Mike told him and the pilot pointed to the aisle and told him to take a seat.

Mike made his way down the aisle and all he saw was officers. He continued to walk to the rear of the plane. A private was sitting by a window. Mike pointed to the seat next to the guy. "Is that seat taken?"

"No, sit down. Glad to have you. I feel out of place with all the brass on this plane."

"Yeah, I know what you mean." Mike sat down and put his hand out. "I'm Mike Ryan."

The private shook his hand. "Bob Brandon, most of my friends call me Tank. Where you headed Mike?"

"I really don't know other than Japan. They handed me some orders and away I went."

"Hey, that's exactly what they did to me. I don't care as long as I'm getting out of Korea. That's one mean place."

Mike nodded. "I know what you mean."

The plane took off and Mike visualized Zug and Rick back at the positions watching him leave.

He kept thinking of them until Tank said. "Mike, we got to put these life jackets on." Mike shook his head and came back to reality.

"Thanks, I was thinking of my friends. Too bad they can't get this war over with."

"You're right there." Mike put on his life jacket and started laughing. Tank asked him what was so funny? He told him how Rick pulled the tab on the life jacket and scared Leroy. Tank smacked his knee. "Man I bet that scared hell out of that guy." He started laughing out loud. Some officers turned around and stared at him. He didn't care, he kept laughing. "Man I wish I could of seen that."

They were airborne for awhile and not much conversation. Tank stood up. "Excuse me, Mike, I got to use the head. Mike slid his knees in the aisle and Tank squeezed passed him. Mike looked up. No wonder they call him Tank. The guy must be all of six foot three and close to three hundred pounds. They nick named him right.

The wheels hit the ground with a thumping sound and the plane taxied to a small hanger. "Well, Tank we made it to Japan. I sure wish I knew what is going to happen next."

Tank nodded. They waited till the officers got off, then they left. They stood on the tarmac and the place was deserted. A black sedan pulled up and a lieutenant and a master sergeant got out. The lieutenant shouted. "You guys Ryan and Brandon?"

"Yes sir." They answered in unison.

"Well, come on, get in the car."

The sergeant got behind the wheel. The lieutenant sat in the front with his arm over the seat looking at Mike and Tank. Mike noticed the thick neck on the lieutenant and he looked in good shape. The master sergeant was a big guy and his nose was out of line. It must of been broken a few times. Mike looked at the lieutenant. "Sir, could you tell us what's going on?"

The lieutenant ignored the question and opened up a folder. "Ryan you're a quarterback on offense, and a linebacker on defense? Is that right?"

"Yes sir, that's what I played in high school."

"That's a piss poor combination. A quarterback playing linebacker. I never heard of that."

He turned the page in the folder and looked at Tank. "You, Tank, you're a tackle, right?"

Mike thought, they even know his nickname. Tank said. "No, I'm a quarterback too."

Mike busted out laughing but the two in the front didn't think it was funny.

The sergeant yelled. "Your ass better move like a quarterback or you won't be here long."

No more was said. The car slowed down as they approached the large gates with a small house on an island dividing two lanes of traffic. Two military police saw the car, saluted and waved it through with their white gloves. Mike looked at the large sign. "Camp Zama."

The sergeant said. "Welcome to the prettiest army camp in the Far East and the meanest-assed football team on earth."

The ride continued till the car stopped in front of an impressive wooden building surrounded by a six foot white picket fence. The lieutenant got out first and instructed Mike and Tank to follow him. Mike looked at Tank and Tank shrugged his shoulders and said. "Let's do what the man says." The sergeant heard this and scowled at Tank.

They entered the beautiful building and walked down a hall on the second floor. On both sides of the walls were glass cases filled with sports trophies. Mike asked the sergeant. "Sergeant, where are we going?"

"You're going to meet the owner."

Mike squinted and shook his head. "The owner?"

"Don't worry about it. You'll find out in a minute."

They walked into a well-furnished office and the receptionist smiled as they passed her. Mike saw a sign. "Post Commander, General Marvin." The lieutenant knocked on the door and a deep rough voice shouted from inside. "Come in."

The lieutenant opened the door and motioned for Tank and Mike to go inside. They walked in and a middle-aged burly built man dressed in Class A uniform stared at them. Mike looked at the stars on his shoulders. He never saw a general and a frightened feeling came over him. Mike immediately came to attention and saluted. Tank did the same. The general half saluted and said. "Damn it, sit down." Mike quickly grabbed a chair and sat. The general shouted, "Relax, damn it. I got some questions to ask and I don't want any bullshit. Is that understood?" Mike and Tank nodded.

The general pointed at Mike. "You're a quarterback. Where did you play ball?"

"Sir, I played at Woodward High School in Toledo, Ohio.

"High school? And where in the hell is Toledo?"

Mike didn't answer.

"It says here you made Allstate."

"Yes, sir, I made Allstate."

"Why didn't you go to college? You figure you couldn't make it?"

"No, sir, I didn't want to go to college. If I'd went, I'm sure I could of made the team."

"How many scholarships were you offered?"

"I received scholarships."

"How many?"

"I didn't count them because I wasn't interested in going to college."

"Maybe you were scared of getting hit by the big boys, huh?"

Mike could feel the blood racing up the back of his neck turning his face red. He wanted to say something but he looked at the stars on the general's shoulder and thought it best he keep quiet.

The general looked at Tank and asked him how much he weighed. Tank said two hundred and sixty five pounds.

"You're overweight. If you think you're going to play here, you better lose it. Where did you play ball?"

"Well, sir, I made All American two years in a row in college and was playing professional ball before I got drafted into this chicken shit army and almost got my ass blown off in Korea. If I didn't come into the army I probably would be in excellent shape. This food is not the best. And furthermore, I'm sure I can make your goddamn team."

The room became silent and very uncomfortable. The general smiled and looked at the lieutenant and the sergeant. "You see the difference? The quarterback kept his cool. The big lineman gets mad and wants to get right back on the offense. Yes sir, I like that." He continued to look at Tank and smile. The lieutenant and sergeant saw the general smile and they too smiled.

The general looked back at Mike. "Most of my men are college and pro players. If you don't make the team you'll find your ass back in Korea. Is that understood?"

Mike was ready to tell him to stick his team up his ass, but changed his mind. He glared at the general and said. "Yes sir, I understand."

The general nodded at the lieutenant. "That's all, take them to the barracks."

In the car, Tank said, "Now I know why you call him the owner. He's something."

"He's something all right. After you get to know him you'll find he's a great man. He wants to be a winner. Isn't that what the army is all about?"

"Yes, Sir, I'm finding it out every day."

The lieutenant and sergeant showed them to their bunks and introduced them to some big, well-fed men sitting around in shorts. They eyed Tank because his reputation must have arrived before he did. One giant named Doug Rucker came over and hit Tank on the back and called him by his name. The lieutenant said. "This is Doug Rucker he made All American and All Pro."

The giant said. "I know Tank. We played against each other many times. He's the toughest and meanest guy I ever met. Glad to have you on our team, Tank."

Tank pointed at Mike. "This here is Mike Ryan, a great quarterback." Mike shook the big guy's hand. Other players came over They all seemed to know Tank. When they left, Tank and Mike sat on the edges of their bed. Mike looked around. Towels, jerseys, jockstraps and socks were hanging and lying all over the place.

"Hey, Tank this isn't what I remember about living in a barracks."

Tank laughed and pointed at a spear sticking in a speaker. A jockstrap was hanging on it. "I wonder what that's all about?"

A soldier overheard him. "Some son-of-a-bitch hooked up that bitch box and it sounded reveille at six in the morning." He pointed at a bed about twenty five feet away. "Apeman fired a spear gun and it stuck where you see it. It hasn't worked since."

Tank looked at him. "Who's Apeman?"

"Oh, you'll get to meet him real soon. He's the craziest guy I ever met. He's T.D.Y. out of his cage during football season."

"Well, what do you think, Tank?"

"Mike, they sure got a lot of talent here from what I see. I heard these service teams are tough." Mike didn't say anything and Tank sensed something was wrong. "Hey, what goes with you Mike? We got it made man. Pick up." Mike looked disgusted. "Come on Mike, what the hell is the matter with you?"

"You heard that general. He only wanted college and pro players. Hell, they won't even look at me. I don't have a big name."

"Mike, you know you can't feel that way when you play sports. Screw the general. Don't worry about a name. When you get on that field, make your name. It's what you can do here that counts, not what you did back in the States. You'll get your chance. They wouldn't of bothered bringing you here if they didn't think you had a chance. Listen to old Tank. Give it your best, and you'll be all right."

Mike nodded. "Thanks."

They lay down in their beds. In the comfort and safety of the barracks they fell asleep. They slept for about ten minutes when a loud bang caused them to jump out of their beds. Someone shouted. "You son-of-a-bitch, Apeman. Why do you always slam that door?" Mike couldn't believe what he was seeing. A huge guy was standing in the aisle. He was six one and must of weighed over three hundred pounds. He wore only shorts. His massive chest and back were covered with dark hair. His eyes were close together. His arms and legs were so big they looked out of proportion.

Someone started singing. "Ape call do le aa ba." Others joined in. Now everyone was chanting "Ape call, do le aa ba." The large hairy guy heard this and started moving his shoulders side to side. He hunched over and let his knuckles drag on the floor. His eyes opened wide and his lips formed like the front of a trumpet. The men sang louder and the big guy rocked back and forth faster and his arms were swinging.   He was worked up and made noises like a wild animal and started leaping from one bed to another, hunched over, with his arms dangling.

Tank squinted. "Would you look at that silly son-of-a-bitch."

The guys kept chanting and Apeman got wilder. He pounded his chest, threw his head back and let out a loud belch. Someone said, "That was the result of four cheeseburgers, three fries, a cake and a quart of milk"

Apeman bounced down the aisle like a wild monkey. Mike and Tank stared at him as he got closer. He circled them twice, all the time hunched over dragging his knuckles and screeching. Mike busted out laughing when he saw Tank with his fists clinched glaring at this wild man. Apeman stared at Tank than recoiled and jumped to a window and grabbed the handle. It flew open with a bang. He let out a loud screech and continued to rock back and forth. People going into the PX across the street looked up at him. He cupped his hands around his mouth and belched again.

Mike and Tank couldn't believe what was happening. They stared at his large hairy back as he continues to act up in front of the window. The other guys in the barracks encouraged him by singing louder. Apeman was now pointing down while he gyrated. Mike walked to another window so he could see what he was pointing at. A full bird colonel was looking up. The colonel was a heavy set man in short pants. An overweight woman, who probably was his wife, was standing beside him. The colonel shouted. "Goddamn it, are you laughing at me?"

Apeman continued to rock. Again, he formed his lips like a trumpet and shrieked a loud wild noise, then laughed. Tank walked over to Mike. "What the hell is going on out there?"

"Man, he's got some colonel down there pissed. There's going to be trouble." Mike walked back to his bed. He shook his head. "I don't want any part of this."

The door flew open and the colonel in Bermuda shorts stood staring at all the jockstraps, undershorts, towels, and other clothing on the floor. Mike quickly got into bed, put his face in the pillow and pretended to be asleep The

252

colonel looked at a soldier lying in bed, reading a magazine. He kicked the bed. "Soldier, what do you do when an officer comes into the room?"

The guy in the bed stared at him and said. "Attention," and went back to reading his magazine. Mike and Tank immediately jumped out of their beds and came to attention. The guy who said "attention" continued to lie in the bed reading his magazine, ignoring the colonel glaring at him.

The colonel screamed. "Soldier, come to attention!"

The guy put down his magazine and continued to lie in the bed. He put his legs together and brought his arms to his sides. His body became rigid and he looked up at the colonel. Tank elbowed Mike. "Man, I can't believe that guy. He's got to be crazy, lying at attention."

The colonel was going berserk. "Goddamn it, I'm coming back with the M Ps. What the hell's going on? I'll straighten out this pigpen." He rushed out the door and slammed it.

Everyone acted like nothing happened. Someone shouted. "Another idiot who likes to slam doors like Apeman."

Mike and Tank sat on the edge of their beds. Mike said, "What do you think?"

"I know what I'm going to do. I'm getting the hell out here. That colonel is coming back with the M Ps. and there's going to be real trouble. I don't want to stick around and see it." Mike agreed and they left.

They went into the PX and wandered around, looking out the windows at the barracks across the street. Two military police cars pulled up then the Provost Marshall's car. The colonel jumped out of the car and pointed to the open window where Apeman had been acting up. They rushed in. "You know, Mike, the fireworks are about to start." Another car pulled up. Small red flags with gold stars flew from both front fenders. The Post Commander, General Marvin, hurriedly jumped out the back door of the car before it came to a stop. He rushed inside the barracks.

"Hey, Tank, I'm sure glad we got out of there."

"Yeah, there's going to be hell to pay."

To Tank and Mike's surprise the MPs came out, got in their cars and drove off. The Colonel and the Provost Marshall came out. They also left. Five minutes later General Marvin came out and his driver opened the back door for him. They drove off.

Tank looked at Mike. "That didn't take long. I think it's safe." They entered the barracks and everything seemed normal, as though nothing happened. The guy who came to attention in the bed was still lying there reading his magazine.

Mike looked startled. "What did that general do when he came in here?"

The guy slowly looked up from his magazine. "Oh, he just dropped in and told a colonel what a great football team he had living in this barracks."

Mike couldn't believe it. "You mean to say he didn't yell at Apeman?"

"Naw, the owner knows Apeman is crazy and he gets a little rambunctious once in awhile."

Tank, nodded. "Man, you can say that again. They ought to hang a tire over his bed so he can get rid of some of that wild shit."

The soldier laughed. "Aw, you'll get use to the nutty bastard after awhile." The guy remained in bed and held up his hand. "I'm Tony Shavanto, I play right end." Tank and Mike shook hands with him. "I'm sorry I didn't get up, but I'm tired. You'll find out about being tired after you go through a couple of practices with this team."

Darkness set in and the barracks progressively got quiet as the men went to sleep. Mike lay in the darkness thinking about the things that happened so fast to him the past few days. Exhaustion took over and he fell asleep. Then he had a nightmare. He and Rick were in a foxhole. In the distance coming down a hill and charging were thousands of North Koreans screaming, with fixed bayonets. Their bayonets were shining in the sunlight. He yelled for Rick to fire the gun. Rick tried to pull the trigger but the barrel of the gun had melted. Rick kept yelling, "The barrel's gone. It won't fire." The enemy overran the position and their bayonets were aimed at his heart. Mike's body was thrashing the sheets and blankets. He fell out of bed and got to his feet still asleep. He started banging on a locker, screaming. "Help us, they're stabbing us to death."

A halfback who was sleeping across from Mike woke up and shouted. "Hey man, hit the lights. There's a cat in here with a blade." Someone turned on the lights and the halfback ran to Mike who was still asleep, screaming and banging the locker. He grabbed Mike by the shoulders. "Come on man, wake up, everything is cool. There ain't no gooks in here."

254

Mike shook his head and stared at the halfback. He realized he had a nightmare. "I'm sorry, you guys, I didn't mean that. I had a bad dream, I didn't mean to wake you up."

The halfback tapped him on the back. "Don't worry about it. It happened to most of us who were in Korea. Don't think nothing about it. Get back in bed and get some sleep. We'll see you in the morning."

"Thanks, I appreciate what you did for me."

They followed the rest of the players to the locker room after breakfast. They were given football gear. It was the best quality equipment Mike had ever seen. After he got dressed he jogged to the practice field with the rest of the team. A group of coaches were in the middle of the field. One had a clipboard in his hand. He blew a whistle and made circles in the air above his head with the clipboard and yelled. "Give me four laps around the field."

The players ran, groaned and bitched at the same time, but nevertheless they kept running. One lap around and someone from the group started singing. "Ape call do le aa ba." Strange animalistic sounds could be heard from someone in the group. More players started singing the song. Mike looked to the side as Apeman broke from the group and ran to the front of the pack.

Apeman slapped his hips and galloped like a horse. He shouted. "Come on, Trigger. Keep the cattle moving nice and slow. We don't want a stampede."

Mike looked at Tank. "He thinks he's on a horse."

Tank stared at Apeman. "He's a horse's ass, the goofy bastard."

The players continued singing and Apeman reacted to it. Someone shouted. "Apeman, cut them off at the pass."

Apeman's head went back and he made a whinny sound. He turned a quick left and ran across the field all the time galloping, slapping his hips and yelling, "Come on, Trigger. We got to get them at the pass." The coaches in the center of the field stared at him. The players were making the turn on the track. Apeman was waiting. He pretended his hands were pistols and yelled. "Bang, bang, I got you doggies."

Tank shouted to Mike. "That bastard probably played without a helmet. The fool has been hit in the head too many times."

The head coach, Captain Wilson, saw Apeman fooling around and yelled, "Apeman, get back in the group and act sane or I'll have you running this track the rest of the day." Apeman saluted and got back in the pack.

Some player started singing again, "Ape call do le aa ba."

Apeman shouted, "Screw you."

After laps Mike went to the end of the field where the backs were practicing. An assistant couch came up to him. "Mike I want you to watch the other quarterbacks. Try to learn the plays and then we'll try to work you in." Mike thought, he was trying to be nice and one day he will tell him they already have enough quarterbacks. For the following days it was the same, stand around and watch. He never got a chance to show what he could do.

After practice, Tank came up to Mike as they walked to the showers. "How's it going?"

Mike shook his head. "I don't think I got a chance. I just stand around and they never let me handle the ball. They don't even know I'm out here."

Tank hit him on the back. "Come on, shake that attitude. Hang in there, you'll be all right. Don't give up."

"That's all right for you to say. They look you over like a prize bull at a live stock auction. You got the credentials, Tank. I don't."

"Now don't get down on yourself. I saw you throw the ball the other day in warm-ups and you had a lot of zing on it. How far can you throw?"

"Well, one game I threw the ball seventy yards."

"Seventy yards! Hell, ninety-five percent of the pro players can't throw that far. Have they seen you throw the ball yet?"

"No, all I do is stand around and watch the quarterbacks hand off the ball on running plays. Like I said before, they already have this team picked. I'm on my way back to Korea. I hope when they send me back, it will be to my old outfit and my friends." They walked back to the locker room without any more conversation.

The next week was the same for Mike, standing on the sidelines, watching. He never got a chance to handle the ball. He knew his days were numbered. He felt helpless because he couldn't do anything about it. Tank ran up to him after practice smiling. "I overheard Coach Wilson say to his assistants that tomorrow they're going to have passing drills. Remember what I told you? Here's your chance. When you get in the huddle, you tell those halfbacks and ends to run long patterns. When they get far down field, rifle that ball."

Mike half-heartily said. "Yeah."

Tank hit him on the shoulder. "Hey, you heard me didn't you? I mean it. It's going to be your chance, so be ready, and do your stuff."

Mike perked up a little. "If only they would give me a chance."

The next day practice started and Tank was right. The head coach pointed to the far end of the field. "I want all the backs and ends to go down there. You're going to run pass patterns. All interior linemen will stay with me in the middle of the field." The assistant coach called the five quarterbacks he had been using for the past weeks. He showed them the pass patterns he wanted them to throw. The quarterbacks in turn, told the receivers the patterns they wanted them to run and threw the ball to one of them.

Someone shouted, "Here comes the owner." A car pulled up and parked. Flags with stars on them were fluttering from each fender. The post commander, General Marvin, got out and walked to Coach Wilson.

When he got about five feet away, the coach saluted and General Marvin returned it and said, "Carry on."

The general had a big smile when he saw the large linemen practicing blocking. The crashing of their pads was heard all over the field. He really enjoyed these big guys pounding on each other. Mike saw Apeman and Tank going at it. They looked like they were so mad they were going to come to blows. Coach Wilson pulled them apart a couple of times for fear they were going to fight. Tank looked at the other end of the field and saw Mike standing on the sidelines. He motioned with his arm like he was passing a football and pointed to the group who were practicing pass patterns. Mike shrugged his shoulders and threw out his hands indicating he was being ignored.

Tank clinched his fist and raised his arm and shouted, "Get with it Mike. Don't let them keep you on the sidelines. Go get your chance."

Mike was burning up inside. Every quarterback got a turn except him. He walked up to the assistant coach. "Hey, coach, I've been standing around for a couple of weeks. When am I going to get a chance?"

The coach looked startled, he hesitated. "Sure kid in a little while, but not right now."

Mike could tell by the coach's expression he was irritated so he didn't press the issue. He went back to waiting. It was getting late and the assistant coach called the backs and ends together. "Men, you did good today, let's take a lap around the field and call it a day."

Mike was mad and ready to explode. He walked up to the coach and stared him in the eyes. "You said you'd give me a chance. I've been waiting for two weeks and I don't even get a chance to put my hand on a ball. This isn't fair."

Everyone stopped and stared at the coach who nodded. "You're right kid, I did promise you. I'm sorry." The coach looked at the other coaches who were walking away. "Hold it everyone. Let the high school quarterback who came here with the All American throw a few passes. I told him earlier he could and it slipped my mind." The coach pointed at a couple of ends and backs and told them Mike was going to throw some passes to them. He looked at Mike. "Do you know the patterns?"

"I know them. I had plenty of time waiting to learn them."

Mike stood in front of the group who were going to be the receivers. He thought back to what his high school coach said. When you 're standing in front of the huddle talk with authority. Show them you're the boss and you know what you 're talking about. Mike looked at the right end. He was tall and rawboned. Mike watched him catch the ball earlier and thought he had good hands. He called the pass play and he looked at the rawboned end. "Instead of going across the middle, go straight down the sideline for a long one." The end nodded. Mike got behind the center and thought how long he had waited for this chance. He was mad about the coach referring to him as the high school quarterback. I want to show them. The adrenalin was blasting through his body. He shouted out the signals in a loud angry voice. The center slammed the ball back into Mike's waiting hands. The players went down field running their patterns. Mike squeezed the ball so hard he could feel the grain in the leather. He pumped the ball as though he was going to throw it to the halfback going across the middle. At the same time he watched the rawboned end running down the sideline. He was half way down the field and he slowed down and looked back at Mike. Mike waved his arm indicating for him to keep going farther. The end looked puzzled like he didn't believe Mike could throw the ball that far.

Mike kept waving his arm telling the end to continue running. The end reluctantly started running again. Mike went into the throwing position. He cocked his arm behind his head all the time keeping a tight grip on the ball. He took aim at the end downfield and put his back, arm and wrist into the throw. The ball released from his hand in a tight spiral. It flew over the large linemen in the middle of the field. Tank pointed at the ball and shouted. "Look at that." Everyone, including the head coach and the General looked up. The raw bone end saw it coming and he had to use every bit of speed he had to get under it and make the catch. When he caught it he was in the end zone. He turned around laughing. He couldn't believe the ball had traveled that far.

The general looked at the head coach. "Who in the hell kicked that?"

Tank yelled. "No one kicked it. That quarterback, Mike Ryan, threw it."

The general shouted. "Threw it. That ball must have traveled seventy yards in the air. Who is this guy?"

The general trotted to the end of the field where the backs and ends were. Coach Wilson was next to him. When they got to the assistant coaches the general shouted. "Where's the guy who threw that pass?"

The assistant coaches looked nervous. One of them said. "What pass?" They weren't watching because they were looking at their clipboards and talking to one another.

The head coach was upset. "Damn it, get that guy who threw that long pass." The assistants looked dumbfounded.

Coach Wilson shouted. "Never mind." He looked at the players. "Who threw that ball?"

Mike raised his hand. "I did, Sir."

"Okay, get out here. I want the same men who ran that pattern and I want you to throw that same pass." The group got into their positions. Mike received the ball from the center. He watched the raw bone end run down the sideline. This time the end didn't hesitate or look back. Mike drew back and threw. Again the ball flew in a tight spiral on a straight line. The end saw it coming and it landed on his outstretched fingers. He caught it and went into the end zone.

He held the ball over his head and shouted. "Beautiful pass."

General Marvin shouted. "He's got an arm like a Howitzer." He pointed to Mike. "Come here, I want to talk with you." Mike walked to him. "Where you from?"

"I'm from Korea."

"Skip that Korean shit. Where did you play ball?"

"I'm the high school player from Toledo, Ohio."

"Where in the hell did you learn to throw a football like that?"

"Well Sir, we play tough high school football in Toledo."

The General nodded. "Yeah, they must. I've been around this game for a long time and I never saw a pass like that. Get back there and do it again, son. That is a beautiful sight."

Mike huddled the group up again. The raw bone end looked at Mike. "Let it fly and I'll bring it in."

Mike again watched the end run down the side line and he fired the ball. The end caught it without breaking his stride. He stood in the end zone breathing hard. Some player yelled. "Throw it back."

The end shook his head. "Are you kidding?" He ran the ball back and handed it to Mike. "Man, that was great passing."

Mike nodded. "Thanks, you got a good pair of hands."

The general and the head coach walked away from the group. They talked and every once in a while one of them pointed at Mike.

Practice was over and a group of players crowded around Mike asking him questions. He noticed not one of the five quarterbacks were there. Tank came up and hit him on the shoulder. "That was the best thing I've seen in a long time. Man, when that ball sailed over that General's head, his eyes got as big as saucers. You did great. I knew you could do it."

"Thanks, Tank, I appreciate everything you did for me."

"Listen, kid, don't thank me. They'll know you now when you come out on this field."

Mike didn't dread practice anymore, now that the coaches weren't ignoring him. It was getting close to their first game and every practice was serious. This day the coaches were in the meeting room. As soon as the players sat down Coach Wilson stood in front of the room.

"This is the day you've been waiting for. We're going to have a full contact scrimmage. We'll separate the men from the boys."

The players smiled. Coach Wilson held up a short sleeved red shirt. "The men I call will wear these shirts and be the red team. The other team will wear blue shirts." Mike and Tank were given red shirts.

Tank held up his shirt, "Let's get'em, Mike." On the field Coach Wilson shouted. "Red quarterback get your team huddled up. You'll be on offense first."

One of the assistant coaches talked to the red team before Mike called the play. "Okay, men, you're my group. Get out there and kick hell out of that blue team. Don't hold back."

Mike called the play and the blue team was waiting for them. Mike looked to make sure his team was ready. He saw Apeman lined up directly across from Tank. Apeman looked mean. He shouted in Tank's face, "I'm going to break your back and tear your lungs out." Tank didn't say anything. He glared and dug his cleats in.

The ball was snapped to Mike and he handed it off to a halfback who ran about five yards before being brought down by a hard tackle. Mike was getting ready to form the huddle for the next play when he heard, "You dirty rotten son-of-a-bitch." A loud slap that sounded like two large sides of beef being slammed together. Tank and Apeman were toe to toe fighting for all they're worth. Apeman was bigger but Tank was faster. Every time one of their fists made contact there was a loud impact sound. Apeman swung and Tank blocked it and then drove his fist into Apeman's stomach. Apeman leaned forward trying to catch his breath. Tank hit him with an upper cut that knocked him off the ground. He reeled backward and Tank went after him to finish him off.

The coaches blew their whistles but Tank didn't pay attention. General Marvin shouted, "Break that up before someone gets killed." It took three assistant coaches and four players to separate them. The general got between them. "You guys, keep that bullshit for the games. I don't want anyone getting hurt in practice. That's your teammate you're kicking hell out of." Tank and Apeman looked like they didn't care what the general said. They glared at one another. The general yelled, "Do you men understand? I don't want any fighting." The big guys continued to glare and looked like they were going to go at it as soon as the coaches and players turned them loose. General Marvin shouted, "Damn it, if you can't control yourself in practice what are you going to do in a game? Fighting causes penalties and penalties can lose a game. Now straighten up and play ball. Use your head instead of your temper. Now get back in there and play smart."

Apeman went back to his defensive position and Tank returned to the huddle. Mike ran a few more plays and was impressed with the intense determination these seasoned players had for the game. He felt it would be a good time to call a draw play. He went back to pass and faked throwing it. The big defensive linemen put up their hands trying to block it. Mike ducked under them and ran up the middle. Momentarily he was in the open. A would be tackler came from the right. Mike stiffed-armed him and spun away. The safety man came running full stride and put his head down to tackle Mike. Mike saw him and it was too late to dodge. He put his head down and their helmets came together with a loud crack. Flashing streaks exploded in Mike's head. His body slammed to the ground. He tried to think but his mind was in a fog. He felt like laying there but the words of his old football coach echoed. 'If they hit you hard don 't give them the satisfaction of letting them know they hurt you. Get up, no matter how it hurts. Let them know you took their best shot and it didn't bother you. If they think they hurt you, they'll give it to you harder the next time.' Semiconscious, Mike managed to get to his feet and walked back to the huddle. He shook his head and the cobwebs started to clear. The other player was still on the ground being attended to.

The scrimmage continued and it was hard hitting throughout. Finally, Coach Wilson yelled. "Okay, men that's all for today."

The warm water from the shower felt like heaven. Mike kept twisting the nozzle to the many sore parts of his body. The stiffness was setting into muscles he didn't know he had. He smelled the rubbing ointments. I'm not the only one who got banged up. Mike was putting on his shirt when Tank walked up. "You looked real good out there today. Keep it up."

"Thanks. You and Apeman really got into it."

"I don't usually lose my temper but that crazy bastard bit my leg." He pulled up his pant leg and there was a perfect imprint of teeth marks. "I hit him with a clean block and knocked him down. The next thing I know his teeth were in my leg. Man, I don't remember anything after that. We'll go at it again because that guy don't have any sense."

Mike was tired and walked a slow pace back to the barracks. He dropped on his bunk and felt he would fall asleep after the tough practice. Instead, he stared at the ceiling. Memories floated through his mind. First his mother, then Rick, Zug and Hillbilly. Mitzko appeared. He tried to erase her face but it didn't work. Her image was indelible and it wouldn't go away. He remembered her sitting at the table laughing, and the night he will never forget when she walked through those strands of beads in his bedroom. He jumped up and it was a matter of minutes, he was on a bus headed for the Ginza.

The bright lights from the club made his legs move faster. He ran up the steps two at a time. A strange girl was taking the cover charge. He threw down his money and asked, "Where is Mitzko?"

The girl shook her head. "Mitzko, no know." Mike tried to explain that Mitzko worked at this club.

The girl shrugged her shoulders. "I not know."

Mike walked into the bar area and looked around. The familiar surroundings stimulated his memory. He remembered the good times he had here. If only he could relive them. He saw the table where they sat at on those happy nights. He could see everyone laughing, the bandstand where Zug had everyone in the place clapping for him, the hallway leading to the bedroom that he will never forget. He continued to reminisce till a voice kept saying, "Joe, Joe you want table?"

He shook his head and looked down at a hostess staring at him. "Yes, yes please." She led him to a table and he sat and looked up at her. "Where is Mitzko?"

She had a hard time understanding, then she said. "No, Mitzko."

"You know Jimmiesan?" She looked puzzled. Mike made his hand look like he was holding a cigarette and brought it to his mouth. "Jimmiesan light cigarettes."

The girl's face lit up. "Ah, so, Jimmiesan." Mike's hopes rose. "Jimmiesan, go sayonara, no more." Mike stared at her and was going to ask her more but he thought, what's the use. He ordered a beer and wiped the moisture from the bottle, all the time thinking of Mitzko. He started to leave and he looked at Owner Mike's office. He smiled and quickly walked to it and knocked.

A voice inside shouted. "Joe ta ma tay." (Just a minute.)

Mike heard footsteps inside, then the door partially opened and an eye stared at him. The door exploded open. "Mike, Mike what are you doing here?" Owner Mike put out his hand and Mike shook it. Owner Mike pulled him into his office. "Where's Rick and Zug?" Mike explained how he was picked to come to Japan and Rick and Zug were still in Korea. Mike asked him where Mitzko was?

"Well, Mike, right after you guys went back she left."

Mike interrupted him. "

"Where is she now? How can I find her?"

"I don't know. She probably went back to college, but I can't say for sure. Once they quit I don't keep track of them anymore."

"What about Jimmiesan?"

"I really don't know about him either. One day he didn't show up for work and I haven't seen him since. He was a slick and someone was probably looking for him. I still got some money he earned but he never came around to pick it up." Owner Mike got up and opened the door. "Come on, let's have a few drinks."

They went to the same table they sat the night they met. Owner Mike pointed at the bandstand. "Every day I come in here and I look at it. I think of Zug and the night he put on that show. That man played the sax and had the customers standing and cheering. When he went onto that bandstand and played every instrument, it was unreal. If he didn't have to go to Korea, I would of made him a rich man. I asked him to write me but I never received a letter. He probably forgot me."

Mike shook his head. "Oh, no, he didn't forget you. Many times we talked about you and this wonderful place and all the fun we had. They're catching hell over there. They use every minute thinking of ways to survive. I know when Zug gets a chance, he'll write. I can guarantee when they come back on R&R this will be the first place they will come."

"I hope you're right. I thought a lot about you guys. Those few days when you were here I never laughed and enjoyed myself so much in all my life. Remember when that crazy Rick got up and pretended he could play the trumpet? He couldn't play a note. All he could do was make loud noises." Owner Mike slapped his knee and laughed out loud. "Oh, how I wish they were here."

Mike was quiet and had his head down. "I wish they were here, too."

Owner Mike got serious. You miss them, don't you? I can see it in your face."

"Yeah, I sure do. It seems like since I came into the army every time I get to know someone I get separate from them. I heard older soldiers talk about it and they said it's just the way army life is. It's a lonesome feeling."

"Well, you listen, Mike. I'm your friend and I'll be here for a long time. You feel free to come here any time you want. You're always welcome, my friend."

"Thanks a lot. I appreciate it."

Owner Mike yelled for the waitress. "Get the best wine we have." In a short time she came back with a bottle and glasses. Mike put his hand up and tried to explain he didn't want wine. Owner Mike wouldn't take no for an answer. He ignored Mike and pulled the cork from the bottle. "It's great to see you, Mike. We have to have a toast to our friendship and our friends in Korea." Mike felt guilty not taking the drink after hearing this. Mike raised his glass and they toasted. The wine was sweet and went down smooth. He no sooner put his glass on the table and Owner Mike filled it again. Another toast, then another, the two of them reminisced about their friends and drank. More bottles were brought to the table.

Mike stared at the chairs that Mitzko, Zug, and Rick sat in. "Wouldn't it be nice if we had the power to bring back everyone who was sitting here that night? Everything was so right and happy. I would pay anything just to relive it."

Owner Mike pondered for a moment. "You're right, it would be nice, but life is not that way. We get the bad times, so when the good times come we enjoy them much more."

Mike stared at the chair Mitzko had sat on. He slurred, "That was the chair she was sitting in. Where is she now?"

"Let's don't dwell on the past. We can't do anything about it. We can do something about the present and the future. Forget about the girl. Another one will come along." The wine started to take hold of Owner Mike. His face became redder and he laughed a lot. He jumped up and shouted to a group of hostess girls. "One of you get over here." They looked at each other and one came to the table. Owner Mike pointed to a chair next to Mike. She immediately sat. "This is Mike, my camadotchie (friend). Mike, this is Marceko."

She sat down and Mike could tell she was nervous about being at the same table with her boss. She bowed and smiled. Mike bowed back. "Hey, wait a minute. It's all right, I don't need a girl sitting here. Let's just you and me talk."

Owner Mike laughed. The music started and he put the girl's hand into Mike's. "You two get up and dance."

Mike hesitated. He didn't know what to do. The girl stood up. They went to the floor and started dancing. Owner Mike felt good and yelled to the rest of the hostess girls telling them to get behind Mike and dance with him. Eight of them walked to the dance floor and followed Marceko and Mike as they danced. Each one tapped the girl dancing with Mike on the shoulder and took turns dancing with him. He blushed as the girls kept changing. He looked at Owner Mike and shrugged his shoulders and put out his hands.

Owner Mike shouted. "You want more women? I can arrange it."

"No this is enough. Everything is okay." Mike walked back to the table and the girls followed. "Hey, call them off. I appreciate this but it's too much. Let's you and me talk." Owner Mike said something to the girls and they smiled and left. He grabbed the wine again and filled their glasses. Mike tried to refuse but it was no use.

A waiter came with a stainless steel cart. He lifted the large lid and steam came from the food. Mike looked at the fish and vegetables on a bed of rice. His stomach turned with the thought of eating with all the sweet wine he drank. The waiter put a generous amount on a plate and placed it in front of Mike. He looked at it and Owner Mike smiled. Mike wanted to say he wasn't hungry but he didn't, for fear he might hurt Owner Mike's feelings. Owner Mike spoke, "Come on Mike eat up. There's more where that came from."

Mike took the chop sticks and tried to get the food to his mouth but it kept falling off. Owner Mike apologized. "Mike, I'm sorry." He called to a waiter and told him to bring a spoon and fork. Mike did much better with the fork and spoon. Owner Mike looked at him eating. "Good, huh, Mike?"

Mike forced another spoonful into his mouth. "Yeah! yeah! real good." He struggled to eat the rest of the food.

"Owner Mike motioned the waiter to serve him more. Mike put his hand over the plate. "Please, I've had enough. It was very good." The waiter stood with the large spoonful of food ready to put it on Mike's plate. Mike shook his head. "No more, thank you." The waiter looked at Owner Mike who waved him off. "I have to get going Mike said. The wine was good but it's making me woozy. I have to get back to camp, I got a big day tomorrow. If I get a letter from Rick or Zug I'll bring it with me the next time I come. I'll write and tell them what a great time we had."

"Thanks, Mike I appreciate that. Be sure to tell them I am thinking about them and to be careful."

Mike stood. The dizziness was bad. He steadied himself by grabbing the edge of the table. He shook his head a couple of times to clear it. Owner Mike stood. "Wait, I'll walk you outside and help you catch a cab." They both staggered as they left the club. The hostess girls smiled and waved. Mike waved back. Outside Owner Mike threw his hands up and shouted at a cab. The

266

driver put on his brakes immediately. The cars following slammed on their brakes. Mike thought there would be an accident. Owner Mike, laughed. "Don't worry these cab drivers are the best in the world. They may scare you but you always make it to your destination." They shook hands as Mike got in the cab.

The driver looked back. "Where to, Joe?"

Mike laughed. He thought of the last time they were in a cab and the driver said that to Rick. The driver was waiting for an answer. Mike tried to talk but the wine and food kept trying to come up. He sort of burped and held his breath then blurted out, "Camp Zama." The driver put the cab in gear and they were on their way.

Mike kept making burping noises and taking deep breaths. The driver looked in the rear view mirror. "Hey, Joe, you get sicky, sicky you tell me and I stop cab. No fucky up my cab." Mike shook his head and motioned with his hand to keep going.

The ride took forty-five minutes. Every time Mike breathed hard or burped the driver slowed down and looked in the rear view mirror. "I stop, Joe. You sick." Each time Mike reassured him he wouldn't mess up the cab. The cab pulled up in front of Mike's barracks. He was glad to get out and breathe fresh air. He reached in his pocket took out a handful of Yen and gave it to the driver. Seeing so much money the driver smiled. "Domoageigato (thank you.) I hope no hangover for you tomorrow, Joe." Mike didn't answer, but ran into the barracks and straight for the head.

The sweet, sick feeling was terrible. It felt like everything he ate was stuck in his throat. He stood over a toilet for ten minutes but nothing happened. He got so dizzy he sat down. He felt as though it would be better dead then to feel like this. He managed to get up and walk through the dark barracks. He found his bed and dropped on it. The bed felt like it was rocking and spinning. He put one foot on the floor and hoped it would stabilize. Somehow, he managed to fall asleep for a couple of hours. He woke up with the dry heaves and ran for the head in the darkness. Again, he stood over the toilet and nothing happened. He sat down on it and fell asleep.

Tank walked into the latrine in the morning and saw Mike asleep on the stool with his head against the wall. "Mike, Mike, wake up. What the hell are you doing sleeping in here?" Mike's bloodshot eyes opened slowly. "Man, what you been doing, a little celebrating? You must of pissed a good one last night."

Mike shook his head. "Oh no, I didn't mean to. Man, I'm really sick. I went into town and saw a friend that I met on R&R."

"What in the hell were you drinking to get tore up like this?"

Mike leaned over and rubbed the back of his neck. "Sweet wine and it was terrible stuff."

Tank laughed. "That shit will kill you."

Mike moaned. "It did."

"Come on, get up. We're going to breakfast. Get something to eat, it'll make you feel better."

Mike gagged and waved him away. "Please, don't talk about food."

Tank grabbed Mike under his armpits and pulled him to the sink. "Get your head under the faucet and turn on the cold water. That will straighten you out."

Mike let the water run over his head. It helped relieve part of the headache but the nauseated feeling remained. Tank threw him a towel. "Come on, let's go to the mess hall and get some food and you'll straighten up."

Mike shook his head. "Food is the problem. It's still stuck in me from last night and I can't get rid of it. I don't want to eat more, it will make it worse. Let me go back to bed for a while."

Tank looked concerned. "Remember Mike, we got practice in two hours. Pull yourself together."

"I'll try. Will you wake me when you get back?" "Sure."

Mike laid down and fell asleep immediately It seemed like Tank had just left when he shook him. "Get up, Mike."

Mike's eyes slowly opened. "Man, I'll never touch wine again." He got out of bed, all the while holding his head.

They walked to the locker room and it even hurt to put on his equipment. He stared at the helmet for a long time before he put it on. Coach Wilson shouted, "Two laps." Mike grimaced when he heard this. The heat outside was almost unbearable.

He started to run around the field and every time his foot hit the ground he could feel the rice, vegetables, and wine sloshing from his stomach to his throat. He thought,This is the beginning of a very painful day. I'll try to stay as inconspicuous as I can and maybe they won't notice me and let me alone. I don't want to be hit today. As soon as Mike was done with his laps he ran to the water bucket. He couldn't ever remember being so thirsty.

Tank watched him drink. "Go easy, Mike. That wine is still in your system and you'll get drunk all over drinking like that." Mike put down the cup.

Again, Coach Wilson passed out shirts, Mike got a red one. Tank smiled when he saw Mike slowly and painfully put it on "Come on Mike, get moving. This heat will sweat that crap out of you." Mike didn't say anything, he just shook his head. The assistant coach running the red team motioned for Mike to come to him.

"Listen, I want you to throw a few passes then come back with the draw play." Mike didn't answer. "Did you hear me?"

Mike swallowed hard. "Yes, sir, I heard you." The coach stared at him. "Are you all right? What's the matter?"

"I'm all right, sir."

Tank saw Mike was having a problem. He got the coach's attention. "Sir, don't you think it would be wise to start out running, then go to the pass? We did good against them yesterday and they'll think we're going to start out throwing today."

The coach turned to Tank. "I don't think so. I thought about it last night. We'll pass till they stop it and then we'll go to the run." The coach hit Mike on the back. "Okay, go out there and wing it."

Mike leaned over the center and slowly put his hands under him. Perspiration dripped from his face. He called the signals and the ball came back. He dropped back and completed a short pass. The coach came up to Mike. "That's how you do it. Great pass."

Mike held his breath but didn't say anything. He didn't want the coach to smell his breath. "Keep throwing, Mike. I'll tell you when to start running the ball." Mike completed two more passes and both were painful. He felt bloated. The water, rice and wine was churning in his stomach causing a sour taste in his mouth. The coach came up again. "Okay, Mike, go back like you're going to pass, pump the ball and run up the middle. You guys up front, open the hole. You got it?" Everyone in the huddle nodded.

Mike called the signals and dreaded running the ball. He took the snap from the center. He dropped back and faked. The defensive men put their arms up trying to block the pass. Mike brought the ball back down and cradled it in his arm and started running for the large hole in the line. For some reason his knee hit the ball and it dropped to the ground. Someone yelled. "Fumble!" Mike leaned over and tried to scoop the ball. Apeman saw the ball on the ground and bent over running as fast as he could toward Mike. Mike managed to pick up the ball, at the same time Apeman drove his shoulder into Mike's stomach. Mike was carried backwards on Apeman's shoulder and slammed to the ground. Apeman's weight crushed into Mike's stomach. Other players dove on. Mike felt his body being spun, twisted and squashed. He had a hard time breathing, his mouth was pressed against Apeman's neck right below the back of his helmet. He felt everything in his stomach coming up.

He made a gurgled, muffled scream. "Let me up." It was too late. Mike's mouth erupted. The stale wine, rice, and vegetables mixed with digestive fluids spewed from his mouth. The rancid smell was sickening.

Apeman felt the hot mixture running down his back and smelled it. He screamed. "Puke, puke, fuck'in puke. Get off me, you son-of-a-bitches." The other players on the pile smelled it and quickly got up. Apeman jumped to his feet and wiped the back of his neck. He brought his hand in front of his face and squinted at the swelled rice. He slung it to the ground and kept shouting. "Maggots, maggots, fuck'in maggots." He dove on the ground, rolled over on his back and rubbed in the dirt.

Coach Wilson stared at him and looked at his assistants. "You know that guy is actually crazy." They stared in disbelief.

Tank knew what happened. He slapped Mike on the back. "I never saw anything so funny in all my life. Boy, I bet you feel better now, getting rid of that shit. It couldn't a went on a better person."

Mike felt better, but was embarrassed. He tried not to laugh. Apeman stood in a creek. He was waist deep, shouting, "Maggots, puke." and throwing water over his shoulders trying to wash himself off.

Three days before the first game the team was given their uniforms. Some of the pro and college players demanded their uniforms fit perfectly. Tailors, and shoemakers adjusted the shirts, pants, and shoes. Mike's uniform was a little loose. He didn't say anything. I'm lucky to have made this team and I better keep quiet. He looked at the pro and college players having their uniforms adjusted. The professional teams must really cater to their players. They must get anything they ask for. Back in high school, you were given a uniform and if it didn't fit that was tough. You played with it anyway. Really, what do I care if it's loose. I'll probably be sitting on the bench watching the game. And on the bench it don *'t* matter how your uniform fits.

270

Coach Wilson came into the locker room. "Men, stay in your game uniforms. We're going to take team pictures. Come out in an hour and sit in the stands. The photographer will tell you what he wants you to do." After hearing this, Mike saw Apeman rush into the latrine with his comb. He watched him standing in front of the mirror combing his hair and practicing smiling. He stayed in front of the mirror for a half hour trying to get every hair in place and making sure he had the right smile for the picture.

The team stood in front of the stands. The photographer instructed the smaller players to sit in the first row. The bigger men were told to take a seat in the back according to their size. Mike watched Apeman pat his hair as he went to the third row. Another group sat behind him. The photographer made adjustments on his camera then told the group to get ready. He took the picture and Apeman shouted at the same time. "You son-of-a-bitch, I'll kill you." Everyone turned around. Apeman's was standing with his hair in his face. Someone in the row behind messed his hair just when the picture was taken. The guys behind him all looked innocent. Apeman pointed at them. "I'll find the bastard who did it and I'll kick his ass." The picture was put in the program, and Apeman looked wild.

Chapter 20
The first game

Game day and the players came into the locker room. It wasn't noisy.
No one joked or teased. They talked in low tones just above a whisper and kept
to themselves and didn't say much. Mike thought back to his high school days.
It was the same type of atmosphere in the locker room before a game. Even
though these players were seasoned, they had the same emotions. After they got
dressed, Coach Wilson called them into the conference room. The player's
cleats clicked on the tile floor as they walked in. No one said a word. This was
all business today. Even Apeman understood that.

Coach Wilson stood in front of the room. He looked different dressed
in his sports jacket and tie. He waited till everyone sat down. "Men, this is the
day we've been waiting for. We worked hard to get here. This Navy team also
worked hard but we worked harder and we will prove it today. Is that
understood?"

A loud roar from the players. "Yes, sir." Mike could feel the emotions
progressively being lifted.

Coach Wilson waited till it got quiet. "Remember men, Today you'll be
making memories that will last the rest of your life. If we win, it will be happy
memories and you'll enjoy thinking back about it. If we lose - damn I hate that
word- you'll try to forget it but it won't go away. So when you're out on that
field make yourselves good memories. When we come back here after the game
we'll be winners."

Another loud yell. "Yes, Sir."

Coach Wilson spoke for about five more minutes, working up the team.
"Okay, men, here is the starting team. Mike stared at the ceiling. This will be
the first game I ever sat on the bench. It will be hard to take, but that's the way
it is. They don't want a high school quarterback running a team of pros and
college stars.

Coach Wilson called out a position and then a player's name. The
player smiled and nodded. The quarterback was the last position to be called.

The coach hesitated and looked around the room and pointed. "Our quarterback will be Mike Ryan."

Mike was stunned. He couldn't believe it. He looked at Coach Wilson and nodded. His body tingled. He felt as though everyone in the room was staring at him.

Coach Wilson shouted. "Okay men, let's take the field and win this game."

Tank and Mike jogged to the stadium. "Congratulations Mike, I knew you could do it."

"I just hope I can. It sure is something, me a high school player leading this team."

Tank laughed. "You don't have anything to worry about. You proved yourself."

"But, you know what I mean. You All Americans and pros and me just a high school quarterback leading you guys. Man, I'm overwhelmed."

"That's why these guys are great and made the pros. They play as a team. You call the plays and they'll make them work."

"Thanks, Tank. I'm going to do my best."

"That's all you can do. Now get out there and do it."

The team rushed onto the field and warmed up. Coach Wilson and the assistants stood on the sideline watching. After warm-ups, the players gather around the coach. He pointed to one of the goal posts. "I want the starting eleven to go under that goal post and wait till your name is called. They're going to introduce you. When your name is called, run onto the field and take your spot for the kickoff." Mike could feel the butterflies forming in his stomach.

The large trumpet shaped speakers came alive with shrill static sounds. After the squeaking subsided the announcer said. "Good afternoon ladies and gentlemen, welcome to Camp Zama football field. We have a great game in store for you on this clear day. The United States Navy from Atsugie Naval Base against the United States Army team from right here at Camp Zama. I will introduce the players from Atsugie first.

Mike listened as the announcer called out the Navy players. A lot of them were college and pro players. When a Navy player ran onto the field with his dark blue and gold uniform the band played his college fight song. Mike thought, This Navy team is loaded with talent. After the last Navy player took his kickoff spot the announcer shouted.

"And now the United States Army, Camp Zama Ramblers." The soldiers in the stands stood and cheered. One after another the Camp Zama players were introduced and the history where they played football. It was unbelievable. So and so from Notre Dame made All-American and now playing for the Cleveland Browns. So and so from Southern California now playing with the Los Angeles Rams. Most of the Ramblers were All-Americans.

Mike thought, The owner, General Marvin must of had a lot of men screening for his players in Korea. When the player heard his name he ran onto the field and the Army band played his college song. Everyone had a title and a college.

Mike thought, This must be a dream.

He was the last to be announced. "At quarterback Mike Ryan.—." The announcer stuttered. The stands were quiet. The band didn't know what to play. Mike felt uneasy. Finally the announcer shouted. "Starting at quarterback, Mike Ryan from Ohio." The band immediately played the Ohio State fight song. Even though Mike didn't play for Ohio State, he felt proud to be running onto that field with that spirited song playing for him. He felt like he was floating ten feet above the field as he ran to his team mates.

Camp Zama had won the toss and chose to receive. The Navy team kicked the ball and it was returned for twenty-five yards by a Zama receiver. Mike huddled his team. Tank grabbed his wrist. "Mike, be cool. Try to catch these guys sleeping. Go for the long pass and throw it on the first play." Mike looked uncertain. "I mean it, throw the bomb, take a chance. You can do it."

Mike debated with himself. Should he throw the ball and risk an interception or play it safe and run it. He stood in front of the huddle and Tank nodded and winked.. Mike looked at the raw-boned end. "You ready Tony?"

"Always."

"Okay, gang, long pass divide right."

The Zama team clapped in unison, came out of the huddle and faced the Navy team. Mike looked at the line before calling signals. Apeman was staring at the Navy player directly across from him. Apeman shouted in his face. "It's going to be a long day for you, Asshole."

The Navy player didn't blink. "Show me, Jerk."

Tank shouted. "Knock off the bullshit, Apeman."

Mike called signals and when the right number was shouted the ball was pounded back into his hand by the center. He back pedaled to the pocket. He looked away from Tony, the end, going down the sideline. He pumped the ball like he was going to throw to a halfback going across the middle. The line was doing their job keeping the Navy players off him. Mike looked to Tony who now was about forty-five yards down the field and running fast. Mike brought his arm back and noticed the defensive halfback was slowing down. Mike smiled. He saw this before. The defensive back didn't believe he could throw it that far. Mike whipped his arm forward putting his back and wrist into it. The ball released in a tight spiral. Tony kept running and the defensive man slowed down, anticipating the ball would fall short and he'd make an interception. He saw the ball coming but it didn't slow down and drop. It flew over his head with a lot of velocity and good trajectory. He tried to regain the distance to Tony but it was too late. He made a dive for the ball but it continued into the outstretched hands of Tony, who pulled it in and ran into the end zone for a touchdown.

The soldiers from Camp Zama stood and cheered. The announcer blurted out, "Camp Zama strikes first on a beautiful seventy-five yard pass from Ryan to Agreo."

Mike sensed that wonderful feeling that he experienced so many times when he played in high school. He jogged off the field and the whole team was waiting to shake his hand. They tapped him on the back and some of them said, "Nice pass, Mike. It was perfect."

Mike sat on the bench and Coach Wilson stood over him. He hit Mike on the helmet. "That was the prettiest throw I ever saw. Keep up the good work, kid."

The Navy team moved the ball down the field but Camp Zama held. The pounding in the line was fierce and it could be heard in the stands. The big linemen from both teams were going toe to toe against each other. A Navy halfback ran into the Army line. There was a large pileup. Everyone got up except one Zama player who was lying on his back rocking back and forth gasping for air. Someone shouted. "Apeman is down."

Some of the players started singing. "Ape call do le aa ba." The big guy rolled on to his stomach and got to his knees. He was in pain, but the chanting seemed to make him try harder to stand up. The fans were chanting with the players. Even though he was hurting he called off the trainers running to assist him. Mike saw the pain on Apeman's face as he limped back to the sideline. The chanting from the players and the spectators got louder. Apeman hunched over and started rocking back and forth. He let his knuckles drag the ground. His lips looked like the front of a trumpet. He tried to make animal calls but it was too painful. He made it to the bench and dropped down on it.

An assistant coach ran to him. "What's the matter with you?"

"My fuck'in ribs are broke."

The coach yelled. "Hell, I thought it was something serious. You're not going to stop for something like that, are you?" Apeman stared at him. The coach glared back. "You want to play, or sit down like a puss?"

"Play, man. I want to play."

Two trainers grabbed Apeman and stood him up. One of them shouted. "Throw your arms above your head." Apeman did, and they pulled his shirt up exposing his huge hairy chest. They wrapped wide white adhesive tape around his massive chest and back. Every time the tape stuck to the rib area where Apeman was injured he grimaced, and took a deep breath. When the trainer was done, Apeman's chest looked like a mummy's. The trainer tapped him on the back and said, "All done. How does it feel?"

"It hurts like hell."

"Get back in there. It'll feel better as the game goes on."

Apeman made a screechy noise and ran back on the field. The people in the stands erupted cheering and singing. Apeman responded by bending over and letting his arms dangle and his knuckles drag the ground all the way to the huddle. The fans went crazy and gave him another big cheer. The Navy team just stared at him in disbelief.

Mike's confidence grew with every play. He looked at Tony the raw-boned end. "Tony, we burnt their defensive back on that long pass. This time go down field like you're going to run that long pattern. After you get about fifteen yards, buttonhook. I'll hit you with a pass then you lateral to the right halfback, who will be trailing."

The defensive halfback saw Tony coming straight down the field and thought Tony was going for the long pass again. This time he would not underestimate the strength of the Army quarterback's arm. He didn't let Tony get behind him. He was surprised when Tony stopped and turned and the football came into his chest. The defensive halfback dashed back and tackled Tony. As soon as Tony felt he was being tackled he pitched the ball to the trailing halfback. The speedy halfback caught the ball and ran down the sideline for another Army touchdown.

Tony came up to Mike and hit him on the helmet. "Mike, it worked like a charm. It faked that guy out of his jockstrap." He put his arm on Mike's shoulder and they walked off the field to the people cheering them.

Coach Wilson met them as they came off the field. "You guys are a great combination. You're playing a hell of a game."

The game was winding down and Camp Zama was still winning fourteen to nothing. Mike knew the Navy team was playing defense against the pass. He called the draw play. He went back to pass, then faked it. He ran up the middle and then headed for the sideline. He was open and going for the goal. A Navy player was running toward him. A Zama man threw a block on him. Mike continued running and scored. The Army fans were on their feet cheering. The announcer shouted over the speakers. "A fifty yard touchdown run by Quarterback Mike Ryan from Ohio. What a day this boy is having."

The rest of the game was strictly defense and both teams continued to battle each other. The final gun sounded and the Camp Zama team walked off the field victorious with a twenty-one to nothing win. Mike thought this was one of the best games he had ever played. These great players on his team made him look good. What a privilege to be part of them.

Mike was walking to the showers and he heard someone call. He turned and saw General Marvin in his dress uniform. "Come here, Mike, I want to talk with you." He stared at the stars on the general's shoulders. He still felt uneasy with him.

Mike took off his helmet and slowly walked to him. He raised his hand and started to salute. "That's not necessary, Mike." The general tapped Mike on his chest with the back of his hand. "That was a great game you played today, son."

Mike nodded., "Thanks, Sir."

"Are you sure you never played college ball?"

"No, Sir, just high school."

General Marvin smiled. "Well before you go home, I guarantee there'll be colleges begging for you to come to their schools, if I have anything to do with it. You may be playing in Japan, but I assure you they'll be hearing about you."

"Thank you, sir."

Frenzy in the locker room was unbelievable. Guys were patting each other on the backs celebrating. General Marvin entered slapping his swagger stick on the side of his pants. The room became quiet, all eyes were on him. Someone shouted, "Throw the owner in the showers." Two big sweating linemen made a move for him.

The General pointed his swagger stick at them and they stopped in their tracks. "They'll be none of that bullshit." There was no more talk about throwing the General into the showers. The room got quiet and the players studied the man's serious expression. He stayed that way for awhile, then he busted out laughing. "Men, you played a hell of a game today and I'm very proud of you." The players relaxed and gave him a loud cheer. He yelled, "Bring on the Marines and the Air Force and we'll kick their asses too." The team gave another loud roar.

General Marvin said a few more encouraging words and left. The players settled down and dressed. Mike stayed in the shower letting the warm water run over his sore spots. When he was done most of the players were gone. He walked back to his locker and heard someone in pain. "Ew, ouch, wow, damn, ah, wow." He went to where the voice was coming from. Apeman was naked leaning against the wall and looking up. He was covered with sweat and slowly pulling tape off his chest. He'd pull a little, then with a razor blade he'd cut the thick hair sticking to it. When he pulled he'd jerk his head back, grimace, and cuss. Mike walked back to his locker and put on his under-shorts. Apeman kept groaning and Mike felt sorry for him. Mike knew how much it hurt when you pull tape off bare skin. It must really hurt when you got all that thick hair under that tape like Apeman.

Mike thought he'd help. He hunched over and snuck behind Apeman. When Apeman shut his eyes and started to pull the tape, Mike grabbed it and yanked as hard and as fast as he could. The big man jumped and let out an ear-splitting scream. Everyone stopped doing what they were doing except Mike who kept pulling the tape. Apeman was on his tip toes screaming and looked like a giant top spinning as Mike yanked. He didn't stop pulling till every strip was off.

Mike stood in front of Apeman holding the large ribbon of white tape with black hair stuck to it. He dangled it in front of the big guy. "Now, don't that feel better?"

'I'll, I'll, I'll kill you, I'll kill you. You bastard." He lunged for Mike's throat and Mike ducked and ran. He dashed down the aisle and Apeman was behind, cussing and threatening. Mike got to the doors and stopped. He turned and Apeman was still after him. From the mean expression on Apemans face Mike thought it would be best to get out of there. He pushed the panic bars and the doors flew open. Mike quickly shut them hoping Apeman would stay inside. Almost immediately the doors blasted open and Apeman rushed out naked, charging like a wild bull. "I'm going to break your neck you little bastard when I get you."

Mike was faster and he ran for a block and thought Apeman would give up the chase. He looked back and Apeman was still following, cursing and threatening. "I'll get you, bastard, you."

Mike let him get about twenty yards away. "Apeman, listen, I didn't do that to be funny. I wanted to help you."

There was no reasoning with the big guy. "When I get my hands on you, I'll kill you."

Mike knew it was useless trying to talk to this madman. He had to find a way to make him stop. He ran, again putting distance between the two of them. People stared at Mike running barefooted in his undershorts. They didn't stare long at him when they saw the big naked hairy guy. Mike noticed this and he headed for the PX. There will be plenty of people there. He'll surely realize he's naked and stop when he sees them. The next block Mike turned left and made a dash for the large store a hundred yards away. There was a crowd in front. He ran right in the midst of them. Someone pointed at Apeman. "That guy doesn't have any clothes on." Everyone stopped and stared at the big hairy naked guy.

Apeman saw the people. He stopped dead in his tracks and doubled over. "Oh, no, shit." He put one hand over his privates and the other on his buttocks. He turned around and galloped away. Mike, laughed, I better not go back to the locker room, he'll be waiting for me. He ran to his barracks and got a new change of clothes.

He dressed and left. Tank and a few of the other players were walking down the sidewalk. Tank shouted for Mike to join them. He did and they went to the service club. They were sitting at the table enjoying themselves, rehashing the game and drinking beer when Mike felt a large hairy arm go around his neck. "You may be faster than me but I got you now." Mike's eyes widened. He tried to think of a way to get out of Apeman's hold. The other players looked and then they broke out laughing. The pressure was released and Apeman removed his arm and swung Mike's chair around. Mike was relieved when he saw Apeman laughing. He grabbed Mike's hand and shook it. "No hard feelings, quarterback. You played a great game."

"Thanks a lot."

"Tell me one thing. Why in the hell do you have to mess with me? First you puke on me, then you tear my skin and hair off. What goes with you?"

Mike shrugged his shoulders. "I'm not messing with you, Apeman. I just wanted to help."

"Help?" He lifted his shirt and exposed his chest. It looked as though someone with a small lawn mower went around his chest and back. There was a white path in the dark hair where the tape ripped out his hair. Everyone at the table laughed except Mike.

Mike, told him he was sorry. Apeman pulled his shirt down and Mike patted him on the back. "I want to thank you and the rest of you guys for giving me all that protection when I was passing. It was great and I really appreciate it."

Apeman smiled, then grabbed everyone's drinks and chugged them. After he'd empty one glass he'd wipe his mouth with his big hand and grab another. Mike couldn't believe a man could drink so fast. A couple of times he swallowed the ice, too. When he finished the last glass he belched and said, "Man, you guys drink good stuff. Why don't you order another round?"

Tank looked at his empty glass and said to Mike. "I got a good notion to hit that crazy son-of-a-bitch so hard I'd drive him through the wall."

"Take it easy. He's just playing around. You know how he is." Tank glared at Apeman but didn't say anything.

Chapter 21
Coincidence

Everyone was having a good time. A pretty American girl walked up to their table. "Which one of you guys is Mike Ryan?" The players looked at Mike.

"I am."

"Could I please talk with you in private?" She pointed to a table.

Mike, got up and followed her. The guys at the table shouted. "Man, I wish I was a quarterback."

Mike sat down with her. "I hope you don't think I'm too forward, but this is a real coincidence. I have the same name as you. My name is Michelle Ryan. I saw you play today and that announcer kept saying your name. You're a football star. We have the same name. I had to tell you."

Mike blushed. Well, I don't know about the football star but I know you're a lot prettier Mike Ryan than I am."

"I graduated from college last year and was a majorette. I love football games, they're so exciting. I'm working in Japan as a DAC."

"DAC, what's that?"

"It's a civilian employed by the government. It's interesting work and I get to do a lot of traveling."

They danced and got to know each other. When it was time to leave Mike looked at her. "If we were back in the states I'd have a car, and if you would of let me I'd drive you home. But we're in Japan and I don't have a car so I guess this is the end of the evening. It was nice meeting you."

She laughed, "Don't worry about that. I've got a car."

"You mean to say you have your own car, here in Japan?"

"Sure, my father sent it to me. I'd be glad to drop you off at your barracks."

"Well, that would be nice of you. I'd appreciate that."

They walked toward the door. The players saw them leaving and started howling and making remarks. Mike told her to ignore them. She shook her long blond hair and laughed. "That's all right, I think it's cute." Mike hurriedly got her outside.

Michelle led him to a new shiny yellow convertible. She handed him the keys. "Here, you drive, you wanted to take the lady home." Mike felt awkward but he took the keys. He opened the passenger door and she got in. He walked around the back of the car and admired it and thought how many times he wished he had a car like this. He got in and started it. Michelle slid next to him. "What time is your curfew?"

"No curfew tonight. The coach was satisfied about the game today and we can stay out as late as we want."

She pointed to the mountains which were illuminated by a full moon. "It sure is a romantic night. Mike, you see that little cluster of lights on the side of that mountain?"

"Yes, I see it."

"Well, there's a nice nightclub and restaurant up there. Would you like to go?"

"With you, I'd go any place."

She laughed. "Great."

She pointed to a road. "It will lead right to the base of the mountain. They exited the camp and Mike drove on the right side of the road. "Hey, Mike, you're in Japan. You have to drive on the left side."

"Oh, that's right. I'm sorry."

The night air was warm and smelled of pine trees. Michelle snuggled up closer to him. She turned on the radio to the Armed Forces Station. It was playing slow moody music. Mike thought he better pinch himself to see if this was real.

He looked at the pretty girl and said, "Please don't wake me up. This has to be a dream."

She smiled and gave him a soft kiss on his neck. "It's real."

The road leveled off into a parking lot. Mike parked the car, got out and opened the door for her. "You're a real gentleman, Mike."

"And you're a beautiful lady." He held her arm and they walked to the dimly lit nightclub. They were met by an attractive oriental woman in a tight fitting dress with a slit up the side that exposed a well shaped leg. She bowed and led them to a table next to a picture window. Mike looked out the window. "What a spectacular sight. It reminds me of Colorado."

Michelle agreed. "Look at those lights down there, aren't they beautiful?"

"Yeah, they look like embers of a dying fire."

"You have a good imagination."

"When I see something beautiful it automatically makes my imagination work. It's working overtime when I look at you."

She reached across the table and put her hand on his. "You got my imagination working."

Mike could feel the short hairs on the back of his neck rise and the blood rushing to his face. He smiled at her and a crazy thought ran through his mind. If Rick were here he'd be crawling across the table after her. He started to laugh and tried to hold it back.

"What are you laughing about?"

"Oh, I just thought of a friend of mine who is in Korea. He used to do some crazy things. I'll introduce you to him when he comes over on R&R."

All through the night she stared at him and smiled. He liked it but it made him feel uncomfortable. He looked away and every time he looked back at her she was staring and smiling. She asked him where he went to college? He thought, if he told her he didn't go to college she'd know he was younger than her. "Well it's a long story. Right now let's talk about you. I'm sure it will be more interesting."

"You got a girl back home waiting for you, don't you?"

"No, believe me I don't have a girl. I had a few dates but never got serious with anyone."

"Now, come on, Mike, you're a good looking football player. You have to have a girl friend."

"No, honest there's no one." Mike's face showed he was uncomfortable with these questions.

"You don't like talking about yourself, I can see that. I won't question you anymore."

"Oh, I don't mind but there are so many other things we could talk about, like that beautiful view, or how fate gave us the same names and we meet in a land half way around the world."

She smiled. You're right, Mike. And before we go any further I have to make a confession. Please forgive me for what I did."

Mike shrugged his shoulders and squinted. "Go ahead and tell me."

She stirred her drink and looked down at the table. "Well, my name isn't Michelle Ryan. My name is Betty Pierce. I feel like a fool for what I did. I saw you playing today and I needed an excuse to meet you. I thought, if I told you my name was the same as yours it would get me acquainted. When I came into the club tonight and saw you, I got up enough nerve to tell you that lie." She looked up. "Are you mad, Mike?"

"Naw, what's in a name. You're still as pretty with this name as you were with the other one."

She put her hand on his. "I'm so glad you're not mad at me, Mike." She started rubbing the calf of his leg with her foot under the table.

Mike looked around to see if anyone was watching. He took her arm. "Let's dance." He escorted her to the terrace and a dark spot. Stars Fell On Alabama was playing.

They held each other closely and danced. She looked into his eyes. "That is the perfect song for tonight."

"It sure is."

She placed her head on his shoulder and pressed her body so tight against him he could feel every muscle of hers when she moved. "Please, Mike, don't let this night end." She stood on her tip toes, kissed him and whispered, "You're not only a good athlete, you're a wonderful dancer. She started to say, "I bet you're a wonderful lov— ." But caught herself.

Mike felt his temperature rising. Everything was going perfect till he straightened up. He grimaced. Betty pushed him away. "What's the matter? Did I do something wrong?"

"No, it's nothing. It will go away in a minute. I got a cramp in my back."

She rubbed his back. "Mike, those muscles are as hard as stone."

"It's nothing. A lot of players get cramps after a game. I guess it's from the pounding and stress." They walked back to the table. Mike picked up his glass. "If I get enough of these in me, it will go away."

They drank and listened to the music and stayed till dawn. The mountains turned different shades of reds. Mike and Betty were fascinated by this incredible view and gazed till the sun came up completely. They left the table and again were met by the attractive lady in the dress with the split up the side. She looked at Mike. "Is everything all right? I saw you limping."

He explained he played football and was sore. She pointed to the large window. "Come, I want to show you something." They followed her. She pointed downward. "You see that white building next to the river?" They nodded. "That is a very good Japanese steam bath and hot pool. You go there and you will get rid of the soreness."

Betty smiled. "That's wonderful. I haven't had a steam bath for a long time. Want to go, Mike?"

Mike shrugged his shoulders. "Hey, I'm game for anything."

Betty smiled. "Anything?"

Mike didn't reply. He drove down to the building. They got out of the car and as soon as they got to the door it slid open. An old man bowed to them. He pointed to a pool, then to thick wooden doors where the steam rooms were. "You like?"

Betty pointed at the steam rooms and in fluent Japanese told him they wanted a steam bath. The old man looked surprised and bowed. Mike asked, where she learned to speak Japanese so well? "I studied it in college and took courses here in Japan."

The old man escorted them down a hall. He opened a door to a dressing room. Betty went in and Mike started to follow. The old man put out his arm blocking Mike and said something in Japanese. Mike looked at him.

Betty laughed. "He said, you'll have to go down the hall to the little boys' room."

The old man led him to another room and handed him a large towel. Mike took off his clothes and wrapped the towel around his waist. He waited in the hallway. Betty slid the door open and came out with a towel wrapped around her. Mike could see she was a well- built woman. He walked to her and she whistled. "Well if it isn't the big football player."

The old man motioned for them to follow him. He pulled a thick wooden door open that had a small glass window three quarters the way up. They entered and Betty sat down on one of the tiers. She patted the seat next to her. "Right here, sit next to me." The old man left and immediately steam hissed from pipes along the walls. Betty pointed at the steam. "That's what you do to me."

Mike bent over and kissed her.

The heat in the room increased and Mike felt the perspiration running down his face and body. He looked at Betty. Her blond hair was wet and sticking to her head. She tapped him on his knee. "Feels good doesn't it? This should do wonders for your back."

"It feels better already."

Betty didn't talk, she just smiled at him. He looked at the wet towel clinging to her body. It outlined every curve she had. He felt uneasy and looked back at her face. She still had that smile. He looked away and put his elbows on his knees and his hands under his chin. He wanted to look at her and say something but he felt awkward. It was uncomfortable. A towel dropped on his foot and he heard a soft giggle. Mike stared at the towel and got nervous. He reached down to pick it up and give it back to her. She got up and stood on it. He gasped, then slowly looked up. Her beautiful wet naked body glistened. She was the best developed woman he had ever seen. She still had that smile on her face. "You like what you see?"

Mike reached out and put his hands around her slim waist and pulled her to him. He slid his hands up and down her soft moist back that felt like velvet. She wrapped her arms around his neck and kissed him hard. He twisted her and slowly laid her on the wooden bench. Mike's hands caressed her warm soft skin. He looked down into her eyes and she whispered.

"Oh, Mike." He couldn't believe how spontaneous things were happening. He was in another world. Nothing mattered now. Betty was screaming, "Mike, Mike, oh, Mike, don't ever stop." The couple was in ecstasy till loud pounding sounded on the door. Mike looked through the steam and barely made out the face of the old man staring in the small window shouting something in Japanese.

Mike waved his hand. "Get out of here."

The old man opened the door slightly and screamed, "Domie you, no do, no do."

Mike tried to wave him off again. "Get the hell out of here, you old fool. What's the matter with you?"

Betty kept gyrating her body shouting "Mike, oh Mike."

"What goes with this guy? What's he saying?"

Betty kept maneuvering and panting. "He's saying, we'll die if we do this in the steam."

"Tell him to get out of here, we don't care."

She shouted something in Japanese but the old guy didn't go away, he kept yelling. "He says our hearts will explode and he doesn't want us to die in his place." Mike told her to ignore him and he'll go away.

She smiled. "That's what I'm doing."

The old man left but not for long. He grabbed a bucket and ran outside to a cold mountain stream. He dipped the bucket and filled it to the brim with ice water. He ran back to the steam room and pulled the door open and slung the cold water through the steam onto the two naked bodies. The wave of cold water hit its targets. Two shrieking screams erupted in the dense steam. Mike found he was standing on his feet and didn't realize he got up. "Where you at, you crazy old man?"

Betty was standing beside him shivering. "Oh, Mike, I never felt anything so cold in all my life." She hugged him to get warm. Mike opened the door and looked into the hallway.

"Get back, Betty he's coming with another bucket."

Betty yelled, "Oh, no," and hid behind Mike. Mike quickly closed the door and held the handle to keep it shut The old man pulled the door but couldn't open it. He looked into the small glass window and Mike was looking directly into his face.

"Betty, tell him to quit." She shouted something in Japanese and the old man quieted down. Mike continued to hold the door shut and watched him. The old guy kept shouting and pointing to his heart. "Betty tell him it's over and there's no need to throw any more water." Betty convinced the old man and he slowly walked away with the bucket. They left the steam, showered and got dressed.

The sun was high and they squinted until they got into the car. Mike looked at her and laughed. "Man, that cold water sure put a damper on it."

"You're right there."

He drove back to his barracks and got out. Betty slid behind the steering wheel. "Will I be seeing you again, Mike?"

"Sure, but I hope under different circumstances." She drove off and he walked to the barracks.

A couple of players were standing outside. "Hey, Mike, that's a fine looking broad and she got some flashy wheels."

Mike smiled, "Yeah, you can say that again."

"You want to tell us about last night? We're good listeners."

287

"No, you guys wouldn't believe it. And besides you're too young."

The next week was hard work at practice preparing for the game against the Fuji Marines. Couch Wilson was worried about this game. There was a bitter rivalry between Camp Zama and the Fugi Marines. General Marvin was at practice every day. The curfew was ten thirty and the assistant coaches checked every bed to make sure the guys were in them. Mike knew this game would be harder since the Marines scouts watched the game with the Navy. He wouldn't have the element of surprise like he did in the opening game. Every day Betty drove by the practice field with the top down on her convertible. Her long blonde hair blew in the wind. The players shouted wolf calls and whistled. General Marvin saw them not paying attention to the coaches, he shouted, "Whoever belongs to that broad in heat, tell her to wise up and stay the hell away from the practice field. There's not going to be any bullshit until we kick hell out of those Marines. Is that understood? Those Marines are going to be tough and we better be ready for them or they'll kick our asses."

Every day after practice Mike walked to the barracks and dropped on his bed exhausted and fell asleep. One day he noticed someone put the mail on his bed. He saw an envelope. It came from Korea. Rick's name was on the upper left corner. He opened it and sat on the side of his bed.

Hello Mike:

Well we finally got a lull between the shooting and all the bullshit. Mike this place is wall to wall gooks. There are so many waves attacking us it feels like we're in a hurricane.

Where are all these bastards coming from? They must not have TVs in their homeland. They have to be multiplying twenty four hours a day. You can't believe all the guys we took basic with who got it. Zug and I are old timers now.

Mike, you're not going to believe this but I'll tell you anyway.

They made me a sergeant. Can you imagine that? Me, a sergeant. The other day I looked right in this guy's face and gave him an order and the damn fool laughed. I thought it was funny so I laughed too.

We got the Stars And Stripes Newspaper and we saw your picture scoring that touchdown. Zug and I showed everyone in the company.

We 're proud of you, Mike. I hope everything is going great for you.

You deserve good things. You're a good person, the best I ever met. I can't wait till we go on R&R again. I've been studying this Japanese book every day. Bring on those broads now. I'll be able to talk do - do, just watch me operate when I get there.

Mike, I got to get serious. This place is really bad. Guys are getting killed like flies. We fight these gooks all the way to the Thirty-Eighth Parallel and then we have to stop. Whole new armies join the ones we pushed up there. They regroup and it's unbelievable how many soldiers they come back at us with. When they do this we are so outnumbered it is almost impossible to stop them. We have to retreat and regroup and then go back at them. There's not going to be an end to this war. Korea is just a big killing field where soldiers are pushed at each other so they can slaughter one another. I guess it's a good way to reduce the population. I just want you to know you are the best friend I ever had. I mean this from my heart. If something should happen and it probably will, please remember me as a good guy once in awhile. Think of all the fun we had. I enjoyed it. Please say one of those prayers your mother taught you for me, I'd sure appreciate it. Maybe you could tell your mother about me and maybe she would remember me in her prayers. God likes prayers from mothers. I would really appreciate it and I'm sure it would do me good if I should meet my Maker. Thanks Mike.

Your friend, Rick

Mike put the letter on his footlocker. He shook his head. Rick and Zug must be going through some rough times. It has to be bad over there for Rick to write a letter like that. I've got to think of a way to bring up their spirits. So many times they made me feel good when I was depressed. I feel bad I got it so good here and they're in that damn war. I can't tell them how nice it is here.

He opened up his foot locker and took out a pad of paper and a pen.

Hello Rick:

Great hearing from you. It sure sounds like you're busy. It's the same way over here. I have never practiced so hard in all my life. These guys are big and when you get hit by them it hurts. I'm trying my best, but I hurt in places I never knew existed. I think I got an answer on how to keep the gooks north of the Thirty-Eight Parallel. See if you can get your girlfriend Big Bertha to come to Korea. When you chase the gooks north of the Thirty Eighth Parallel have Big Bertha waiting for them when they start coming back down. You know I feel bad talking about your girlfriend and I apologize. You probably write her a letter every day and beg her to wait for you, so that when you get home you can marry her.

The other day I went into Tokyo and saw Owner Mike. He said to be sure to say hello to you and Zug. He can't wait till you guys get over here on R &R. He said he's going to have a big celebration when you get here. All the girls and Jimmiesan are gone. Owner Mike couldn't tell me how to get in touch with them. He still can't get over how you and Zug played those horns. Owner Mike pushed a lot of drinks and food on me. Man, I was really full. I was never so sick in all my life. I had to practice the next day and it was hot. Well this big guy tackled me in the stomach and everything went down the back of his shirt. You ought of seen him run to a creek and jump in.

Thanks for showing my picture around to the guys. I really appreciate it. We have a good team here. There are some great players and they make me look good. I read the paper and I know the fighting is fierce over there. Believe me I'm thinking and praying for you guys. Friend, you don't have to ask me to pray for you. Like I said before I say a prayer for you and Zug every day. I'll ask my mother to do the same. I'm sure she will.

I know it's bad over there. Think about R&R and all the fun we'll be having. After R&R is over you'll be a short timer and you'll be getting discharged. Of course you'll probably re-up. Just kidding.

Again, Rick, tell all the guys thanks. If I score a touchdown it will be for you guys. Don't any of you let your guard down for a minute. Stay well and get out of that hell hole. One more thing. When it gets tough, you adapt to the situation. Well, so long for now and I'll see you in a couple of months. If you and Zug get time, write a letter to Owner Mike. He is concerned about you guys. God be with you.

Hang in there, Mike.

Mike folded the letter and put it in an envelope. He walked to the mailbox by the PX, dropped it in and started walking back to the barracks. He felt helpless because he couldn't do anything for Rick and Zug except pray for them. Betty drove by and slowed when she saw him. Mike was so engrossed thinking about his friends he didn't see her. She drove in front of him and shouted as he walked by. "Hey, Mike."

Mike looked and immediately recognized the yellow convertible. He walked over and leaned his head in the window. "Hi, Betty, how you been?"

"Oh, I've been doing all right. I saw you sending off a letter to your girlfriend back home."

"Like I told you before. There's no girlfriend back home."

"What's the matter, big football player? You feel guilty about the other night and you sent her a letter confessing and telling her what a bitch I am?"

Mike was mad. "No, Betty, you got it wrong. That letter I sent was to a friend in Korea."

"Korea, what's so important about Korea? Who you kidding? You've been ignoring me for the past week." Mike looked at her and shook his head. He wanted to shout something, but he controlled himself. He glared. She smiled and patted the seat next to her. "Come on, get in, I'll forgive you." He turned and walked back to the PX and stayed inside till he cooled off. He bought a few things he didn't need and walked out the back door. He went back to the barracks and thought about his friends in that brutal war.

The game with the Marines was tough and Apeman didn't make it easier. He kept taunting them. When Camp Zama broke the huddle on the first play, Apeman ran to the line of scrimmage rocking back and forth dragging his knuckles. The Marine players stared at him and one of them said, "Stupid ground-pounding idiot."

Apeman pointed at them and shouted, "I'd rather have a sister in the cat house than a brother in the Marine Corps."

The Marines shouted, "Kill that goofy looking bastard. Kick that balloon head's ass."

Mike could see the anger in the Marines' eyes. They're going to be tough enough to play and now he riles them up by saying something like that. This is going to be a mean game. Why can't he keep his mouth shut. Mike got the ball and handed it to the halfback. He was immediately tackled by the Marines. Mike tried to pass but was dropped for a loss. The Marines were hitting hard and when they tackled there were four or five of them hitting the Zama ball carriers at once. The first quarter came to an end and the score was tied zero to zero. A Zama halfback gained five yards and there was a big pile of bodies. Someone screamed from inside the mass. "Aw,wa, awww, hurry up and get off me. The players unpiled and a Marine was dancing around rubbing the calf of his leg. "Some son-of-a-bitch bit me." The referee came to him and the Marine pointed to a perfect set of red teeth marks on his leg. "Some bastard bit me."

The referee asked. "Who bit you? Point him out."

"How in the hell do I know. 1 was at the bottom of that pile. If I knew, I'd punch his fuck'in teeth out."

Mike had his team in a huddle waiting for the game to start again. He noticed Apeman laughing. Tank saw him and grabbed him by the shirt and stuck his fist in his face. "Knock off that bullshit right now. You better keep that big mouth shut or I'll beat you to a pulp you big dummy."

Apeman glared at Tank and started pounding his chest. He yelled, "Try it, Asshole."

Tank lunged at him, but Mike and a couple of other players grabbed him. Mike shouted, "Hey, what's the matter with you guys? You keep it up and we'll lose this game." The coach saw what was going on and he yelled for Mike to call a time out. The players walked to the sideline and Coach Wilson pointed at Tank and Apeman.

"You two stay out of the game till you get control of yourselves. This kind of crap will cost us the game. Don't go back in till I tell you." Mike studied the Marine team before he formed the huddle.

From the looks on their faces they were going to rush hard. The screen pass would be a perfect play if they're coming hard. "Okay gang, they're going to be rushing. I want a screen pass to the fullback going right." They broke the huddle. Mike got the ball and dropped back deep, sucking the Marines after him. It felt like every one of their players were chasing him. He quickly jumped up and lobbed a pass to the fullback who had wandered to the right side of the field. Zama's linemen were in front of him and they blocked the remaining Marine defensive men. The fullback scored.

It didn't take the Marines long to come back with a touchdown of their own. The score was tied again. Tank and Apeman came back in the game and joined the huddle. Mike said, "Their defense is rushing everyone except their secondary. The trap, draw and screens are working. Let's pay attention to our assignments and make these plays work. We can win this game, if every man does his part."

Tank yelled out. "You're right, Mike. Remember, we play hard, not dirty." Apeman made a mocking noise.

Mike shouted, "Knock it off, you guys." I got to find a way to stop these guys. They're going to disrupt our whole offense. I'll call a play that they 're both involved in. "Okay, gang, T 22 trap double spin. Apeman, make the guy across from you think he's got a clear shot into our backfield. Tank, when the guy comes across cut him down from his blind side." The play worked perfectly. Camp Zama scored another touchdown. Mike patted Apeman and Tank on the back. "You guys did a good job." They both nodded. Mike thought they were calmed down since they both helped get that touchdown.

Everything was going good until Apeman looked at the Marine across from him. "Hey, Puss, we're going to come across your chicken shit ass and score another touchdown."

The Marine dug in his cleats and yelled. "I'm going to kill you. You stupid bastard."

Mike took the ball from the center and handed it to a halfback. Apeman and the Marine made no attempt to play football. They stood toe to toe punching each other. Tank quickly got between them and tried to break it up. Apeman saw the referee running toward them blowing his whistle. He knew, if he got caught fighting he'd get thrown out of the game. He grabbed Tank by his shoulder pads and shouted. "Quit fighting, Tank. Don't hit him again."

The referee heard this and pointed at Tank and the Marine. "You're both ejected from the game for fighting."

Tank looked the referee right in the eye. "You're throwing out the wrong guy. I didn't do anything. I was trying to break it up."

The referee was irritated. "I said you're out of the game. Say one more word and I'll penalize your team fifteen yards."

Tank stormed off the field and when he got to the bench he threw his helmet down. "I'll kill that nutty bastard." He pointed at Apeman and yelled. "I'll get you for this."

Apeman laughed and shook his index finger. "You got to learn to hold your temper. You see what happens when you don't."

Mike quickly grabbed Apeman by the arm. "What's the matter with you? Knock it off." The half came to an end and

Camp Zama was ahead fourteen to seven. The team followed the coach into the locker room for the half time talk.

293

The players sat on benches and on the floor. Coach Wilson walked to the front of the room and was ready to say something when a loud bang in the back of the room got everyone's attention. They turned and saw Apeman bounce off a locker and Tank dive on him like a tiger. "You dirty rotten son-of-a-bitch pulling a stunt like that."

Coach Wilson shouted, "Break them up." Five players jumped up and managed to pull Tank off Apeman. Coach Wilson yelled, "Wait till after the season to do it, we need him right now."

Coach Wilson gave instructions for the second half. With a loud roar the players almost busted down the door to get back on the field. Tank continued to glare at Apeman. Apeman was going to shout something but Mike ran up to him. "Come on Apeman settle down. You're doing real good. You could do a lot better if you stop fooling around. You're too good of a player to be acting like this."

Apeman straightened up. "You're right Mike. I'm sorry, I don't know what makes me act this way. No more, I promise."

Ten minutes pased and Apeman was behaving. Camp Zama was in the huddle and all at once the people in the stands chanted, "Ape call do lee aa ba." Apeman stepped in front of the huddle hunched over and let his knuckles hit the ground. He jumped up and circled the huddle like a big ape.

Mike was disgusted. He glared at Apeman. "Is that how you keep your promise?"

"Ah man, I'm sorry, Mike."

The chant came from the stands again. Apeman ran to the middle of the field. He threw up his arms and both his middle fingers and shouted,. "Fuck, all you people." General Marvin and the head coach rushed onto the field. Coach Wilson grabbed Apeman by his shirt. Both he and the general chewed him out. The referee saw the general and allowed him to hold up the game.

Apeman came back to the huddle. Someone asked,

"Hey, Apeman, what did Coach Wilson and the general have to say to you?"

Apeman's head quivered. "Don't want to talk about it. Don't want to talk about it."

Mike stood in front of the huddle. "Okay you guys, let's get back to the game. Concentrate and make every play count. Let's walk off this field winners."

294

The game became a defensive battle. Both teams almost scored but couldn't cross the goal line. Camp Zama won fourteen to seven. The teams congratulated each other on a hard-fought game. A Marine player shook Mike's hand and pointed at Apeman. "What do you guys do after the game with that guy, lock him back in the mental ward and give him a stalk of bananas?"

"You're right. He was on his best behavior today. "

Mike was talking to the Marine players when Betty walked up. She waited till he was done. "You played a good game, Mike. Are you still mad at me?"

"No, I'm not mad. I was in a bad mood when I saw you at the PX. A couple of my friends are fighting for their lives in Korea. I tried to send them a letter to cheer them up. I don't understand why you keep asking me about having a girl back home. Please don't say it again."

"I won't, Mike. I'm sorry about what I said. What are you going to do tonight?"

"Most of the players are going to the service club and have a few drinks."

"Hey, that's great. A few of my girl friends and I are going there too. We'll see you."

Chapter 22
Apeman finds a mate

Mike got a beer and joined the other guys. Betty and her friends walked in and Tank nudged Mike. "Hey, look who just came in and she's got some good lookers with her. Why don't you call them over and have them join our table?"

Mike waved and Betty waved back. She and her friends walked over and she introduced them. Mike introduced the guys. More chairs were brought to the table and the girls sat down. In no time the guys and girls were paired off. One heavy set girl sat at the end of the table by herself and appeared to be bored and didn't want to be bothered.

Mike asked Betty. "Your friend doesn't look like she's having any fun. What's the matter with her?"

"Oh, she's a real stick in the mud. She's one of those intellectuals. She's always that way. I don't think she has ever been with a man and wouldn't go out with one if she was asked. She'd rather be reading a book. She's the type of person you don't want around you. I don't like her."

Mike didn't like this kind of talk and felt Betty had a sharp tongue. He didn't ask her anything else. For the next hour all she talked about was how rich her father was and all the great things about her life. Mike thought this girl must of had everything she ever wanted in life. He felt like leaving but he looked at his friends and everyone was happy and he didn't want to ruin the party, so he stayed.

Someone from the table yelled, "Apeman's here." They turned to the door. Apeman took off his baseball hat and waved it at the table.

Mike heard Tank. "Look at the way that silly jerk is dressed."

Mike tapped Tank on the shoulder. "Be cool. Let's not have any trouble. Let's all get along tonight and enjoy ourselves."

"Don't worry 1 won't start anything. I got this chick and things are looking pretty good. When I get that dummy, there's not going to be anyone around. Just me and him." Tank glared at Apeman when he came to the table. Apeman had on a white sports jacket, black dress shirt, white tie, olive drab fatigue pants, white high top tennis shoes and a multi colored baseball cap. Apeman looked at all the drinks grunted a couple of times, and walked to the only empty chair at the table next to the heavy set girl. The girl looked up at him.

He smiled. His eyes went up into their sockets and he started sucking air through his lower teeth. The girl leaned backwards. He took off his hat and bowed. "I'm Apeman, pretty lady. What's your name?"

The girl was startled but she smiled. "I'm ... I'm Wilma."

Tank and Mike watched what was going on at the end of the table. When Apeman took off his hat, Tank said, "Look at that goof's hair shine. He's got a pound of grease on it. Someone must of put a grease gun in his ear and filled his empty head, and it's seeping out." Mike broke out laughing when he looked at Apeman's glistening hair.

Wilma looked intrigued by this strange guy and she smiled. Someone at the table said, "Let's sing him the chant." The players put their hands up and shook their heads.

One of them said. "Don't get him going."

Apeman got the attention of the waitress. She asked Wilma what she would like to drink?

"I would like a soda."

Apeman started shaking his head. "I'll order the pretty lady a good drink." He got up and whispered to the waitress. Then sat down. "Now listen, pretty lady, old Apeman will get you something you'll like." The waitress came back to the table. Apeman took the drinks off the tray. He chugged his and then handed Wilma hers.

Wilma smelled it, then looked at Apeman. "This won't get me intoxicated will it?"

Apeman smiled, "Nah, it's a mild drink."

She took a sip and nodded. "This has a nice taste." She put the glass back to her mouth and took a drink. Apeman looked at Mike and winked.

Betty saw Apeman sitting next to Wilma. "Isn't that the repulsive slob that made those obscene gestures, and cursed the fans at the game today?" Mike didn't get to answer.

Tank blurted out. "That's the fool. You're a good judge of people."

Wilma had a few more drinks. Apeman got up and grabbed her by the wrists. "I want to dance with you, pretty lady."

" I never danced in my life. I don't know how."

"I don't know how either. This is a good time to learn."

She was reluctant but she went to the dance floor with him. Everyone at the table laughed when they got a good look at Apeman's suit with his white high-top tennis shoes and baseball cap. He didn't care. He wrapped his arm around Wilma, grabbed her other hand and extended their arms straight out. The music started and they rocked side to side, their straight arms went up as far as they could then dropped almost to the floor. Mike couldn't stop laughing.

Tank stared in disbelief. "Look at that jerk, he looks like he's working a water pump."

Apeman ignored other couples on the floor as he bumped into them. The dancers saw him coming and they got out of his way. Wilma was enjoying herself, Apeman made her laugh.

Betty shook her head. "I don't believe this is happening. I never saw her act this way."

Mike smiled. "She looks like she's enjoying Apeman."

"It sure does. It's probably the first man that ever got close to her, if you can call him a man."

The slow songs continued and Apeman held Wilma close. The music ended and he continued to hold her. Wilma grabbed the back of his head and pushed his lips to hers and kissed him hard. They embraced for a time and Apeman broke loose and started shaking. His lips looked like a trumpet squeaking all kinds of strange sounds.

Tank shook his head. "That broad is in heat and that dummy is sending out his mating call."

The guys at the table started chanting. "Ape call do lee aa ba." More people joined in. Apeman hunched over, his knuckles dragged along the floor. Wilma was baffled as he circled her. The people on the dance floor moved away in shock. The band played a fast tune. Apeman put his baseball cap on backwards, bent over and rolled up his pant legs. He licked his lips and rubbed his hands together. "Let's get with it baby."

Betty just sat there shaking her head. She looked at Mike. "Please tell me I'm not seeing this."

The band stopped for intermission. Apeman had his arm around Wilma when they came from the dance floor. They sat down and Wilma slurred. "Get me one of those drinks please. I'm thirsty."

298

"Mike, I never saw her act this way. She never drank alcohol before. What's got into her?"

"She's enjoying herself. It's probably the most fun she had in a long time."

Wilma kept asking for more drinks, her voice progressively grew louder. People were staring at her, but Apeman didn't care. Betty shook her head. "I wish I had a camera and a tape recorder so I could show Miss Goody-Two-Shoes how she acted."

Apeman was getting very serious and Wilma loved it. He whispered into her ear. She smiled and every once in awhile she rubbed his cheek. She again grabbed his head and pulled his face close to hers and gave him a lingering kiss. They stayed in this embrace for a long time till Apeman jumped up and shouted, "She stuck her tongue down to my liver, hot damn." He quickly bent over and kissed her again.

Betty called out. "Wilma, quit, not here, what's the matter with you?" She looked at Mike. "What should we do? She never acted this way before."

Mike shrugged his shoulders. "Leave them alone. They're not hurting anyone."

Apeman and Wilma separated from the kiss and she shouted. "Another drink, Monkey."

Apeman's head shot back. "Monkey, who the hell you calling Monkey? It's Apeman, not Monkey."

"Okay, Apeman, monkey, orangutan or whatever you are. Get me a drink."

Betty yelled. "No more, Wilma you're drunk. Don't drink anymore."

Wilma's head wobbled. "I'm all right. I can handle myself, can't I Apeman?"

"Yeah, yeah, yeah, keep drinking you're all right. I'll take care of you."

As usual, all eyes were on Apeman the rest of the night. No one knew what he would do next. Wilma stood and went to the restroom and Apeman followed her. He had his hands a couple of inches away from her buttock like he was going to grab it. When she turned around he quickly raise them and patted her on her shoulders and smiled. She smiled back and gently rubbed his chin. He let out some animal calls and walked back to the table. The guys saw him coming and they grabbed their drinks for fear he might chug them. Wilma came out of the rest room and walked across the dance floor back to the table.

Apeman jumped up and held out his arms and grunted. She laughed and ran to him and they hugged.

Tank shook his head. "You know Mike, I should hit him just once to drive some sense into his hollow head."

Wilma was having a wonderful time with Apeman. He kept encouraging her to drink more. Everyone at the table knew what he had in mind for later. The band played *Good Night Sweet Heart.* The last song of the evening. Wilma started shouting she didn't want it to be the last song. She yelled for the band to continue. Betty tried to settle her down but Wilma didn't pay any attention. The group from the table exited the club and Apeman helped Wilma navigate. She kept kissing him on the cheek and that turned him on till she said. "Monkey, you're the nicest guy."

"The damn name ain't Monkey. It's Apeman, Apeman, goddamn it, call me Apeman."

"I'm sorry, you're such a big strong man I just love being with you. She kissed him on the cheek.

He was overjoyed. He saw a large manhole cover in the sidewalk and wedged his fingers around the sides of it and managed to loosen it. He sucked in a lot of air expanding his chest. In one jerk he lifted the heavy cover over his head. The group was surprised. They couldn't believe one man could lift something that heavy.

Mike shouted, "Apeman put it down, you'll strain yourself."

Apeman smiled and started pumping the cover up and down over his head. All at once his legs buckled and he staggered and fell into the hole. The cover came down on the hole. Apeman shouted. "Get the damn thing off so I can get out of here." Tank stood on top of the cover and laughed.

Mike motioned for Tank to get off and yelled for the other guys to help him lift the lid. Tank said, "Never mind, let that half wit stay down there and cool off."

Mike reached down and started to lift the cover. Tank reluctantly stepped off and they slid the cover off the hole as Apeman crawled out. His pants were wet, the elbows of his white sports jacket had large holes. He must have torn them on the sides of the hole when he fell in. Mike asked, "Are you all right Apeman?"

He didn't answer. He started to lift the cover again. Mike stepped on it and shouted, "No."

Apeman nodded and went to Wilma. "I could of held that thing over my head as long as I wanted to. I just tripped and fell in that damn hole."

She looked at him and giggled. Wilma was drunk.

Betty asked Mike if he would help her get Wilma home, and he said he would. They got her into the back seat and Apeman immediately got in with her. Betty looked to Mike. "He's not going, is he, Mike?"

Mike didn't say anything. He looked in the back seat and Wilma had her arms around Apeman kissing him. Mike pointed to what was going on. Betty cussed as she got behind the steering wheel. She headed for the DAC. billets. She told everyone to open the windows. Whatever Apeman fell into stunk. It was quiet in the backseat except for some heavy breathing. Betty parked in front of the billets. "Wilma, you're home. You can get out now." There was no reply from the back seat. Mike didn't want to look back, for fear of what he might see.

He yelled. "Hey, Apeman, are you going to walk the lady to the door?"

No answer. Then Apeman said, "Oh, yeah, come on baby, me and you are going to your pad."

Mike helped Apeman get her out of the car. Wilma slurred something then started staggering for the billets. Apeman picked her up and carried her.

Betty shook her head as she watched. "I don't believe it. I never saw her act like this. Wait till tomorrow, she won't believe what she did." Betty screamed when she saw Apeman carry Wilma into the billets. "Good grief, there's other girls in there. He's not allowed in there."

Mike laughed. "Well, he did. Let's go, they'll be all right."

No one ever found out what happened in that bedroom between Wilma and Apeman. They did learn that Apeman walked naked to the bathroom that night and one of the girls saw him in the hallway. She screamed and woke the other girls. Apeman grabbed his clothes and jumped out Wilma's bedroom window. When the military police arrived the girl described the guy as a big hairy thing. She said he looked like Big Foot.

Hard work on the practice field paid off. The team was undefeated. Mike sent letters to Rick and Zug but none were answered. He read the papers and the fighting was worse in Korea.

Apeman continued to slam the large door every night and make everyone jump. One night he came in drunk at two thirty in the morning and slammed it so hard Mike thought the door shattered. Everyone woke up and cussed. Apeman laughed and took off his clothes and dropped in bed. Tank turned on the lights and yelled.

I've had enough of this door slamming. A few of the other guys got up and asked what he was going to do? Tank pointed at Apeman who was laying naked, sound asleep.

"We pick up this bed with that drunken fool and carry it to the grassy area in front of Headquarters Building and let him sleep there."

A loud shout. "That's a great idea." They placed a blanket over Apeman and carried him and the bed. People on the sidewalk watched them carry the bed.

Tank led them to the middle of the grassy area in front of the Headquarters Building and pointed. "Put him down right here, this is perfect. There's a lot of windows where people can see him when they come to work. Hurry, grab the blanket and let's get the hell out of here."

They laughed and one of them asked. "Are you sure you want to take the blanket from him?"

Tank shouted, "Hell, yes, that's the only way." They ran back to the barracks.

The sun was bright. Apeman felt the heat. He lifted his arm and shielded his eyes. A mild breeze crossed his back and he reached for the blanket. He couldn't find it and thought it must have fallen on the floor. He dropped his hand down searching for it. Instead of feeling the wooden floor his hand passed over grass. His eyes opened wide and he looked to where his hand was in the grass. He rolled over and saw the Headquarters Building. People were walking on the sidewalk about twenty feet from him.

"Oh, shit." He sat up and put his hands over his privates trying to convince himself he was dreaming. He realized he was naked in front of the Headquarters Building and one of the offices in there was General Marvin. At the end of the bed there was a note that said. "See if you can find a door to slam out here." He jumped out of the bed, grabbed the note and covered his privates with it and ran for the barracks. People on the sidewalk got out of his way as he ran toward them. The players were looking out the windows and shouted when they saw him running to the barracks. Tank locked the door. Apeman made one jump and was on the porch cursing. He pulled the handle but the door wouldn't open. He shouted, "Open the damn door."

The players heard him begging. They shouted, "If we open the door are you going to slam it?"

"No, no, I promise I won't. Just let me in, I'll never slam a door again. Come on, man, let me in." Tank, let him stand outside a while longer and then he unlocked the door. Apeman rushed in. He glared at Tank but didn't say anything. He mumbled that the general saw him running without any clothes on and he was in a lot of trouble and didn't want to be in the barracks when the general came looking for him. He grabbed his clothes and ran out. He looked like he was going to slam the door but at the last moment he changed his mind.

Chapter 23
Bad News

The football team was still undefeated. Mike was playing excellent ball. General Marvin encouraged him after every game. He told Mike there would be scholarships to colleges when he got discharged. Every time the general brought this to his attention Mike thanked him. The general smiled. "Son, if you play as well in college as you do here. You'll make All American, for sure." Mike took a real liking to this rough old guy, who really cared about his players.

Everything seemed to be going well for Mike, until one day a corporal came into the barracks. "You Mike Ryan?"

"Yes. What's the matter?"

"Mike, I'm Corporal Tom Willard, the chaplain's assistant. Will you come with me to his office? He wants to talk with you."

"What happened? Did something happen to my mother?"

"I'm sorry Mike, I don't know. When we get to the church the chaplain will explain." Mike quickly left and got in the corporal's jeep. They entered the church and when they crossed in front of the altar they both bowed and went into the chaplain's office. The chaplain got up from his desk and walked to Mike.

"Mike, it's nice to meet you. I'm Captain Weber. I saw you play football and you're a credit to our team." He pointed to a chair. "Have a seat please, we have to talk."

Mike sat on the edge of the chair. "What's the matter? Is it my mother? Tell me, Sir."

The chaplain looked Mike directly in his eyes. "Your mother is fine, Mike. It's bad news from Korea. Your old outfit suffered heavy casualties. The Chinese and North Koreans made a massive attack with heavy losses to both sides."

Mike jumped up. "Who got it? Who got killed?"

The chaplain bowed his head. "Zug was killed, Rick Miller is critically wounded and at this time they don't know if he's going to make it."

Mike shut his eyes and exhaled. He felt the tears trying to escape. He stood up and looked at the ceiling. The chaplain put his hand on Mike's shoulder and told him to sit down. Mike felt like running out of the office and just keep running till he dropped.

"Sit down, Mike, the best thing to do is talk this matter out. I have more to tell you."

Mike slowly sat down. "How did they get it?"

"They were manning their position when the enemy attacked. It's reported as the largest offense the enemy has ever made. Your outfit was the first to get hit and it took a pounding. There are a lot of heroes in your outfit. They were outnumbered but they held their ground. A mortar made a direct hit in Zug and Miller's foxhole. Both were badly wounded but they continued to fire their machine gun. When reinforcements reached them, enemy soldiers were dead all around their foxhole. Rick and Zug were badly wounded. The medics tried to bring them around but Miller was the only one who responded. All their ammunition was gone. Both had their bayonets in their hands."

"Sir, where was Rick hit?"

"I don't know Mike. They didn't go into detail concerning the locations of his wounds. They just reported he was in critical condition. If I get any more information I will get in touch with you at once."

Mike shook his head. "Sir, why does this have to happen? What does it prove?" He wanted to shout but stopped short when he looked into this kind man's face.

The chaplain knew what Mike was thinking. "Say it, son. That's why I'm here. There are some things I have answers for and some I don't. Let's get it out in the open." Mike looked at him, confused. "Mike, there are things we will never understand. That is the reason we have faith. If we knew all the answers there would be no need for faith."

"Sir, where's Rick now?"

"He's probably in a M.A.S.H unit and, when they get him stable, he'll be sent to one of our hospitals here in Japan."

Mike looked down at the table and mumbled. "Zug's dead, Hillbilly's dead. Rick, you got to make it." Mike thought of all the times they were together. The tough times and the laughter. It will never be the same. Is this what war is about, only tragic and sad things?" Tears streamed down his face. It was no use, he couldn't hold them back.

"You'll get over it, Mike. Time will heal this tragedy. If I can be of any help please come and see me. We'll work it out. I'm always here."

"Thanks, Sir. You will contact me if any more information comes in about Rick?"

"I will, Mike. Would you like to go into the chapel and we'll say some prayers for them?"

"Yes, sir, I would appreciate it."

They knelt in the first pew and looked at the altar. The chaplain said the prayers out loud and Mike said them in a whisper. He thought, Rick, you wanted me and my mother to say a prayer for you and now the chaplain is praying for you. You can't get any better than that. After they were finished they slowly walked out of the chapel. They shook hands. "Mike, is there anything you'd like to say?"

"Yes, sir. You don't know how important saying those prayers were." He told the story about how Rick said the Lord would never answer his prayers because he thought he was too bad for the Lord to listen to him.

The chaplain smiled. "I won't forget, Rick, Zug and Hillbilly in my prayers. You drop in the chapel and do the same. It will do you good. Remember, I'm here all the time, Mike. Get back out on that football field and do your best. You entertain our soldiers and that gets their minds off their problems."

"I will, Sir. Thank you."

Mike started walking. Memories flashed by. *Rick talking Zug into playing the sax on that hill when they were on bivouac. The night Zug played the sax at Owner Mike's nightclub. Big Bertha chasing Rick in that motel. Rick and Hillbilly walking on their hands. The tattoo parlor.* He shook his head and wondered, "why." So many happy times and now they're gone. His eyes shut and he shivered when he visualized the Chinese and North Korean attack on Rick and Zug's position. It was like being there. He could see thousands of men in quilted jackets blowing horns, shouting and shooting at them. He could see his friends at the machine gun bleeding, trying to fight them off. Hillbilly's face with that terrible wound flashed in his head. He started running. *I got to get these thoughts out of my mine or I'm going to lose it. I'll run till I get so tired I won't be able to think.*

Everything was a blur. He stopped running and bent over to get his breath, then ran out of the camp and was near a highway. A car pulled up and it was Betty. At first he thought he was dreaming. She kept shouting. "Mike, Mike, what's the matter with you? Mike, don't you hear me? Are you sick?"

Mike was in a daze but he figured she must have been following him. Betty got out of the car and opened the passenger door. "Get in, Mike." Mike was confused. He got in and just stared. She talked to him. He didn't answer. She became angry, shouting and driving fast. Mike didn't answer, he just stared at her. "What the hell is the matter with you? Did you get a Dear John letter from your bitch back home?"

Mike shook his head. "Please, not now Betty."

She screamed, "I'm tired of your bullshit and that broad back home. The only person you love is yourself and that goofy bitch."

Mike glared at her and shook his head, mumbling, "No, no. Please."

She continued her tantrum, screaming and cussing him. The car swerved from one side of the road to the other. "I'll see how much guts you got, big football player. She pushed the accelerator down further. "If we hit something at this speed we'll both be killed."

Mike's expression didn't change. He put his foot over hers on the gas pedal and pushed it to the floor. "Now, you spoiled brat, I'll show you about death." Her eyes got wide and her knuckles turned white as she gripped the steering wheel. She screamed for him to get his foot off hers so she could reduce the speed. Her face was full of fright as they swerved in and out of traffic. A couple of times they almost hit a truck and car head on. "Have you had enough of this?"

Betty screamed. "Yes, Mike, please slow down."

Mike lifted his foot off hers and put the car in neutral and removed the keys. The car slowed down and came to a stop. Betty put her face on the steering wheel. Mike got out and threw the keys in her lap. "Leave me alone. Do you understand?" She looked up at him. Her lips quivered.

He walked down the road and she pulled up next to him. "Mike. Mike, I just want to talk with you."

He glared at her. "Get away from me." She drove off, looking at him through the rear view mirror.

Mike went to the service club and sat at a stool in an empty part of the bar. He drank and thought about his friends. Fate has funny ways. The four of them were thrown together over a damn war. Each one was different, yet they became good friends. How quickly they were taken away. He cannot believe

Zug and Hillbilly were gone and Rick might go. He remembered their smiling faces and he kept repeating, "Why? Why?" He drank till his head became heavy and dropped to the bar. He got up and was leaving; People called his name. He ignored them and walked out. In the barracks he fell on his bed, fully clothed and passed out.

Morning came and Tank shook him. "Hey Mike, come on, get up, we got to make practice." Mike raised his head slowly. Tank laughed. "What's the matter kid? Did you go out and get your head bad?" Mike nodded. Tank said, "I'll meet you at the locker room."

Each morning Tank had to wake Mike because he spent every night at the service club till it closed. He tried to drown the thoughts of his friends with alcohol. Tank saw what was happening and had a good talk with him. Mike realized that drinking was not helping him. He remembered what the chaplain said. *When you get down, work hard on the football field and it will help.*

The coaches noticed that Mike drove himself extra hard at practice. Instead of passing the ball he seemed to be running a lot when it wasn't necessary. Coach Wilson called him over. "I don't know what got into you Mike, but I don't want you running that ball so much. If you break your arm we're going to be in a mess. Is something bothering you? You know my door is always open. Come in and we'll talk it over."

Mike nodded. He didn't want to tell the coach that running the ball and getting tackled helped relieve how he felt.

The championship game with the Air Force came up. This was for all the marbles. Coach Wilson gave his stimulating talk and the team ran to the field. On the way General Marvin called Mike. "Mike, I want you to meet General Black who is the head of the Eighth Army." Mike looked at the General's shoulders. On each side were four stars. Mike never got accustomed to seeing those stars. General Black stuck out his hand and Mike shook it.

"Mike, I'm glad to meet you. You're a great football player. I played at West Point and I can appreciate a good player. Good luck today and win one for the Army."

"Thank you, Sir. I'll try my best."

Mike ran to the entrance of the field. The Army team was congregated in front of it. There were four tanks facing each another When the team ran between them their large cannons fired volley after volley. The ground shook and smoke filled the air. This brought the Army fans to their feet, cheering.

The Air Force wasn't going to be out-done. Jet fighters swooped down and roared as they skimmed the stadium. Blue uniformed Airmen in the stands jumped to their feet cheering *their* team. There was electricity in the air. Everywhere Mike looked there were high ranking officers. He felt pumped up as he got caught up in the game's atmosphere. This was the first time his spirits rose since he got the bad news about his friends. The only thing that mattered now was winning the game.

No sooner had the game started, it had to be stopped. Some Army fans went into the Air Force stands and started cheering for the Army. A brawl broke out. The Army men were outnumbered and the soldiers on the other side of the field saw this. Someone shouted. "Let's help." They jumped over the railing, ran across the field and climbed into the Air Force stands and swung at the first blue uniform they saw. The coaches quickly got their teams to their sidelines. Mike watched as the khaki and blue uniformed men brawled. *This must be the biggest fight ever.*

The announcer shouted. "You men will immediately stop that fighting." No one listened. This time he yelled. "Knock off that goddamn fighting, do you hear me?" They kept fighting.

General Marvin got out of his seat and jumped over the rail and went to the leader of the Army Band. He yelled something and the band quickly assembled in the middle of the field. He ran to the Air Force Band and they too went to the middle of the field. The general shouted. *"Play the National Anthem. "* Immediately the bands aimed their instruments at the brawl and started playing. Every soldier and airman stopped fighting and came to attention. The MPs saw their chance and rushed into the stands. They filtered out the Army men and sent them back to their side. Order was restored and both teams were instructed to resume the game.

The game was scoreless. The Air Force punter went back to kick. Tank rushed so hard he almost beat the ball back to the kicker. The Air Force player started to kick and Tank dove and hit him. The ball went straight up in the air and it came down in Apeman's surprised arms. No players except Apeman knew he had the ball. It was funny to see this big awkward guy running with the ball toward the goal line. A couple of fast Air Force players realized what had happened. They chased and jumped on Apeman's back. Apeman carried them over the goal line with him. At first the thought of him scoring a touchdown hadn't sunk in. All at once his big body started quivering and he let his knuckles drop to the ground. He hunched over and jumped in small circles.

The Army fans started chanting, "Ape call do lee ah ba."

Hearing this, Apeman shimmed up the center pole that held up the goal post. He grabbed one of the cross bars and hung on with one arm and with the other one started scratching his arm pit and privates.

The fans chanted louder. Coach Wilson yelled to his assistant coaches. "Get that screwball down." The assistants ran to the goal post and escorted Apeman back to the bench. Even Tank shook his hand.

Apeman hit Tank on the back. "Nice going big guy, you fucked up that punter."

Tank smiled. "Great catch. Was that the first time you ever scored?"

"Damn right. You know us linemen never get to score. When we do, we got to enjoy it."

"Yeah, I know what you mean."

The score was seven to nothing. The Army got the ball back. All week at practice the coach kept saying, "The Air Force is aware that we can throw the long pass and they'll be looking for it." He designed a play that would trick them. Mike called the play. He got the snap from the center and immediately lateraled to the right halfback who ran right. Mike ran to the left and down the sideline. The halfback stopped and threw the ball to Mike who was wide open. He ran into the end zone for a touchdown. The Army led fourteen to nothing.

The Air Force was giving it all they had but they couldn't score. It was the last quarter and Mike threw a pass. When he released the ball a big Air Force lineman drove his shoulder into Mike's mid section. When they hit the ground, Mike's back slammed down and his head whipped back, striking the ground. Mike didn't move. Tank was first to grab him and bring him to his feet. Mike was groggy but his instincts took over. His old coach's voice echoed in his head. *No matter how hard they hit you, get up and pretend it don't hurt.* He made it to the huddle. "Okay, quarterback draw play."

Tank noticed Mike slurred when he called the play and his eyes weren't focused. Tank was ready to call a time out when Mike shouted. "Okay, let's go." Mike got the ball and everything went blank. He just stood there. His team mates were yelling for him to run. The Army line was doing their best to block and keep the other team off him. Two large Air Force players broke through and smashed into Mike, who was standing still. He took the whole impact of these rushing giants. The Air Force players got up but Mike stayed on the ground. Tank ran to him and tried to help him up, but Mike's body was limp and bright blood was running out of his mouth. Tank turned Mike on his side so the blood would drain and yelled for the trainers. As soon as the trainers saw Mike's condition they yelled for a stretcher.

Coach Wilson ran to Mike. He shouted at the trainers. "Where's he hurt?"

"He has a bad head injury. He's coughing up bright blood which indicates broken ribs and a punctured lung." Mike was rushed to the hospital.

The emergency room people were waiting for him. The head doctor saw his condition and ordered. "Don't waste any time. Get him to surgery."

Hours passed but there was no word from the operating room. The coaches and the team were all in the waiting room. Tank was pacing back and forth and every once in a while he'd slam his fist into his hand. Coach Wilson put his hand on Tank's shoulder. "Tank, this isn't doing anyone any good. Sit down and take it easy."

"I should of called a time out. He was out on his feet in that huddle. He didn't know what he was doing. Damn, if only I would of called a time out that kid wouldn't be up there right now."

"Don't talk like that. How many times have you got hit that bad and you continued to play?"

Tank didn't say anything. He just looked at the floor and shook his head.

The waiting room was quiet. The players talked in whispers. Apeman sat with his elbows on his knees and his face in his hands. This didn't look like a team who had just won the Far East Armed Forces Championship.

The chaplain came in and went immediately to the coach. They talked for a short time and the coach turned to his players. "Men, Chaplain Webber is going to say some prayers for Mike." They all dropped to one knee and bowed their heads.

After prayers the chaplain said to the coach. "That was bad news Mike got last week about his old outfit in Korea."

"What do you mean?"

"Didn't he tell you about his best friends? One was killed and the other is badly wounded. Most of the men in his old outfit got killed."

When they heard this the room became silent. These football players were American soldiers. They knew how bad it was over there and they felt for that unit. They understood how men can become close friends in the Army. They knew how Mike felt. Coach Wilson stared at the chaplain. "I knew that boy had something bothering him. He wanted to be in the thick of things. He was trying to get it off his mind. I wish I would have known."

The chaplain bowed his head. "I should have told you. I'm sorry."

The wait continued and no one left. Finally a doctor in scrubs came in. His mask dangled on his chest. Everyone stood up. "We got a seriously injured boy. His ribs are broken and some of them speared his internal organs. He's in a coma. For the next couple of days it's going to be touch and go. He's in excellent condition and that's a plus factor for him recovering. No one will be able to visit him till his condition improves. There's nothing you can do for him. We did all we could and now it's in the hands of the Lord."

Chapter 24
Reunion

As the chaplain walked to his car flashing red lights caught his attention. A convoy of ambulances led by a military police car pulled into the hospital driveway. He felt his services might be needed and ran to the admitting area. He asked the MP. "Where are all these injured coming from?"

"Sir, they were flown in from Korea. They're some of the wounded who were caught up in that big offense the North Koreans and Chinese pulled. That doctor over there has more information about it."

The chaplain thanked him and ran to the doctor. "Doc. Let me help."

The doctor saw the small golden crosses on the chaplain's uniform. "Yes, glad to see you. We're starting to give these men a quick examination to determine what we'll have to do for them. You can accompany me, they need all the help they can get. I'm Colonel Hill."

"I'm Captain Weber." They walked into a large room where stretchers with wounded men lined the floor. The colonel dropped to one knee near a stretcher and the chaplain knelt on the other side. The colonel lifted the bandages and studied their wounds, then wrote on his clipboard. If the soldier could talk he would ask him questions. After he was done, the chaplain said a prayer and asked the soldier if he could help him in any way. The colonel checked out seven severely wounded soldiers. The next soldier had his face completely bandaged. The doctor knelt next to him. The chaplain stared at the blanket that was covering the soldier's body. He noticed one side was flat. The soldier had lost his leg.

"Soldier, can you hear me? I'm Doctor Hill and I'm going to remove the bandages from your face."

A weak raspy voice. "Go, ahead."

While the doctor removed the bandages, he asked, "Your right eye is the one that is injured. Am I right?"

The weak voice. "Yes, Sir, the right one."

When the bandages were removed, the left eye blinked a couple of times and squinted. The soldier's voice grew a little stronger. "Hey, Doc, you remember me? Your old lady puked on my head."

The doctor quickly looked at the chart for the soldier's name. "I sure do, Rick. You're going to be with us for a while and we're going to make you good as new."

"Man, you don't know how happy I am to see a familiar face."

The doctor smiled. "It's good seeing you again, too." He slowly removed the bandage from where Rick's eye use to be. He wanted to shake his head when he saw the wound but he didn't. He knew the boy was watching every expression he made. The chaplain saw it and turned away.

The doctor slowly lifted the blanket and folded it. He examined the area where once the leg was attached to Rick's body. He pulled the blanket back over Rick and tapped him on the shoulder. "You listen to me. I'm going to be with you as much as possible. If you ever want to see me, tell the nurses and I'll come. I promise. Do you remember my name?"

"Oh, yes sir, Major Hill."

"Well, you got the Hill right, but I'm now a colonel."

"Hey, that's great. Congratulations. I made sergeant and fucked up the next week and got busted."

Colonel Hill nodded and looked at the chaplain who smiled.

"Well from what you and the rest of your company did in Korea you'll be getting those sergeant stripes back."

"Instead of stripes, see if you can get me an eye and a leg."

The doctor put fresh bandages over Rick's face. "Now, I want you to rest. We're going to do everything we can for you."

"Thank you, Sir."

The doctor examined the remaining men. The chaplain asked, "Colonel, can I talk with you?" "Sure go ahead."

"That soldier you called Rick, is his last name Miller?"

Colonel Hill ran his finger down the clip board. "Yes, his name is Miller. Why do you ask?"

"Sir, there's a football player by the name of Mike Ryan who is fighting for his life. The boy's in a coma. Rick Miller is his best friend. They were in the same outfit. The army took Mike out of Korea to play football. I would like to talk with Rick and maybe we could put them together. I believe it would be good for both of them."

"I think it's a good idea. Let's wait a couple of days then we'll talk to Rick. Right now I don't want to shock him."

"Yes, sir, I understand. When you break the news to Rick about his best friend I'd like to be there."

"I'll contact you. Thank you for your help tonight."

A week passed and Mike didn't regain consciousness. Colonel Hill called the chaplain. "Captain Weber, Rick Miller is doing pretty good considering his wounds. If you'd like to come to the hospital we can talk with him and arrange for both soldiers to be put in the same ward."

The doctor and the chaplain entered Rick's room. Rick sensed that someone had come in. He raised and twisted his head so he could see with his left eye from under the bandages. Colonel Hill spoke, "Lay down, Rick, it's only me." Rick smiled and his head dropped back on the pillow. "I got a visitor for you. This is Chaplain Weber."

Rick raised again and mumbled. "Aw, shit, I'm going to die."

Colonel Hill and the chaplain both laughed. Chaplain Weber grabbed Rick's hand and shook it. "I'm Captain Weber. You're not going to die. I've got some information and I want you to do us a favor. Rick cocked his head and looked at the chaplain. "Son, your friend Mike Ryan" ... Rick raised up. Colonel Hill put his hand on Rick's chest.

"Lay back down, let the chaplain finish."

Rick yelled, "What happened to Mike. Is he dead?"

"He's in the hospital like you. He got hurt bad playing football."

"Hey, Colonel, can I see him? Take me to him."

"You'll see him. I'm making plans for you to be moved next to him. Right now listen to the chaplain."

Rick looked back and the chaplain spoke. "Mike has been in a coma for a week. We believe that if you're in the room with him and he hears your voice, it might bring him out of it."

"Take me to him."

They rolled him into the ward and put his bed next to Mike's. Rick said to the nurse, "Turn me over on the right side so I can see him." Rick stared at Mike who was on his back and in a deep sleep. "Hey, Mike, it's me, wake up and look at me." Mike didn't flinch, he just lay there. "Come on, Mike, wake up. We're here together again. Mike, you can do it. Wake up and we'll raise hell." Rick continued talking into the night but Mike just lay there.

The head nurse on the night shift walked up to Rick's bed. "What do you think you're doing, soldier, making all that noise?"

"Get lost."

"You don't know who you're talking to. There will be no more noise the rest of the night. There are other men in here trying to sleep." Rick ignored her and kept calling Mike.

The nurse bent over so Rick could get a good look at her. She showed him her collar with the silver bars on them. I want you to understand I'm an officer and I'm ordering you to stop this. What do you have to say to that, *Soldier!"*

"Get the hell out of here officer, or you're going to get hit in the head with this bed pan."

She grabbed his chart from the end of the bed. "I'm writing you up for insubordination."

"Write it big."

She went back to the desk and called for another nurse. A nurse came running from a room. "You come with me and listen to this soldier. I need a witness. They went to Rick's bed and she screamed at Rick. "I ordered you to stop that noise."

Rick reached over to the night stand and grabbed the bed pan and threw it at her. She ducked and ran out of the room. She screamed to the other nurse. "Did you see that?" The other nurse nodded. "I'm getting an orderly and a doctor. We'll shut him up."

Rick heard this and yelled, "Screw you, and the orderly." He quickly turned toward Mike when he heard a moaning sound. "Hey, Mike, is that you? You got to get me out of trouble again. Some chicken-shit nurse is going to have me court martial right here in this goddamn hospital." Rick knew Mike heard because a faint smile came on his face. "You're doing it, Mike, keep it up." Mike's head slowly turned to Rick. He blinked a couple of times and his eyes partially opened but his face didn't show any expression. Rick screamed. "Mike, it's me. They got me wrapped up like a damn mummy. Mike, it's me, Rick. You remember me. I jumped in bed with that big ugly broad, Bertha. Damn, Mike, say something. Don't shut your eyes. Come on, Mike, say something."

The head nurse led two large orderlies and three nurses into the room. She stood in front of Rick and he yelled. "Get the hell out of my way." She didn't move. He reached for a water pitcher.

She yelled to the orderlies. "Get him, he's out of control."

One of the nurses said. "His eyes are open." She ran to Mike and rubbed his forehead. "Soldier can you hear me?"

His lips moved and in a soft whisper he said. "Rick, is that you?"

"It's me, Mike. I'm in the bed next to you. There's some crazy bitch giving me a bunch of shit. I'm under all these bandages It's me. Stay awake, Mike."

Mike smiled and a nurse quickly turned on the overhead lights. An orderly called the doctor. The head nurse slowly retreated from the room.

One doctor arrived, followed by two more. They examined Mike and smiled. One of them walked over to Rick and tapped his shoulder. "Nice work, soldier." Mike was rolled out of the room to be examined further. Four hours passed and he was back, awake but groggy. He asked if he could be raised so he could see Rick.

Rick shouted, "What the hell happened to you, Mike?" Mike shrugged his shoulders.

He wanted to ask him about Zug and Korea but he really didn't want to know. It felt good to hear Rick's voice again, it gave him strength. Rick noticed Mike staring at the flat part of his bed where his leg use to be. "It's gone Mike. They're going to give me a wooden one. You won't call me shit on a stick, will you? They're going to give me a glass eye too. I asked them if they would put a small light bulb in it. Can you imagine what the broads will do when I blink them. You got to adapt to the situation."

Mike laughed and grimaced. He had his hands on his ribs. "Knock it off, Rick, it hurts when you make me laugh." Rick kept it up and Mike put his fingers in his ears so he couldn't hear him.

"Okay, Mike, I'll knock off the bullshit." Mike slowly brought his hands down. Rick grinned and was going to say something. Mike quickly brought his hands over his ears again.

"Please quit. My ribs are broken and it hurts like hell when I laugh. I mean it, no more joking."

Word got back to the team that Mike had regained consciousness. The next day the whole team visited him. Rick stared at them. He couldn't believe the size of these guys. After they left he told Mike. "No wonder you got messed up, getting hit by *them* guys."

Apeman came every day. When he walked through the ward he looked down at the floor. He didn't like to see the wounded soldiers with missing arms and legs. He sat in a chair next to Mike's bed. He always had a sad look and didn't say much. When he left he'd tap Mike's shoulder. "I'll be back tomorrow, Mike. Do you need anything?"

Mike couldn't believe the change in him. He told Rick about Apeman and all the fun he use to be. Rick liked the part about how Apeman reacted when he heard the chant. He told Mike he had an idea on how to liven up the place.

The next day Rick called a soldier named Brodie, who had both his arms in casts. "Hey, Brodie, you know that big black haired guy that comes here every day to see my friend?"

"Yeah, that big football player. What about him?"

"Well, when you pass the other beds tell the guys to start singing Ape call do lee ah ba when the big guy comes in."

"Hey, Miller, have they examined your head? Something is the matter with you."

"No, now hear me. That guy turns on when he hears people singing that." Rick pointed at Mike. "Isn't that right, Mike?"

"Yes, he sure does, but I don't think it's wise to do it in here."

Brodie laughed, "Why not?" He walked away and went to every bed in the ward informing the wounded soldiers.

The next day Apeman came in and started walking down the aisle with his head down. Someone started singing. "Ape call do lee ah ba." The wounded turned and saw the big guy. They joined in chanting the song. Apeman stopped and looked startled. His eyes went up into their sockets. His body quivered and his large shoulders swayed back and forth. Seeing this, the soldiers chanted louder. Apeman hunched over, his knuckles dropped to the floor. His mouth looked like a trumpet. He screeched some strange animal sounds and jumped in small circles. The men cheered.

Rick shouted to Mike, "Hey, that guy is great."

The nurses at the station desk heard the uproar and ran to the ward. They were startled when they saw the big guy jumping and screeching, reacting to the wounded soldiers' chanting. A doctor came running and shouted to the nurses. "What's going on in here?" He saw Apeman acting up. "Who is he? Is he from the mental ward?" The nurses went to stop Apeman but the doctor put out his arm. "Let him go. It's the first time these boys have laughed in a long time."

Apeman became a big hit with the guys. The nurses and doctors always knew when he came. The chant would echo though the hallways. They'd smile, shake their heads and someone would say. "Apeman has arrived." The head nurse just rolled her eyes. She wanted to say something but didn't since all the doctors liked him. Rick treated him like a long lost friend. Apeman liked Rick and did anything Rick told him to do. Mike tried to put a stop to this for fear they'd get into trouble, but it didn't do any good.

One day Mike was sleeping and Rick had compresses over his eyes. General Marvin walked up to Mike's bed and stood there. He didn't wake Mike and thought he'd come back later. The head nurse stared at the general from the doorway and couldn't understand what a general was doing in the ward.

Rick felt someone near his bed. He lifted the compresses and squinted his good eye and saw the stars on the man's shoulders. "Wow, a goddamn general." After he said it he knew he did something wrong. General Marvin walked over to Rick's bed. Rick stuttered and rubbed his hand over his eye. "Ah, Sir, I'm sorry. You surprised me. I never was this close to a general."

General Marvin stood there and in his gruff voice said. "Now take a good look." Rick stared at him and was lost for words. General Marvin grabbed Rick's hand and shook it. "You're Corporal Miller, is that right, Son?"

"Yes Sir, I mean, General Sir."

General Marvin put his hand on Rick's shoulder. "Are you being treated all right, soldier?"

"Yes, Sir. Everyone is real nice. They're bringing me around."

"Listen, Son. I heard about your outfit and I'm sorry about your losses. You people were outnumbered but you held your position. I'm proud of you, and the rest of the men from your outfit. If there is anything I can do for you, just let me know."

Hearing this, the head nurse walked away from the doorway. Rick was stunned seeing the general so close, and he couldn't answer. "Did you hear me soldier?"

Rick stuttered. "Yes Sir, ah, General Sir, I mean.... Ah shit, I'm all messed up looking at you."

"Don't you worry about me. Take care of yourself and get better. That's an order. Again, you let me know if I can do anything for you."

"Thank you, Sir."

Mike coughed and General Marvin walked to his bed. "I guess your friend and I woke you up, Mike. I'm sorry about that."

"No Sir, I wasn't sleeping that sound. When you get your bell rung you just drop off for a minute and then you wake up. The doctors told me it will clear up in a few days and I'll be as good as new."

General Marvin reached into his jacket and pulled out an envelope. "Mike, you'll be leaving here in about a week to go back to the States. When you get discharged go to the university and hand this letter to the football coach. He's aware of you, because I talked with him by phone."

"Thanks a lot, Sir."

"Now, you get your life together and make something out of yourself. You got the talent, I'll be reading the sports sections looking for your name." He shook Mike's hand. "You take care, Son. If you play ball like you did for us, you'll make Ail-American. I'll never forget the best quarterback we ever had. He was a high school player."

"I'll never forget you, General and the team. It was a great experience."

"Mike, if you get time, drop me a letter. I want to know how you're doing."

"I will, Sir."

General Marvin turned and looked at Rick. "Soldier, what's my name?"

Rick shook his head. "Ah, shit, why don't you come back in civilian clothes. Man, all those ribbons and stars shakes the shit out of me. Sir, General, Sir."

General Marvin, smiled and stared at Rick. "You're a hero Son and like I said, I'm proud of you and your outfit. Good luck, Son." He pointed at his stars on his shoulders. "You get well quick. That's an order. Do you understand, Soldier?"

"Yes, Sir, thank you, Sir."

General Marvin walked to each wounded soldier in the ward and talked with him before leaving. Mike stared at him. "Rick, that's one fine man. He's rough, but a fair and caring person."

"I know what you mean. He has a chest full of ribbons and most of them were combat."

Chapter 25
Going Home

Time passed and the two were healing. A nurse came in smiling. "We're going to be missing you two handsome men."

Mike and Rick knew what she meant. Mike asked, "When are we leaving?"

"Day after tomorrow."

"Can you believe it, Rick? We're going home? It's going to be great to be back in the States." Rick didn't answer. "Hey, Rick did you hear me?"

In a low voice he said. "Yeah."

The nurse picked up on his answer. "What's the matter Rick? Don't you want to leave us?"

"Yeah, I want to go back but I'm going to miss all you pretty women and how nice you were. You treated me just like you were my mother."

"Hey, you and Mike were the best patients we ever had."

Rick smiled and turned his head. Mike could tell something was bothering him and he changed the subject.

Departure day came. Mike limped out but Rick had to be carried to one of the many ambulances waiting outside. Military police cars with red lights flashing escorted the convoy of ambulances to the large, white hospital ship. At the dock in Yokohama a nurse helped Mike hobble aboard. He limped to the railing and stared at the city. *Mitseko you 're out there someplace. I wonder what you're doing. Would you be here if you knew I was going back home? Do you ever think about me? I'll never forget that wonderful night when you walked through those beads. Boy, it's a lonesome feeling not seeing you and being able to say goodbye.* He stood by the railing till the ship started to move. He shook his head. "Sayonara, Mitseko, I'm leaving part of myself here. I'll never forget you."

Other than listening to the guys telling what they were going to do when they got home, nothing much happened.

Hearing these stories Mike felt reality settling in. It won't be long and he'll be home.

Rick was looking at him. "Hey, Mike, I bet your mother and uncle will be waiting at the bus station for you. She'll probably hug and kiss you. Your uncle will shake your hand." Mike nodded. "I bet she washed all your clothes, cleaned your room, and washed your bedding so your room will smell fresh."

"Hey, hey, don't start asking all those questions about my mother again. Why do you want to know those things?"

Rick shrugged his shoulders. "Oh, I often wondered how it would feel to have a mother."

"Did your mother die when you were little?" Mike could tell this question hurt Rick. He was bound up and couldn't talk. "I'm your best friend, Rick. You've been holding something about your mother inside since I met you. Maybe if you'd let it out, it will do you good."

Rick remained silent and Mike was ready to walk away. "I was eleven years old and we were in a bus station. She told me to go to the restroom before we got on the bus. When I came out, she was gone. She abandoned me. I never saw her again. The only thing that woman did for me was give me a name."

"What about your father?"

"I never saw him. She wouldn't talk about him. When I went to school the kids used to ask about him. I didn't know what to say. They teased me and it caused a lot of fights."

Mike shook his head and squinted. "How did you survive?"

"I left the bus station and just wandered. When I got hungry I stole what I could. The cops would catch me and throw me in a reform school. If I could escape, I would. If I couldn't, I'd act nice and they'd put me in an orphanage or a foster home. It was easy to run away from them. The only reason I ended up in the army was the last time I got arrested the judge said, 'What's it going to be, the army or the penitentiary?' When he gave me that choice I thought it would be easier to escape from the army than the penitentiary."

"Why didn't you go AWOL? You had a lot of opportunities."

Rick looked at the floor. Well, because of you, Zug, and Hillbilly. You guys were the closest thing I ever had to a family. You were like brothers to me. Before meeting you guys no one ever cared about me. I never trusted no one. Man, you guys were sincere. You were worried about me and kept me out of trouble. I never had people like you guys around me. Now it looks like it's back to where I started."

"Hey, Rick I'm still here. Just because we're getting out of the army doesn't mean our friendship ends. I'll never forget you. If it wasn't for you I wouldn't be making this trip back home. You don't know how many times I was lonesome and ready to go over the hill. You always perked me up. In Korea you kept those gooks from killing us the way you fired that machine gun. As soon as you get better come to my house and stay till you get your life in order."

Rick smiled. "You really mean that, don't you, Mike?"

"You know I do."

Rick reached over and grabbed Mike's hand and squeezed. "You don't know how important it is to have another person who cares if you live or die. Like I said, I never had anyone like you guys. The only thing that woman gave me was a name. Every time those sergeants called me names I'd think back to one Christmas Eve. I was walking and it was raining and snowing. I had no place to go, I was wet, hungry and cold. I watched a father drive up in his driveway and open the trunk of his car. He took out Christmas presents. He went inside his home and his kids ran up to him and pulled at his legs. The mother hugged him. It was cold out there but I stood on the sidewalk and watched them through a big window. I cried and walked away and broke into a warehouse and huddled up next to a furnace. I laid there and thought, I do have a name and that's part of family.

"Mike took a deep breath. "Now I understand why you got so mad when they called you shithead. I would have acted the same way."

"It hurt, Mike. The only little thing I had that was part of a family was my name and those bastards tried to take it away from me."

The next day was clear. The sea was calm and the air was warm. The captain of the ship looked to a couple of his officers. "In a few hours we'll be in port. Put all the wounded topside."

Mike, Rick, and some of the other soldiers were reminiscing about Korea when an officer along with some orderlies walked into their quarters. Rick saw them first. "Now, what the hell are they up to?"

The room got quiet. The officer broke the silence, "Men, I need your attention. The captain wants everyone on deck."

Rick laughed out loud. "You want me to run up the steps."

The officer saw Rick was missing a leg. "That's no problem, soldier. Our people will carry you topside. You men, who can manage on your own power, leave now. The others will be helped."

Mike hobbled up the steps and stood by the rail and looked at the blue water. There wasn't a cloud in the sky. Slowly the deck was filled with stretchers. Some of the wounded hadn't been in the sun for weeks. They shielded their eyes and squinted. Mike sat next to Rick who was on a stretcher and had his hand over his eye. "Man, this is typical Army. If they know you're comfortable they got to mess with you,"

"Come on, Rick, quit bitching. You know it feels good."

"Hey, Mike, I wonder if I could get sun glasses with only one lens? You know like those Nazi officers use to wear."

"You mean a monocle?"

"Yeah, a monocle. I could wear that on my good eye, and on the other side I'd wear a black patch. People would see me and they wouldn't know if I was a Nazi, or a pirate."

"Don't start up that crazy talk again."

"Why not? You got to adapt to the situation."

Mike looked at him and shook his head. *All busted up and he still manages to laugh. I wonder how I would feel if I lost a leg and an eye? How can he be this way? What does he have to look forward to?*

The PA system came alive. "Men, this is the captain. I want to tell you how proud my crew and I are of you. You did your job in an honorable way. Thank you, from a brother American. In a little while you'll see a dark line forming on the horizon. That soldiers, is your home — The United States Of America. Welcome back, and good luck." A loud cheer went up from the deck.

The wounded watched in front of the ship. Someone yelled. "There it is." Orderlies lifted the men on the stretchers so they could see. A loud cheer erupted. Mike raised Rick and they watched the dark line get bigger, then buildings and landmarks appeared. No one said anything. They just stared at the wonderful sight.

The ship approached the Golden Gate Bridge. Everyone looked up. A woman in a white formal stood in the middle and music played from large speakers The lady started to sing, "God Bless America." Almost every soldier on deck had tears streaming down his face. In a low tone they started singing the beautiful song. Mike listened to the words and thought how true they were.

People walking on the bridge looked at the lady singing and at the ship below. One man asked another. "What's going on?"

The man pointed down at the white ship with the large red cross on it. "They're bringing American soldiers back who were wounded in Korea."

The guy shrugged his shoulders and said. "Is that all." And walked on.

The lady finished the song. Cheering could be heard from the ship going under the bridge. The singer wiped her eyes and shouted, "Welcome home and God bless all of you."

Doyle stood on the dock and watched the lone ship come in. *Where are you America? Why aren't you here to greet your heroes?* He shook his head and straightened the medal with the blue ribbon on his neck. The ship docked and the men who could walk came off first. Mike waited on the dock for Rick. He felt a hand on his shoulder and quickly turned around. "Sergeant Doyle."

Mike noticed he had on his dress uniform with a chest full of ribbons and the Medal of Honor on his neck. He grabbed Mike's hand and shook it. "Good to have you back, Michael."

"Thanks Sergeant. It's great to be back."

"You men did great over there. I'm sorry about Hillbilly and Zug."

Mike's smile drained from his face. "Yeah, I sure wish they could of made it. They were great friends. I'll never forget them."

"How is Rick?"

"He lost a leg and an eye. He's holding up pretty good. I just hope he'll be okay."

"He'll be all right, Mike. That boy is tough. He had a lot of mean things happened to him before he came into the army. He knows how to handle himself. The army will take care of him, I'll see to that. What are *your* plans? Rick wrote and told me how well you played football. He even sent me the picture of you scoring a touchdown."

"Well, I'll have to see how I heal up. I'll probably go to college and maybe play ball again."

"That's good thinking, Mike."

"Sergeant, will Rick be all right? He needs a break. In my eyes he's a hero. I hope they treat him like one."

"Like I said, the army takes care of their own. I will watch over him. Don't worry about it."

325

Two soldiers carried Rick off the ship on a stretcher and were walking to an ambulance. Mike ran up to them. "Hey, Rick, look who is here."

Rick saw Doyle. He shouted to the stretcher-bearers. "Put me down."

The two privates carrying him looked at Doyle and saw the Medal of Honor. Doyle nodded. "It's okay men, put him down."

Rick stared at him. "You came to see me, Sergeant Doyle?"

"Yes, I wanted to see you and Michael." Doyle bent over and shook Rick's hand. Rick touched the Medal of Honor. "Sergeant, is this one of those special days you wear it?"

Doyle nodded. "Yes, this is one of those special days." Rick kept staring at the medal but didn't say anything. "You know Rick, I called Bertha and she said she couldn't make it. She said she'll see you later." Doyle burst out laughing when he saw Rick's expression.

"You don't have to do me any favors."

"Do you know where you're going now, Rick?"

"Some hospital here in California. I guess they got some spare parts for me."

"What about you, Mike?"

"I think they're going to check me out here in California, and then I'll be sent to Fort Sheridan in Illinois to be discharged."

They talked a while longer and Mike handed Rick an envelope. "My address and phone number is inside. If you ever want anything, give me a call. When they let you out of the hospital come to my house. We got an extra room and you can stay as long as you want."

Rick took the envelope. "I appreciate this, Mike."

Mike picked up his overnight bag and was getting ready to say good bye. Rick stopped him. "Don't say good bye. Please say, I'll be seeing you."

Mike nodded. "You're right, that's the best way. I'll be seeing you, Rick and you too, Sergeant Doyle."

Rick and Sergeant Doyle nodded. "We'll be seeing you, too."

Mike turned and started to walk away. The same lonesome feeling came over him, like when he left his mother and uncle in the bus station and the time he left Zug and Rick back in Korea. He didn't want to see Rick being loaded into the ambulance but a loud shout from behind caused him to turn around. A lieutenant was yelling at the two young soldiers who had been carrying Rick's stretcher. "You goddamn shitheads, who the hell said you could put that stretcher on the ground?"

The two young soldiers stood at attention and the lieutenant kept yelling at them. Mike saw Rick's hand go into his pocket and come out with a cigarette lighter. He put the flame to the lieutenant's pants. In a short time the lieutenant was jumping up and down slapping at the fire crawling up his pant leg. Mike smiled, turned around and mumbled. "You got to adapt to the situation."

CPSIA information can be obtained at www.ICGtesting.com
Printed in the USA
LVOW13s0950211013

357766LV00002B/9/P